Writing Essays about Literature

A GUIDE AND STYLE SHEET

SEVENTH EDITION

Kelley Griffith

University of North Carolina at Greensboro

THOMSON

WADSWORTH

Australia • Canada • Mexico • Singapore • Spain • United Kingdom • United States

For Gareth,
Kelly, Bronwen,
and Graham

THOMSON
━━━★━━━ ™
WADSWORTH

Writing Essays about Literature:
A Guide and Style Sheet, Seventh Edition
Kelley Griffith

© 2006 Thomson Wadsworth, a part of The Thomson Corporation. Thomson, the Star logo, and Wadsworth are trademarks used herein under license.

Printed in Canada

1 2 3 4 5 6 7 09 08 07 06 05

For more information about our products, contact us at:
Thomson Learning Academic
Resource Center
1-800-423-0563
For permission to use material from this text or product, submit a request online at
http://www.thomsonrights.com
Any additional questions about permissions can be submitted by
email to **thomsonrights@thomson.com**

Library of Congress Control Number: 2005922185

ISBN 1-4130-0395-8

Publisher: *Michael Rosenberg*
Acquisitions Editor: *Aron Keesbury*
Development Editor: *Mary Beth Walden*
Technology Project Manager: *Cara Douglass-Graff*
Marketing Manager: *Carrie Brandon*
Advertising Project Manager: *Patrick Rooney*
Project Manager, Editorial Production: *Brett Palana-Shanahan*
Senior Print/Media Buyer: *Mary Beth Hennebury*
Permissions Editor: *Kiely Sisk*
Production/Design/Composition: *Graphic World, Inc.*
Cover Designer: *Ross Carron*
Text/Cover Printer: *Transcontinental*

Thomson Higher Education
25 Thomson Place
Boston, MA 02210-1202
USA

CONTENTS

PREFACE

Over twenty years ago, I wrote the first edition of this book in response to questions students asked when I assigned essays in my literature courses: "What should I look for?" "What's an essay?" "How long should it be?" "Do we have to use outside sources?" "How should I document sources?" Many students had little or no experience writing arguments, not only about literature but about anything. They struggled to get started. This book was my answer to their questions. The initial edition gave a brief introduction to the study of literature, defined key critical terms, explained details of usage (the "style sheet" part of the book), and included sample essays that would illustrate good student writing.

Writing Essays about Literature: A Guide and Style Sheet has evolved over the years, and this, the seventh edition, still strives to answer key questions students raise about studying literature and writing about it. First, in Part One (Chapters 1 through 6), this book provides extensive guidance about reading literature. Chapter 1 (Strategies for Interpreting Literature) poses the question that undergirds the entire book: How can we interpret literature? Chapters 2 through 5 are discussions of the nature of literature and the three major literary genres—fiction, drama, and poetry. These chapters define the elements of literature and provide heuristics—questions, "Thinking on Paper" exercises, and "Now It's Your Turn" assignments—that lead readers toward their own interpretations. Chapter 6, with its brief discussions of critical approaches, invites readers to study all aspects of literature.

Second, the book offers guidance for writing about literature. Chapter 7 (Writing about Literature) serves as an introduction to Part Two and poses the question, How can we write about literature? The primary focus of Part Two is the interpretive essay, but Chapter 7 and subsequent chapters also give attention to more "personal" kinds of writing, such as free writing, notes, and journals. Chapters 8 through 10 are arranged according to the four stages of the writing process: inventing, drafting, revising, and editing. Chapter 8 (Choosing Topics) suggests strategies for generating topics. Chapter 9 (Drafting the Essay) emphasizes the argumentative nature of essays about literature. It covers strategies for reasoning, organizing, and developing an essay from early drafts to a final draft. Chapter 10 (Revising and Editing) provides advice about revising, rules for quotations and other matters of usage, and guidelines for the essay's appearance and format.

Third, the book serves as a style guide. Both Chapter 10, with its treatment of usage, and Chapter 11 (Research and Documentation) carry out this purpose. Chapter 11 explains what research papers are, how to find information and opinions, how to incorporate them into essays, and how to document sources using the MLA style. The book concludes with a chapter on taking essay tests and a chapter containing four student essays—one on a poem, one on a short story, one on a play, and one on a novel.

This edition, extensively revised, features many new elements.

SUBHEADS

Additional subheads indicate where specific terms and concepts are treated. They make these discussions more visible and easy to find.

CHECKLISTS

Checklists at the end of relevant chapters (especially the chapters on fiction, drama, poetry) serve as overviews of the chapters and lists of key things to do.

GLOSSARY

A glossary of critical terms, located at the back of the book, gives brief definitions of critical terms discussed in the text.

NOW IT'S YOUR TURN

A new heuristic, "Now It's Your Turn," also joins the "Questions about . . ." and "Thinking on Paper about . . ." directives that appear after discussions of generic elements. "Now It's Your Turn" invites readers to explore complete works, printed in the book, such as Mary Robison's short story "Yours," Susan Glaspell's play *Trifles,* and numerous poems. The assumption is that readers, having read the discussion of a generic element, would enjoy the challenge of applying the concepts on their own, without prompts from the author.

COMPLETE REVISION OF THE CHAPTER ON FICTION

This revision includes concepts that are now staples in narratology. New discussions include:

❖ The place of the author in the text
❖ Point of view (new terminology, treatment of narratees)
❖ Plot ("plot" and "story," beginnings and endings, embedded stories, frame stories, summary narration, scenic narration)
❖ Characterization (methods of representing characters' thoughts)

"Yours," a complete short story by Mary Robison, serves as discussion matter for "Now It's Your Turn" prompts.

COMPLETE REVISION OF THE CHAPTER ON POETRY

New to this edition are poems by Matsuo Basho, Elizabeth Bishop, Louise Bogan, Emily Brontë, Gwendolyn Brooks, Robert Browning, Taniguchi Buson, e. e. cummings, Emily Dickinson, George Herbert, Langston Hughes, Kobayashi Issa, Jane Kenyon, Amy Lowell, Edna St. Vincent Millay, and Ezra Pound, plus an anonymous ballad, "The Daemon Lover."

New or expanded treatments include:

❖ How to read a poem the first time
❖ The role of the speaker (including the speaker's connection to the author)
❖ Syntax (how to cope with fractured syntax)
❖ Lines as a structural feature of poetry
❖ Enjambment
❖ Ballad and common (hymn) meter
❖ The haiku
❖ Visual poetry
❖ Rhythm
❖ Word sounds
❖ Free verse

UPDATING OF GUIDELINES AND RESOURCES

The sections on usage and documentary style have been revised according to the latest edition of the *MLA Handbook for Writers of Research Papers*. All resources listed in the book, including Internet sites, have been checked for accuracy.

I have written this book out of a long-standing love for literature. My hope is that the book's information and suggestions will help readers get as much pleasure from literature as it has given me over the years. The book can serve several related purposes. Teachers can use it as a textbook in introductory courses and as a supplement in advanced ones. Students can use it on their own as an introduction to the study of literature, as a guide to writing essays about literature, and as a reference manual.

I welcome comments and suggestions from users of this book. My e-mail address is <kelley_griffith@uncg.edu>. Regular mail is English Department, University of North Carolina at Greensboro, Greensboro, NC 27412.

ACKNOWLEDGMENTS

I owe many people gratitude for their help. I am indebted to the writers whose works I have consulted. For past editions, very helpful were the insightful comments of Laurence Perrine, Frank Garratt (*Tacoma Community College*), George Gleason (*Southwest Missouri State University*), John Hanes (*Duquesne University*), Jacqueline Hartwich (*Bellevue Community College*), Irving Howe (*Hunter College*), Edward Pixley (*State University of New York at Oneaonta*), Dexter Westrum (*Ottawa University*), Jeff Bagato (*Virginia Polytechnic Institute*), Helen O'Grady (*University of Wyoming*), Karen Meyers (*University of North Carolina at Greensboro*), William Tucker (*University of North Carolina at Greensboro*), Walter Beale (*University of North Carolina at Greensboro*), Thomas C. Bonner (*Midlands Technical College*), Nancy Hume (*Essex Community College*), Gretchen Lutz (*San Jacinto College*), Robbie Clifton Pinter (*Belmont University*), Wallace Watson (*Duquesne University*), Judy Brown (*University of British Columbia*), Gaye Elder (*Abraham Baldwin Agricultural College*), Albert J. Griffith (*Our Lady of the Lake University*), James M. Hutchisson (*The Citadel*), Ellen N. Moody (*George Mason University*), John David Moore (*Eastern Illinois University*), Tyler Smith (*Midlands Technical College*), Judith Corbin (*Eastern Illinois*), P. R. Dansby (*San Jacinto College*), Jim Dervin (*Winston-Salem State University*), Isabella DiBari (*Diablo Valley*

College), Bruce Gans (*Wright College*), and Becky Roberts (*Mt. San Antonio College*).

For this edition I wish to acknowledge the valuable suggestions of

John Carroll
California State University–Stanislaus
William Davis
College of Notre Dame of Maryland
Glenn Hutchinson
University of North Carolina–Charlotte
Homer Kemp
Tennessee Technological University
Lisa Ray
Thomas Nelson Community College
Ronn Silverstein
Florida International University
Roberta Stagnaro
San Diego State University

At Thomson Wadsworth I thank Mary Beth Walden, who oversaw the editing of the book and kept me on schedule. I would also like to thank Aron Keesbury, acquisitions editor, Brett Palana-Shanahan, production project manager, Cara Douglass-Graff, technology project manager, and Matt Heidenry at Graphic World, Inc. who helped produce this book.

Finally, I am deeply grateful to my family for the encouragement they always give me.

INTRODUCTION

Literature is all around us. We find it in school courses, where we study great masterpieces of the past. We run into it in drugstores, where best sellers occupy long ranks of shelves. We experience it in the poetry slams of coffee houses and night spots. The devices of literature show up in popular media. Hip-hop music incorporates its rhythms and rhymes. Movies and television shows co-opt its mythic stories and character types. Internet websites reinvent its plot strategies. Graphic artists enhance its psychological explorations with powerful visual illustrations. Politicians clothe themselves in its images of competence and authority. Every day, even when we aren't aware of it, literature gives our lives zest and imparts its wisdom.

Like all art, literature gives pleasure. It has a certain magic that transports us from the "real" world to seemingly remote and enjoyable places. We can experience this quality without thinking about it. But literature also poses intellectual challenges that do demand thought. For most readers, grappling with these challenges enhances the pleasure of literature. By studying literature, we "see" more of it to appreciate. We learn that, far from being remote from life, literature reflects the real world and helps us locate our places in it.

This book addresses two related questions: (1) How can we read literature? and (2) How can we write about it? The questions are related because we have to read literature skillfully in order to write about it. In turn, writing about literature stimulates our understanding of it.

There are many ways to read and write about literature. This book focuses on one way—interpretation. *Interpretation* is the act of making sense of something, of establishing its meaning. When we interpret literature, we explore its meaning. To do this well, we employ strategies of discovery, analysis, and reasoning. Exploring those strategies—for reading and writing—is the subject of this book.

Part One of the book takes up the first question, how to read. Chapter 1 discusses the process of interpretation and follows up with some basic strategies for interpreting literature. The rest of Part One concentrates on "places" in literature to look for meaning: the properties of literature itself (Chapter 2) and of fiction (Chapter 3), drama (Chapter 4), and poetry (Chapter 5). The concluding chapter of Part One examines specialized strategies of interpretation, each of which illuminates potential sources of meaning in literature.

Part Two considers the question of how to write. It is organized according to a process many writers follow: inventing (deciding what to write about), drafting (writing first drafts), revising (writing more drafts), and editing (producing a final draft for "publication"). Throughout Part Two, and most notably in the final chapter, samples of student writing illustrate interpretative writing.

Although each part of the book follows an orderly path—a step-by-step process for reading and writing—you can also use the book as a handbook. Part One covers such things as the elements of literature and of genres (fiction, drama, and poetry), as well as theoretical approaches such as historicism, New Criticism, structuralism, deconstruction, new historicism, and feminist and gender criticism. Part Two gives information about, among other things, generating topics, organizing essays, using logic, doing research, documenting sources, handling quotations, and taking tests. The location of all of this material is easy to find, especially when you use the Glossary and the Index of Concepts and Terms located at the back of the book. If you do not remember where a definition or explanation is, just look it up in the Glossary and in that index.

We begin, then, with reading.

PART ONE

Interpreting Literature

PART ONE

1

Strategies for Interpreting Literature

WHY DO PEOPLE READ LITERATURE?

We read literature for pleasure and for meaning—because it is fun and because it speaks to us about important things.

Reading for fun. When we read purely for pleasure, we do not usually care what the work means. We just want to escape from the concerns of the day and let the work perform its magic on us. You may remember your first great reading experience, when you were so caught up in a work that you were oblivious to everything else. Reading just for pleasure is like that. We sit down with a book and say to ourselves, "I don't want to think. I just want to enjoy."

Reading for meaning. But on a more thoughtful level, reading for pleasure and reading for meaning are related. Part of the pleasure of reading comes from the meaning it gives us. On first reading a Raymond Chandler* detective novel, for example, we may be gripped

---

*Dates of authors' lives and publication dates of works cited in this book can be found in the author-title index at the back of the book.

by the suspenseful plot. We eagerly turn pages just to find out what will happen next. But upon rereading the novel, and especially reading other works by him, we discover a thematic and artistic richness we may not have noticed before: how he uses conventions of the detective story—wise guy dialogue, intrigue, suspense, urban settings, stereotypical characters, a melancholy hero—to render a moral dimension to his fictional world. We notice his poetic language, his mastery of tone, his insights about American cities, about American obsessions, about high life and low life, wealth and poverty, innocence and crime. As we continue to read Chandler, we move from one level of enjoyment—reading for "escape"—to another—reading for meaning. Or, put another way, we read not just for pleasure and meaning but for pleasure *because* of meaning.

Reading for fun and meaning.　In this book we will explore how to uncover the meanings of works of literature. These include the themes of a work (the issues it raises about the human condition) as well as the nature and effectiveness of literary devices like characterization, setting, plot, and imagery. We will consider how the aesthetic qualities of literature—the devices authors use to give us pleasure—embody meaning. They are the means by which authors deliver ideas and influence our response to these ideas, and their appeal often arises from the ideas they embody. We like the ideas in a work because of its artistic devices; we admire the devices because we like the ideas. Form and content, beauty and truth—they can hardly be separated.

How do we discover meaning in works of literature? We do so through interpretation.

WHAT IS INTERPRETATION?

Definition.　*Interpretation* is a process. It is the process of examining the details of works of literature in order to make sense of them. John Ellis, the literary theorist, describes the goals and process of interpretation in this way: interpretation "is a hypothesis about the most general organization and coherence of all the elements that form a literary text." This "organization and coherence" emerges from a "synthesis" between a work's themes and its details. "The most satisfying interpretation," he says, "will be that which is the most inclusive. The procedure of investigation will be that of any inquiry: a continual move between general notions of the coherence of the text, and consideration of the function within the whole of particular parts of it. General conceptions will change in the light of particular observations, and new particular observations will then become necessary in the light of the changed conceptions" (202).

Interpretation as process.   Ellis is saying here that as we read, we encounter details of a work and develop hunches about how they relate to one another, what they mean. As we continue to read, we encounter more details. These may confirm our hunches or cause us to replace them with new ones. Once we have finished reading the work, we can decide which hypotheses (hunches) account for the most details; those hypotheses, Ellis says, constitute the best interpretations.

Many critics today would disagree with Ellis that the best interpretation "covers" or accounts for the most details in a work or that it establishes a "coherence" that unifies the whole work. For one thing, it is hard to say which interpretation covers the most details. For another, the most comprehensive interpretation may not be the most satisfying to a particular reader. We might, for example, want to focus on just one aspect of a work, such as the motivation of a character or the importance of setting. Many works, furthermore, stubbornly resist complete "coherence." But Ellis is correct about how the process of interpretation works. Interpretation is a quest for ideas manifested by a work's details. To be believable, interpretations must emerge from the details of the work. If we encounter details that contradict our interpretations, we must adjust the interpretations to accommodate those details.

Interpretation is something we do with more than just literature. It is an unavoidable process in any thinking person's life: Why is Miriam angry with me? Why did Jonathan go to pieces when he took the test? Would this job be better for me than that one? How will my blowup with Lucy affect our relationship? Is the defendant guilty? Should we legalize late-term abortions? What were the causes of World War II? Do human beings have free will? Answering questions like these, from the trivial to the profound, requires interpretation.

A crime scene, for example, demands a similar interpretive process as a work of literature. You, the detective, have just arrived at the scene of the crime. As you examine the details of the scene, you formulate hypotheses about what happened and who is responsible. With the discovery of new evidence, you adjust your hypotheses until, having sifted through all the evidence, you decide who committed the crime. A key difference between crime scenes and works of literature, however, is that literature has authors. Criminals may be "authors" of a sort; they create the crime scene, but they do not want us to know what they have done. Authors, in contrast, want to reach us.

The communication process.   The following diagram represents this process of communication:

Authors have ideas, express them in works of literature, and "send" the works to us, their readers. We read ("receive") the works.

As receivers, our challenge is to understand authors' ideas. But this challenge is complicated by the nature of literature. Instead of just telling us what their ideas are, authors use "literary" devices— metaphor, symbol, plot, connotation, rhyme, meter, and so forth—to convey ideas. Such devices communicate meaning indirectly. They force us to figure out authors' ideas. It is as if an author says to us, "I want to state my ideas about something, but instead of saying them straight out, I will tell a story and let you figure out what I'm trying to say." Or the author says, "The woman I'm in love with is wonderful, but instead of telling you directly how this is so, I'm going to say, 'My love is like a red, red rose.'" Most authors impose the task of "figuring out" on us, the readers. Such a task requires interpretation. The craft of interpreting literature is called *literary criticism.* Anyone who interprets literature is a literary critic.

HOW DO WE INTERPRET?

Interpretation of works of literature is the process of thinking about their details in order to see how the details interconnect and what ideas they convey. Interpretation requires us to read actively rather than passively. When we read purely for fun, we are "passive," letting the work wash over us, not trying to figure it out. But when we interpret, we pay close attention to the potential meaning of details. We might even imagine the author as a wily rascal who uses literary devices to manipulate our emotions and our beliefs. Do we agree with the ideas authors foist on us?

The following are suggestions about how to be active, interpreting readers.

1. **Get the facts straight.** A fundamental step in interpreting anything is to see a work's "facts." For some works, this is easy; the

details in them are accessible and understandable. But for other works, getting the facts straight may not be so easy. The poetry of seventeenth-century poets like John Donne and George Herbert is notoriously dense and requires close study to understand. Modernist and Post-Modernist authors such as T. S. Eliot, Virginia Woolf, James Joyce, Thomas Pynchon, and Toni Morrison employ innovative techniques that obscure the details of their works. The language of Chaucer and Shakespeare is not quite our language. To understand it we have to rely on glosses (definitions) that editors often place at the bottom of the page. In short, we sometimes have to work hard just to recognize the facts of literary works. When we read, then, we should look up words we do not know. We should track down allusions (references to myths, religious texts, historical and biographical events, other works of literature). We should read works slowly and more than once.

2. **Connect the work with yourself.** For each of us, the most important meanings of works of literature will arise from our own experience and beliefs. This does not mean that the reasons people value great authors like Sophocles, Sappho, Virgil, Dante, Shakespeare, Goethe, Emily Dickinson, and George Eliot are unimportant. Such reasons are part of our cultural heritage. Not to be interested in them is to deny ourselves the wisdom of that heritage. Even worse, to care only about our own "meanings" is to cut ourselves off from the rest of humankind. But, that said, unless we can connect a work of literature to our own experiences and interests, it will not live for us.

Use the "connection" strategy to project yourself into works of literature, especially ones that seem disconnected from you. Ask, "How would I live under these circumstances?" The writings of the New England Puritans may seem remote and forbidding. But imagine yourself in the Puritan world. Capture its connection to your life. How would you think and feel had you lived then—about your family, the wilderness around you, the difficulty of scraping out a living, the harsh winters, the imperatives of your religion? What would your psychological state—emotional conflicts and tensions—have been? Authors like Nathaniel Hawthorne (in his novel *The Scarlet Letter,* 1850); Arthur Miller (in his play *The Crucible,* 1954); and Maryse Condé (in her novel *I, Tituba, Black Witch of Salem,* 1986) have done just this—projected themselves into Puritan culture and produced intriguing rethinkings of it. As readers, we can do the same. By asking questions like the following, we can recover the appeal of works of literature that may at first seem distant from our own lives:

- ❖ How are things in the work (characters, incidents, places) similar to things in our lives?
- ❖ How does this work challenge our beliefs, and lead us to reconsider what we thought was true?
- ❖ What new issues does the work bring up for us?
- ❖ How does this work give us pleasure?
- ❖ What is upsetting or unpleasant about it?

3. **Develop hypotheses as you read.** As John Ellis says in the passage on pages 4–5, when we read works of literature, even for the first time, we generate ideas about them. The "hypothesis" strategy makes this action intentional and constant. As you read, raise questions about what the details mean: Why does a particular character act the way she does? What ideas does a character espouse? Why does the author keep using a particular image? rhyme scheme? metrical pattern? As you read, do not feel that you have to give final answers to these questions. Plan to come back to them later. Such questions and tentative answers get us thinking, help us pick up important details that pop up later, and make reviewing the work easier.

4. **Write as you read.** Writing generates ideas and helps us think creatively. By putting concepts in our own words, we make them our own and embed them in our memory. If you own copies of works of literature, write in them: underline passages, circle words, draw arrows from one passage to another. In the margins, write questions, summaries, definitions, topics the author addresses, and tentative interpretations. If something is repeated in a work, note where it first appears (i.e., "see page 123") and make comparisons later. Such notations help us generate ideas about what we are reading. Our markings are very helpful when we review the work for tests and writing projects.

5. **Learn from the interpretations of others.** Although we read alone, interpretation is most fruitful as a shared activity, something we do with others. Knowing what others think helps us decide what we think. One critic wrote that even blurbs on book jackets helped him get his bearings in a work. By learning from the insights and knowledge of others, we place ourselves in a dialogue with them. We listen, agree, disagree, share, and thereby clarify

what we believe. Interpretations by professional critics are readily available in books and articles. Equally stimulating are the ideas of people we know—friends, classmates, teachers, colleagues. These people are often nearby, ready to share what they think.

6. **Analyze works of literature.** To *analyze* is to examine the "parts" of something and discover the relationships among them. Analysis is a powerful, necessary strategy for generating and communicating interpretations of anything, not just literature. If you sell computers, you will do it better if you can analyze them—know how they work and what they can do, thus what they "mean" (how they can help your customers). The same is true for interpreting literature. Being able to analyze literature helps us see how each "part" contributes to the meaning of a work.

In the next chapter, we will consider the "parts" of literature itself.

Checklist for Interpreting Literature

❖ Understand all the details of the work. Clarify any confusion about what goes on in the work.

❖ Use your imagination to relate the work to your experiences.

❖ Develop hunches (hypotheses) about the meaning of the work as you read.

❖ If you own the work, mark it (underline, draw arrows, etc.) and write comments in the margin to help you generate ideas and to remember key passages when you review the work.

❖ Seek out ideas of others—critics, teachers, and other students. Compare your ideas with theirs.

Work Cited

Ellis, John. *The Theory of Literary Criticism: A Logical Analysis.* Berkeley: U of California P, 1974.

2

What Is Literature?

Is a Batman comic book "literature"? What about a physics textbook? a restaurant menu? a university catalog? a television sitcom? a political speech? the letters we write home?

Back about the middle of the twentieth century, critics thought they knew what literature was and thus the answer to such questions. The so-called New Critics, who flourished in the United States from the 1920s until the 1960s, believed that literature had certain properties that experts trained in the writing and studying of literature could identify—such things as imagery, metaphor, meter, rhyme, irony, and plot. The New Critics confidently identified and evaluated works of literature, elevating the "great" works of literature to high status. Literature for them consisted, with but few exceptions, of poetry, drama, and fiction and would definitely *not* have included the kinds of writing listed at the beginning of this chapter.

Older definitions. Beginning in the 1960s, however, critics questioned the concept of literature expounded by the New Critics. The New Critics, they noted, seemed narrow in policing the literary "canon"—that unofficial collection of works that critics deem worthy of admiration and study. The New Critics were mostly male and Eurocentric, and the works they admired were written for the most part by males who wrote within the European literary tradition. Largely excluded from the canon were works by females, persons of color, and persons who lived outside Europe. Excluded, also, were the genres (kinds) of "literature" that such outsiders preferred. Because women often lacked access to the means of publishing, many wrote in genres that would not normally be published: letters, diaries, journals, memoirs, autobiographies. Why, critics asked, were these genres not "literature"? Because people of color were often politically active, they wrote in genres that furthered political ends: speeches, autobiographies, essays. Why were these not thought of as "literature"? And because some people belonged to "traditional" cultures, their works were often meant to be spoken, not written. Were these works not "literature"?

Recent definitions.   As a result of such questions and because of the emergence of new theories about language, critics wrestled anew with the question, "What is literature?" At stake were a number of related issues: Which works would get published? Which works were available—in textbooks and paperbacks—to be taught? What groups of people would be valued (because their works were read and appreciated)? If we compare textbook anthologies of English and American literature published circa 1960 with those published today, we can see that the canon now embraces a much broader variety of authors, works, and genres.

Such a comparison reveals how much the concept of "literature" has changed in the past forty years. Some theorists have challenged even the concept of literature. John Ellis argues that literature is not definable by properties, such as rhyme, meter, plot, setting, and characterization. "Nonliterary" works often have such properties—advertisements, popular songs, jokes, graffiti. Rather, the definition of literature is like that of weeds. Just as weeds are "plants we do not wish to cultivate" (38), so literature is identifiable by how people use it. People use works of literature not for utilitarian purposes—to get something done—but as objects of enjoyment in themselves. Ellis says that a work becomes literature when it is no longer "specifically relevant to the immediate context of its origin" (44). If a physics textbook is no longer read for information about physics but instead is read for some other reason—say, the elegance of its prose style—then it transcends the "immediate context of its origin" and becomes literature.

Terry Eagleton, another contemporary critic, claims that literature is a social construct: "Literature, in the sense of a set of works of assured and unalterable value, distinguished by certain shared inherent properties, does not exist" (11). Literature—and the literary "canon"—are constructs, established by society: "Anything can be literature, and anything which is regarded as unalterably and unquestionably literature—Shakespeare, for example—can cease to be literature" (10).

Ellis and Eagleton represent a skeptical reaction to the categorical pronouncements of the New Critics, whose definitions excluded many works we value today. Nonetheless, as interpreters of literature, it is helpful for us to know about properties traditionally identified with literature. Not every work may contain all of these, but most will have one or more of them. We can think of these characteristics as "places" to look for meaning in literature.

LITERATURE IS LANGUAGE

The word *literature* has traditionally meant written—as opposed to spoken—works. But today, given the broadened meaning of the word, it includes oral as well as written works. The works of Homer emerged from an oral tradition. The author "Homer," whether a single individual or a group of people, may even have been illiterate and spoken his works to a scribe, who wrote them down. What Homer and other oral storytellers have in common with writers is language. The medium of literature, whether oral or written, is language. This raises questions about the "literariness" of media that rely heavily on other means of communication: film, dance, physical theater (mime, slapstick, farce), graphic (pictorial) narrative, musical plays. Most critics believe that language is a key aspect of literature and that there has to be enough language in a work for it to be considered literature.

Denotation and connotation. Some theorists claim that authors of literature use language in special ways. One of those ways, according to René Wellek, is an emphasis on connotative rather than denotative meanings of words. Scientists, for example, use language for its *denotative* value, its ability to provide signs (words) that mean one thing only. For scientists, the thing the sign represents—the referent—is more important than the sign itself. Any sign will do, as long as it represents the referent clearly and exactly (11). Because emotions render meanings imprecise, scientists strive to use signs that eliminate the emotional, the irrational, the subjective. Writers of literature, in contrast, use language *connotatively*—to bring into play all the emotional associations words may have. *Connotation* is the meaning that words have in addition to their explicit referents. An example of connotation is the word *mother,* whose denotation is simply "female parent" but whose connotations include such qualities as protection, warmth, unqualified love, tenderness, devotion, mercy, intercession, home, childhood, the happy past. Even scientific language becomes connotative once it enters everyday speech. When we see Albert Einstein's equation $E = mc^2$, we no longer think just of "Energy equals mass times the speed of light squared" but of mushroom clouds and ruined cities. Or the term *DNA,* which denotes the genetic code of life, connotes the alteration of species or the freeing of innocent people from death row. Some kinds of literature (poetry, for example) rely more heavily on connotation than others. Realistic novels, in contrast, may contain precise denotative descriptions of physical objects. Most authors of literature are sensitive to the emotional nuances of words.

Defamiliarization. The Russian Formalists, a group of theorists who flourished in the Soviet Union in the 1920s, claimed another use of language as a defining quality of literature. The key to literature, they said, is "literary" language, language that calls attention to itself as different from ordinary, everyday language. The term for this quality, invented by Viktor Shklovsky, is *defamiliarization* (literally, "making strange"). "The technique of art," he said, "is to make objects 'unfamiliar,' to make forms difficult, to increase the difficulty and length of perception, because the process of perception is an aesthetic end in itself and must be prolonged" (quoted in Selden 31). Shklovsky's idea of defamiliarization can apply not just to language but other aspects of literary form—plot, for example, or techniques of drama.

The principle of defamiliarization is to "foreground"—give prominence to—something in the work of literature that departs from everyday use or familiar artistic conventions. When authors foreground language, they in effect say, "Hey! Look at my language! See how different it is from ordinary language!" They focus on language for itself. They are fascinated by its sounds, its rhythms, even its appearance on the page. Sometimes they become so interested in these qualities that they subordinate meaning to them. Some nursery rhymes, for example, exhibit a delight in language that virtually eliminates meaning, like this one, "Swan":

> Swan, swan, over the sea:
> Swim, swan, swim!
> Swan, swan, back again;
> Well swum, swan!

Here, the anonymous author revels in the repetition of sounds that key off the word *swan*. People who use language in everyday, nonliterary speech and writing also show sensitivity to its sounds and subjective qualities, but writers of literature exploit these qualities more fully, more consciously, and more systematically.

⌒ QUESTIONS

Language is one of the "places" we can look for meaning in literature. Be alert to how writers convey ideas in their subtle and complex language.

1. How does an author use language to signal ideas?

2. What seems significant about such things as the author's choice of words *(diction)*, ways of constructing sentences *(syntax)*, word sounds, repetitions of key words and phrases, archaisms of diction or syntax (as in language that echoes the King James Bible or Shakespeare)?

LITERATURE IS FICTIONAL

We commonly use the term *fiction* to describe prose works that tell a story (for example, fairy tales, short stories, and novels). In fact, however, many works of literature are "fictional" in the sense that something in them signals that readers may set them apart from the context of real life.

Invented material.   A work can be fictional in two ways. First, authors make up—imagine—some or all of the material. This property explains why literature is often referred to as "imaginative literature"; it features invented material that does not exist in the real world. In fantasy fiction, for example, human beings fly, perform magic, remain young, travel through time, metamorphose, and live happily ever after. But even historical fiction, which relies on actual events, is fictional. It includes characters, dialogue, events, and settings that never existed. The three main characters of Hilary Mantel's 1992 novel *A Place of Greater Safety*—Camille Desmoulins, Maximilien Robespierre, and Georges-Jacques Danton—were real people. But the author, while following the outline of their participation in the French Revolution, makes up much of what they do and say.

Stylized material. Second, the fictionality of literature lies also in the artistic control the writer exercises over the work. This artistic control has the effect of stylizing the materials of the work and thus setting it apart from the real. This effect occurs even when the material does accurately mirror the facts of real life or when it states ideas that can be verified in actual experience. Such works would include autobiographies like those by Benjamin Franklin and Frederick Douglass and "true crime" narratives like Truman Capote's *In Cold Blood* (1966) and Norman Mailer's *The Executioner's Song* (1979).

Compare, for example, how a newspaper reporter and a poet would describe the same event. Assume that both would describe the event accurately. The reporter would make his or her account correspond as exactly as possible to the event. Just like the poet, the reporter "controls" his or her account by arranging events in order, by choosing apt words, by leaving out details. There is an art to what the reporter does. But the reporter wants us to experience the details of the event, not the report of it. The poet, in contrast, makes his or her *poem* the object of experience. Through the play of language, selection of details, inclusion of metaphor, irony, and imagery, the poet makes the work an artifact, an object of enjoyment and contemplation in itself.

Consider Walt Whitman's "Cavalry Crossing a Ford" (1867), a poetic account of an event he no doubt witnessed during the American Civil War:

CAVALRY CROSSING A FORD

Walt Whitman

A line in long array where they wind betwixt green islands,
They take a serpentine course, their arms flash in the sun—hark to
    the musical clank,
Behold the silvery river, in it the splashing horses loitering stop to
    drink,
Behold the brown-faced men, each group, each person a picture,
    the negligent rest on the saddles,
Some emerge on the opposite bank, others are just entering the
    ford—while,
Scarlet and blue and snowy white,
The guidon flags flutter gayly in the wind.

Although there are no end rhymes or regular metrical patterns in this poem—it is free verse—readers sense, even if they are not sure why, that this is a work of literature. The way it looks—lines separated, not run together, as they would be in prose—signal its difference from utilitarian writing. Also, such devices as unusual word choice ("array," "betwixt," "behold," "guidon"), alliteration ("flags flutter"), repeated vowel sounds ("silvery river," "horses loitering"), repeated phrases ("Behold the silvery river," "Behold the brown-faced men"), and colorful imagery ("Scarlet and blue and snowy white") call attention to *how* Whitman describes the event, to the poem itself. In this way, the work becomes "fictional." It transcends the event described. Long after people have forgotten the event, they will take pleasure in the poem.

Stylized nonfiction. Even works that are not supposedly fictional, that purport to be about real people and events, become "fictional" by means of literary devices. Two well-known autobiographical examples are Henry David Thoreau's *Walden* (1854) and Richard Wright's *Black Boy* (1945). Thoreau really did live in a cabin at Walden Pond, and we can be fairly sure the events he records in *Walden* did happen. But Thoreau does so many "literary" things with those events that he causes us to conceive of them in aesthetic and thematic terms. His prose style is highly stylized and "poetic." He emphasizes his own feelings. He collapses the two years he actually spent at Walden into one year, and organizes that year around the four seasons of the year, thus giving the book a kind of "plot." He retells events to illustrate philosophical themes. The text is heavily metaphoric and symbolic.

As with Thoreau, Richard Wright records events that actually happened. But here, too, the author employs "literary" devices to make these events vivid. He conveys his intense feelings through first person narration. His language is charged with emotion. He constructs "novelistic" scenes that have extensive dialogue and minute descriptions of physical actions and details. These scenes are almost certainly "fictional," because it is unlikely the author could have remembered the exact words these people said and the physical details he records. We can believe the scenes happened, but Wright fills in details to give them aesthetic impact.

The fictional quality of literature is a second "place" to look for meaning in literature. The fantasy element in literature is fun in itself, but fiction grants authors the option to fill in gaps that always exist in historical events, to make connections that historians cannot. The stylized quality of literature often underscores ideas. Whitman's "Cavalry Crossing a Ford" conveys the impression of lightheartedness, vigor, and gaiety, largely through his selection of details of color, sound, and light.

QUESTIONS

1. What, then, seems fictional about the work, whether imagined or stylized?
2. What ideas do those qualities suggest?

LITERATURE IS TRUE

Factual accuracy. Even though works of literature are "fictional," they have the capacity for being "true." This paradox creates one of the most pleasurable tensions in literature: its imaginative and stylized properties (fictionality) against its representation of the human condition (truth). There are at least three ways that literature can be true. First, literature can be true to the facts of reality, as in descriptions of real people, places, and events—Napoleon's defeat at Waterloo, the operations of a coal mine, the building of the Brooklyn Bridge, the details of human anatomy, the biology of a forest.

Directly stated ideas. More important, literature can be true by communicating ideas about life. The model we presented in Chapter 1 is relevant here:

Authors have ideas they want to communicate to readers. They embed them in works of literature and "send" the works to readers. We can most readily spot this purpose when authors directly state their ideas, as in this poem, "My Friend, the Things That Do Attain," by Henry Howard, Earl of Surrey, written in 1547:

MY FRIEND, THE THINGS THAT DO ATTAIN

Henry Howard, Earl of Surrey

My friend, the things that do attain
The happy life be these, I find:
The riches left, not got with pain;
The fruitful ground; the quiet mind;

The equal friend; no grudge, no strife;
No charge of rule, nor governance;
Without disease, the healthy life;
The household of continuance;

The mean° diet, no dainty fare;   °*simple*
Wisdom joined with simpleness;
The night discharged of all care,
Where wine the wit may not oppress:

The faithful wife, without debate°;   °*argument*
Such sleeps as may beguile the night;
Content thyself with thine estate,
Neither wish death, nor fear his might.

Here the poet tells us straight out his ideas about how to live the "happy life." Even when authors employ obvious elements of fantasy, they can state their ideas directly. Aesop's animal characters are like no animals in real life: They reason, talk, and act like human beings. But the author uses these fantastic characters to state "morals," shrewd commentaries on the human experience.

Indirectly stated ideas. More typically, however, authors refrain from directly stating their ideas. Instead, they present them indirectly by means of literary conventions such as plot, metaphor, symbol, irony, musical language, and suspense. All the details of a work make up an imaginary "world" that is based on the author's ideas about the real world. The world of George Orwell's *Nineteen Eighty-Four* (1948), for example, is filled with crumbling buildings, frightened people, children who betray their parents to the police, procedures whereby truth is systematically altered, masses of people trapped by their ignorance and selfishness, and officials who justify any deed to achieve power. It is a world without love, compassion, justice, joy, tradition, altruism, idealism, or hope. The facts of this world are patently imaginary—Orwell placed them in the future—but we infer from them that Orwell had a pessimistic view of human nature and human institutions. We sense that he is warning us: the terrible society in *Nineteen Eighty-Four* has already existed in places like Nazi Germany and Stalinist Russia and could spread to other places as well.

Typical characters, probable actions. Since most works of literature tell stories, two prominent conventions for communicating ideas are *typical characters* and *probable actions*. You may have heard the phrase "stranger than fiction," as if the characters and events in works of fiction are abnormal and bizarre. But, ironically, it is real life that gives us freakish events and inexplicable people. In contrast, authors impose order on the chaos of real life. To do this, they present characters who typify real people, and they recount actions that would probably happen in real life. J. R. R. Tolkien, for example, offers an array of fantasy creatures and kingdoms in *The Hobbit* and its sequel, *The Lord of the Rings*. Yet his characters, whatever they may look like, represent recognizable types of people. The protagonists, Bilbo and Frodo Baggins, for example, typify those gentle, kindly people who would prefer to live in domestic obscurity but who instead play heroic roles in cataclysmic dramas. And the way they behave is probable because it fits the types of people they are. They do not suddenly become supermen with supernatural powers. Like average people, they are vulnerable to superior strength and to their own fears. They succeed because they exhibit the strengths of average people: perseverance, shrewdness, unselfishness, courage, and honesty.

Allegory.   So prominent in literature are typical characters and probable actions that most works of literature are to some extent allegorical. *Allegory* is a kind of literature in which concrete things—characters, events, and objects—represent ideas. Here is a very short allegory:

> Fear knocked at the door.
> Faith answered.
> There was no one there.

In this story, the character "Fear" stands for the idea of fear, and the character "Faith" is equivalent to the idea of faith. The setting of the story is a house, which symbolizes our psychological selves. Fear's knocking at the door shows an emotion that everyone experiences. Faith's opening the door shows a possible response to fear. The "moral" of the story, implied in the conclusion, is that we should all have faith because faith makes fear disappear.

In longer allegories, such as John Bunyan's *Pilgrim's Progress* (1678), Edmund Spenser's *The Faerie Queen* (1590–1596), and the anonymous medieval play *Everyman* (c.1485), the characters, places, and events are more complexly developed but nonetheless, as in this allegory, have names that directly indicate the ideas they represent. But even in nonallegorical works, the characters, locations, and events are so typical and probable, that they could almost be given names to represent ideas: Hamlet could be named "Melancholy," Othello could be called "Jealous," Ophelia "Innocent," Romeo "Love Sick," Iago "Sinister," and so forth. We can infer authors' worldviews from the "allegorical" qualities of their works—typical characters, suggestive places, and probable actions.

Literature as expression. The near-allegorical quality of literature underscores its expressiveness. Literature is always an expression of the individuals who compose it. Their personalities, emotions, styles, tastes, and beliefs are bound up in their works. As interpreters, our task is to determine objectively what the ideas of a given work may be. We do not, however, have to agree with them. Orwell's worldview is very different from Tolkien's. Orwell shows an average man rebelling against social corruption and failing miserably to do anything about it. He is weak, ineffectual, and controlled by forces outside himself. In Orwell's world, good loses because people are too stupid or greedy or weak to overcome evil. Like Orwell, Tolkien also shows the weakness of average people, but in his worldview, the average person is innately good and potentially strong. Such individuals can band together with others and overthrow evil. Orwell is pessimistic about human nature and the future of humanity; Tolkien is optimistic.

Literature as experiential. Still another kind of "truth" conveyed by literature is the *experience* of reality. Whatever the experience might be—white-water rafting, losing a loved one, falling in love, going hungry, overcoming a handicap—authors put us in the midst of it, make us feel it. Such feelings can teach us about experiences we have never gone through.

Scientists do not often write novels about their research, but one who did was Björn Kurtén, the Swedish paleontologist. His novel *Dance of the Tiger: A Novel of the Ice Age* (1980) features the interaction of *Homo sapiens* and Neanderthal peoples during the Ice Age. Kurtén has published many scholarly books on Ice Age peoples. "Why," he asks in his preface, "write a novel about prehistoric man?"

> In the last three decades, it has been my privilege to be immersed in the life of the Ice Age. More and more, I have felt there is much to be told that simply cannot be formulated in scientific reports. How did it feel to live then? How did the world look to you? What were your beliefs? Above all, what was it like to meet humans not of your own species? That is an experience denied to us, for we are all Homo sapiens (xxiii).

In his novel, Kurtén brilliantly succeeds in bringing Ice Age people to life. Through the thoughts, conflicts, and daily activities of his characters, we *feel* what it was like to live 35,000 years ago.

Another example is Jessamyn West's novel *The Massacre at Fall Creek* (1975). In the afterword she says she was intrigued by an event that occurred in Indiana in 1824. A white judge and jury convicted four white men of killing Indians, and the men were hanged. Although this event marked the first time in United States history that white men convicted other white men for killing Indians, West could find little information about it. She wondered: What was it like to be convicted for something previously condoned? How did the Indians and whites feel about the event? West's novel is her answer to these questions. Drawing upon her understanding of what most people would go through under those circumstances, she shows us what they *probably* experienced. Furthermore, she causes us to *feel* what they experienced. We live through the gruesome killings. We share the fear of Indian reprisal. We see the callousness of Indian killers. We experience the dawning consciousness of some whites that Indians are human and have rights. We suffer the alienation caused by taking unpopular moral stands. We inhale the circus-like atmosphere of the hangings. With the judge, we puzzle over ambiguous ethical dilemmas. We stand on the scaffold with the condemned.

⌐ QUESTIONS

The truth of literature is the most important "place" to look for meaning in literature. The following questions encapsulate the points we have made here about truth in literature.

1. What ideas does the author state directly?

2. How are the characters typical of human behavior? What ideas do they espouse or seem to represent? Which characters—and thus the ideas associated with them—predominate at the end of the work?

3. What ideas are associated with places and other physical properties?

4. Authors sometimes signal ideas through devices like titles, names, and epigraphs. (An *epigraph* is a pertinent quotation put at the beginning of a work or chapter.) Examples of suggestive titles are *The Grapes of Wrath* (taken from a line in "The Battle Hymn of the Republic"), *All the King's Men* (from the nursery rhyme "Humpty-Dumpty"), *Pride and Prejudice, Great Expectations,* and *Measure for Measure.* What ideas seem embedded in titles, chapter heads, epigraphs, names, and other direct indications of authors' ideas?

5. What do other works by the author suggest about the meaning of this work?

6. As with Björn Kurtén and Jessamyn West (discussed above), authors sometimes comment on their own work. What light does such comment shed on the ideas in the work?

7. What feelings does the work elicit in each of us? What do we experience in the work that we have never gone through? What have we experienced that the work brings powerfully to life?

LITERATURE IS AESTHETIC

Order and form in literature. Literature is "aesthetic"; it gives pleasure. The aesthetic quality of literature—its "beauty"—is hard to define and describe. In a sense, it just *is*. Like various other art forms—music, patterns of color in paintings, photographs of sunsets, dance—literature is an end in itself. The pleasure of literature rests in the way authors use literary conventions, such as metaphor, plot, symbolism, irony, suspense, themes, and poetic language. Taken together, they constitute the *form* of the work, the order authors impose on their material. Such order is not typical of real life. In real life, events can be random, disconnected, and inconsequential. Problems can remain unresolved. The murderer may not be caught, the cruel parent may continue to be cruel, the economic crisis may persist, the poor but honest youth may not be rewarded. We cannot be aware of all the things that happen to us, much less remember them. Nor do we always know which events are important, which trivial. But literature can give order to events in the form of a *plot*. Unimportant events are excluded, cause-and-effect relationships established, conflicts resolved. Events are arranged in logical order so that they form a sequence with a beginning, a middle, and an end. Plot is but one of a multitude of ways that artists give order to material. They may also arrange language into patterns, reduce characters to recognizable types, connect details to ideas, elegantly describe settings. In works of literature, all of the elements combine to form an *overall* order, an *overall* coherence.

The aesthetic quality of literature is thus another "place" to look for meaning in literature. Experiencing the beauty of literature may itself be a kind of meaning. But the aesthetic qualities of literature are bound up with the other kind of meaning, the ideas conveyed by a work. Authors use pleasurable conventions to enhance and communicate ideas.

Chapter 2

QUESTIONS

1. What conventions (of language, plot, characterization, etc.) does the author use to give us pleasure?

2. Why does the author's manipulation of these conventions affect us so strongly?

3. How does the author use pleasurable conventions to communicate ideas and make them appealing?

LITERATURE IS INTERTEXTUAL

Genre

Literature is intertextual: It relates to other works of literature, it incorporates established literary conventions, and it belongs to at least one genre of literature. *Genre* is a French word that means "type" or "kind." Literary genres are identifiable by their literary conventions. *Conventions* are features of literature, whether of language, subject matter, themes, or form, that readers can easily recognize.

As an example of intertextuality, consider these two poems. The second, by Sir Walter Raleigh, is a response to the first, by Christopher Marlowe.

THE PASSIONATE SHEPHERD TO HIS LOVE

Come live with me and be my love,
And we will all the pleasures prove
That valleys, groves, hills, and fields,
Woods, or steepy mountain yields.

And we will sit upon the rocks,
Seeing the shepherds feed their flocks,
By shallow rivers to whose falls
Melodious birds sing madrigals.

And I will make thee beds of roses
And a thousand fragrant posies,
A cap of flowers, and a kirtle
Embroidered all with leaves of myrtle;

THE NYMPH'S REPLY TO THE SHEPHERD

If all the world and love were young,
And truth in every shepherd's tongue,
These pretty pleasures might me move
To live with thee and be thy love.

Time drives the flocks from field to fold
When rivers rage and rocks grow cold,
And Philomel becometh dumb;
The rest complains of cares to come.

The flowers do fade, and wanton fields
To wayward winter reckoning yields;
A honey tongue, a heart of gall,
Is fancy's spring, but sorrow's fall.

A gown made of the finest wool

Which from our pretty lambs we pull;

Fair lined slippers for the cold,

With buckles of the purest gold;

A belt of straw and ivy buds,

With coral clasps and amber studs:

And if these pleasures may thee move,

Come live with me, and be my love.

The shepherds' swains shall dance and sing

For thy delight each May morning:

If these delights thy mind may move,

Then live with me and be my love.

Christopher Marlowe (1600)

Thy gowns, thy shoes, thy beds of roses,

Thy cap, thy kirtle, and thy posies

Soon break, soon wither, soon forgotten—

In folly ripe, in reason rotten.

Thy belt of straw and ivy buds,

Thy coral clasps and amber studs,

All these in me no means can move

To come to thee and be thy love.

But could youth last and love still breed,

Had joys no date nor age no need,

Then these delights my mind might move

To live with thee and be thy love.

Sir Walter Raleigh (c. 1600)

These poems are intertextual in the three ways mentioned above. First, Raleigh's poem is an almost line-for-line response to Marlowe's. We can understand Marlowe's poem without knowing Raleigh's, but we would miss a lot in Raleigh's poem if we did not know Marlowe's. Second, Marlowe's poem belongs to a genre called pastoral poetry. Third, in composing his poem, Marlowe incorporated the conventions of the pastoral genre: a peaceful, simple rural setting; carefree shepherds (the word *pastor* means "shepherd"); a season of eternal spring; an absence of the difficulties of life—hard work, disease, harsh weather, betrayal; lovers who talk genially about love; and a playful, witty, charming poetic style. Raleigh knows the conventions of pastoral poetry so well that he can challenge their basic assumptions.

QUESTIONS

The intertextuality of literature is a rich source of meaning for the interpretation of individual works. We can pose questions that help us mine this meaning.

1. **What can we learn about a work by considering works related to it?** Authors often have specific works of literature in mind when they compose their own. Sometimes they signal this by means of *allusions*: explicit references to other works. Such allusions are always invitations to compare the author's work with the other works. Dante, for example, by featuring the Latin poet Virgil as a

prominent character in *The Divine Comedy,* signals that Virgil's writings and especially *The Aeneid* were significant for his work.

Sometimes authors make no overt references to other works, but we infer from the work itself or learn from outside sources, that the author drew from other works. We know, for example, that Dostoevsky was influenced by the works of Charles Dickens, but he does not necessarily say so in his novels. Whether or not authors tell us what other works serve as their reference points, we can ask what ideas and artistic devices from these other works are applicable to the work under study. Raleigh, in "The Nymph's Reply to the Shepherd," openly invites us to compare his poem to Marlowe's. When we do, we see the stark difference between his ideas and Marlowe's.

2. **Can we understand the genre in which the work is written?** Genres are indispensable for both writers and readers of literature. Alastair Fowler, in his comprehensive treatment of genre, *Kinds of Literature: An Introduction to the Theory of Genres and Modes,* says that genres are similar to language. The conventions of each genre constitute a "grammar" that allows us to "read" the genre and works written in it (20). Just as we must learn the structure of a language in order to read it, so must we learn the conventions of genres in order to read literature.

People learn popular genres as they grow up—by being read to, watching television, going to movies. But some genres require special training to understand. One reason is that genres are products of particular cultures and times. We can read narrative fiction, for example, because we know its conventions. But a culture could conceivably have no tradition of fiction. If so, its members would find fiction baffling, just as people brought up in the Western tradition usually find Japanese Nō plays and Kabuki theater puzzling. Another reason is that genres change over time or cease to exist. We may encounter genres even in our own language that puzzle us because we do not know them. To read some works of literature, we have to *recover* their genres. Pastoral poetry, a genre that was enormously popular in Christopher Marlowe's day, is virtually dead as a genre today. To recover it, we can read other poems in the pastoral tradition. And we can refer to historical works, such as M. H. Abrams's excellent *A Glossary of Literary Terms,* for information about pastoral poetry and other unfamiliar genres.

3. **What values does the genre convey?** Genres are cultural phenomena. In contrast to works by an individual author, they emerge

from many authors and reflect the interests, ways of life, and values of particular cultures.

Detective fiction, for example, became a recognizable genre in the nineteenth century. Critics contend that its conventions mirror the values, troubles, and circumstances of Western culture in the nineteenth century. The detective hero, for example—Edgar Allan Poe's Dupin, Arthur Conan Doyle's Sherlock Holmes—represents Western culture's enormous respect for science. These detectives are dispassionate, analytical, and brilliant. Holmes, in fact, publishes treatises on forensic science. The setting of detective fiction is typically the great industrial cities, which were by-products of nineteenth-century capitalism. These cities, with their mazelike streets and heterogeneous populations, were perfect environments for intrigue and crime. Dupin works in Paris, Holmes in London. The crime is almost always murder or threat of murder. The pursuit and punishment of the murderer upholds the nineteenth century's respect for the individual. The murderer destroys the individual's most valuable possession, life itself. But the murderer destroys more than just lives. At stake also are the institutions held dear in the nineteenth century—the family, religious communities, boards of trade, governmental agencies, universities. The detective, by capturing the murderer, purges these institutions of those who would corrupt and destroy them.

Other genres reflect their own cultural contexts. The epic trumpets heroic deeds and national solidarity. The medieval romance inculcates a code of chivalry. Why, then, did the author choose to compose in this genre? What ideas associated with the genre carry over to this work?

4. **Why is or was the genre appealing?** It is a cold, rainy night. You are home for vacation. Everyone else in the house has gone to bed. You have been saving Stephen King's latest gothic thriller for just such a time. Perfect. You settle in for two hours of uninterrupted escape. The book, of course, need not be horror. It could be science fiction, romance, western, detective, adventure, spy, thriller. Maybe you do not care who the author is. You just picked the book off the shelf because it belongs to a genre you like.

When we do this—read something because it is a kind of literature—we have succumbed to the pleasures of genre. The reasons we like certain genres are part of the "meaning" of what we read—the pleasures the genres give as well as the ideas they convey. We can pinpoint that meaning by investigating the appeal of genres. Why do we and other people like them?

The same question applies to genres from the past. We can discern meanings authors may have intended by asking why people liked the genres in which the authors wrote. Authors and readers of pastoral poetry during Christopher Marlowe's time lived in the city. They liked pastoral poetry because the fantasy of an idealized rural life, with pretty scenes, images, and language, allowed them to escape the grimy, dangerous, and changing cities where they lived.

5. **How does the author challenge or change the genre?** Before authors can compose a work of literature, they have to know its genre well. But when they compose, they almost always rebel against generic formulas. Alistair Fowler describes the process in this way: The "writer who cares most about originality has the keenest interest in genre. Only by knowing the beaten track, after all, can he be sure of leaving it" (32). Because authors and readers hunger for innovation, every literary work, Fowler says, "changes the genre it relates to." Consequently, "all genres are continuously undergoing metamorphosis. This, indeed, is the principal way in which literature itself changes" (23). An example of a recent "new" genre is "magic realism," a form of fiction that has been popularized by Latin American authors such as Gabriel García Márquez (*One Hundred Years of Solitude,* 1970), Isabel Allende (*The House of the Spirits,* 1985), and Laura Esquivel (*Like Water for Chocolate,* 1992). Combining the characteristics of two genres—realistic fiction and fairy tale—these authors couch trenchant political and social criticism within the delights of erotic romance and supernatural happenings.

Most authors alter the formulas of genres on purpose. What shifts in values and aesthetic effects do these changes contribute to the works we want to interpret? Raleigh, by having his female character respond to Marlowe's shepherd in terms of the harsh realities of life, cleverly changes the pastoral genre into a new genre, one we might call the antipastoral. He criticizes not only the ideas that undergird pastoral poetry but the pastoral genre itself.

6. **How do individual conventions of a genre add meaning to a work?** Alistair Fowler says that the nucleus of all literary genres is three huge, amorphous categories: fiction, drama, and poetry (5). Within these genres are numerous subgenres. *Subgenres,* Fowler says, "have the common features of a kind—external forms

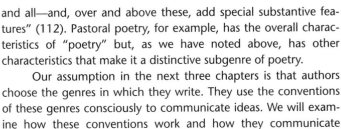

and all—and, over and above these, add special substantive features" (112). Pastoral poetry, for example, has the overall characteristics of "poetry" but, as we have noted above, has other characteristics that make it a distinctive subgenre of poetry.

Our assumption in the next three chapters is that authors choose the genres in which they write. They use the conventions of these genres consciously to communicate ideas. We will examine how these conventions work and how they communicate ideas. Like the properties of literature discussed in this chapter—language, fictionality, truth, aesthetics, and intertextuality—each literary convention is a "place" to look for meaning in works of literature.

Checklist for the Elements of Literature

❖ Note the qualities of language that make the work you're studying "literary." (Literature is language, pages 13–15.)

❖ Spot the ways in which the author uses invented materials. (Literature is fictional, page 15.)

❖ Explore how the author stylizes the work to make it seem "fictional." (Literature is fictional, pages 16–18.)

❖ Underline those places where the author states ideas directly. (Literature is true, pages 18–19.)

❖ Explore how the work might be allegorical—how characters, actions, and physical details embody ideas. (Literature is true, pages 20–21.)

❖ Explain how the characters are typical or atypical of real human beings. (Literature is true, pages 19–20.)

❖ Show how the events and actions of characters are probable or improbable. (Literature is true, pages 19–20.)

❖ Indicate how the work makes you experience its subject matter. (Literature is true, pages 21–22.)

❖ Explain how the work gives you pleasure. If it does not, say why. (Literature is aesthetic, pages 23–24.)

❖ Compare works that are alluded to in the work or that are similar to it. (Literature is intertextual, pages 24–29.)

❖ Identify the genre of the work. (Literature is intertextual, pages 24–29.)

❖ Note how the work abides by and departs from the conventions of the genre. (Literature is intertextual, pages 24–29.)

❖ Speculate about why the author chose this genre to present the ideas of the work. (Literature is intertextual, pages 24–29.)

Works Cited

Abrams, M. H. *A Glossary of Literary Terms.* Fort Worth: Harcourt, 1999.

Eagleton, Terry. *Literary Theory: An Introduction.* Minneapolis: U of Minnesota P, 1983.

Ellis, John. *The Theory of Literary Criticism: A Logical Analysis.* Berkeley: U of California P, 1974.

Fowler, Alastair. *An Introduction to the Theory of Genres and Modes.* Cambridge: Harvard UP, 1982.

Kurtén, Björn. *Dance of the Tiger: A Novel of the Ice Age.* New York: Pantheon, 1980.

Selden, Raman, and Peter Widdowson. *A Reader's Guide to Contemporary Literary Theory.* 3rd ed. Lexington: U of Kentucky P, 1993.

Wellek, René, and Austin Warren. *Theory of Literature.* New York: Harcourt, 1942.

West, Jessamyn. *The Massacre at Fall Creek.* New York: Harcourt, 1975.

3

Interpreting Fiction

This chapter begins an analysis of the three major genres of literature: fiction, drama, and poetry. The word *genre* in French means "type" or "kind." Our purpose in this and the next two chapters is to show how elements of the three very broad "kinds" of literature provide opportunities for interpretation. After the discussions of each element, you will find questions and suggestions for exploring on your own. In this chapter, we take up the most popular genre, fiction.

THE ELEMENTS OF FICTION

Fiction belongs to a large category of communication called narrative. *Narrative* is the telling of a story, a recounting of events in time. The distinguishing characteristic of narrative is the presence of a teller, a narrator. The "teller" can be any medium through which a story is revealed. Images (films, cartoons, paintings), bodily movements (dance, mime), sounds (singing, musical instruments)—all of these tell stories. The kind of narrative most people associate with literature is fiction. In contrast to nonfiction narrative (biography, memoir, autobiography, history), *narrative fiction,* whether written in poetry or prose, features a telling of made-up events. We now take up those conventions and aspects—elements—that typify narrative fiction.

Theme

Themes are ideas about the human condition that we draw from works of literature—not just from fiction but from literature in all genres. The following discussion continues the treatment of "truth" in literature begun in Chapter 2. Here we offer guidelines for stating themes and strategies for identifying them.

Guidelines for stating and describing theme

1. **Subject and theme.** Although the terms *subject* and *theme* are often used interchangeably, they are different. The *subject* is what the work is about. You can state the subject in a word or phrase: "The subject of Shakespeare's Sonnet 116 is love." In contrast, theme is what the work *says* about the subject. Stating a theme requires a complete sentence, sometimes several sentences: "A theme of Sonnet 116 is, 'Love remains constant even when assaulted by tempestuous events or by time.'"

2. **Reference to reality outside the work.** A theme applies to the world outside the work. The claim, "Rapid change in Rip Van Winkle's environment threatens his identity," is thoughtful and interesting, but it does not state a theme. It applies only to something inside the work. State themes so they refer to reality outside the work: "Rip Van Winkle's experience shows that environment causes *many people* to feel their identity is threatened." Like all claims about theme, this one seizes upon concrete situations within the work to make generalizations about reality outside the work. Literature thus becomes a form of "philosophy"—universal wisdom about the nature of the world.

3. **Theme as dilemma.** Theme may present an intellectual dilemma rather than a "message" that neatly solves the dilemma. Robert Penn Warren's novel *All the King's Men,*[*] for example, raises the problem of morality in politics. How, the novel seems to ask, can political leaders in a democratic society do good when citizens are apathetic and easily misled? The character who embodies this question is a well-meaning and gifted politician who uses corrupt and violent means to attain good ends. By telling his story, Warren dramatizes the question. But he never really answers it. You cannot pull a neat moral out of the story of this character's rise and

---

[*]Publication dates of works of literature cited in this book and dates of authors' lives can be found in the author-title index at the back of the book.

fall. Rather, to state the "theme" of this novel—or one theme—you need to summarize as accurately as you can the problem Warren presents in the way he presents it. You could explain how the problem is worked out in this one character's life, but you could not necessarily generalize from that to all people's lives. Or the generalization might be that politics is morally contradictory, never simply right or wrong.

4. **Multiple themes.**   In many works, especially complex ones, there may be several, even contradictory themes. A subject of Tolstoy's *Anna Karenina* is sacred love versus profane love. But another, equally important subject is social entrapment. One theme of *Anna Karenina,* then, seems to be that people should not abandon "sacred" commitments, such as marriage and parenthood, for extramarital "loves," no matter how passionate and deeply felt they may be. This theme emerges from Anna's desertion of her husband and child for Count Vronsky. An alternate theme is that people, through little fault of their own, can become trapped in painful, long-lasting, and destructive relationships that they want desperately to escape. This theme emerges from Anna's marriage. When she was very young, Anna married an older man whom she now realizes is too petty, prim, and self-absorbed to satisfy her generous and passionate nature. So discordant is her relationship with her husband that it seems no less "immoral" than her affair with Vronsky. Tolstoy, in other words, draws complex, even contradictory lessons from Anna's adultery. She is not simply the sinful person; she is also the driven person. This combination of traits characterizes the condition of many people.

5. **A lack of themes.**   Some works have no clear themes. They may display images, actions, atmosphere, and characters that have no apparent relationship to the world outside the works. Or their ideas may be incompletely developed. Don't feel, then, that you have to state themes in a work when they don't seem to exist.

6. **A work's themes vs. our values.**   When writing about a work's themes, our task is to represent them fairly—with well-supported explanations of what we think they are. To do this, however, is not necessarily to agree with them. You are always free to disagree with authors' world views.

7. **Themes and the author.**   Are the themes we detect in a literary work equivalent to the author's ideas? Wayne C. Booth says no, they are not the same. In *The Rhetoric of Fiction,* he argues

passionately for the existence of themes in works of literature. A work embodies a "value system which gives it its meaning" (112). The author's "voice," which establishes this value system, "is never really silenced. It is, in fact, one of the things we read fiction for" (60). But Booth makes a now well-known distinction between "real" authors and "implied" authors. He reasons that real authors are rhetoricians. They craft works of literature to persuade us of their values. In order to persuade, they project an idealized concept of themselves in each of their works. Booth calls this idealized author, manifested by the work, the implied author: "The 'implied author' chooses, consciously or unconsciously, what we read; we infer him as an ideal, literary, created version of the real man; he is the sum of his own choices" (73–75).

Booth seems to imply that we can set aside the real author and, instead, attribute the values of a work to an implied author, whose existence we glean from the work itself. The "Jane Austen" of her novels is not the real Jane Austen but the "implied" author, unique to each novel.

But we might counter Booth's argument by saying that the identity of any human being is multiple. We all play different roles in life. We are different as family members from how we are at school or work. When we make sales pitches or political speeches, we advance versions of ourselves that we hope will sit well with our audience. Why aren't these "selves" all real, all part of our identity? Why can't we assume that the "self" an author projects in a literary work is an aspect of the real author, just as the selves each one of us manifests in different situations is an aspect of our real selves?

Learning about authors' lives and concerns, furthermore, often provides insight into the meanings of their works. Sometimes authors even comment on their works. In a lecture at Hollins College, Flannery O'Connor explains some of the ideas she had in mind when she wrote her short story "A Good Man Is Hard to Find" (109). Her elucidation of the story is highly compelling. But she added "that there are perhaps other ways than my own in which this story could be read, but none other by which it could have been written" (109). In other words, when we see connections between authors and their works, we don't lock out other interpretations. But we can at least see connections between ideas held by the real author and themes in the work.

QUESTIONS ABOUT THEME
(STRATEGIES FOR IDENTIFYING THEMES)

Two broad questions about theme are: What subjects does the work address? What does the work seem to say about them—what are its themes? The following are some strategies for answering these questions:

1. **Comments made by narrators and characters.** Sometimes narrators and characters state one or more of a work's themes. In the final chapter of Hawthorne's *The Scarlet Letter,* the narrator says, "Among many morals which press upon us from the poor minister's miserable experience, we put only this into a sentence: 'Be true! Be true! Be true! Show freely to the world, if not your worst, yet some trait whereby the worst may be inferred!'" How believable are such statements? If they square with the philosophical and moral concepts of the work, then you can claim them as themes. If they are mouthed by untrustworthy speakers or are contradicted by evidence, they are questionable as themes. Further questions: Do the narrator and characters state other possible themes? Do other aspects of the work suggest themes?

2. **Areas of philosophical inquiry.** Philosophers and theologians have for generations raised questions about the human experience. You can seize upon these to interpret works of literature. Here are four rich areas of inquiry:

   Human nature. What image of humankind emerges from the work? Are people, for example, generally good? deeply flawed?

   The nature of society. Does the author portray a particular society or social scheme as life-enhancing or life-destroying? Are characters we care about in conflict with their society? Do they want to escape from it? What causes and perpetuates this society? If the society is flawed, how is it flawed?

   Human freedom. What control over their lives do the characters have? Do they make choices in complete freedom? Are they driven by forces beyond their control? Does Providence or some grand scheme govern history, or is history simply random and arbitrary?

   Ethics. What are the moral conflicts in the work? Are they clear cut or ambiguous? That is, is it clear to us exactly what is right and exactly what is wrong? When moral conflicts are ambiguous in a work, right often opposes *right,* not wrong. What rights are in opposition to one another? If right opposes wrong, does right win in the end? To what extent are characters to blame for their actions?

3. **Moral center.** Another strategy for discovering a work's themes is to answer this question: Who, if anyone, serves as the *moral center* of the work? The *moral center* is the one person whom the author vests with right action and right thought (that is, what the *author* seems to think is right action and right thought), the one character who seems clearly "good" and who often serves to judge other characters. Not every work has a moral center; but in the works that do, its center can lead you to some of the work's themes. In Dickens's *Great Expectations,* for example, the moral center is Biddy, the girl who comes to Pip's sister's household as a servant. She is a touchstone of goodness for Pip, and when he strays from the good, Biddy and his remembrance of her helps bring him back to it. *Great Expectations* is largely about morality (subject), and by studying Biddy we uncover some of Dickens's ideas about morality (theme).

When identifying a work's moral center, answer questions such as these: How can we tell that this person is the moral center? What values does the moral center embody? Is the moral center flawed in any way that might diminish his or her authority? What effect does the moral center have on the other characters and on us?

THINKING ON PAPER ABOUT THEME

1. List the subject or subjects of the work. For each subject, see if you can state a theme. Put a check next to the ones that seem most important.

2. Explain how the title, subtitle, epigraph, chapter titles, and names of characters may suggest themes.

3. Describe the work's depiction of human behavior.

4. Describe the work's depiction of society. Show the representation of social ills and how they might be corrected or addressed.

5. List moral issues raised by the work.

6. Name the character who is the moral center of the work. List his or her traits.

7. Mark statements by the narrator or characters that seem to state themes.

Now It's Your Turn

Explain one or more of the themes in Mary Robison's "Yours" (pages 43–44), "The Daemon Lover" (pages 146–48), or Frost's "The Death of the Hired Man" (pages 262–66).

Point of View

Point of view is the narrator's relationship to the world of the work. The term is a metaphor that indicates the location (point) from which the narrator sees (views) everything in the narrative. Another term that some critics prefer is *perspective*. Authors employ four basic points of view.

Third-person omniscient point of view. In the third-person omniscient position, a narrator from "outside" the story world tells the story. This point of view is "third person" because the narrator refers to all the characters in the third person, as "he" and "she." It is "omniscient" because the narrator assumes near complete knowledge of the characters' actions, thoughts, and locations. Omniscient narrators move at will between places, historical periods, and characters. They sometimes even speak directly to the reader. Needless to say, their godlike knowledge exceeds what any of us knows about the real world. It is as if the omniscient narrator hovers above the story world, seeing and hearing everything, including characters' thoughts. Many famous eighteenth- and nineteenth-century novels use an omniscient perspective. Examples are Hawthorne's *The Scarlet Letter,* Hardy's *Tess of the D'Urbervilles,* Fielding's *Tom Jones,* and Eliot's *Adam Bede.*

Third-person limited point of view. As with omniscient narrators, narrators of the third-person limited point of view refer to characters as "he" and "she," and still have more knowledge of the fictional world than we do of our worlds. But they restrict (limit) their perspective to the mind of one character. This character may be either a main or peripheral character. Names for this character are "central consciousness," "reflector," and "filter." A plot device that often accompanies this point of view is the character's gradual discovery of some truth that climaxes with an epiphany. (See page 55 for an explanation of "epiphany.") Examples of third-person limited perspective are Hawthorne's

"Young Goodman Brown," Stephen Crane's "The Open Boat," and James Joyce's "Araby."

Sometimes the author restricts this point of view so severely that we see everything solely through the mind of a single character, like sunlight filtered through a stained glass window. Henry James experimented with such severe restrictions in his later fiction, as in "The Beast in the Jungle" and *The Ambassadors*. Usually, however, the limited point of view is a mixture of omniscient and limited. In Jane Austen's *Pride and Prejudice*, for example, the narrator manifests an omniscient perspective but, for the most part, gives us the thoughts of just one character, Elizabeth Bennet.

Third-person objective (dramatic) point of view. Narrators in the objective point of view refer to characters in the third person and display omniscient knowledge of places, times, and events. They do not, however, enter the minds of any character. We see the characters as we do people in real life or as we might observe them in a play (thus the term "dramatic"). We learn about them from what they say and do, how they look, and what other characters say about them. But we do not learn what they think unless they tell us. Examples are Ernest Hemingway's "Hills Like White Elephants" and "The Killers," Stephen Crane's "The Blue Hotel," and Shirley Jackson's "The Lottery."

First-person point of view. In the first-person point of view, one of the characters tells the story and uses the first-person pronoun, "I." Whereas in the third-person limited point of view, the narrator reveals anything about one character—even things characters may be dimly aware of—here, the narration is restricted to what one character *says* he or she observes. The narrator may be a major character located at the center of events or a minor character who observes the action from the side. The character's narration may be about events that have recently occurred (Twain's *Huckleberry Finn*, Fitzgerald's *The Great Gatsby*) or about events that happened well in the past (Dickens's *Great Expectations*, Poe's "The Cask of Amontillado"). An unusual use of first-person point of view is the epistolary narrative, which reveals action through letters. (An *epistle* is a letter; *epistolary* means "written in letters.") Samuel Richardson's *Pamela*, Henry James's "A Bundle of Letters," Choderlos Laclos's *Dangerous Liaisons*, and Alice Walker's *The Color Purple* are all epistolary narratives.

Tone.   Tone is also an aspect of point of view since it has a great deal to do with the narrator. *Tone* is the narrator's predominant attitude toward the subject, whether that subject is a place, event, character, or idea. The narrator conveys his or her attitude through the way narrative devices are handled, including choice of words. Sometimes the narrators state point blank how they feel about a subject; more often, the narrator's attitude is conveyed indirectly. Jack Burden, the narrator of Robert Penn Warren's *All the King's Men,* maintains a flippant and cynical tone through most of the narration. Jake Barnes, the narrator of Hemingway's *The Sun Also Rises,* manifests a stoical, hard-boiled tone. Dr. Watson, the narrator of the Sherlock Holmes stories, displays a bemused, surprised tone.

Multiple points of view.   Authors sometimes include several points of view in the same work. Dickens in *Bleak House* shuttles back and forth between a first-person narrative and an omniscient narrative. We see that the first-person narrator has a more limited view of things than the omniscient narrator. Point of view here becomes a means of developing characters and of making a point about the limits of human perception.

Reliability of narrators and centers of consciousness.   Some narrators and centers of consciousness are more reliable than others. You can almost always trust omniscient narrators. But be suspicious of first-person narrators and characters who serve as centers of consciousness. These characters may distort what they tell us or observe. They may be self-deceived, or untruthful, or gullible, or mentally troubled, or limited in understanding (children, for example), or self-serving.

In *The Adventures of Huckleberry Finn,* there is a marked difference between the narrator's (Huck's) naive view of reality and the author's more sophisticated and realistic view. When Huck sees the Grangerford house, he says, "It was a mighty nice family, and a mighty nice house, too. I hadn't seen no house out in the country before that was so nice and had so much style." He proceeds to describe the interior with awe and reverence. Although Huck is impressed with the furnishings, Twain clearly is not. We recognize Twain's attitude from the details Huck provides: the unread books, the reproductions of sentimental paintings, the damaged imitation fruit, the crockery animals, the broken clock, the painted hearth, the tablecloth "made out of beautiful oilcloth," the piano "that had tin pans in it" (85–88).

Huck also shows his admiration for Emmeline Grangerford's poetry by reproducing some of it to share with us (87–88). But we see, as Twain wants us to see, that the poetry is terrible.

Finally, Huck is awestruck by the family's aristocratic bearing: "Col. Grangerford was a gentleman, you see. He was a gentleman all over; and so was his family. He was well born. . . . He didn't have to tell anybody to mind their manners—everybody was always good mannered where he was" (89). Yet he fails to see, as Twain and we see, the ironic contrast between the family's good manners and its irrational and murderous feud with another family. Twain's handling of point of view in this novel helps to develop both character and theme. By presenting Huck's credulous view of things, it develops Huck as an essentially naive and innocent person. By ironically contrasting Twain's view to Huck's, it underscores the author's harsher and more pessimistic perception of "reality."

The student essay on Poe's "The Cask of Amontillado" (pages 362–67) explores another example of a possible unreliable narrator. See if you agree with the author's assessment.

Narratees. When we define *narrative* as a story told by a teller (narrator), we assume the existence of an audience—one or more people who listen to or read it. The term for this audience is *narratee(s)*. In first-person narratives, the audience may be specified. Chaucer's *The Canterbury Tales* presents a motley collection of people who, while making the pilgrimage to Canterbury, tell one another tales. Marlow, the narrator of Joseph Conrad's *Heart of Darkness,* tells his story to men sitting in a living room. The duke in Browning's "My Last Duchess" (pages 120–22) addresses an ambassador from another family. But often the narratee of first-person narratives is not specified. Who is Huck's audience (in Twain's *The Adventures of Huckleberry Finn*)? Huck has apparently written the story. To whom is he writing? Charlotte Brontë's narrator Jane Eyre addresses a narratee whom she calls "Reader." Whom does she have in mind? Why is she writing this story?

The identity, character traits, motives, and inclinations of the audience for first-person narratives often illuminates other elements in the story, especially the narrator. The narratee of Poe's "The Cask of Amontillado" (pages 362–67) is referred to only as "you" and is not identified or described. But, as the student essay on this story indicates (pages 368–73), speculating about who this person is and why Montresor tells him the story, leads to provocative ideas about Montresor and his expectations.

The narratee of third-person works is harder to discern. Third-person narrators may indicate, directly or indirectly, an audience—people, for example, who until now have been ignorant about certain experiences, such as slavery, apartheid, imprisonment, and warfare. The narrator may seem to have an identifiable audience in mind—people with specialized knowledge, with certain political views, with a particular social bias, with certain experiences. An example is the author of *Beowulf,* who assumes his audience is familiar with the history and legends of sixth-century Scandinavian tribes. The author seems also to assume that his audience consists of Christians who would favorably compare their religion to that of the pagan characters of the narrative.

Works may have multiple narratees. Folk epics like *Beowulf* and *The Odyssey* have at least three categories of narratee. One is the characters who listen to other characters tell stories. Another is the audience for the oral versions of the epics, before the epic was written down. A third is the audience for the written version. Speculation about the settings, occasions, and audiences of such narratives often throws light on possible meanings of the work.

Narrators and authors.   Is a narrator of a work of fiction equivalent to the author? First-person narrators are clearly not the author. They may resemble the author, but they are nonetheless fictional. Otherwise the work would be nonfiction—a memoir or autobiography. More problematic are third-person narrators, especially omniscient narrators, who seem to have the same knowledge as authors. Suzanne Keen says that the "temptation with omniscient narrators is to equate them and their opinions with their creators, a move that is rarely justified and often misleading" (38). She argues that we should see *all* narrators, even ones that refer to themselves as the work's creator, as fictional. They are as much "characters" in the story as the other characters.

QUESTIONS ABOUT POINT OF VIEW

1. Why did the author choose the work's point of view? How would the story be changed or affected by a different point of view?

2. What effect does the point of view have on us? If, for example, the point of view is first person, how does this character (rather than another character) affect our reception of the story? How would the story be different if told by another character? If the point of

view is objective (dramatic), what do we gain or lose by not being able to enter the characters' minds?

3. If the work includes more than one point of view, how are they different? Why does the author use each one?

4. How reliable is the narrator? If a narrator is unreliable, how can you tell what the truth is?

5. What do we learn about human perception from the author's handling of point of view? Henry James's third-person limited point of view, for example, often shows people to be blind to the needs and desires of other people and blind to their own nature as well.

6. Who is the narratee (listener or reader)? Is it one person or a group of people inside the story? What characterizes this audience? Why does the narrator tell the story to this audience? If the narratee is not inside the story, does the author or narrator seem to have a special audience in mind? What characterizes this audience?

THINKING ON PAPER ABOUT POINT OF VIEW

1. Identify the point of view of the narrative. Describe how the narrative would change if it were told from each of the other points of view.

2. List the main characters in the narrative. Write a paragraph on one or more characters, explaining how the narrative would be different if that character were narrating it.

3. Mark places where the narrator or central consciousness differs from our view of reality or fails to see important truths that we or other characters see.

4. Mark places that are particularly expressive of the narrator's tone. List the characteristics of tone.

Now It's Your Turn

Explain what the point of view is in Mary Robison's "Yours" (pages 43–44). Explore how her choice and use of point of view affects other elements in the story—characters, actions, and themes.

YOURS

Mary Robison

Allison struggled away from her white Renault, limping with the weight of the last of the pumpkins. She found Clark in the twilight on the twig-and-leaf-littered porch behind the house.

He wore a wool shawl. He was moving up and back in a padded glider, pushed by the ball of his slippered foot.

Allison lowered a big pumpkin, let it rest on the wide floor boards.

Clark was much older—seventy-eight to Allison's thirty-five. They were married. They were both quite tall and looked something alike in their facial features. Allison wore a natural-hair wig. It was a thick blonde hood around her face. She was dressed in bright-dyed denims today. She wore durable clothes, usually, for she volunteered afternoons at a children's day-care center.

She put one of the smaller pumpkins on Clark's long lap. "Now, nothing surreal," she told him. "Carve just a *regular* face. These are for kids."

In the foyer, on the Hepplewhite desk, Allison found the maid's chore list with its cross-offs, which included Clark's supper. Allison went quickly through the day's mail: a garish coupon packet, a bill from Jamestown Liquors, November's pay-TV program guide, and the worst thing, the funniest, an already opened, extremely unkind letter from Clark's relations up North. "You're an old fool," Allison read, and, "You're being cruelly deceived." There was a gift check for Clark enclosed, but it was uncashable, signed, as it was, "Jesus H. Christ."

Late, late into this night, Allison and Clark gutted and carved the pumpkins together, at an old table set on the back porch, over newspaper after soggy newspaper, with paring knives and with spoons and with a Swiss Army knife Clark used for exact shaping of tooth and eye and nostril. Clark had been a doctor, an internist, but also a Sunday watercolorist. His four pumpkins were expressive and artful. Their carved features were suited to the sizes and shapes of the pumpkins. Two looked ferocious and jagged. One registered surprise. The last was serene and beaming.

Allison's four faces were less deftly drawn, with slits and areas of distortion. She had cut triangles for noses and eyes. The mouths she had made were just wedges—two turned up and two turned down.

By one in the morning they were finished. Clark, who had bent his long torso forward to work, moved back over to the glider and looked out sleepily at nothing. All the lights were out across the ravine.

Clark stayed. For the season and time, the Virginia night was warm. Most leaves had been blown away already, and the trees stood unbothered. The moon was round above them.

Allison cleaned up the mess.

"Your jack-o'-lanterns are much, much better than mine," Clark said to her.

"Like hell," Allison said.

"Look at me," Clark said, and Allison did.

She was holding a squishy bundle of newspapers. The papers reeked sweetly with the smell of pumpkin guts.

"Yours are *far* better," he said.

"You're wrong. You'll see when they're lit," Allison said.

She went inside, came back with yellow vigil candles. It took her a while to get each candle settled, and then to line up the results in a row on the porch railing. She went along and lit each candle and fixed the pumpkin lids over the little flames.

"See?" she said.

They sat together a moment and looked at the orange faces.

"We're exhausted. It's good-night time," Allison said. "Don't blow out the candles. I'll put in new ones tomorrow."

That night, in their bedroom, a few weeks earlier in her life than had been predicted, Allison began to die. "Don't look at me if my wig comes off," she told Clark. "Please."

Her pulse cords were fluttering under his fingers. She raised her knees and kicked away the comforter. She said something to Clark about the garage being locked.

At the telephone, Clark had a clear view out back and down to the porch. He wanted to get drunk with his wife once more. He wanted to tell her, from the greater perspective he had, that to own only a little talent, like his, was an awful, plaguing thing; that being only a little special meant you expected too much, most of the time, and liked yourself too little. He wanted to assure her that she had missed nothing.

He was speaking into the phone now. He watched the jack-o'-lanterns. The jack-o'-lanterns watched him.

Plot

Events, plot, and story.   *Events* are things that happen in a narrative—actions, statements, thoughts, and feelings. In a general sense, the word *plot* means events of a narrative. When someone asks you to tell them the plot of a work, they usually want you to say what happened. The terms *plot* and *story* are often used interchangeably in this general sense. But in literary studies the terms have more restrictive meanings. E. M. Forster distinguishes between plot and story. A "story," he says, is "a narrative of events arranged in their time-sequence. A plot is also a narrative of events, the emphasis falling on causality. 'The king died and then the queen died' is a story. 'The king died, and then the queen died of grief' is a plot. The time-sequence is preserved, but the sense of causality overshadows it" (86).

Expanding on Forster's distinction, we propose two concepts of events in fictional narratives: plot and story.

1. **Plot.** *Plot* consists of three things. First, it is the work itself, the author's arrangement of events from the first page to the last. By reading the work, we experience the events as the author has arranged them. Second, plot includes the linkage of events by cause and effect. This is Forster's concept of plot. An inevitable byproduct of cause and effect is conflict. Third, plot is the author's presentation of events so as to engage readers intellectually and emotionally. Authors do this through such devices as pacing, intense conflict, surprise, rising action, climax, withheld information, and foreshadowing of later events.

2. **Story.** The *story* is all the events we encounter in the narrative, arranged in the order of their occurrence. Again, this is Forster's concept of story. Sometimes the arrangement of events in the plot and story are the same. We read the events in chronological order. Usually, however, authors arrange events out of chronological sequence. We learn about past and future events by means of *flashbacks* and *flashforwards*. We cannot assemble the events into their chronological order until we have read the plot. And usually we cannot see patterns of cause and effect or, at least, speculate about them until we understand the chronological sequence of events.

A classic example of the difference between plot and story is the detective narrative. First we read the work, the events as the author gives them to us: A murder occurs; a detective uncovers clues; the detective investigates suspects; puzzling events occur; the murderer is exposed; the detective reveals the causes of the murder. As we read, flashbacks inform us of events preceding the murder. The author employs suspense and mystery to keep us turning the pages. Having read the work, we can now place everything that happens in the narrative—the "story"—into chronological order. Once we have done that, we can establish the chain of causes and effects that leads up to the murder.

Numerous theorists of narrative treat the function of events in fiction. Two clearly presented discussions are Suzanne Keen's *Narrative Form* (73–77) and the entry under "plot" in Ross Murfin

and Supryia Ray's *The Bedford Glossary of Critical and Literary Terms*
(286–88).

Plot patterns

A traditional pattern. Although authors arrange events into
many patterns, a traditional and well-known pattern is illustrated by
the *Freytag pyramid:*

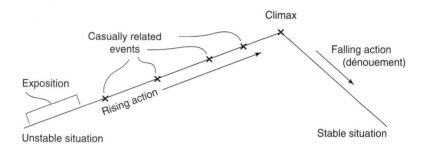

This diagram was developed by the German critic Gustav Freytag in
1863 to illustrate a typical five-act tragedy (114–5). But it applies to
many, perhaps most, works of fiction.

At the beginning of this pattern is an *unstable situation,* a conflict
that sets the plot in motion. The narrator's *exposition* here explains the
nature of the conflict. He or she introduces the characters, describes
the setting, and provides historical background. The narrator next introduces a series of *events,* all related by cause. One event may cause
another event, which in turn causes another event, which causes the
next event (husband gets angry with wife, who gets angry with kids,
who get angry with dog, who sulks in the basement). Or several events
may be linked to the same cause (a series of deaths at the beach, all
caused by a monstrous shark). Whatever the causal relationship
among events, each event intensifies the conflict so that the plot
"rises" toward a *climax.*

The climax is the most intense event in the narrative. The rest of
the story—the *falling action*—is usually brief. It contains events that are
much less intense than the climax and that lead toward the resolution
of the conflict and toward a *stable situation* at the end. Another term for
falling action is *dénouement,* a French word meaning "unraveling."

An example of the Freytag pyramid is the stereotypical fairy
tale in which the youngest son must seek his fortune (unstable situation: He has no source of income, no home). He goes into a far
country whose king is offering a prize, the hand of his daughter, to

anyone who can accomplish three tasks. The hero completes all three (rising action and climax: Each task is increasingly difficult, but the third is a humdinger and is therefore the climax). The remaining part of the story may contain obstacles, but they are easily overcome. The king praises the hero but does not want his daughter to marry a commoner. The hero reveals that he is not, as he seems, a mere peasant but the son of a nobleman (falling action/dénouement: The conflicts now are minor and easily resolved). The hero marries the princess and lives happily ever after (stable situation: The hero has eliminated the initial conflict; he now has a wife, a source of income, and a home).

Other plot patterns.   Other plot patterns are possible. A work might have muted conflicts and so many digressions that it seems only to meander toward an understated climax. Or the work may be open ended and thus have unresolved conflicts and no climax. Or the work may have multiple plots, some of which may be left unresolved. A famous example of a meandering, open-ended novel is Laurence Sterne's *Tristram Shandy.* Sterne published this multivolume novel over a number of years (1759–1767) and died before he brought it to closure.

Multiple plot lines.   A narrative may have more than one plot line. A *plot line* is a single chain of events linked together by cause and effect. In the detective narrative, the events that cause the murder constitute one plot line. But another one might be the love relationship between the detective and another character. The events leading up to the outcome of their relationship make up a second plot line that may or may not intersect with the murder plot line. If the murderer threatens the detective's love interest, or if the love interest provides crucial evidence that leads to the capture of the murderer, then the two plot lines are related. Our task as interpreters is to discern the various plot lines and explain how they relate.

Beginnings and endings

Beginnings.   The plot and the story, as we have said, are different. Sometimes the plot follows the chronological order of the story. In that case, the beginning of the plot is the same as the beginning of the story. But often the plot starts with a later event. Only after reading for awhile do you learn when the sequence of events that constitute the story begins. An often cited example is the *in medias res* (in the middle of things) device of epics like *The Odyssey, The Iliad,* and

The Aeneid. In *The Odyssey*, the plot begins with Athena's plea that Zeus will allow Odysseus to go home. Calypso has been keeping him on her island against his will. This is the unstable situation that opens the plot, the last bit of unfinished business of the Trojan War. But the story of *The Odyssey* begins ten years before this, when Odysseus and his countrymen leave Troy. We don't learn about these events until later, when Odysseus recounts them. After Odysseus tells his tale, the author returns us to the present.

It sometimes requires interpretation to establish the beginning of a plot, the key event that sets in motion the chain of causes and effects that constitute the plot. When does the plot of *The Odyssey* really begin? When Odysseus and his men set sail from Troy? When they incur the wrath of powerful gods? During the war?

Endings. Endings propel us to read narratives. We want to know how they will end. The plot of a narrative is like a pathway that constantly branches in two or more directions. As we read, we know those branches are there. We read on because we want to see which ones authors will take. This is especially true toward the end. As we read, we intuit the different ways the plot can end. We resist certain endings—the hero's defeat, the hero and heroine's permanent separation, the innocent child's death. But since *we* can't end the narrative, we keep reading to see what the author will do.

Authors choose endings. By so doing, they signal ideas about their narratives. Studying the endings of narratives helps uncover those ideas. To do this, think of other ways the author might have ended the narrative. Why didn't the author choose any of those? Some endings may not feel right to you. In the nineteenth century, readers expected novelists to provide happy endings. Sometimes these endings seem forced, given the causes and effects of the plot. Charles Dickens, for example, wrote two endings for *Great Expectations.* In the first ending Pip and Estella part, never to marry. But upon the insistence of a friend, Dickens provided a "happy" ending—the one published at the time—in which Pip and Estella marry. Now we have both endings. Which is better? How does each ending influence our interpretations of the novel? Jane Austen provides a happy ending to *Pride and Prejudice,* Elizabeth's marriage to Darcy. But what if Elizabeth had not married him? How would that unhappy and perhaps more realistic ending color our understanding of the novel?

Usually the plot and story of a narrative conclude at the same time. But sometimes the conclusion is open-ended: the conflicts of the plot are left unresolved. This time, you really are left on your own. You have to provide your own ending.

Internal and external conflict.   Conflict is an essential element of plot. Without conflict we would not want to keep reading. The greater the conflict, the more intense our desire to know what happens next.

There are two general categories of conflict: external and internal. *Internal conflicts* take place within the minds of characters. An example is the good person who wrestles inwardly with temptation. *External conflicts* take place between individuals or between individuals and the world external to individuals (the forces of nature, human-created objects, and environments). The climactic shootout in an American western is an example of a physical, external conflict. But not all external conflicts are physical or violent. A verbal disagreement between two people is also an external conflict.

Protagonist and antagonist.   The forces in a conflict are usually embodied by characters, the most relevant being the protagonist and the antagonist. The term *protagonist* usually means "main character," but think of the protagonist also as someone who fights for something. The *antagonist* is the opponent of the protagonist; the antagonist is usually a person, but can also be a nonhuman force or even an aspect of the protagonist—his or her tendency toward evil and self-destruction, for example. Although a protagonist sometimes fights for evil—Macbeth, for example—we usually empathize with the protagonist and find the antagonist unsympathetic.

Embedded stories and frame stories.   *Embedded stories* are narratives that appear within the work and that digress from the main plot line—or seem to. Typically the main narration stops while a character tells a story, sometimes a long story. When you come across these, you might wonder, Why doesn't the author get on with it? Why do I have to read this "extra" story? Near the beginning of *The Odyssey*, for example, Odysseus escapes to the kingdom of Phaeacia. While there he tells a whopper of a story. This long embedded story—actually, a series of stories—recounts Odysseus's adventures since he left Troy ten years before. Other works that feature embedded stories are the Old English epic *Beowulf*, Cervantes's *Don Quixote*, Madame de Lafayette's *The Princesse de Clèves*, and Herman Melville's *Moby-Dick*.

Embedded stories may seem irrelevant, but in these works and many others, they serve important functions: They can reveal information about the past. They can predict the future. They can provide valuable information about characters and settings. They can parallel events and characters in the main plot. They can establish themes. Take, for example, the embedded stories in *Beowulf.* The main plot of *Beowulf* is straightforward: the hero fights three monsters: Grendel, Grendel's mother, and a dragon. But woven into this plot are embedded stories about Scandinavian history. When we take the trouble to understand these stories, *Beowulf* becomes a richer, more interesting work. The apparently simple tale of Beowulf's heroic deeds belongs to a much more complex and troubling story that began before Beowulf's birth and will continue after his death.

Frame stories "surround"—provide a frame for—other stories in the work. In Boccaccio's *The Decameron,* ten people travel from Florence to escape the plague that ravages the city. When they arrive at their country destination, they agree to tell stories that will center on different topics. Each person will tell ten stories (thus the "deca," ten, in the title). Between each grouping of ten stories, the author returns to the frame story, telling us what the characters do and say and what the next topic will be. After all the stories are told, the characters return to Florence. Mary Shelley's *Frankenstein* also begins and ends with a frame story—Robert Walton's account of his exploration in the Arctic seas and his meeting with the monster and Victor Frankenstein. Frankenstein, upon arriving on Walton's ship, tells his story—the primary story of the novel—of how he created the monster.

Frame stories are similar to embedded stories in that they often relate meaningfully to the other story or stories in the narrative. The topics and stories of *The Decameron* comment on the circumstances of the plague. Frankenstein's story, because it parallel's Walton's, calls into question Walton's motivations and goals. The stories in Chaucer's *Canterbury Tales* reflect the traits of their tellers and of the medieval society they typify.

Summary narration and scenic narration. Two devices that affect the speed and focus of plots are summary narration and scenic narration. *Summary narration* relates (sums up) events that take place over a period of time:

> From that time forward not a day passed without the young officer making his appearance under the window at the customary hour, and between him and her there was established a sort of mute acquaintance. . . . After about a week she commenced to smile at him. (Pushkin, "The Queen of Spades," 8)

Scenic narration presents events in real time. An event takes about as long to read as it takes to happen. Scenic narration typically features dialogue:

> Three days afterwards, a bright-eyed young girl from a milliner's establishment brought Lizaveta a letter. Lizaveta opened it with great uneasiness, fearing that it was a demand for money, when suddenly she recognized Hermann's handwriting.
>
> "You have made a mistake, my dear," she said. "this letter is not for me."
>
> "Oh, yes, it is for you," replied the girl, smiling very knowingly. "Have the goodness to read it."
>
> Lizaveta glanced at the letter. Hermann requested an interview.
>
> "It cannot be," she cried, alarmed at the audacious request, and the manner in which it was made. "This letter is certainly not for me."
>
> And she tore it into fragments. (Pushkin, "The Queen of Spades," 11)

Summary and scenic narration affect readers in different ways. Summary narration provides emotional distance from events and speeds up the passage of time. Scenic narration is more vivid and emotionally involving. It slows down the passage of time. Authors typically alternate between the two: speeding up time here, slowing it down there; giving us distance from events here, drawing us into them there. Such alternation establishes a kind of rhythm in the unfolding of a plot.

QUESTIONS ABOUT PLOT: CONFLICT

1. What conflicts does the work dramatize?
2. What is the main conflict? What are minor conflicts? How are all the conflicts related?
3. What causes the conflicts?
4. Which conflicts are external, which internal?
5. Who is the protagonist? Who or what is the antagonist?
6. What qualities or values are associated with each side of the conflict?
7. Where does the climax occur?
8. How is the main conflict resolved? Which conflicts go unresolved?

An example of how questions about conflict help interpret fiction is Ernest Hemingway's short story "Hills Like White Elephants." The story consists almost entirely of a dialogue between a young woman and man who are waiting for a train at a tiny station in the Spanish countryside. We learn that they have traveled widely and are lovers—but they are in conflict. About what? The conflict they bring out into the open and discuss aloud concerns an abortion. The woman is pregnant. The man urges her to have an abortion. He keeps telling her that the abortion will be "simple," "perfectly natural," will make them "all right" and "happy." But she resists. She asks if after the abortion "things will be like they were and you'll love me" (275). She says that they "could get along" without the abortion (277).

Gradually we realize that although the immediate conflict is about the abortion, there is an unspoken conflict over the nature of their relationship. The man wants the abortion because it will allow him to continue the rootless and uncommitted relationship he has enjoyed with the woman up to now. The woman wants a more stable relationship, one that having the child would affirm, one that she has apparently believed the man wanted too. Hemingway resolves the conflict by having the woman realize, in the face of the man's continued insistence on the abortion, that the relationship she wants with the man is impossible.

Examining the story's main conflict in this way helps reveal important things about the story. At first glance, it seems to have little "action," but examining the conflict reveals what its action is. Studying the conflict also helps illuminate the characters: The man is selfish and obstinate; the woman is idealistic and somewhat innocent. Analyzing the conflict points to the meaning or theme of the story. Hemingway seems to support the woman's view of the way a loving relationship should be. He makes her the protagonist, the more sympathetic character of the two. Examining conflict in works of literature is crucial to understanding them and is thus a rich source of interpretations.

OTHER QUESTIONS ABOUT PLOT

1. How are the "story" and "plot" different? Why does the author arrange events out of chronological order? Can you retell the story in chronological order? Does the plot have gaps—events that are omitted or only hinted at in the text. In "Hills Like White

Elephants," for example, we have to guess information about the couple's relationship before the text begins.

2. If the work has multiple plot lines, what links them together?

3. If the work has embedded or frame stories, how are they related to the main stories?

4. When does the author use summary narration and scenic narration? Is the work primarily one or the other? How do the two kinds of narration complement one another?

5. Does the ending follow logically from the plot? Can you think of a better or equally good ending?

THINKING ON PAPER ABOUT PLOT

1. On one side of a piece of paper, list the external conflicts of the work. On the other side, list the internal conflicts. Draw a line between the external and internal conflicts that seem related.

2. List the key conflicts. For each conflict, list the ways in which the conflict has been resolved, if it has.

3. Describe the turning point or climax. Explain what conflicts are resolved. List the conflicts that are left unresolved.

4. List the major structural units of the work (chapters, scenes, parts). Summarize what happens in each unit.

5. List the qualities of the protagonist and antagonist.

6. Describe the qualities that make the situation at the beginning unstable. Describe the qualities that make the conclusion stable.

7. List the causes of the unstable situations at the beginning and throughout the work.

8. Compare the arrangement of events in the plot and the story. Speculate about why the author arranges the plot this way.

9. Using the graph of the Freytag pyramid as a model, draw a graph of the plot. If it's different from the Freytag pyramid, draw the graph to reflect those differences.

10. If there is more than one plot line, describe each one. Indicate how the plot lines are related and how they intersect at the end.

11. Mark passages of summary narration and scenic narration. Explain why the narrator shifts from one to the other.

12. Write a different ending for the narrative.

Now It's Your Turn

Discuss the presentation of events in Robison's "Yours" (pages 43–44). What are the conflicts? Does the Freytag pyramid work for this story? Can you reconstruct the "story" of the work? How is the "plot" different from the "story"?

Characterization

Definition. Characters are the people in narratives, and *characterization* is the author's presentation and development of the traits of characters. Sometimes, as in fantasy fiction, the characters are not people. They may be animals, robots, or creatures from outer space, but the author endows them with human abilities and human psychological traits. They really are people in all but outward form.

Flat and round characters. There are two broad categories of character development: simple and complex. The critic and fiction writer E. M. Forster coined alternate terms for these same categories: *flat* (simple) and *round* (complex) characters (67–78). Flat characters have only one or two personality traits and are easily recognizable as stereotypes—the shrewish wife, the lazy husband, the egomaniac, the stupid athlete, the shyster, the miser, the redneck, the bum, the dishonest used-car salesman, the prim aristocrat, the absent-minded professor. Round characters have multiple personality traits and therefore resemble real people. They are much harder to understand and describe than flat characters. No single description or interpretation can fully contain them. An example of a flat character is Washington Irving's Ichabod Crane, the vain and superstitious schoolmaster of "The Legend of Sleepy Hollow." An example of a round character is Shakespeare's Hamlet. To an extent, all literary characters are stereotypes. Even Hamlet is a type, the "melancholy man." But round characters have many more traits than just those associated with their general type. Because it takes time to develop round characters convincingly, they are more often found in longer works than in shorter ones.

Static and dynamic characters. Characters who remain the same throughout a work are *static*. Those who change are *dynamic* characters. Usually, round characters change and flat characters remain the same, but not always. Shakespeare's Sir John Falstaff (in *Henry IV, Part I* and *Part II*), a round character, is nonetheless static. Dynamic characters, especially main characters, typically grow in understanding. The climax of this growth is an *epiphany,* a term that James Joyce used to describe a sudden revelation of truth experienced by a character. The term comes from the New Testament and describes the Wise Men's first perception of Christ's divinity. Joyce applied it to fictional characters. His own characters, like Gabriel Conroy in "The Dead," perfectly illustrate the concept. Often, as in "The Dead," the epiphany coincides with the climax of the plot.

Direct and indirect revelation.   Authors reveal what characters are like in two ways: directly and indirectly. In the *direct* method, the narrator simply tells readers what the character is like:

> She was a woman of mean understanding, little information, and uncertain temper. When she was discontented she fancied herself nervous. The business of her life was to get her daughters married; its solace was visiting and news. (Jane Austen, *Pride and Prejudice,* 3)

When the method of revealing characters is *indirect,* however, authors show us, rather than tell us, what characters are like through dialogue, external details (dress, bearing, looks), and characters' thoughts, speech, and deeds.

Representing characters' thoughts.   One of the signal methods of modern fiction is access to characters' minds. Before about the seventeenth century, epics, romances, tales, and other forms of fiction did not do this. Such access is something we cannot have in real life. People tell us what they think. We guess from their facial expressions what they think. We know what *we* think—usually. But we cannot enter other people's minds. Surely one of the great appeals of modern fiction is that it allows us to do just this.

The presentation of thoughts in first-person narratives is no different from real life. The narrators—characters in the works—tell us what they think, just as real people do. But third-person narrators place us inside characters's minds. Suzanne Keen describes three ways third-person narrators do this (59–63). In the first, *reported thought* (her term is "psycho-narration"), narrators use their own words to summarize characters' thoughts:

> She [Elizabeth Bennet] perfectly remembered everything that had passed in conversation between Wickham and herself, in their first evening at Mr. Philips's. Many of his expressions were still fresh in her memory. She was

now struck with the impropriety of such communications to a stranger, and wondered it had escaped her before. (Jane Austen, *Pride and Prejudice,* 143.)

Reported thought allows narrators to probe "thoughts"—levels of consciousness—that characters may not fully recognize:

It is impossible to describe the pain she [the Princess of Clèves] felt on realizing, as a result of what her mother had just told her, how much the Duc de Nemours meant to her: she had not yet dared admit it to herself. She saw then that the feelings she had for him were those that M. de Clèves had so often required of her, and she felt the full shame of experiencing them for someone other than a husband who deserved them. (Madame de Lafayette, *The Princesse de Clèves,* 56)

Here, and throughout the novel, the narrator presents the Princess's interior struggle between her love for the Duc de Nemours and her duty to her husband, the Prince of Clèves. Her feelings on these occasions often seem less than conscious thoughts. When the narrator says, for example, that the Princess "had not yet dared admit it to herself," the narrator seems to know more about the Princess's mind than she knows.

In the second way of representing characters' thoughts, *quoted monologue,* narrators cast thoughts in the characters' own words. "These thoughts," Keen says, "though unspoken, are written in such a way that they could plausibly be spoken aloud without violating the reader's sense of grammatical speech" (61). We can be sure that the characters are fully aware of these thoughts because the characters "say" them. Narrators may or may not place quotation marks around the characters thoughts. Either way, the thoughts are a quotation. Here is an example with quotation marks:

"And of this place," thought she [Elizabeth Bennet], "I might have been mistress! With these rooms I might now have been familiarly acquainted! Instead of viewing them as a stranger, I might have rejoiced in them as my own, and welcomed to them as visitors my uncle and aunt." (Jane Austen, *Pride and Prejudice,* 168)

The following example omits quotation marks:

Of course, she [Clarissa Dalloway] thought, walking on, Milly is about my age—fifty—fifty-two. So it is probably *that.* Hugh's manner had said so, said it perfectly—dear old Hugh, thought Mrs. Dalloway, remembering with amusement, with gratitude, with emotion, how shy, like a brother—one would rather die than speak to one's brother—Hugh had always been, when he was at Oxford, and came over, and perhaps one of them (drat the thing!) Couldn't ride. (Virginia Woolf, "Mrs. Dalloway in Bond Street," 20)

A third method of presenting characters' thoughts, *narrated monologue*, is similar to quoted monologue in that the words are "spoken" by a character, but the narrator states them in the past tense and refers to the character in the third person. As in the following example, narrated monologue is usually mixed in with reported thought and quoted monologue. The underlined sentences are narrated monologue:

That night Dave did not sleep. He was glad that he had gotten out of killing the mule so easily, but he was hurt. Something hot seemed to turn over inside him each time he remembered how they had laughed. He tossed on his bed, feeling his hard pillow. N Pa says he's gonna beat me . . . He remembered other beatings, and his back quivered. Naw, naw, Ah sho don wan im t beat me tha way no mo. Dam em all! Nobody ever gave him anything. All he did was work. They treat me like a mule, n then they beat me. He gritted his teeth. N Ma had t tell on me. . . . Dammit, he'd done it! He fired again. *Blooooom!* He smiled. *Blooooom! Blooooom! Click, click. There! It was empty. If anybody could shoot a gun, he could.* He put the gun into his hip pocket and started across the fields. (Richard Wright, "The Man Who Was Almost a Man," 25–26)

Stream of consciousness. *Stream of consciousness* is a narrative device whereby authors place us within different levels of characters' conscious minds. "Consciousness," Robert Humphrey says (in *Stream of Consciousness in the Modern Novel*), "indicates the entire area of mental attention, from preconsciousness on through the levels of mind up to and including the highest one of rational, communicable awareness" (2). Stream of consciousness narration typically deals with "those levels that are more inchoate than rational verbalization—those levels on the margin of attention" (2–3). These "prespeech levels of consciousness are not censored, rationally controlled, or logically ordered" (3). William James, in his influential treatise *Principles of Psychology* (1890), coined the phrase, "stream of consciousness." The mind, he said, is like a river with debris—thoughts—floating on the surface. The thoughts are not necessarily related to one another.

Ever since James published this work, authors—Dorothy Richardson, Virginia Woolf, James Joyce, William Faulkner, and numerous others—have devised methods to represent the apparently incoherent flow of prespeech thoughts. Sometimes their methods take the form of quoted monologue:

> Through the fence, between the curling flower spaces, I could see them hitting. They were coming toward where the flag was and I went along the fence.

In this, the opening lines of Faulkner's *The Sound and the Fury,* we are inside the mind of Benjy Compson, a grown man who has the mind of a three-year-old. Although Benjy is "speaking," he is not capable of speaking aloud this way. Rather, his interior "speech" is Faulkner's method of rendering his stream of consciousness.

Stream of consciousness can also take the form of reported thought or a combination of reported thought and quoted monologue:

> She meant to wave good-by, but it was too much trouble. Her eyes closed of themselves, it was like a dark curtain drawn around the bed. The pillow rose and floated under her, pleasant as a hammock in a light wind. She listened to the leaves rustling outside the window. No, somebody was swishing newspapers: no, Cornelia and Doctor Harry were whispering together. She leaped broad awake, thinking they whispered in her ear. (Katherine Anne Porter, "The Jilting of Granny Weatherall," 122)

In this example, the narrator includes not just "words" in Granny Weatherall's mind but sensuous experiences as well—images and sounds. As here, stream of consciousness can enter characters' dreams or seem dreamlike.

In real life, the prespeech thought of people may indeed be irrational and disconnected. But in stream of consciousness narration, the images and thoughts only seem to be incoherent. Ironically, authors take great pains to establish logical connections between their characters' prespeech thoughts. Benjy Compon's narration, for example, features confusing shifts between present and past events and from one past event to another past event. It leaves out information—that, for example, the "hitting" in the opening sentence is done by men playing golf. It focuses on images and smells—his sister's muddy drawers, her smell, objects of nature—that at first seem without meaning. It sets us down in the middle of Benjy's mind without any preparation or explanation. We have to figure things out as we go. But once we do figure them out, we see that every time shift, every image, every thought fits together into a coherent and brilliantly conceived whole. Stream of consciousness narratives are puzzlelike. Part of the fun of interpreting them is solving the puzzle.

QUESTIONS ABOUT CHARACTERS

The main questions about characters are: What is the character like? What are the character's traits?

Consider the example of the woman in Hemingway's "Hills Like White Elephants," discussed previously. Hemingway drops hints that indicate something about her personality. She compares the Spanish hills to white elephants, a comparison that at first seems capricious but later suggests an imaginative, even artistic, quality that the man cannot comprehend. After she senses the man's true motivation for wanting the abortion, she looks out over the fields of ripe grain, the trees, the river, and the mountains beyond, and tells the man that "we could have all this" but that "every day we make it more impossible." She seems to connect the appreciation of nature—the sympathy they could feel for it—with the moral quality of their relationship. But because their relationship must remain superficial, she says that the landscape "isn't ours any more" (276). Once again, the man lacks the imagination to make the connection, and he fails to grasp her moral point. Hemingway seems to admire the woman's ability to make these comparisons. It underscores her more obvious and admirable desire for a profound and lasting relationship. Another thing we learn about the woman is that she is a dynamic character. At the beginning of the story, she does not fully recognize the falseness of her relationship with the man. She seems genuinely to hope for something better. By the end of the story, she knows the truth and, from all appearances, has changed as a result. At the beginning she is innocent and dependent upon the man for her happiness; by the end she has lost her innocence and has become independent.

OTHER QUESTIONS

1. Are the characters flat or round? What types do they represent? What makes them complex? Do they have traits that contradict one another and therefore cause internal conflicts?

2. Are they dynamic or static? What, if anything, changes about them? What steps do they go through to change?

3. What problems do they have? How do they attempt to solve them? Are they sad, happy, or in between?

4. Do they experience epiphanies? When, why, and what do their epiphanies reveal—to themselves, to us? Does what they learn help or hinder them?

5. How do they relate to one another?

6. How do we learn about their inner lives—their conscious and unconscious thoughts, their ambitions, their ideas? Do they have speech mannerisms, gestures, or modes of dress that reveal their inner selves? What narrative devices does the author employ to render characters' thoughts?

THINKING ON PAPER ABOUT CHARACTERIZATION

1. List the traits of the main characters in the story.

2. Describe the ways the author reveals traits of a character.

3. Write a description of a complex character. Explain what makes the character "complex."

4. Describe the emotional reaction a character has to an important event or events.

5. Write a paragraph explaining how and why a character changes.

6. Describe the scene in which a character has an epiphany. Explain what happens and what the character comes to see.

7. Mark the places in which the narrator or characters make revealing statements about a character.

8. Show how the author represents characters' thoughts. Write a paragraph that describes a character's inner life.

Now It's Your Turn

Describe the two characters in Robison's "Yours." Consider how everything we learn about them—their looks, ages, clothing, circumstances, statements, other people's reactions to them, attitude to each other, treatment of each other, narrator's comments—adds to your understanding of their nature.

Setting

Setting includes several closely related aspects of a work of fiction. First, setting is the physical, sensuous world of the work. Second, it is the time in which the action of the work takes place. And third, it is the social environment of the characters: the manners, customs, and moral values that govern the characters' society. A fourth aspect—"atmosphere"—is largely, but not entirely, an effect of setting.

⤳ Questions about Place

Facts about place.   First get the details of the physical setting clear in your mind.

1. Where does the action take place? On what planet, in what country or locale?

2. What sensuous qualities does the author give to the setting? That is, what does it look like, sound like, feel like?

3. Do you receive a dominant impression about the setting? What is the impression, and what caused it?

Interpretation of place.   Once you have the basic facts clear, move on to questions about place. What relationship does place have to characterization and to theme? In some fiction, geographical location seems to have no effect on characters. Indoors or out, in one locale or another, they behave the same. In other works, such as those by Thomas Hardy or Joseph Conrad, place profoundly affects the characters.

In the story, "Among the Corn Rows," Hamlin Garland shows how environment brings about a character's decision.

A cornfield in July is a hot place. The soil is hot and dry; the wind comes across the lazily murmuring leaves laden with a warm sickening smell drawn from the rapidly growing, broad-flung banners of the corn. The sun, nearly vertical, drops a flood of dazzling light and heat upon the field over which the cool shadows run, only to make the heat seem the more intense.

Julia Peterson, faint with fatigue, was toiling back and forth between the corn rows, holding the handles of the double-shovel corn plow while her little brother Otto rode the steaming horse. Her heart was full of bitterness, and her face flushed with heat, and her muscles aching with fatigue. The heat grew terrible. The corn came to her shoulders, and not a breath seemed to reach her, while the sun, nearing the noon mark, lay pitilessly upon her shoulders, protected only by a calico dress. The dust rose under her feet, and as she was wet with perspiration it soiled her till, with a woman's instinctive cleanliness, she shuddered. Her head throbbed dangerously. What matter to her that the king bird pitched jovially from the maples to catch a wandering blue bottle fly, that the robin was feeding its young, that the bobolink was singing? All these things, if she saw them, only threw her bondage to labor into greater relief. (107–8)

Garland shows geographical environment pressuring Julia Peterson into a decision that will affect the rest of her life. Garland has already told us that Julia's parents treat her harshly and force her to work too hard. By emphasizing one sensuous quality, the heat, Garland makes us feel the hardship of her life. She has dreamed of a handsome suitor who will take her away from the farm and give her a life of ease, but the heat makes her feel that anything would be better than this misery. So when a young farmer happens along just after the incident described here and offers her a life of respect and only normal difficulty, she marries him. Garland shows that Julia's environment leads her to settle for less than she really wants. She is not free to choose exactly as she would choose.

 ## QUESTIONS ABOUT TIME

Historical period.   Three kinds of time occur in fiction, thus three types of questions about time are important. First, at what period in history does the action take place? Many stories occur during historical events that affect the characters and themes in important ways. Margaret Mitchell's *Gone with the Wind* and Tolstoy's *War and Peace* are examples. To answer this question, you may have to do background reading about the historical period. Tolstoy and Mitchell give you a great deal of historical information in their fiction, but many authors do not. In either case, you may need to supplement facts in the work with facts from outside sources.

Passage of time.   Second, how long does it take for the action to occur? How many hours, days, weeks, years are involved? Authors often use the passage of time as a thematic and structuring device:

The mere fact that some specific amount of time has passed may be important for understanding characters. Years go by in Alice Walker's *The Color Purple,* allowing her characters to grow and change. But because of her method of telling the stories—through letters—we are not immediately aware of how much time passes until near the end of the book. Because we read the letters one after the other, we get the illusion that time passes quickly. In fact, gaps of time occur between letters, so that we must consciously slow down the time of the novel to understand its effect on the characters. What clues, then, indicate how much time passes? Is the passage of time related to characterization and theme? If an author seems to obscure how much time is passing, why? Does the author use time as a structuring device?

Perception of time.   Third, how is the passage of time perceived? Time may seem to move very slowly or very quickly, depending on a character's state of mind. Our recognition of how a character perceives time helps us understand the character's internal conflicts and attitudes.

In *Jane Eyre* Charlotte Brontë intertwines length of time and perception of time. Jane, the narrator, describes her stays at various "houses." She devotes about one-fourth of the novel to her stays with the Reeds and at Lowood and one-fourth to her stay with the Rivers family. But she devotes over half of the novel to her stay at Thornfield, where she falls in love with Mr. Rochester. The effect of these unequal proportions is to slow down the time spent at Thornfield. This "slow" time emphasizes Jane's emotional reaction to the experiences she has there.

Brontë slows the time of specific events as well. In fact, the novel is a collection of highly charged, intensely felt moments in Jane's life that seem to last far longer than they actually do in real time. The novel opens, for example, with Jane's imprisonment in the hated "red room" of the Reed mansion. As her anger subsides, she becomes aware that the room is "chill," "silent," and "solemn." She recalls that Mr. Reed died there. In a mirror she sees her "glittering eyes of fear moving where all else was still." Daylight "forsakes" the room. She feels "oppressed, suffocated" at thoughts of Mr. Reed's death and the possibility of her own. When she sees a light on the wall, she thinks it is a ghost. She screams. When Mrs. Reed rushes to check on her, she thrusts Jane back into the room and locks the door. Jane faints from the intense stress (45–50). The length of this description corresponds to Jane's perception of time, which in turn corresponds to her fear of the room. Each detail is like the tick of a loud clock.

1. What, then, is the relationship between the length of narrated events and the amount of time in which they occur?

2. Is the author purposely slowing down or speeding up our perception of time? If so, why?

3. What mental states or internal conflicts does a character's perception of time reveal?

Questions about Social Environment

Often the social environment represented in a work is of little importance. There may even be virtually no social environment. When it is important, however, it affects interpretations of the work.

1. What, then, is the social environment portrayed in the work—the manners, mores, customs, rituals, and codes of conduct of a society?

2. What does the author seem to think about them? (Approving? Ambivalent? Disapproving?)

3. How do they affect the characters?

Sinclair Lewis spends much of his novel *Babbitt* describing the social environment of his fictional Midwestern city, Zenith. Then he shows that the pressure to conform to this environment is almost irresistible. His characters sometimes want to rebel against this pressure, but they are too weak to do so without extreme guilt or without threat to their economic and social security. Their social environment determines their behavior and entraps them.

Questions about Atmosphere

Atmosphere refers to the emotional reaction that we and—usually—the characters have to the setting of a work. Sometimes the atmosphere is difficult to define, but it is often found or felt in the sensuous quality of the setting. Our emotional reaction to the Hamlin Garland passage is probably pain, discomfort, weariness, and oppression, mainly because of his emphasis on the thermal sense, the sense of hot and cold. Fruitful questions about atmosphere are:

1. What methods does the author use to create the work's atmosphere?

2. What does the author achieve by creating this atmosphere?

3. Why does the author create this particular atmosphere?

Sometimes, authors want simply to play upon our emotions—give us chills (gothic), make us weep (romances), stir anxiety (thrillers). Garland's purpose, however, is more meaningful. He uses atmosphere to raise a philosophical point: Physical environment affects human behavior. Joseph Conrad in *Heart of Darkness* creates an atmosphere of mystery, foreboding, and imminent danger to reflect his hatred of colonialism and his belief that "civilized" people are capable of terrible deeds.

THINKING ON PAPER ABOUT SETTING

1. Mark descriptions of physical place. Underline telling words and phrases.

2. Characterize physical locales, such as houses, rooms, and outdoor areas.

3. Explain the connection of physical place to one or more of the characters.

4. Arrange key events in chronological order. Indicate when each event occurs.

5. Mark passages where a character's emotional state affects the way the passage of time is presented to us.

6. Explain how historical circumstances and characters are important.

7. List the thoughts and actions of characters that seem to typify the social environment of the work. They drink heavily, go to church, obey rules of etiquette, gamble, throw parties, get in fights, cheat in business, wander restlessly, and so forth.

8. Mark scenes in which the narrator or characters express approval or disapproval of these patterns of behavior.

9. Explain how these patterns influence characters.

10. List traits of the atmosphere.

Now It's Your Turn

Describe the setting and atmosphere of "The Cask of Amontillado" (pages 362–67). What purposes does the setting have?

Irony

Authors use irony pervasively to convey ideas. But irony is a diverse and often complex intellectual phenomenon difficult to define in a sentence or two. Generally, *irony* makes visible a contrast between appearance and reality. More fully and specifically, it exposes and underscores a contrast between (1) what is and what seems to be, (2) between what is and what ought to be, (3) between what is and what one wishes to be, and (4) between what is and what one expects to be. Incongruity is the method of irony; opposites come suddenly together so that the disparity is obvious to discriminating readers. There are many kinds of irony, but four types are common in literature.

Verbal irony.   Most people use or hear verbal irony daily. In verbal irony, people say the opposite of what they mean. For example, if the day has been terrible, you say, "Boy, this has been a great day!" The hearer knows that this statement is ironic because of the speaker's tone of voice and facial or bodily expressions or because the hearer is familiar with the situation and immediately sees the discrepancy between statement and actuality. Understatement and overstatement are two forms of verbal irony. *Understatement* minimizes the nature of something. "Greg Maddox pitched a pretty good game," one says after seeing a no-hitter. Mark Twain's famous telegram is another example of understatement: "The reports of my death are greatly exaggerated." *Overstatement* exaggerates the nature of something. After standing in a long line, you say, "There were about a million people in that line!"

Why do people use verbal irony? Verbal irony is more emphatic than a point-blank statement of the truth. It achieves its effect by reminding you of the opposite reality and thus providing a scale by which to judge the present reality. Verbal irony often displays a mental agility—wit—that people find striking and, as with the Mark Twain retort, entertaining. Verbal irony in its most bitter and destructive form becomes sarcasm, in which the speaker condemns people by pretending to praise them:

> Oh, you're a real angel. You're the noble man who wouldn't dirty his pure little hands with company business. But all along, behind our backs, you were just as greedy and ruthless as the rest of us.

Situational irony. In situational irony, the situation differs from what common sense indicates it is, will be, or ought to be. It is ironic, for example, that General George Patton should have lived through the thickest of tank battles during World War II and then, after the war, have been killed accidentally by one of his own men. It is ironic that someone we expect to be upright—a minister or judge—should be the most repulsive of scoundrels. Authors often use situational irony to expose hypocrisy and injustice. In Hawthorne's *The Scarlet Letter,* the townspeople regard the minister Arthur Dimmesdale as sanctified and angelic when in fact he shamefully hides his adultery with Hester Prynne, allowing her to take all the blame.

Attitudinal irony. Situational irony results from what *most* people expect, whereas attitudinal irony results from what one person expects. In attitudinal irony, an individual thinks that reality is one way when, in fact, it is very different. A frequent example in literature is naïve characters—Fielding's Parson Adams, Cervantes's Don Quixote, Dickens's Mr. Micawber, Voltaire's Candide—who think that everyone is upright and that everything will turn out for the best, when in fact people they encounter treat them unfairly and events are hurtful.

Dramatic irony. Dramatic irony occurs in plays when a character states or hears something that means more to the audience than to the character. An example is the play *Oedipus Rex.* Like all Greek tragedies, *Oedipus Rex* dramatizes a myth the audience already knows. Thus, Oedipus's boast at the beginning that he will personally punish the reprobate who killed King Laius is ironic. He does not know—but the audience does—that he himself is the unwitting murderer of Laius. Although dramatic irony gets its name from drama, it occurs in all forms of literature. The key to dramatic irony is the reader's foreknowledge of coming events. Many works become newly interesting when we reread them because we now know what will happen while the characters do not; this dramatic irony intensifies characterization and makes us aware of tensions that we could not have known about during our initial reading.

QUESTIONS ABOUT IRONY

1. What are the ironies in the work?
2. How are the ironies important?
3. What are their implications?

An example of a work whose ironies suggest themes is Shirley Jackson's short story "The Lottery." The setting seems like everyone's nostalgic image of the ideal American small town, with its agricultural economy, central square, post office, country store, cranky old men, gossipy housewives, laconic farmers, mischievous children, settled routine, and friendly atmosphere. But the townspeople commit horrible deeds. What might Jackson be hinting at with this strange juxtaposition? Do "normal" American communities conduct "lotteries" to destroy innocent people? Yes, perhaps. Not as it's done in the story but with equal arbitrariness and cruelty. If this is one of her themes, she makes it more emphatic through irony than direct comment. She shocks us into rethinking our own ways of life.

OTHER QUESTIONS

1. **Verbal irony.** If characters constantly use verbal irony, why? What do we learn about their attitudes toward the world? Does their verbal irony usually take the form of sarcasm? Are they bitter and disappointed or simply realistic?

2. **Situational irony.** Are the characters aware of the situational ironies? Should we blame the characters for creating situational ironies or not understanding them?

3. **Attitudinal irony.** What attitudes do the characters have that contradict reality? Are we supposed to admire the characters who misconstrue the world, or are we to blame them for being naïve and deluded?

4. **Dramatic irony.** What do you know about coming events or past events in the work that the characters do not know? Why does the author give us this knowledge?

THINKING ON PAPER ABOUT IRONY

1. Mark examples of verbal irony, either by the narrator or other characters. Explain how a character's verbal irony helps characterize him or her.

2. Mark episodes in which a character's beliefs and expectations are contradicted by reality. Explain the importance to characterization of these episodes.

3. List instances of situational irony; identify people, for example, whom we expect to behave in one way but who behave quite differently. Explain the importance to theme of these instances.

Now It's Your Turn

"The Cask of Amontillado" (pages 362–67) has been praised for its masterful handling of irony. Explain the story's ironies and discuss their implications.

Symbolism

In the broadest sense, a symbol is something that represents something else. Words, for example, are symbols. But in literature, a *symbol* is an object that has meaning beyond itself. The object is concrete and the meanings are abstract. Fire, for example, may symbolize general destruction (as in James Baldwin's title *The Fire Next Time*), or passion (the "flames of desire"), or hell (the "fiery furnace"). Symbols, however, are not metaphors; they are not analogies that clarify abstractions, such as the following metaphor from Shakespeare's Sonnet 116:

> love is an ever-fixèd mark,
> That looks on tempests and is never shaken.

Here, the abstract concept (the referent) is "love" and the clarifying concrete object is the stable mark (buoy, lighthouse, rock) that tempests cannot budge. A symbol, in contrast, is a concrete object with no clear referent and thus no fixed meaning. Instead, it merely suggests the meaning and, in an odd way, partly *is* the meaning. For this reason, the meaning of symbols is difficult to pin down.

And the more inexhaustible their potential meaning, the richer they are.

There are two kinds of symbol: public and private. *Public symbols* are conventional, those that most people in a particular culture or community would recognize as meaning something fairly definite. Examples of public symbols are the cross, the star of David, the American eagle, flags of countries, the colors red (for "stop") and green (for "go"), and the skull and crossbones.

Private symbols are unique to an individual or to a single work. Only from clues in the work itself can we learn the symbolic value of the object. There are many examples of private symbols in literature. In F. Scott Fitzgerald's *The Great Gatsby,* there is an area between the posh Long Island suburbs and New York City through which the major characters drive at various times and which Fitzgerald calls a "valley of ashes." It is a desolate, gray, sterile place, and over it all broods a partly obliterated billboard advertisement that features the enormous eyes of Doctor T. J. Eckleburg, an optometrist. Fitzgerald invests this area with symbolic meaning. He associates it with moral decay, urban blight, the oppression of the poor by the wealthy, meaninglessness, hell, and violent death. At one point he connects the eyes with failure of vision, at another with God, who sees all things. But we never know exactly what the valley of ashes represents; instead, it resonates with many possible meanings, and this resonance accounts for its powerful suggestiveness.

QUESTIONS ABOUT SYMBOLISM

Not every work uses symbols, and not every character, incident, or object in a work has symbolic value. You should ask the fundamental question:

1. What symbols does the work seem to have? You should, however, beware of finding "symbols" where none were intended. A second question, then, is necessary to the believability of any interpretation based on symbols:

2. What makes you think that certain things in the work are symbols? (That is, how does the author signal that they are symbolic?) Once you answer this question, you can move on to a third and more interesting question:

3. What does the symbol mean?

In Hemingway's *A Farewell to Arms,* for example, the following dialogue between Frederic Henry and Catherine Barkley suggests that Hemingway intended a symbolic meaning for rain; it also suggests what the symbol represents:

[Frederic says] "It's raining hard."

"And you'll always love me, won't you?" [Catherine replies]

"Yes."

"And the rain won't make any difference?"

"No."

"That's good. Because I'm afraid of the rain."

"Why? . . . Tell me."

"All right. I'm afraid of the rain because sometimes I see me dead in it."

"No."

"And sometimes I see you dead in it. . . . It's all nonsense. It's only nonsense. I'm not afraid of the rain. I'm not afraid of the rain. Oh, oh, God, I wish I wasn't." She was crying. I comforted her and she stopped crying. But outside it kept on raining. (125–26)

Throughout the novel, Hemingway's recurrent association of rain with destruction of all kinds broadens its significance from a mere metaphor for death to other and more general qualities such as war, fate, alienation, foreboding, doom, and "reality." Because of these associations, the last sentence of the novel is more than just a description of the weather: "After a while I went out and left the hospital and walked back to the hotel in the rain" (332). The sentence seems to suggest that Frederic is stoically and bravely facing the harsh realities—including Catherine's death, the war, the arbitrariness and cruelty of fate—represented by the rain.

THINKING ON PAPER ABOUT SYMBOLISM

1. List the symbols in the work.

2. State why you think the objects are meant as symbols.

3. Mark the descriptions or episodes that give the symbols meaning.

4. List each symbol's possible meanings.

Now It's Your Turn

Indicate what you think might be symbols in "The Cask of Amontillado" (pages 362–67), "Yours" (pages 43–44), or "My Last Duchess" (pages 120–22). Explain why you think the author intends them as symbols and what they seem to represent.

OTHER ELEMENTS

In this chapter we have treated the elements most obviously identified with fiction. But other elements are also sometimes important in fiction: dialogue, description, metaphor, poetic use of language, diction. We will discuss these other elements in the next two chapters.

Checklist for Interpreting Fiction

Themes (pages 32–37)

❖ State some of the important subjects.

❖ Formulate themes that emerge from these subjects.

❖ Mark statements by narrators and characters that might serve as themes. Assess the validity of these statements as themes.

❖ Use "philosophical" questions to probe thematic implications of the work.

❖ If there is a moral center, describe that character. Explain why this and any other character could be considered a moral center.

Point of View (pages 37–42)

❖ Indicate the point of view—who narrates.

❖ Describe the narrator's tone.

❖ Assess the reliability of the narrator.

❖ Explain who the audience—narratee(s)—of the narrative is.

Plot (pages 44–54)

❖ Compare arrangements of events in the plot and story.

❖ Outline the pattern of the plot—Freytag's pattern or other patterns.

❖ If there are multiple plot lines, summarize each one. Indicate their connections to one another.

❖ Indicate the true beginning of the plot.

❖ Assess the appropriateness of the ending.

❖ Identify the major conflicts.

❖ Explain what the protagonists fight for and against what or whom (antagonists).

❖ Show how any embedded stories or frame stories illuminate the main plots.

❖ Indicate examples of summary narration and scenic narration. Speculate about why the author uses each.

Characterization (pages 54–60)

❖ Explain the traits of flat characters.

❖ Describe how round characters are complex.

❖ Indicate which characters change and why.

❖ Show what method or methods the author uses to render characters' thoughts.

❖ Summarize epiphanies characters have. Explain what causes and leads to the epiphanies.

❖ Mark passages where the narrator or characters make descriptive and judgmental statements about characters.

Setting (pages 61–66)

❖ Describe the place of the setting.

❖ Indicate how the place affects characters.

❖ Explain the time—historical period, passage of time, perception of time—of the narrative.

❖ Characterize the social environment and how characters respond to it.

❖ Describe the atmosphere. Indicate what causes it.

Irony (pages 66–69)

❖ Explore how irony contributes to other elements—especially characterization, tone, and themes.

Symbolism (pages 69–71)
❖ Describe key symbols.

❖ Explain why you think they are symbols and what they represent.

Works Cited

Abrams, M. H. *A Glossary of Literary Terms.* Forth Worth: Harcourt, 1999.

Austen, Jane. *Pride and Prejudice.* New York: Dodd, Mead, 1945.

Booth, Wayne C. *The Rhetoric of Fiction.* Chicago: U of Chicago P, 1961.

Brontë, Charlotte. *Jane Eyre.* New York: Penguin, 1966.

Faulkner, William. *The Sound and the Fury.* New York: Vintage, 1987.

Forster, E. M. *Aspects of the Novel.* New York: Harcourt, Brace, 1954.

Freytag, Gustav. *Freytag's Technique of the Drama.* 5th ed. Trans. Elias J. MacEwan. Chicago: Scott, Foresman, 1894.

Garland, Hamlin. "Among the Corn Rows." *Main-Traveled Roads.* Signet Classics. New York: New American Library, 1962. 98–121.

Hemingway, Ernest. *A Farewell to Arms.* New York: Scribner's, 1957.

———. "Hills Like White Elephants." *The Short Stories of Ernest Hemingway.* New York: Scribner's, 1966. 273–8.

Humphrey, Robert. *Stream of Consciousness in the Modern Novel.* Berkeley: U of California P, 1954.

Keen, Suzanne. *Narrative Form.* New York: Palgrave Macmillan, 2003.

Murfin, Ross, and Supryia M. Ray. *The Bedford Glossary of Critical and Literary Terms.* Boston: Bedford Books, 1997.

O'Connor, Flannery. *Mystery and Manners.* New York: Farrar, Straus, & Giroux, 1969.

Porter, Katherine Anne. "The Jilting of Granny Weatherall." *Flowering Judas and Other Stories.* New York: Modern Library, 1935. 121–36.

Pushkin, Alexander. "The Queen of Spades." *The Queen of Spades and Other Stories.* Trans. T. Keane. New York: Dover, 1994.

Twain, Mark. *The Adventures of Huckleberry Finn.* Riverside Editions. Boston: Houghton Mifflin, 1958.

Woolf, Virginia. *Mrs. Dalloway in Bond Street.* London: Hogarth, 1973.

Wright, Richard. "The Man Who Was Almost a Man." *Eight Men.* New York: Thunder's Mouth Press, 1987.

4

Interpreting Drama

Drama contains many of the elements of fiction. Like fiction, drama contains plot, characters, theme, and setting. Like fiction, drama uses irony and symbolism. And indeed, you can read a play as you would a short novel, using your imagination to fill in all the "missing" material you typically find in fiction: character description, background information, vivid action scenes. Similarly, drama often contains many of the elements of poetry so that you can read it just as you read any poetry. Because of the great similarity of drama to fiction and poetry, the definitions, questions, and exercises stated in the preceding chapter on fiction and in the following chapter on poetry are all equally valid for drama. Use them to generate your own interpretations of plays.

THE NATURE OF DRAMA

Performance of plays. Drama is different from fiction and most poetry in one essential way: It is meant to be performed. Some theorists of drama argue that a play is incomplete *until* it is performed. According to the critic Bernard Beckerman in *Dynamics of Drama*, "a play is a mere skeleton; performance fleshes out the bones" (3). When you read a play, you miss qualities the playwright intended as a part of the play. For one thing, you miss the audience, whose physical pres-

ence and reactions to the performance influence both the performance and your perception of the play. For another, you miss the set
designers' vision of the atmosphere and physical world of the play. You
miss the interpretive art of the actors and the illusion they create of
real life unfolding before your eyes. You miss the physical and emotional *experience* of drama that a production gives.

Reading of plays.   This is not to say that reading a play carefully is
not worth doing. Sometimes in a performance we miss aspects of plays
that people catch only when reading the play. This is especially true of
plays written in poetry. When Romeo and Juliet⋆ first speak to each
other, they develop a complex metaphor (a pilgrim coming to a shrine)
and speak in sonnet form. It is unlikely that a playgoer, upon hearing
this exchange, would think, "Aha! That was a sonnet!" Rather, we notice such devices by reading carefully. Even if our purpose is to produce the play, we must read carefully because productions are based
on interpretations. "Literary" devices such as a sonnet, perhaps unno-
ticed by an audience, provide clues to a playwright's concept of the
performance. In fact, everything in the play is a clue to its possible performance and thus deserves studious attention.

   To read a play with an eye to how the play might be produced,
therefore, is to understand the play as the playwright conceived it.
Since we examine the elements of fiction and poetry in Chapters 3 and
5, we will concentrate in this chapter on how you can use the potential
performance of drama as a means of understanding its elements.

THE ELEMENTS OF DRAMA

Plot

Plot and story.   As with narrative fiction, *plot* and *story* in drama
have different meanings. (See the discussion of plot and story in
fiction on pages 44–46.) *Plot* is three interrelated things. First, it is the
playwright's arrangement of events, which we experience as the performance or reading of the play. Second, it is the connection of events
by cause and effect, which gives rise to conflict. Third, it is the devices
the playwright uses to engage us emotionally and intellectually, such
as pacing, rising action, climax, surprise, intensification of conflict,

---

⋆Publication dates of works of literature cited in this book and dates of authors' lives can
be found in the author-title index at the back of the book.

and foreshadowing. *Story* is the entire sequence of events, arranged in chronological order, of which the play is a part.

The "plot" of *Oedipus Rex,* for example, is Oedipus's attempt to rid Thebes of a blight and his resulting discovery of who he is and the nature of his crimes. The "story" of the play is Oedipus's entire history, starting with his parents' attempt to kill him when he was an infant and ending with his death at Colonus. Some plays feature a plot that is only a small part (but usually a very important and climactic part) of a story. Other plays feature a plot that is nearly equivalent to the story. Shakespeare's *Macbeth* has almost no important past and future events; nearly all the action occurs within the play itself. Thus the plot and story of *Macbeth* are nearly equivalent. The events in *Hamlet,* however, occur after a murder and a marriage and, long before that, a war between Denmark and Norway, all of which profoundly affect the action within the play itself; the conclusion of the play, furthermore, suggests what the future of Denmark will be like under its new ruler, the Norwegian king Fortinbras.

Simplicity of plot.   Because the playwright has only a short time (two or so hours) to develop plot and because the playwright's audience experiences the play in one sitting, with little immediate opportunity to review it, the playwright must keep the plot simple and clear enough for an audience to grasp during the length of the performance. This means that the playwright cannot indulge in numerous subplots or in intricate plot complications; otherwise the playgoer would become confused. Playwrights, therefore, limit the number of characters in a play. (The fewer the characters, the simpler the plot can be.) Playwrights often emphasize conflict to keep the audience involved in the action and establish discernible patterns of cause and effect.

Dialogue.   Although the playwright can present physical action without having to use words, the action (and the conflict implicit in the action) must be understandable to the audience. The most important and almost inevitable means for doing this is *dialogue*—people talking to people. Playwrights, then, strive to make every word of dialogue help move the plot forward. The near inevitability of dialogue also means that playwrights focus largely on conflicts between people rather than conflicts between people and nonhuman forces. In contrast, fiction need not represent characters' words or thoughts and so is freer to depict conflicts between people and nonhuman forces. Jack London's short story "To Build a Fire" does give the thoughts of the protagonist; but otherwise there is no "dialogue," just the protagonist's conflict with the harsh Yukon landscape. It would be difficult for a play to duplicate this kind of conflict. Plays sometimes do portray conflicts between people and nonhuman forces, but these conflicts are revealed through dialogue and usually through conflicts between the characters.

Represented action.   Because the time and space for a presentation is limited, certain kinds of action—battles and sports activities, for example—cannot be represented fully or literally on the stage. These activities must be concentrated or symbolized. A duel onstage, for example, might represent an entire battle; a plantation house that changes from sparkling new to ramshackled might represent the causes of a grand family's ruin. Sometimes the playwright places activities offstage. A character might describe events that have just taken place, but the audience does not see these events. It learns about them only through the dialogue.

Audience expectations.   Plotting in drama depends in part on establishing *audience expectations* of what will happen in the immediate future, as the play is unfolding. Both fiction and poetry, in contrast, focus more on what has already happened. The playwright, of course, predetermines the events in a play; but as we watch, we experience the illusion that the action is occurring in the present and that neither we nor the characters know what will happen next. This effect of expectation is heightened in drama because as we watch the play we have little time to reflect on what has happened, whereas when we read a novel we can pause and think about what we have read. Playwrights often predict our expectations about certain kinds of action and certain kinds of characters and fulfill our expectations or surprise us by thwarting them.

Structural divisions.   The *structural divisions* of plays affect plot. Playwrights usually provide structural divisions to give playgoers physical relief—a few moments to stand up, walk about, stretch, or reflect (however briefly) on what they have seen. Structural divisions also serve to allow set changes. In addition to such performance considerations, structural divisions also mark segments of the plot. *Formal structural divisions* are those specified in the play or the program—acts and scenes. *Informal structural divisions* can be smaller units within an act or scene, units not identified as such by the playwright but that nonetheless have a self-contained quality. In formal structural units, the playwright might call for the curtain to come down, the lights to go off, or the characters to leave the stage to signal the end of a unit. Shakespeare often ends his units with a couplet. In informal units, none of these things may happen; instead, the units may just flow together. Characteristic of most of them, however, is a rising action, a climax, and possibly a brief falling action. The climax of these units is usually a moment of revelation, either to the main characters, to other characters, or to the audience. An example is Hamlet's recognition at the climax of the play-within-a-play scene that King Claudius has murdered his father, the former king. All of the units of a play contribute to the rising action of the entire play and lead finally to its main climax.

⌒ QUESTIONS ABOUT PLOT

Plot versus story

1. What is the "plot" of the play?
2. What is the "story"?
3. If the plot is only part of the story, why does the playwright choose this part?
4. What has happened before the play begins?
5. What will happen afterward? As Bernard Beckerman points out, if the plot is only part of a larger or continuing story, the characters are more likely to seem at the mercy of forces beyond their control; whereas, if the plot and story are roughly equivalent, the characters will seem more free to choose and mold their own fate (172). The plot of *Romeo and Juliet,* for example, is only one episode—the final episode, we hope—of a generations-long, murderous, and irrational family feud. Romeo and Juliet are therefore "star-crossed" and "death-marked"; try as they will, they cannot escape the undertow of their families' history. Even Prince Escalus, the only person in the play with both power and good sense, can do nothing to avert the tragedy. Macbeth and Lady Macbeth, in contrast, choose to do evil at the beginning of the play and thus give rise to the forces that destroy them.

Simplicity

1. We said that plot in drama needs to be relatively simple and clear. In the play you are studying, is it? If not, why would the playwright want to create confusion about the important conflicts and cause-

and-effect relationships? Sometimes the playwright *tries* to create such confusion. Congreve in *The Way of the World,* for example, establishes a pattern of relationships so confusing that an audience is hard pressed to figure out who has done what to whom, especially at the breakneck speed of a typical performance. He probably does this purposefully to indicate the complicated texture of Restoration upper-class society and the difficulty of finding one's way through it safely and honorably.

2. What are the main conflicts?

3. What has caused the conflicts existing at the beginning of the play?

4. What causes the conflicts that emerge during the course of the play?

5. Who is in conflict with whom? Why?

6. Are any of the characters in conflict with forces larger than just individuals—society, for example, or fate?

7. How are the conflicts resolved?

Location of action

1. What actions occur offstage?

2. Why does the author elect to place some actions offstage and other actions onstage? In *Macbeth,* for example, Shakespeare has the murder of King Duncan (at the beginning of the play) occur offstage, but later he has the murder of Banquo and, in another scene, the murder of Macduff's family (or part of it) occur onstage. Why, then, does he choose to put one murder offstage and other murders onstage?

3. How do the characters react to the offstage events? Shakespeare probably places Duncan's murder offstage because he wants the audience to focus attention on Macbeth and Lady Macbeth's reaction to the murder.

4. What does the playwright use to represent or symbolize action that occurs offstage? When Macbeth returns from killing Duncan, he carries the murder weapons, all covered with blood. His hands are covered with blood. When Lady Macbeth returns from smearing blood all over the sleeping guards, *her* hands are covered with blood. The more we see of this blood and the more they talk about it, the more grisly and physical and sticky the murder seems. Without actually describing the murder, Shakespeare uses a physical image—blood—and the characters' reaction to it to signal what the murder was like.

Audience expectations

1. What expectations does the plot call up in the audience?

2. Does the playwright fulfill those expectations? If not, how and why not? Most traditional comedy, for example, offers young lovers as staple characters. We expect the lovers, after suitable complications, to find happiness together, usually signaled at the end by betrothal or marriage. But sometimes the playwright introduces potential lovers, gives us something like a light comic tone, creates comic complications, but thwarts our expectations that they will marry. Examples are Etherege's *The Man of Mode,* Molière's *The Misanthrope,* and Shaw's *Mrs. Warren's Profession.*

Another example is Chekhov's *The Cherry Orchard,* which he called a comedy, even though it is not always played as such. In this play, the main character, Lopakhin, and the adopted daughter of the family he is trying to rescue from economic disaster, seem meant for each other. There is much talk throughout the play of their marrying. Such a marriage would seem to be good for both of them. They agree to marry. Since they are sympathetic characters, the audience wants them to marry. Yet they never do. Why does Chekhov create the expectation and even hope of their marriage and then abort it? The answer to this question provides insight into Chekhov's purposes in *The Cherry Orchard;* and since he uses the same device in other plays— *Three Sisters,* for example—the answer throws light on his entire dramatic method.

Formal and informal divisions

1. What are the formal structural divisions of the plays? How many are there—three acts? four? five?

2. How do the formal divisions reflect the playwright's purposes and materials? Oscar Wilde's *The Importance of Being Earnest,* for example, is divided into three acts. The first act takes place in London, the second and third in the country. This division reflects the double-identity motif in the plot because the main character pretends to have two identities: a city identity and a country identity. The first two acts reflect these opposing identities. The third act, however, synthesizes the first two. Events and revelations allow the main character to blend his city and country identities into one happy whole. The structure of the play neatly reflects a "thesis, antithesis, synthesis" pattern of oppositions and resolution of oppositions.

3. What are the informal units of the play?

4. For *all* the units, what are the climaxes of each? What is revealed in the climax—to the main character featured in the unit, to other characters, to the audience?

5. How is a particular unit important to the whole play?

6. What is the main climax of the play? What do you learn from it?

THINKING ON PAPER ABOUT PLOT

1. List the conflicts revealed in each major section of the play (usually acts, but sometimes scenes).

2. Explain how one or more of these conflicts is first made evident. Pay close attention to dialogue.

3. Summarize how a conflict is developed throughout the whole play and how it is resolved.

4. Summarize the events, either in the past or present, that cause conflict. If there is one event that caused or causes all the conflicts, summarize it in detail and explain why and how it is so important.

5. List the external conflicts. How are they represented on stage? Through dialogue? Through physical action? Through symbolic stage props?

6. List the events that precede the action of the play. Explain the effect, if any, of these prior events on the action.

7. Summarize the events in each major structural unit of the play. Explain the relationship of the play's units to the plot's structure. Show how the action in each unit rises to a climax.

8. Mark some informal structural divisions in the play. Note the rising action and climax of these units. Explain how each is important.

9. Describe one important scene in detail. Explain how the characters' actions and dialogue reveal conflict. Explain the importance of the scene to the whole play.

10. Describe the climax of the play. Explain what conflicts are resolved.

11. List the main plot and the subplots. Explain the relationship of the subplots to the main plot.

12. List the events that occur offstage. Explain why the playwright has one or more of these occur offstage rather than onstage.

13. Summarize the situation at the beginning of the play and state what you expect to happen. Explain how the play does or does not fulfill those expectations.

Now It's Your Turn

Discuss the plot elements in *Trifles* (pages 373–85). What are the conflicts? Are the "plot" and "story" different? What happens offstage? Although this is a one-act play, are there informal divisions in it? Where does the climax occur?

Characterization

Stock characters. As with plot, the playwright must keep character portrayal simple enough for an audience to understand during the course of a single performance. The playwright must therefore rely heavily on flat characters, especially stereotyped ("stock") characters, whose personalities and moral traits are easily caught and remembered by the audience. The playwright may even use unsubtle stratagems of dress, dialect, physical movements, and names to communicate these traits. In Restoration and eighteenth-century comedy, for example, the names signal the traits of comic flat characters: Mrs. Loveit, Sir Fopling Flutter, Snake, Pert, Mr. Oldcastle, Lady Wishforit, Lady Sneerwell, Smirk, Handy. The playwright must also rely on static characters more heavily than dynamic characters because time-restricted performance limits the opportunity to make character changes plausible.

Flat and round characters. Edward Pixley suggests that when a play is dominated by flat characters, the plot hinges mainly on external conflicts; the focus is on action. When the play includes round characters, the plot deals largely with internal conflicts, the focus is on characterization (12).

In Wilde's *The Importance of Being Earnest*, all the characters are flat; the charm of the play lies not in character development but in the witty language, in the mild satire rippling through the dialogue, and in the plot complications resulting from the confusion of identities. In contrast, Ibsen's *Hedda Gabler* presents a complex, round character, Hedda herself; and the interest of the play lies in what she will do next and why she will do it. Hedda does not change during the play, but her character traits intensify and become clearer to the audience. Round characters, therefore, hold the audience's attention by changing or, if they don't change, by becoming more intense. In either case, continual revelations about the characters grip the audience's interest.

Text and subtext. Although the playwright may depend to an extent on exterior details to reveal character traits, the playwright's most important device for character development is dialogue—what the characters say and what they say about one another. But performance time is limited; the words of the dialogue cannot describe the character fully. Playwrights, therefore, rely heavily on implication in the dialogue and on "gaps"—information left out—to indicate what characters are like and what physical things they do. Some critics mark this distinction with the terms *text* for the written words of the play and *subtext* for the implications and gaps. All literary genres make use of implication and gaps, but drama and poetry almost *must* rely on them because both genres are such compressed forms of communication.

A simple example of text and subtext is the scene near the beginning of *Hamlet* in which Hamlet, after a long absence, meets his university friends Horatio and Marcellus. The night before this meeting, Horatio and Marcellus have seen the ghost of Hamlet's father. But Hamlet doesn't know about the ghost; instead, he complains about his mother's marrying so soon after his father's death:

> HAMLET: Would I had met my dearest foe in heaven
>   Or ever I had seen that day [the wedding day], Horatio!
>   My father—methinks I see my father.
> HORATIO: Where, my lord?
> HAMLET: In my mind's eye, Horatio.
> HORATIO: I saw him once. 'A was [he was] a goodly king. (1.2. 182–8)

If you were the actor playing Horatio, how would you say the line "Where, my lord?" The "gap" here is the nature of Horatio's response to Hamlet's statement, "My father—methinks I see my father." To fill the gap, you have to determine from the context how Horatio takes that statement (Shakespeare does not tell you how, as a novelist might), and you have to communicate his reaction to the audience by the way you say the line and by your physical demeanor. You might phrase the line as an incredulous question: "What? You see your father? But how could you, he's dead?" Or you might say it as a reflection of what you take to be Hamlet's witty mood: "I know you're joking, Hamlet. But tell me anyway. Where do you see your father?" But another possibility is that you would say it in astonishment, as if you take it literally. After all, *you* had seen the ghost of Hamlet's father just a few hours before. You probably think Hamlet has now spotted the ghost, and so you say, "Good Lord, do you see it, too? Where?" And you look fearfully around, trying to see the ghost too. When Hamlet indicates that he is only remembering his father, you calm down. At this point you might pause and make appropriate gestures to indicate your shift from fear and astonishment to calmness. The fact that you *have* made such a shift is indicated by your response to Hamlet: "Yes. Once, when the king was alive, I saw him too. He was an impressive-looking king." This last statement shows that Horatio has moved from thinking about a supernatural phenomenon (the ghost) to thinking about a natural one (Hamlet's father when he was alive).

This brief example illustrates the greatest value of understanding a play's subtext. By "reading" implications and gaps in the play, you uncover inner states of the characters—what is going on in their minds and what their hidden nature is. You also establish a correspondence between a character's inner state and what the character says and does (the character's outer state). Interpretation of subtext is essential for actors, who must figure out how to say the dialogue and what to do onstage. But it is important for readers, too, even though a reader may not work out intonation and physical movements in as much detail as actors do.

A character's inner life is the key to the character's nature and actions. Horatio, in the example above, is a flat character. His inner state is relatively uncomplicated. But exposing it gives the performance—whether seen by an audience or imagined by a reader—vividness. Horatio springs to life. As for round characters, the difficulty of uncovering their inner states is much greater, yet their complexity of inner state makes them fascinating. Great characters like Oedipus, Macbeth, Hamlet, and Hedda Gabler grip our imaginations just because their inner states are mysterious. The only way we can expose these inner states is by interpreting the subtext of the play.

Mask wearing.   Closely related to subtext in drama is *mask wearing.* Nearly every play employs the mask as a device for developing plot and characterization. Juliet wears a "mask"—pretends to be different from the way she really is—in order to fool her parents and run away with Romeo. Hamlet puts on a mask of madness to root out the murderer of his father. Hedda pretends to be the contented housewife in order to secure the wealth and social status she thinks she deserves. Macbeth and Lady Macbeth pretend to be the loyal servants and gracious hosts of King Duncan while plotting his murder. The audience may be fully aware of the mask and thus the disparity between appearance and reality, as, for example, in Juliet's case. Or the audience may at first be as unaware of the mask as are the other characters in the play, as in Hedda's case. And sometimes the mask wearers are themselves unaware or partially unaware of their masks; that is, they deceive themselves. Oedipus, for example, does not know that he is masking his true identity of king murderer. In all cases, both plot and characterization turn on revelation—the tearing away of the mask. At these moments of revelation, the audience and at least some of the characters see the reality behind the mask. Often the final unmasking comes at the climax of the plot. In *Othello* the climax occurs when Iago's mask is ripped away before Othello's shocked eyes.

QUESTIONS ABOUT CHARACTERIZATION

1. If the characters are flat, what are their dominant traits? What is their function in the plot? How do they help establish the conflicts in the plot?

2. If the characters are dynamic, how do they change—from what to what?

3. If they are static, do their traits intensify or become clearer as the play moves on?

4. If the characters are round, what can you learn from the subtext of the play about their inner states?

5. What "masks" are the characters wearing? Who is hiding what from whom? When are the masks removed? What causes their removal, and what are the results?

6. How would you play a particular character if you were the actor? What physical devices would you use? Hedda Gabler is aristocratic, proud, and forceful; she seems strong but has an inner fragility. Her rival, Thea, is hesitant, unsophisticated, and afraid; she seems weak but has an inner strength. If you were to act these characters, how

would you present yourself physically to convey these qualities? How would you show that Hedda seems strong but is in fact weak? You may not actually act Hedda but determining a physical presence for her helps you analyze and understand her.

THINKING ON PAPER ABOUT CHARACTERIZATION

1. List the character traits of each major character.

2. List the devices, such as dress, names, and gestures, that help establish the traits of a character.

3. Describe in detail the traits of a complex character, especially contradictory and seemingly inexplicable traits.

4. Explain a character's motivations for doing the things he or she does. Focus especially on what the character seems to want. Explain the situations from which the character's motivations seem to emerge.

5. Describe the strategies a character devises for getting what he or she wants. Explain how effective those strategies are.

6. Describe the miscalculations a character makes and the effect they have.

7. Summarize how a character intensifies, changes, or comes into sharper focus for the audience. Trace the intensification, change, or focus through each major unit of the play. Explain what causes it.

8. Summarize a scene in which a major character faces a crisis. Explain what we learn about the character from the character's words and actions.

9. Summarize a scene in which a major character has a startling or affecting revelation. Explain what the revelation is, what causes it, and its effect on the character's future.

10. Explain how you would portray one of the characters in an important scene. Show how your performance would reveal the character's inner state.

11. Explain the relationship a major character has with the other major characters. Describe the alliances and conflicts the character has with the other characters. Describe the attitudes the character has toward the other characters and their attitudes toward him or her.

12. If there is one character who exerts control—intentionally or unintentionally—over other characters, describe that character in detail and explain the source and nature of that control. Describe the other characters' reactions to that control.

13. List the masks characters wear. Explain why a character wears a mask.

14. Trace one or more of these masks throughout the play. Explain how effectively the mask accomplishes the character's purpose.

15. Summarize the scene in which the mask is dropped. List the effects of the mask being dropped.

Now It's Your Turn

Explore aspects of characterization in *Trifles* (pages 373–85).

Setting

Because of the limited time and space of dramatic productions, a play cannot create a "world" in the same detail and breadth a novel can. The worlds of novels like Tolstoy's *War and Peace* and Hugo's *Les Miserables,* with their multitude of characters, scenes, physical places, and battles, are impossible to show in drama. Rather, such worlds can be represented only fragmentarily. The playwright must use a shorthand method of presenting the setting so that the playgoer grasps enough information about it to understand whatever relationship it might have to characterization and theme. Sometimes the relationship is minimal, sometimes very close. *Setting* in drama is the same as in fiction: the social mores, values, and customs of the world in which the characters live; the physical world; and the time of the action, including historical circumstances.

Dialogue. The playwright has three main ways of communicating setting to an audience. First, we learn about setting from the characters' dialogue, dress, and behavior. In Sheridan's *School for Scandal,* we know immediately that the world of this play is leisured upper-class English society. We know this from the elaborately polite and mannered way in which the characters carry themselves and from the names they so freely drop—Sir Harry Bouquet, Lord Spindle, Captain Quinze, Lady Frizzle, the Dowager Lady Dundizzy. In *Hedda Gabler* the conversations between Hedda and Judge Brack let us know that they are aristocrats and that Hedda's husband and his family are middle class.

Sets. Second, we learn about setting from the sets produced by the set designer. Sheridan doesn't tell us what the interiors for *School for Scandal* should look like. He says simply that throughout the play the setting is "London" and that in act one it is "Lady Sneerwell's house." A set designer, however, would do research on the interior design of fashionable homes in late-eighteenth-century England and produce that image on stage. The set, in short, should "say" that these people are aristocrats.

Audience's knowledge. Third, we learn about setting from the knowledge we *bring* to the performance. The playwright alludes to the nature of the setting and assumes we will fill in the details. As Americans, for example, we have relatively little trouble understanding the setting of Arthur Miller's *The Crucible,* even though it is set in seventeenth-century New England. Miller expects us to know something about the Salem witch trials and about the McCarthy "witch-hunts" of the 1950s, and most Americans who see that play do know something about them.

A problem surfaces, however, when the audience does not have the supplemental information to complete the setting of the play—audiences from other cultures or other periods. Chekhov's plays are a case in point. *The Cherry Orchard,* for example, plays against a background of Russian history that Chekhov assumes we know: the reform acts of Czar Alexander II (1855–1881), including the freeing of the serfs in 1861 and the establishing of the *zemstvo* system of local self-government; Alexander's assassination by anarchists in 1881; the rigid autocracy of the next czar, Alexander III (1881–1894); and the ineffectual and repressive reign of his successor, Nicholas II (1894–1917), which revived revolutionary movements in the late 1890s. *The Cherry Orchard* focuses on the passing of a decrepit aristocratic order and the rising of a vigorous middle class and financial order. For us even to recognize this concern, it helps to know a little Russian history. Otherwise, we may be confused about why the aristocrats are so nostalgic, whimsical, and impractical in the face of imminent financial disaster. Chekhov wants us to see that their attitude is both a result and a cause of this historical change.

Sets as symbolic. Playwrights and set designers can choose to give their sets symbolic value. Sets need not be symbolic. The sets in *School for Scandal* will usually be a literal suggestion of aristocratic drawing rooms and mean nothing more than that. To create the illusion of real rooms, the set designer can use physical detail lavishly—furniture, wallpaper, decorative doodads, architectural features, paintings, and clothes. But aspects of sets can take on symbolic or representational meaning. The simplest representational set is a bare stage, which can represent anything the playwright wants—a battlefield, a heath, a forest, or a gothic cathedral. The playwright can be blatantly symbolic, assigning obvious meanings to physical objects. Thornton Wilder does this in *Our Town* when he uses stepladders to represent houses.

The playwright can also combine a realistic with a symbolic method. In *Hedda Gabler,* for example, Ibsen calls for solidly "real" things to be put in the two rooms we see of the Tesman house—an armchair, footstools, sofa, tables, French windows, and flowers in vases. But certain objects—Hedda's pistols, the portrait of General Gabler (Hedda's father), and the piano—become closely associated with her and her psychological disorders. Equally suggestive are the two rooms: one a large, elegant drawing room located in the front part of the stage and the other a smaller sitting room located in back. In act one Hedda's piano is in the drawing room, but in act two it is out of sight in the back room. In fact, as the play proceeds, the back room becomes more and more "Hedda's room" and the drawing room "Tesman's room." Even the portrait of General Gabler is in the back room. At the end of the play, Hedda retreats to the back room, pulls the curtains, frantically plays the piano, and shoots herself. It is as if the back room represents an increasingly restricted physical and emotional space for Hedda, until at last it becomes her prison and coffin.

QUESTIONS ABOUT SETTING

1. What do you learn about the setting from characters' behavior and dialogue?

2. What kind of sets does the play seem to call for?

3. What costumes would you have the actors wear?

4. What costumes would best fit particular characters?

5. Does the play seem to require background knowledge on your part to understand its setting?

6. What are the symbolic possibilities in particular objects or in larger portions of the set?

7. What relationships does the setting have to characterization?

8. What emotional feel—atmosphere—does the setting have?

9. What relationships does the setting have to theme?

⤳ THINKING ON PAPER ABOUT SETTING

1. For each major unit of the play, describe the place where the action occurs. If the playwright gives a description of the place, summarize the description. If the playwright does not give a description, use information from the dialogue to construct a description. Explain the relationship of place to action, characterization, and theme.

2. Identify the time of day of each unit of the play. Explain how the time of day is represented on stage and its effect on the characters and the action.

3. Identify the time of year of each unit of the play. Explain the relationship of time of year to action, characterization, and theme.

4. Identify the historical period of the play. Give any background information that would be useful for understanding the play. Explain the relationship of the historical period to action, characterization, and theme.

5. Describe the atmosphere of each major unit of the play.

6. Describe the costumes the characters wear. Explain the relationship between costumes, characterization, and theme.

7. Describe your design for the physical world—sets, costumes, sounds, lighting, the works—of one major unit of the play. Explain the reasons for your choices.

8. List the details of setting that have symbolic value. Explain what each symbolizes. Explain the relationship of symbolism to characterization and theme.

9. Explain each major character's attitude toward the setting.

Now It's Your Turn

Susan Glaspell makes setting almost like another character in *Trifles* (pages 373–85). Explain the meanings setting has in the play.

Theme

Playwrights build themes into their plays through the development and interrelationship of all the elements of drama, most of which are the same as for fiction. Three methods of developing theme, however, are particularly noteworthy: repetitions, symbols, and contrasts. All three lend themselves well to drama. Audiences pick up on them easily during performances.

Repetitions. *Repetitions* take many forms—a character's performing the same gesture over and over again, repeating the same phrase, stating the same idea, or appearing at regular intervals. But for repetitions to relate to theme, they must develop ideas. Shakespeare does just that in *Hamlet* by repeating and intertwining three concepts: Denmark as "rotten," human beings as sinful, and the king's role as crucial to the health of the state. He characterizes Denmark by repeatedly comparing it to a garden overrun with weeds and to a diseased body, analogies borne out by Hamlet's partial madness and Ophelia's complete madness and suicide. He has key characters dwell on the sinful nature of humankind. The queen says that her own soul is "sick," "as sin's true nature is" (4.5.16). The king says that his "offense is rank, it smells to heaven" because it has "the primal eldest curse" upon it (Cain's murder of Abel, 3.3.36–37). And Hamlet says that even the best people seem to have "some vicious mole of nature in them" that leads them from purity to corruption (1.4.24). (All three of these statements connect sin to sickness.) The corrupt state of Denmark, Shakespeare implies, is the result of the king's sin. For, as one character says, the king is like the hub of a wheel whose spokes connect to "ten thousand lesser things" (3.3.11–23). Whatever the king does affects everyone in the state.

Symbolism. As we noted, *symbolism* can enrich setting. In fact, symbolism bears on both characterization and theme as well. It is often hard to separate the effect of symbolism on all three elements. In *Hedda Gabler,* for example, Ibsen contrasts Hedda's and Thea's hair to symbolize their different character traits. Hedda's hair is thin and dull; Thea's is thick and luxuriant. Hedda dates her long-standing rivalry with Thea from their school days, when Hedda threatened to "burn off" Thea's hair. Hedda seems at times to want to inspire people to create, but her efforts end up as destructive; whereas Thea has an innate and unconscious gift for inspiring creativity. This wellspring of inspiration and fertility is symbolized by Thea's hair, which helps explain Hedda's animosity toward it. It's hard to say just what Ibsen's themes in *Hedda Gabler* are; he may simply be trying to present, not explain, Hedda's mysterious perversities. But one implication of the hair symbolism may be that creativity is a mysterious quality existing even in someone as innocent and nonintellectual as Thea and that it may not have anything to do with the intellectual sharpness and forcefulness of people like Hedda. Whatever Ibsen's themes are, they are inextricably bound up with his characterization of Hedda and Thea.

A simpler—that is, easier to interpret—example of thematic symbolism occurs in Lorraine Hansberry's *A Raisin in the Sun*. Mrs. Younger, the main character, is the mother of a large extended family, but her environment—a stultifying, roach-infested, inner-city tenement—has kept her from giving the best of life to her children. The house she wants to buy in the suburbs becomes equivalent to new "earth" in which her children and grandchild can "grow," because, as she says, they are her "harvest." To emphasize the analogy between the house and a garden, Hansberry shows Mrs. Younger constantly dreaming of working in the garden at the new house and, as a moving present, her children give her garden tools. The most visible symbol of Mrs. Younger's frustrations and aspirations is a sickly houseplant she has been trying for years to nurture. The audience sees the plant sitting in the window. Mrs. Younger fusses over it. Her children chide her for messing with it, but she persists. The last thing we see her do is say goodbye to the oppressive apartment and carry the plant out the door. At the new house, it will revive in the sunshine and clean air of a better world. The message seems clear: People are like plants; they become healthy—mentally, morally, and physically—only in hospitable environments.

Contrast.   Like symbolism, *contrast* helps develop not just theme but characterization and plot. We have already seen many examples of contrast in the plays we have discussed so far: romantic love (Romeo and Juliet) versus social requirements (the Montagues and the Capulets), Thea versus Hedda, Macbeth versus Duncan, old Russia versus new Russia, Hamlet's father versus the new king. Often, playwrights repeat situations but vary them in such ways that the differences have thematic implications. In *Macbeth,* for example, Shakespeare places nearly identical events at the beginning and end. At the beginning, Scotland has just defeated Norway. The traitorous Thane of Cawdor is executed, and Macbeth triumphantly displays the head of another rebel by putting it on a stake. As a reward for valor, the king designates Macbeth the new Thane of Cawdor. At the end of the play, another battle is fought; Macbeth is killed as a "usurper," and his head is cut off and held aloft as a sign of revenge and victory. Ironically, Macbeth has changed places with the first Thane of Cawdor in both name and nature, and the circumstances of their deaths are almost identical.

A more far-reaching example of contrast is the Surface brothers in Sheridan's *School for Scandal.* Joseph Surface pretends to be good, but he is in fact selfish and destructive. Charles Surface leads a carefree and careless life; he seems to be a wastrel, but he is in fact generous and honest. Their uncle and benefactor, Sir Oliver Surface, a brusque but warmhearted man, has just returned to England after a long absence and wants to ferret out the true nature of his two potential heirs. To do this he visits each brother separately, disguised as someone else. Both scenes are so similar that an audience cannot fail to notice the similarity; Sheridan uses the similarity to contrast the brothers. The first scene, with Charles, does indeed expose his good qualities. The audience now knows how the scene will go and gleefully awaits the second scene, in which the despicable Joseph will unwittingly reveal his selfishness and pride. This contrast not only develops plot and character, it also points a moral—that the appearance of goodness is worthless without the practice of goodness.

ᴄ᷎ QUESTIONS ABOUT THEME

1. What repetitions occur in the play? What meanings can you draw from these repetitions?

2. What symbols does the author deliberately establish? How do you know they are symbols? What do the symbols seem to mean?

3. What contrasts does the playwright establish? Which are the obvious contrasts and which are the not-so-obvious contrasts? In *Romeo and Juliet,* for example, we easily spot the contrast between the lovers and the parents, but other contrasts are suggestive: Romeo is different from Juliet (less mature) and is perhaps partly to blame for their deaths; Prince Escalus is different from the parents. The nurse's attitude toward love contrasts starkly with Juliet's. The friar's attitude toward love is different from Romeo's. Any one or a combination of these contrasts would make a good focus for interpretation.

4. How is contrast related to the conflicts in the plot? Hedda and Thea are not only different from each other, they are in conflict. What values, then, do the contrasting sides of a conflict manifest?

THINKING ON PAPER ABOUT THEME

1. List the subjects of the play (the issues or problems the play seems to be about). State themes for each of these subjects (what the play seems to be saying about these issues and problems).

2. Mark speeches and sections of dialogue that help develop a particular theme. Look especially for "the big speech," which will typically be longer than most and will forcefully state a theme. Hamlet's "To be or not to be" speech is an example. There may be more than one "big speech." Summarize them and explain how the actions of the play develop their ideas.

3. Explain in detail how an important scene helps develop themes.

4. Trace the development of one theme throughout the play. Mark all the passages that help develop this theme. Summarize the plot as it relates to this theme.

5. List the images (sensuous images, metaphors) that recur in the play. Explain the ideas they seem to develop.

6. List other repetitions (characters' actions and words, characters' obsessions, scenes, details of setting). Explain their relationship to characterization and theme.

7. List the symbols in the play. For each symbol, list its meanings.

8. Describe the important contrasts in the play (of characters, scenes, values, actions, physical objects). Explain how these contrasts help expose character traits and develop theme.

Now It's Your Turn

Explore how repetitions, symbols, and contrasts help develop themes in *Trifles* (pages 373–85).

Irony

Presence of an audience. The presence of an audience at performances of plays affects profoundly the way plays are written and the way productions are conceived. The actors, of course, pretend to be real people involved in real human relationships. But unlike real life, these fictional activities are witnessed by an audience of total strangers. It is as if the front wall of your neighbor's house were taken away and the whole neighborhood were witnessing your neighbors' lives, actions, and speech.

The playwright or producer must decide whether to exclude or include the audience as participants in the play. If the choice is to exclude the audience, the production assumes that no one is watching. The production establishes a physical and psychological distance between the performance and the audience (the performance lighted, the auditorium dark; the performance up on stage, the audience down and away from the stage), and the actors pretend the audience is not there. If the choice is to include the audience, then measures are taken to bring the audience "into" the play. The physical distance between performance and audience may be reduced (by building the stage out into the auditorium or by having the actors circulate among the audience). The actors may look at the audience, gesture to it, or talk to it as if the audience were another person. Shakespeare's drama includes these possibilities with its numerous asides and soliloquies.

Dramatic irony.　One prominent device that relies entirely on the presence of an audience, and on what the audience is thinking, is dramatic irony. *Dramatic irony* in effect does acknowledge the presence of the audience because it gives the audience the privilege of knowing things that characters do not know. Dramatic irony occurs when characters say or do something that has meaning the audience recognizes but the characters do not. The concept of dramatic irony can be extended to all situations in which characters are blind to facts the audience knows. Sometimes only the audience is aware of the ironic contrast between the character's words or actions and the truth; sometimes the audience shares this knowledge with other characters onstage.

In the two parallel scenes in *School for Scandal,* for example, the audience knows that Sir Oliver Surface is wearing a mask to test his nephews—and, of course, Sir Oliver knows—but the nephews do not. So the audience recognizes as ironic everything the nephews do and say that works for or against their self-interest, particularly in the case of Joseph, who would treat Sir Oliver with meticulous courtesy if only he knew who he was. In another scene from this play, Lady Teazle hides behind a screen while her husband, unaware of her presence, talks about her. When he says that he wants to leave her a lot of money upon his death, but that he does not want her to know about it yet, we recognize his statement as ironic because we know—and he does not—that Lady Teazle hears everything.

A powerful example of dramatic irony occurs in the last scenes of Shakespeare's *Othello.* Before Desdemona goes to bed, she sings a song about a man who accuses his love of being promiscuous. She asks Emilia, her lady-in-waiting, if any woman could so treat her husband. Emilia says that some might for the right "price," but Desdemona says that she could never do so "for the whole world." The audience recognizes her comments as ironic, because Othello, unbeknownst to Desdemona, is nearly insane with the belief that she is a "whore" and plans to kill her for it. Later, when Othello strangles Desdemona, he boasts that even if he is "cruel" he is at least "merciful" because he will kill her quickly without allowing her to "linger in . . . pain." But his "mercy" contrasts horribly with our knowledge of her innocence and the quality of mercy she deserves. When he defends his murder to Emilia, he says,

> Cassio did top her. Ask thy husband [Iago] else.
> O, I were damned beneath all depth in hell
> But that I did proceed upon just grounds
> To this extremity. Thy husband knew it all. (5.2. 137–40)

We know, and poor Othello is about to find out, that Iago has betrayed him and that he has in truth had no "just grounds" for the "extremity" of his deed.

QUESTIONS ABOUT IRONY

1. To what extent does the playwright seem to want the audience involved in the action?

2. How would you perform such audience-involving devices as soliloquies and asides? To whom, for example, would you have the actors make asides?

3. What advantages are there in performing the play as if the audience is not there?

4. Like fiction and poetry, drama uses all kinds of irony. Verbal irony is very prevalent simply because drama relies so heavily on dialogue. Sometimes the director and actors themselves must decide whether particular lines are ironic. When Thea, for example, tells Hedda about inspiring Loevborg to write his book, Hedda interjects comments such as "Poor, pretty little Thea"; "But my dear Thea! How brave of you!"; "Clever little Thea!" (284–9) Hedda means these statements ironically. The actress would say them with enough sarcasm to let the audience know how Hedda really

feels about Thea's successes, but without allowing the slow-witted Thea to pick up on the irony.

What are the ironies, then, in the play you are studying? How do they relate to characterization and theme?

5. Most important, what dramatic ironies does the playwright build into the play?

6. Do the dramatic ironies—such as Othello's repeated description of Iago as "honest"—create a pattern of revelation or meaning?

7. Why do the dramatic ironies appear where they do in the play?

ꙮ Thinking on Paper about Irony

1. Explain the extent to which the play seems to invite audience participation.

2. Mark the instances of dramatic irony in the play. Explain what the dramatic irony reveals about characterization and theme.

3. Mark the instances of verbal irony. Explain what the verbal irony reveals about the characters who use it.

4. List the instances of situational irony. Explain the importance of situational irony to characterization and theme. (For a definition of situational irony, see Chapter 3.)

5. List the instances of attitudinal irony. Explain the importance of attitudinal irony to characterization and theme. (For a definition of attitudinal irony, see Chapter 3.)

Now It's Your Turn

Where do you see dramatic irony in *Trifles* (pages 373–85)? How important is dramatic irony and other ironies in the play?

Subgenres

The best-known subgenres of drama are tragedy and comedy, but there are many others: melodrama, theater of the absurd, allegory, comedy of manners, the spectacle, the masque, modern drama, farce, and tragicomedy. Some, like musicals, opera, and ballet, shade into other art forms.

Tragedy. Definitions of subgenres can lead to fruitful interpretations of individual works. The definition of *tragedy* began with the first and most famous discussion of it, that in Aristotle's *Poetics*. Aristotle based his definition on an inductive examination of Greek tragedy, and he seems in particular to have had Sophocles's plays in mind. His definition focuses primarily on the effect of the play on the audience and on the nature of the tragic hero. The hero, he says, inspires "pity" and "fear" in the audience: pity because the hero doesn't deserve his fate and fear because the hero's fate could be anyone's. The audience, in other words, identifies deeply with the tragic hero. The hero is noble but flawed. He has one principal flaw—in Sophocles, usually the flaw of pride. This flaw Aristotle called a *hamartia,* literally a "miscalculation." Because of the hero's flaw, he suffers emotionally and experiences a reversal of fortune, moving abruptly from a high place (high social position, wealth, responsibility, purity) to a low place. Before this reversal occurs, the hero understands for the first time his flawed state and his error-filled ways. This moment is the "recognition" and usually occurs at the climax of the play. The hero recognizes that he is responsible for his deeds and that they contradict a moral order inherent in the entire cosmos. The effect of the play on the audience is to induce a *catharsis,* a feeling of emotional release and exuberance.

Comedy. Aristotle planned to write as comprehensively on *comedy* as on tragedy, but either that part of the *Poetics* was lost, or he never got around to it. It is hard to see, however, how he could have made comedy any less enigmatic than it still appears to us, for the nature of comedy is difficult to pin down, both artistically and psychologically. Numerous critics have speculated about why people laugh. Laughter is only one of the puzzling aspects of comedy. Most critics agree on some of the aspects of comedy. Comedy is the depiction of the ludicrous; that is, a gross departure from the serious. Therefore, in order to see something as comic, you must first understand what is "serious." The comic in drama is related to what playgoers *think* is serious. If the community of playgoers thinks that proper attire for men is a business suit, tie, and polished shoes, then a gross distortion of that dress—by a clown in a circus, for example—would be comic.

Methods of comedy. Two methods of signaling the ludicrous are incongruity and exaggeration. It is incongruous for a haughty, spiffily dressed man, walking nose in the air, to slip and fall face first into a mud hole or to be hit in the face with a cream pie. Further, comedy must cause no pain to the audience. This means that the audience cannot identify as deeply with comic figures as it does with tragic figures and that the method of presentation—language, acting, setting—must communicate an air of "fantasy." Through its methods and style, the production constantly says, "This isn't true. It's only a joke." The fantasy element in comedies helps explain why they almost always end happily, whereas tragedies end unhappily. Finally, the characters in comedy are more "realistic" than in tragedy. They are more like us, whereas in tragedy they are, even in their flawed state (sometimes *because* of their flawed state), far nobler than we are.

QUESTIONS ABOUT SUBGENRES

Definitions of genres and subgenres are useful only if they help you understand specific works. Aristotle was trying to understand Greek tragedy, so it does non-Greek tragedies an injustice to rigidly apply his definition to them. The same goes, really, for anyone's definition of a subgenre because literature is too varied and complex a phenomenon to fit neatly into categories. Use definitions like Aristotle's as insights into the probable nature of a work and base your questions on those insights.

Turn definitions of tragedy, comedy, and subgenres into probing questions aimed at a specific work:

1. What is the character's major flaw? Does he or she have more than one flaw?

2. When does the recognition scene occur? What does the character recognize?

3. What incongruities cause the comedy?

4. What do the incongruities reveal about the playwright's attitude toward the characters and setting?

5. Are there hints of satire in these incongruities?

6. How does the playwright establish the detachment necessary for us to laugh?

Try applying definitions like these to works that do not quite fit the categories and see what you come up with. Some people regard *Hedda Gabler* as like a "tragedy" but not exactly an Aristotelian tragedy. Will any parts of Aristotle's definition apply to *Hedda Gabler?* Which fit well? Which do not? Does Hedda have a "tragic flaw"? Is she responsible for her actions? Is she to blame for the harm she causes? Does she have a moment or moments of recognition? Is she nobler than we are? Does she experience a "reversal"? How does the audience feel after seeing or reading the play? Does the audience experience pity and fear for Hedda?

Some of the most interesting questions about subgenres emerge from plays that mix subgenres. Why, for example, are there comic elements in Shakespeare's tragedies? Is *The Cherry Orchard* a comedy? a tragedy? both? Are we supposed to laugh or cry at the fate of Chekhov's ineffectual aristocrats? If Aristotle's definition or someone else's provides no explanation for some feature of a play, can you invent an explanation of your own?

 Thinking on Paper about Subgenres

1. If you know the subgenre to which the play belongs (tragedy, comedy, farce, and so forth), find a good definition of the subgenre. List the characteristics of the subgenre.

2. Take one item from the list and explain how well it applies to the play. If Hamlet is a tragic character, for example, what might be his tragic flaw? What constitutes his reversal? When does he experience a recognition? How does the audience respond to him?

Now It's Your Turn

Susan Glaspell wrote a short story version of *Trifles* titled "A Jury of Her Peers." She seems to suggest that the play (and the story) belongs to the "trial" subgenre. It is also a kind of detective story. What conventions of these subgenres does the play utilize? Does Glaspell alter the subgenres any, bend them to her own purposes? Are there other subgenres to which the play might belong? In short, explore Glaspell's possible use and alteration of one or more subgenres.

Checklist for Interpreting Drama

Plot (pages 78–85)

❖ Note the actions that occur off stage. Explain why the playwright places them off stage rather than on.

❖ Indicate the conflicts and how you learn about them (through dialogue, the characters' actions, and other means).

❖ Compare the "plot" to the "story." Determine to what extent events of the past influence actions in the play.

❖ Speculate about how the playwright anticipates audience expectations.

❖ Characterize the structure and content of formal and informal structural units. Indicate any that seem especially important.

Characterization (pages 85–90)
❖ Identify traits of stock characters.

❖ Explain what makes round characters complex.

❖ Indicate which characters change and which do not. Speculate about what causes the dynamic characters to change.

❖ Specify how subtexts influence your understanding of characters, conflicts, and themes.

❖ Indicate when and how characters wear masks. Show where and how the true nature of characters becomes clear. Speculate about why the characters wear masks and how their masks affect others.

Setting (pages 90–93)
❖ Determine how you learn about the setting—from dialogue, sets, stage directions, and other means.

❖ Describe the sets the playwright calls for or that you would design.

❖ Speculate about how the audience's knowledge before they attend the play influences their concept of the setting.

❖ If the setting or sets are symbolic, show how.

Theme (pages 94–97)
❖ Point out repetitions and explain their significance.

❖ Explore the meanings of symbols.

❖ Indicate telling contrasts.

Irony (pages 97–100)

❖ Consider different "locations" of the audience in relationship to the performance—up close or back away, lights up or down, on stage with the players or down away from the stage, ignored by the players or directly addressed. Explore how any of these arrangements would affect the performance of the play and the audience's response to it.

❖ Note occurrences of dramatic irony. Explain their probable impact on the audience.

❖ Indicate other kinds of irony and the extent to which the playwright employs irony. Show how irony develops characters and themes.

Subgenres (pages 100–103)

❖ Indicate the subgenre to which the play seems to belong.

❖ Show how the play employs conventions of the subgenre and how it alters any of them.

❖ Speculate about why the playwright chose this subgenre for the play.

Works Cited and Consulted

Abrams, M. H. *A Glossary of Literary Terms.* Fort Worth: Harcourt, 1999.

Aristotle. *Aristotle's Poetics: A Translation and Commentary for Students of Literature.* Trans. Leon Golden. Commentary O. B. Hardison, Jr. Tallahassee: UP of Florida, 1981.

Beckerman, Bernard. *Dynamics of Drama: Theory and Method of Analysis.* New York: Drama Book Specialists, 1979.

Corrigan, Robert W., ed. *Tragedy: A Study of Drama in Modern Times.* New York: Harcourt, 1967.

———. *Comedy: Meaning and Form.* New York: Harper, 1981.

Hansberry, Lorraine. *A Raisin in the Sun.* New York: New American Library, 1987.

Ibsen, Henrik. *Hedda Gabler and Other Plays.* Trans. Una Ellis-Fermor. New York: Penguin, 1988.

Pixley, Edward, George Kernodle, and Portia Kernodle. *Invitation to the Theatre*. 3rd ed. San Diego: Harcourt, 1985.

Shakespeare, William. *Hamlet*. Ed. Willard Farnham. Pelican Shakespeare. Baltimore: Penguin, 1957.

———. *Othello*. Ed. Gerald Eades Bentley. Pelican Shakespeare. Baltimore: Penguin, 1958.

Sheridan, Richard Brinsley. *The School for Scandal. Four English Comedies*. Ed. J. M. Morrell. Harmondsworth, England: Penguin, 1950.

5

Interpreting Poetry

WHAT IS POETRY?

What is poetry? As with the question we raised in Chapter 2, What is literature?, there are no certain answers to this one. If you look at a poem published in the *New Yorker* magazine, you might think, "There is no rhyme in this poem, no meter, no apparent structure. It is arranged in lines, but why couldn't I take any paragraph, arrange it in lines, and call it 'poetry'? What makes this poem, or any poem, 'poetry'?"

A mystical definition. Edward Hirsch, author of the best-selling *How to Read a Poem and Fall in Love with Poetry* (1999), claims that the defining characteristic of poetry is its spirituality. Poetry, which originated in prehistoric religious worship (86, 135), has never lost "its sense of sacred mystery" (16). The vocation of poets is thus "Orphic" (that is, mystical; associated with the miraculous gift for music manifested by Orpheus, a figure from Greek mythology). Poets enter "the mystery of a world riven with *anima,* with process, a world that awakens to the Orphic calling of the poet. The impulse [of the poet] is shamanistic" (78).

Hirsch concludes that since the essence of poetry is spiritual, it can transform us. Poetry is "the most intimate and volatile form of literary discourse" (xi). It can deepen "our capacity for personhood, our achievement of humanity" (xiii). It induces insights in which "the self is both lost and found" (243). When "I encounter and interiorize the poem, when I ingest it, dreaming it and letting it dream its way into me," then "I can feel the Orphic enchantment, the delirium and lucidity, the swoon of poetry" (261). Poetry "activates my secret world" (8).

A poem that Hirsch feels represents the mystical nature of poetry is this poem by Emily Brontë★:

THE NIGHT IS DARKENING ROUND ME

Emily Brontë

The night is darkening round me,
The wild winds coldly blow;
But a tyrant spell has bound me
And I cannot, cannot go.

The giant trees are bending
Their bare boughs weighed with snow,
And the storm is fast descending
And yet I cannot go.

Clouds beyond clouds above me,
Wastes beyond wastes below;
But nothing drear can move me;
I will not, cannot go.

Brontë's poem, he says, is "spellbound," the "poetry of trance." It enacts "a sense of transfiguration and dark initiation" (66). Hirsch hails Emily Dickinson's famous definition of poetry as a fitting complement to Brontë's poem:

> If I read a book [and] it makes my whole body so cold no fire can ever warm me I know *that* is poetry. If I feel physically as if the top of my head were taken off, I know *that* is poetry. These are the only way I know. Is there any other way? (7)

We should read poetry the way Dickinson does, by letting "its mysteries breathe through us" (157).

Definition by element.   Many people would disagree with Hirsch's claim for the spirituality of poetry, but most commentators posit special qualities for poetry that are hard to define. Writing in the *New Princeton*

---

*Publication dates of works of literature cited in this book and dates of authors' lives can be found in the author-title index at the back of the book.

Encyclopedia of Poetry and Poetics, T. V. F. Brogan says that "a poem conveys heightened forms of perception, experience, meaning, or consciousness in heightened language." As "a heightened mode of discourse" (938), poetry exhibits "intensified speech" (939). What does he mean by "heightened" and "intensified"? Furthermore, what causes such special qualities? An answer lies in the conventions poets use to create poetry, conventions that poets have used for centuries and that are often cited as defining characteristics of poetry. Poets must learn such conventions in order to use them, to depart from them, and to invent new conventions. Even Hirsch says that poetry is a "conscious craft," not just something composed by "unconscious invention" (27).

We will explore these conventions—or elements—in this chapter. As with literature in general, traditional characteristics of a genre do not singly or collectively "define" it, but they help us recognize, read, and write it. Brogan orders these conventions into three broad categories: sense (elements that convey meaning), sound (elements that underscore the musical qualities of language) (939–40), and sight (elements that affect the appearance of poems). Although the sense, sound, and sight of poetry are interwoven in any given poem, we will for the sake of clarity deal with them separately. We begin with "sense," because we have already seen some of these devices in the chapters on fiction and drama.

SENSE IN POETRY: ELEMENTS THAT CONVEY MEANING

Getting Started: Reading a Poem the First Time

Here are some simple strategies for reading a poem the first time:

1. Read the poem through once without stopping. Don't try to understand every word or phrase. Just get the general sense of the poem.

2. Reread the poem, looking up words you don't know. See *Diction* below.

3. Read the poem again. This time identify the normal word order of all the sentences. See *Syntax* below. "Normal" word order is subject-verb-object: Jane loves Joe.

4. Track down any allusions in the poem. An *allusion* is a reference to historical events and people, to mythological and biblical figures,

and to works of literature. Allusions invite comparison between the work at hand and the items referred to. An example of an allusion is Matthew Arnold's reference to Sophocles in "Dover Beach" (pages 117–18). Arnold invites us to bring the weight of Sophocles' tragedies to bear on the subject matter of his poem. An allusion is a compact way of adding meaning to the work.

Diction

Diction refers to the poet's choice of words. Poets like words, some-times unusual words. Most people, even experienced readers, have to look up such words. Don't feel ashamed that you might have to as well. Knowing the poets' understanding of the words they use is cru-cial to understanding the meaning of their poems.

Poets are sensitive to the subtle shades of meanings of words, to the possible double meanings of words, and to the denotative and connotative meanings of words. As we say in Chapter 2, *denotation* is the object or idea—the referent—that a word represents. The deno-tation of a word is its core meaning, its dictionary meaning. *Connotation* is the subjective, emotional association that a word has for one person or a group of people. See pages 13–14 for a more thorough discussion of these two concepts. Poets often choose words that contribute to the poem's meaning on both a denotational and a connotational level.

✒ QUESTIONS ABOUT DICTION

Meanings of words. Examine the words in a poem for all their possible shades and levels of meaning. Then ask how these meanings combine to create an overall effect. Note, for example, the effect that connotation creates in William Wordsworth's "A Slumber Did My Spirit Seal."

A SLUMBER DID MY SPIRIT SEAL

William Wordsworth

A slumber did my spirit seal;
I had no human fears—
She seemed a thing that could not feel
The touch of earthly years.

No motion has she now, no force;
She neither hears nor sees;
Rolled round in earth's diurnal course,
With rocks, and stones, and trees.

In order to create the stark contrast between the active, airy girl of the first stanza with the inert, dead girl of the second, Wordsworth relies partly on the connotative effect of the last line. We know the denotative meaning of "rocks, and stones, and trees," but in this context the emotional or connotative meaning is unpleasant and grating. Rocks and stones are inanimate, cold, cutting, impersonal. And although we usually think of trees as beautiful and majestic, here the association of trees with rocks and stones makes us think of tree roots, of dirt, and thus of the girl's burial. The rocks and stones and trees are not only not human, they confine and smother the girl. Another example of connotation is the word *diurnal,* which means "daily." But the Latinate *diurnal* has a slightly more formal connotation than the prosaic *daily.* The effect of the word is to make the processes of nature—death, the revolving of Earth, the existence of rocks and stones and trees—seem remote, remorseless, and inevitable.

Wordplay. Be alert for wordplay—double meanings and puns. The speaker in Andrew Marvell's "To His Coy Mistress," for example, tries to persuade a reluctant woman to make love with him. His argument is that time is running out. Unless we take opportunities when they appear, we will lose them. He concludes his speech with a pun:

Thus, though we cannot make our sun
Stand still, yet we will make him run.

That is, we cannot stop time (make the sun stop), but we can bring about new life (a child: "son"), who will "run," and thus defeat decay and death. Some poets, such as e.e. cummings, make imaginative wordplay a dominant trait of their poetry. In "anyone lived in a pretty how town," cummings uses pronouns on two levels of meaning. The words *anyone* and *noone* mean, on the one hand, what we expect them to mean ("anybody" and "nobody"); but on the other hand they refer to two people, male (anyone) and female (noone), who fall in love, marry, and die.

THINKING ON PAPER ABOUT DICTION

1. Circle all the words you do not know. Look them up in the dictionary. Write brief definitions in the margin.

2. Underline words that seem especially meaningful or well chosen. For each word, explain denotations and connotations.

3. Underline any wordplay such as double meanings and puns. Explain what the wordplay adds to the sense of the poem.

4. Underline any uses of "unusual" words—slang, profanity, archaisms, foreign language words, made-up words. Say what qualities and meanings these words add to the poem. Explore how the poem would be different without them.

5. Identify the level of diction in the poem (formal, informal, colloquial, slangy, dialect). State what the poem gains from the use of this level. Say what it would lose by changing to a different level.

6. Indicate how the choice of words contributes to the speaker's tone (attitude).

Now It's Your Turn

Analyze Sir Walter Raleigh's diction in "The Nymph's Reply to the Shepherd" (pages 24–25). How fitting are the nuances of his words as a response to the rosy picture of love painted by Marlowe in "The Passionate Shepherd to His Love"? Assess the implication of Raleigh's allusion to Philomel, a character from Greek mythology.

Syntax

Syntax in poetry can be profoundly meaningful but also confusing.

Independent clauses. *Syntax* is sentence structure, the way words go together to make sentences. The basic unit of any English sentence is the *simple sentence* or *independent clause*. The normal word order of independent clauses is subject-verb (Jane loves) or subject-verb-object (Jane loves Joe). Poets often invert the normal word order of independent clauses. They do so to make the sentence rhyme, to fit a metrical pattern, or to emphasize an idea. An example is "A slumber did my spirit seal," the first line of the preceding Wordsworth poem.

The normal word order of this sentence would be "My spirit did seal a slumber"—subject (spirit)-verb (did seal)-object (slumber). But by inverting the word order, Wordsworth gains the end-rhyme he wants, the iambic metrical pattern he wants, and an emphasis on the speaker's state of mind, "slumber."

Complex sentences. Poets also often (usually) include complex sentences—sentences containing independent and subordinate (dependent) clauses. *Subordinate clauses* begin with relative pronouns (that, what, which, who), subordinating conjunctions (because, since, although, whereas, once, wherever, etc.), and prepositions (to, in, by, along, behind, with, etc.). Such clauses are always part of an independent clause; they do not stand alone. In poetry, complex sentences can be richly suggestive but confusing. The subordinate clauses may be long, there may be more than one per sentence, they may be located between subject and verb, and their normal word order—subject-verb-object—may be inverted to meet metrical and rhyme schemes.

Further causes of confusion are sentences that are so long we forget how they begin, sentences in which words are left out, and sentences marked by eccentric punctuation.

〰️ *Questions about Syntax*

Do yourself a favor. *Unscramble these sentences!* You really have to in order to understand the meaning of any poem. Initial questions, then, are:

1. What is the normal word order of the sentences in the poem?

2. What words have been left out?

The syntax of many poems is easy to follow. But most poems have some complexity of syntax that needs your alert attention. Arnold's "Dover Beach" (pages 117–18), for example, starts off with lucid syntax: "The sea is calm"; "The tide is full"; "the moon lies fair"; "the light gleams"; "the cliffs of England stand." But when the speaker's thoughts become more complicated (in line 7), so does the syntax: "Only, from the long line of spray/ Where the sea meets the moon-blanched land,/ Listen! You hear the grating roar/ Of pebbles which the waves draw back, and fling,/ At their return, up the high strand,/ Begin, and cease, and then again begin,/ With tremulous cadence slow, <u>and bring</u>/ The eternal note of sadness in" (ll. 7–14). The heart of this long sentence is the phrase "you [subject] <u>hear</u> [verb] the <u>roar</u> [object]" plus what the "roar" does. (See the underlined words in the sentence.) But to find this structure, you have to pare away the subordinate clauses from the independent clause.

3. A follow-up question is: Why does the poet diverge from normal word order or make the syntax abnormally complicated? Mary Kinzie (in *A Poet's Guide to Poetry*) says that poets' games with syntax are "thresholds of invention" that "are closely bound up with thematic suggestion. It makes as little sense to work toward complexity and tension in a poem that aims to express contentment as to compose the lines simply and uniformly in a poem of fretful brooding. Form should follow theme" (87).

4. How, then, is a poem's syntax related to its ideas?

 Thinking on Paper about Syntax

1. Write out all the sentences in the poem in normal word order.

2. Fill in the "missing" words. Put them in brackets.

3. If you remember how to diagram sentences, do so for all the complex sentences. At least, indicate the relationship of the subordinate clauses to the parts of the independent clause.

4. Speculate on how the poem's ideas would be altered were the syntax "normal."

Now It's Your Turn

Louise Bogan's "Song for a Lyre" is notable for its complicated syntax. Identify the independent clauses in her sentences. Explore the relationship of syntax and meaning in the poem.

SONG FOR A LYRE

Louise Bogan

The landscape where I lie
Again from boughs sets free
Summer; all night must fly
In wind's obscurity
The thick, green leaves that made
Heavy the August shade.

Soon, in the pictured night,
Returns—as in a dream
Left after sleep's delight—
The shallow autumn stream:
Softly awake, its sound
Poured on the chilly ground.

Soon fly the leaves in throngs;
O love, though once I lay
Far from its sound, to weep,
When night divides my sleep,
When stars, the autumn stream,
Stillness, divide my dream,
Night to your voice belongs.

Characterization, Point of View, Plot, and Setting

Fiction and drama as poetry. Poetry shares many elements with its sister genres, drama and fiction. Indeed, many works of drama and fiction are written in poetry. Plays by Sophocles, Shakespeare, and Goethe are poetry, as are epics by Homer, Dante, and Milton. Poetic narratives and dramas are similar to prose fiction and drama in their handling of characterization, point of view, plot, and setting. Thus the same questions one asks about a short story, novel, or play to probe their meanings are relevant to these poems. See the discussions of these two genres in Chapters 3 (fiction) and 4 (drama).

Most poems, however, do not offer a "story" in the conventional sense. They are usually brief and apparently devoid of "action." Even so, a plot of sorts may be implied, a place and time may be important, a point of view may be operating, and characters may dramatize the key issues of the poem.

The speakers in poems. In any poem there is always one "character" of the utmost importance, the speaker or "I" of the poem. T. S. Eliot, in an essay entitled "The Three Voices of Poetry," says there are three possible speakers or voices:

The first voice is the voice of the poet talking to himself—or to nobody. The second voice is the voice of the poet addressing an audience, whether large or small. The third is the voice of the poet when he attempts to create a dramatic character speaking in verse; when he is saying, not what he would say in his own person, but only what he can say within the limits of one imaginary character addressing another imaginary character. (96)

How can you tell the difference between these speakers? It is often easy to spot Eliot's third "voice": a speaker who is fictional, not at all equivalent to the poet. The speaker of Robert Browning's "Porphyria's Lover," for example, is a deranged killer who speaks to another character. He is clearly not Robert Browning. The "speaker" of Langston Hughes's "Vagabonds" (page 154) is plural, a group of people, so not Langston Hughes. But what about the speaker of Emily Brontë's poem that we read at the beginning of the chapter? Although the scene is dreamlike and thus possibly fictional, she may have had the dream and be writing about herself. The speaker of Matthew Arnold's "Dover Beach" (pages 117–18) is addressing another character, but even so this speaker may be mouthing the beliefs of the poet.

Speaker and author. The only way to know for sure if speakers are similar to poets is by means of biographical information. Consider, for example, this poem by the American poet Jane Kenyon.

IN THE NURSING HOME

Jane Kenyon

She is like a horse grazing
a hill pasture that someone makes
smaller by coming every night
to pull the fences in and in.

She has stopped running wide loops,
stopped even the tight circles.
She drops her head to feed; grass
is dust, and the creekbed's dry.

Master, come with your light
halter. Come and bring her in.

Is the speaker like the poet? Probably yes. We know that she took care of her mother in her mother's final illness and wrote elsewhere about this experience. Similarly, we can be fairly sure that the speaker of Edna St. Vincent Millay's sonnet, "I, Being Born a Woman" (page 145), is like Millay. We know enough about Millay's life to make the connection. But often we don't know. Is the speaker of Shakespeare's sonnets a stand-in for Shakespeare? Lacking biographical information, we cannot be sure.

Does it matter? Yes, if you want to understand a poem in the context of the poet's philosophy or view of life. Knowing about a poet's life and beliefs can often make the meaning of poems more visible. A poet's experiences and attitudes may touch you and lead you to rich understandings of individual poems. But even when a speaker manifests beliefs and traits of the poet, you should probably think of the speaker as fictional, as a projection of the poet's imagination, as a voice not quite the same as the poet. In this sense, the speaker becomes a "character" in the poem, subject to the same questions you would pose about characters in narratives and plays.

QUESTIONS ABOUT CHARACTERIZATION, POINT OF VIEW, PLOT, SETTING, AND THEME

In analyzing poetry, your first step should be to come to grips with the "I" of the poem, the speaker. Answer questions such as these:

1. Who is speaking?
2. What characterizes the speaker?
3. To whom is he or she speaking?
4. What is the speaker's emotional state?
5. Why is he or she speaking?
6. What situation is being described?
7. What are the conflicts or tensions in this situation?
8. How is setting—social situation, physical place, and time—important to the speaker?
9. What ideas does the speaker communicate?

Matthew Arnold's "Dover Beach" provides an example of how you can use most of these questions to get at the meanings of a poem.

DOVER BEACH

Matthew Arnold

The sea is calm to-night.
The tide is full, the moon lies fair
Upon the straits; on the French coast the light
Gleams and is gone; the cliffs of England stand,
Glimmering and vast, out in the tranquil bay.   5

Come to the window, sweet is the night-air!
Only, from the long line of spray
Where the sea meets the moon-blanched land,
Listen! you hear the grating roar
Of pebbles which the waves draw back, and fling,   10
At their return, up the high strand,
Begin, and cease, and then again begin,
With tremulous cadence slow, and bring
The eternal note of sadness in.

Sophocles long ago   15
Heard it on the Aegean, and it brought
Into his mind the turbid ebb and flow
Of human misery; we
Find also in the sound a thought,
Hearing it by this distant northern sea.   20

The Sea of Faith
Was once, too, at the full, and round earth's shore
Lay like the folds of a bright girdle furled.
But now I only hear
Its melancholy, long, withdrawing roar,   25
Retreating, to the breath
Of the night-wind, down the vast edges drear
And naked shingles° of the world.

Ah, love, let us be true
To one another! for the world, which seems   30
To lie before us like a land of dreams,
So various, so beautiful, so new,
Hath really neither joy, nor love, nor light,
Nor certitude, nor peace, nor help for pain;
And we are here as on a darkling plain   35
Swept with confused alarms of struggle and flight,
Where ignorant armies clash by night.

°beaches covered with pebbles

  Because Dover is an English port city, one of several points of departure for the European continent, the speaker has apparently stopped
for the night on his way to Europe. As he looks out of his hotel window,
he speaks to another person in the room, his "love" (last stanza). Arnold
traces the speaker's train of thought in four stanzas. In the first stanza,
the speaker describes what he sees, and his tone is contented, even joy-

ous. He sees the lights on the French coast and the high white cliffs of Dover "glimmering" in the moonlight. He invites his companion to share the glorious view. As he describes the sound of the surf to her, his tone alters slightly; the sound reminds him of "the eternal note of sadness." This melancholic tone deepens in the second stanza. There the speaker connects the sea sound with a passage in a Sophocles tragedy.

In the third stanza, the remembrance of the Sophocles passage leads the speaker to make a disturbing comparison. He likens the sea to faith—apparently religious faith, both his own and that of his age. He says that at one time the "Sea of Faith" was full but now has withdrawn, leaving a "vast," "drear," and coarse world. By the fourth stanza, the speaker has fallen into near despair. He says that what merely looks beautiful—the panorama seen from his window—is only a false image of the world, which in reality is absurd and chaotic. He has only one hope, his companion, whom he now urges to be true to him as he is true to her.

The speaker, in short, is an erudite, thoughtful, but deeply troubled person. The poem takes him from momentary contentedness to near hopelessness. The stimulus for his train of thought is the place of the poem—Dover Beach—and the companion to whom he addresses his remarks. All these elements—thoughts, place, and companion—are interrelated.

THINKING ON PAPER ABOUT CHARACTERIZATION, POINT OF VIEW, PLOT, SETTING, AND THEME

Many of the exercises one does on poetry consist of marking the poem itself. You might photocopy the poem and even enlarge it. That way, you can see the poem well and have plenty of space to write. If helpful, make more than one copy of the poem. Use different copies to mark different aspects of the poem.

1. Paraphrase the poem. This helps you understand every sentence or, at least, the major sections of the poem. The two paragraphs immediately following "Dover Beach" are a paraphrase of the poem.

2. Identify the speaker of the poem. Underline the words and phrases that help characterize the speaker and bring out the speaker's concerns. Describe in detail the traits of the speaker and of any other characters in the poem.

3. Describe the situation of the poem: where the speaker is, what time of day it is, what season of the year, what historical occasion,

to whom the speaker is speaking, and why. List the external and internal conflicts of the poem.

4. State the issues that concern the speaker. Explain the speaker's ideas. Note any changes in the speaker's mood or ideas as the poem moves from unit to unit. Explain what the speaker is trying to accomplish.

5. Describe the speaker's tone (angry, lyrical, hopeful, bitter, nostalgic, sarcastic, compassionate, admiring, sorrowful, amused, and so forth). Note any changes of tone.

6. If the speaker is fictional—not the poet—estimate the poet's attitude toward the speaker and toward the issues raised by the poem. Indicate any differences between the poet's attitude and the speaker's.

7. Relate the poem's title to its themes.

8. Explain any allusions in the poem.

Now It's Your Turn

Characterize the Duke of Ferrara and his deceased wife in Robert Browning's "My Last Duchess." Show how physical details, social circumstances (such as class and gender status), the duke's manner of speaking (word choice, syntax), lead you to your conclusions. The poem, based on an actual event, is set in sixteenth-century Italy. The duke negotiates to marry the young daughter of another aristocrat. Speaking to an ambassador of the girl's father, he attempts to convince the ambassador of his merits as a husband. Does he succeed? The artists the duke mentions, Frà Pandolf and Claus of Innsbruck, are fictional.

This poem has been described as a highly condensed short story or even a novel. Using the clues in the poem, can you construct a "plot" for the duke and duchess's marriage? Try a plot from the duchess's point of view, then one from the duke's.

MY LAST DUCHESS

Robert Browning

Ferrara

That's my last Duchess painted on the wall,
Looking as if she were alive. I call
That piece a wonder, now: Frà Pandolf's hands
Worked busily a day, and there she stands.
Will 't please you sit and look at her? I said   5

"Frà Pandolf" by design, for never read
Strangers like you that pictured countenance,
The depth and passion of its earnest glance,
But to myself they turned (since none puts by
The curtain I have drawn for you, but I)   10
And seemed as they would ask me, if they durst,
How such a glance came there; so, not the first
Are you to turn and ask thus. Sir, 'twas not
Her husband's presence only, called that spot
Of joy into the Duchess' cheek: perhaps   15
Frà Pandolf chanced to say "Her mantle laps
Over my lady's wrist too much," or "Paint
Must never hope to reproduce the faint
Half-flush that dies along her throat": such stuff
Was courtesy, she thought, and cause enough   20
For calling up that spot of joy. She had
A heart—how shall I say?—too soon made glad,
Too easily impressed; she liked whate'er
She looked on, and her looks went everywhere.
Sir, 'twas all one! My favor at her breast,   25
The dropping of the daylight in the West,
The bough of cherries some officious fool
Broke in the orchard for her, the white mule
She rode with round the terrace—all and each
Would draw from her alike the approving speech,   30
Or blush, at least. She thanked men—good! but thanked
Somehow—I know not how—as if she ranked
My gift of a nine-hundred-years-old name
With anybody's gift. Who'd stoop to blame
This sort of trifling? Even had you skill   35
In speech—(which I have not)—to make your will
Quite clear to such an one, and say, "Just this
Or that in you disgusts me; here you miss,
Or there exceed the mark"—and if she let
Herself be lessoned so, nor plainly set   40
Her wits to yours, forsooth, and made excuse
—E'en then would be some stooping; and I choose
Never to stoop. Oh sir, she smiled, no doubt,
Whene'er I passed her; but who passed without
Much the same smile? This grew; I gave commands;   45
Then all smiles stopped together. There she stands
As if alive. Will 't please you rise? We'll meet

The company below, then. I repeat,
The Count your master's known munificence
Is ample warrant that no just pretense   50
Of mine for dowry will be disallowed;
Though his fair daughter's self, as I avowed
At starting, is my object. Nay, we'll go
Together down, sir. Notice Neptune, though,
Taming a sea horse, thought a rarity,   55
Which Claus of Innsbruck cast in bronze for me!

Imagery: Descriptive Language

Definition. When applied to poetry, the term *imagery* has two
meanings. First, imagery represents the descriptive passages of a
poem. Although the word *imagery* calls to mind the visual sense, poetic imagery appeals to all the senses. Sensuous imagery is pleasurable
for its own sake, but it also provides concreteness and immediacy.
Imagery causes the reader to become experientially involved in the
subject matter of the poem. Further, the poet often uses descriptive
imagery to underscore other elements in a poem, such as tone, meaning, and characterization.

An example of descriptive imagery is the first stanza of John
Keats's narrative poem "The Eve of St. Agnes":

St. Agnes' Eve—Ah, bitter chill it was!
The owl, for all his feathers, was a-cold;
The hare limped trembling through the frozen grass,
And silent was the flock in woolly fold;
Numb were the Beadsman's fingers, while he told
His rosary, and while his frosted breath,
Like pious incense from a censer old,
Seemed taking flight for heaven, without a death,
Past the sweet Virgin's picture, while his prayer he saith.

This stanza appeals to the thermal sense (the chill of the evening, the
frozen grass), the sense of touch (the beadsman's numb fingers), the visual sense (the beadsman saying his rosary before the picture of the
Virgin), the sense of motion (the hare trembling and limping through
the grass, the beadsman's frosted breath taking flight toward heaven),
and the sense of sound (the silent flock, the sound of the beadsman's
monotonous prayer). The dominant sensuous appeal, however, is to the

thermal sense. Keats uses every sensuous image in the stanza to make us feel how cold the night is.

Another example is the scene in Christina Rossetti's "Goblin Market" when the heroine Lizzie withstands the temptation of the evil goblins' fruit.

> One may lead a horse to water,
> Twenty cannot make him drink.
> Tho' the goblins cuffed and caught her,
> Coaxed and fought her,
> Bullied and besought her,
> Scratched her, pinched her black as ink,
> Kicked and knocked her,
> Mauled and mocked her,
> Lizzie uttered not a word;
> Would not open lip from lip
> Lest they should cram a mouthful in:
> But laughed in heart to feel the drip
> Of juice that syruped all her face,
> And lodged in dimples of her chin,
> And streaked her neck which quaked like curd.

The dominant appeal here is to the sense of touch. Rossetti conveys the physical pain Lizzie suffers as well as the icky, sticky quality of the forbidden fruit.

Imagery: Figurative Language

Rhetorical figures of speech.   Critics today use *imagery* in a second sense. They use it to mean figurative language, especially metaphor. *Figurative language* is the conscious departure from normal or conventional ways of saying things. This could mean merely a rearrangement of the normal word order of a sentence, such as "Sir Gawain the dragon slew" or "With this ring I thee wed." Such unusual rearrangements are called "rhetorical" figures of speech.

Similes.   But much more common and important to poetry is a second category of figurative language: tropes. *Tropes* (literally, "turns") extend the meaning of words beyond their literal meaning. The most common form of trope is metaphor. *Metaphor* has a general and a specific meaning. Generally, it means any analogy. An *analogy* is a similarity between things that are basically different. Specifically, metaphor means a particular kind of analogy and is contrasted with the simile. A *simile* uses *like* or *as* to mark similarities; for example, "Her tears were like falling rain." The following stanza from Shakespeare's "Fair Is My Love" contains several similes (indicated by the underlining):

> Fair is my love, but not so fair as fickle;
> Mild as a dove, but neither true nor trusty;
> Brighter than glass, and yet, as glass is, brittle;
> Softer than wax, and yet, as iron, rusty;
>   A lily pale, with damask dye to grace her;
>   None fairer, nor none falser to deface her.

Metaphors. A metaphor also claims similarities between things that are essentially unlike, but it eliminates the comparative words (such as *like*) and thus equates the compared items. For example, "My heart was a tornado of passion" (not "My heart was like a tornado of passion"). The poem "Love Is a Sickness" by Samuel Daniel contains three metaphors—love is a sickness, love is a plant, love is a tempest—indicated here by the underlines:

LOVE IS A SICKNESS

Samuel Daniel

Love is a sickness full of woes,
    All remedies refusing.
A plant that with most cutting grows,
    Most barren with best using.
                    Why so?

More we enjoy it, more it dies,
If not enjoyed it sighing cries,
                    Hey ho.

Love is a torment of the mind,
    A tempest everlasting,

And Jove hath made it of a kind
    Not well, nor full, nor fasting.
                    Why so?

More we enjoy it, more it dies,
If not enjoyed it sighing cries,
                    Hey ho.

Personification.   Analogies can be directly stated or implied. The similes and metaphors in the poems by Shakespeare and Daniel are directly stated analogies; but when Daniel in the last lines of each stanza says that love "sighs," he implies a kind of analogy, *personification;* he pretends that love has the attributes of a person.

Extended metaphor.   When the poet develops just one analogy throughout the whole poem, the analogy is called an *extended metaphor.* Thomas Campion's "There Is a Garden in Her Face" contains an extended metaphor comparing the features of a woman's face to those of a garden:

THERE IS A GARDEN IN HER FACE

Thomas Campion

There is a garden in her face,
Where roses and white lilies grow,
A heavenly paradise is that place,
Wherein all pleasant fruits do flow.
There cherries grow, which none may buy
Till "Cherry ripe!"° themselves do cry.

Those cherries fairly do enclose
Of orient pearl a double row;
Which when her lovely laughter shows,
They look like rosebuds filled with snow.
Yet them nor peer nor prince can buy,
Till "Cherry ripe!" themselves do cry.

Her eyes like angels watch them still;
Her brows like bended bows do stand,
Threatening with piercing frowns to kill
All that attempt with eye or hand
Those sacred cherries to come nigh,
Till "Cherry ripe!" themselves do cry.

°A familiar cry of London street vendors

Another example of an extended metaphor is Jane Kenyon's "In the Nursing Home" (page 116). Throughout this poem the woman is compared to a horse.

QUESTIONS ABOUT IMAGERY

Imagery is an important—some would argue the most important—characteristic of poetry. Identify the imagery of a poem.

1. What senses does the poet appeal to?
2. What analogies does he or she imply or directly state?
3. *Why* does the poet use these particular images and analogies?

Descriptive imagery in "Dover Beach."   In "Dover Beach," Arnold uses both descriptive and metaphorical imagery. He emphasizes two senses: the visual and the aural. He begins with the visual—the moon, the lights of France across the water, the cliffs, the tranquil bay—and throughout the poem he associates hope and beauty with what the speaker sees. But the poet soon introduces the aural sense—the grating roar of the sea—which serves as an antithesis to the visual sense. These two senses create a tension that mirrors the conflict in the speaker's mind. The first two stanzas show the speaker merely drifting into a perception of this conflict, connecting sight with hope and sound with sadness.

Figurative language in "Dover Beach."   By the third stanza, he has become intellectually alert to the full implications of the conflict. He signals this alertness with a carefully worked out analogy, his comparison of the sea with faith. In the fourth stanza, he sums up his despairing conclusion with a stunning and famous simile:

> And we are here as on a darkling plain
> Swept with confused alarms of struggle and flight,
> Where ignorant armies clash by night.

This final analogy achieves several purposes. First, it brings the implication of the descriptive imagery to a logical conclusion. No longer can the speaker draw hope from visual beauty; in this image, he cannot see at all—it is night, the plain is dark ("darkling"). He can only hear, but the sound now is more chaotic and threatening than the mere ebb and flow of the sea. Second, the analogy provides an abrupt change of setting. Whereas before, the speaker visualized an unpeopled plain, now he imagines human beings as agents of destruction. He implies that a world without faith must be arbitrary and violent. Finally, the analogy allows the speaker to identify his own place in this new world order. Only loyalty is pure and good. So he and his companion must cling to each other and maneuver throughout the world's battlefields as best they can.

ᴛʜɪɴᴋɪɴɢ ᴏɴ ᴘᴀᴘᴇʀ ᴀʙᴏᴜᴛ ᴅᴇsᴄʀɪᴘᴛɪᴠᴇ ʟᴀɴɢᴜᴀɢᴇ

1. Mark the descriptive images. For each image, name the sense appealed to. Characterize the dominant impression these images make.

2. Explain the relationship of descriptive images to the speaker's state of mind.

3. Describe how the descriptive images create a sense of the time of day and season of the year.

4. Note any progression in the descriptive images; for example, from day to night, hot to cold, soft to loud, color to color, slow to fast.

5. Explain how the descriptive images help create atmosphere and mood. Slow movements, for example, are conducive to melancholy; speed to exuberance and excitement.

ᴛʜɪɴᴋɪɴɢ ᴏɴ ᴘᴀᴘᴇʀ ᴀʙᴏᴜᴛ ꜰɪɢᴜʀᴀᴛɪᴠᴇ ʟᴀɴɢᴜᴀɢᴇ

1. Mark the similes in the poem. Underline or circle the words that signal the comparisons (words such as *like, as, similar to, resembles*). Explain the implications of the analogies (that is, what they contribute to the meaning of the poem).

2. Mark the metaphors in the poem. Explain the implications of the analogies.

3. Mark any personification in the poem. Underline the words and phrases that make the personification clear.

4. Poets often use analogies to help make an abstract quality, such as "love" or "my love's beauty" or "my current predicament" or "the destructive effect of time" or "God's grandeur," concrete and knowable. They do so by comparing the abstract quality to something the reader knows well. Almost always this "something" is a physical object or reality. Name the abstract quality the poet wants

to clarify and the object the poet is comparing it to. List the qualities of the object. Explain how the comparison has clarified the abstraction.

5. List the senses appealed to in each analogy. Describe the dominant sensuous impression created by the analogies.

Now It's Your Turn

Explore the implications of descriptive imagery in Gwendolyn Brooks' "We Real Cool" (page 159) and of figurative language in Shakespeare's Sonnet 116 (pages 144–45). What are the images? What ideas do they convey?

Symbolism

Symbolism appeals to poets because symbols are highly suggestive yet succinct. As we say in Chapter 3, a *symbol* is an object—usually a physical object—that represents an abstract idea or ideas (see pages 69–71). The most powerful symbols are those that do not exactly specify the ideas they represent.

Symbolism in Psalm 23. An example of a symbol in poetry occurs in Psalm 23, quoted on page 151. The poem begins with a metaphor: God is like a shepherd and I (the speaker) am like one of his sheep; just as a shepherd takes care of his sheep, so will God take care of me. But the poem shifts from metaphor to symbol with phrases such as "green pastures," "still waters," and particularly "the valley of the shadow of death." The meanings of "green pastures" (nourishment, security, ease) and "still waters" (peace, sustenance, calm) are fairly easy to ascertain. But the meaning of "the valley of the shadow of death" is more difficult. It does not seem to mean just death, but a life experience—perhaps psychological or spiritual—that is somehow related to death (the "shadow" of death). We must journey through this "valley." Perhaps the indefiniteness of this phrase, combined with its ominous overtones, explains its appeal.

Symbolism in "The Sick Rose." Another example of a symbol in poetry is William Blake's "The Sick Rose":

THE SICK ROSE

William Blake

O Rose, thou art sick.
The invisible worm
That flies in the night
In the howling storm

Has found out thy bed
Of crimson joy,
And his dark secret love
Does thy life destroy.

This poem might be understandable as a literal treatment of horticulture: a real rose beset by an insect that preys on roses. But Blake probably means for us to see the rose, the worm, and the action of the worm as symbolic. For one thing, the poem occurs in Blake's collection of poems *Songs of Experience,* suggesting that it has to do with ominous aspects of human life. For another, much of the poem makes little sense unless it can be taken symbolically. What can we otherwise make of the "howling storm," the bed of "crimson joy," the worm's "dark secret love"?

Blake's diction, furthermore, links to symbolic Christian literature, which he knew well. The archaic meaning of "worm" is dragon, an image of evil that harks back to the devil's appearance to Eve as a snake. In Christian romances the rose represented female beauty and purity and sometimes the Virgin Mary. Blake, then, may symbolize here the destruction of purity by evil. The poem may have sexual implications, since the worm (a phallic image) comes at "night" to the rose's "bed." More generally, the poem may show the destruction of all earthly health, innocence, and beauty by mysterious forces.

The point is that although we get the drift of Blake's meaning, we do not know precisely what the symbolic equivalents are. Yet the symbols are so sensuous and the action so dramatic that the poem mesmerizes.

⌐◦ QUESTIONS ABOUT SYMBOLISM

When you read poetry, keep alert for symbols. But persuade yourself—and your reader—that the objects you claim to be symbols were intended as such by the author. Remember that not *every* object in a poem is symbolic.

1. What are the symbols in the poem you are reading?
2. Why do you think they are symbols?
3. What do they mean? In answer to this last question, offer thoughtful explanations for your interpretations. Stay close to meanings the author seems to have intended.

Thinking on Paper about Symbolism

1. Circle the symbols in the poem.
2. List the possible meanings of each symbol. Explain what evidence suggests these meanings.
3. Explain what each symbol contributes to the overall meaning of the poem.

Now It's Your Turn

Discuss the symbolism in either Ezra Pound's "Xenia" (page 153) or Robert Frost's "The Death of the Hired Man" (pages 262–66). What are the symbols? What makes you think they are symbols? What are their possible meanings?

THE SOUND OF POETRY: MUSICAL ELEMENTS

Rhythm

Rhythm is one of the most naturally pleasing elements of poetry. Edward Hirsch says that rhythm "creates a pattern of yearning and expectation, of recurrence and difference. It is related to the pulse, the heartbeat, the way we breathe. It takes us into ourselves; it takes us out of ourselves. It differentiates us; it unites us to the cosmos" (21).

Meter. All human speech has rhythm, but poetry regularizes that rhythm into recognizable patterns. These patterns are called *meters*. Paul Fussell defines *meter* this way:

> Meter is what results when the natural rhythmical movements of colloquial speech are heightened, organized, and regulated so that pattern—

which means repetition—emerges from the relative phonetic haphazard of ordinary utterance. (4–5)

Metrical patterns vary depending on the sequence in which poets arrange the accented (á) and unaccented (ă) syllables of an utterance. The unit that determines that arrangement is the foot. A *foot* is one unit of rhythm. The most common foot in English poetry is the iamb: an unaccented syllable followed by an accented syllable (ăá).

Here are the most used metrical feet:

iamb (iambic) ăá   ăbóve

    Bĕcaúse Ĭ coúld nŏt stóp fŏr deáth (Emily Dickinson)

trochee (trochaic) áă   lóvelў

    Cíndĕréllă, dréssed iň yéllow (jump-rope rhyme)

anapest (anapestic) ăăá   ŏvĕrwhélm

    Whĕn thĕy saíd, "Doĕs ĭt búzz?" hĕ rĕpliéd, "Yĕs, ĭt doés!" (Edward Lear)

dactyl (dactylic) áăă   róyăltў

    Thís ĭs the̅ forešt přimévăl (Henry Wadsworth Longfellow)

spondee (spondaic) áá   bréak, bréak

    Wé réal cóol (Gwendolyn Brooks)

In practice, iambic and trochaic feet tend to blend together. That is, poets readily switch back and forth between the two, so that you can't always tell which foot predominates. The same is even more true of the "waltz-time" feet, anapest and dactyl. The key difference between the two sets is the number of beats: two for iambic/trochaic, three for anapestic/dactylic. An example of the iambic/trochaic blend is the third stanza of Emily Brontë's "The Night Is Darkening Round Me" (page 108).

> Clouds beyond clouds above me,
> Wastes beyond wastes below;
> But nothing drear can move me;
> I will not, cannot go.

Edward Lear mixes anapestic and dactylic feet throughout "Calico Pie." Here's the first stanza:

> Calico pie,
>   The little birds fly
>   Down to the calico-tree:
> Their wings were blue,
> And they sang "Tilly-loo!"
> Till away they flew;
>   And they never came back to me!
>   They never came back,
>   They never came back,
>   They never came back to me!

Measuring meter.   Fussell indicates four ways in which poets "measure" meter (6). (The word *meter*, he notes, comes from the Greek word for "measure.") Least used in English is *quantitative*, a pattern based on duration of syllables (long sound and short sound) rather than stressed and unstressed syllables. Also little used in English is *syllabic*—the number of syllables per line. An example is the haiku, whose line lengths are based entirely on syllable count. (See pages 149–50 for a discussion of haiku.) Much more widespread in English is *accentual*—the number of stresses per line. Examples are Old English poetry, such as *Beowulf,* and Scottish border ballads. (See pages 145–49 for a description of ballad form.) In this pattern only stresses are counted:

> "O whére hae ye beén, Lord Rándal, my són?
> O whére hae ye beén, my hańdsome young mán?"
> "I hae beén to the wíld woód; móther, máke my bed soón,
> For I'm weáry wi huńting, and fáin wald lie doẃn."

Since ballads were meant to be sung, singers could vary stresses to fit the music or the themes of the poems.

Finally, the most utilized metrical pattern in English poetry is *accentual-syllabic,* a pattern based on the number of stresses *and* the number of syllables per line. The best known such pattern is iambic pentameter, which consists of five stresses (iambs) and ten syllables. Shakespeare wrote his plays and sonnets in iambic pentameter. The following are the names of accentual-syllabic line lengths:

monometer (one foot)

dimeter (two feet)

trimeter (three feet)

tetrameter (four feet)

pentameter (five feet)

hexameter (six feet)

heptameter (seven feet)

octameter (eight feet)

These iambic tetrameter lines from Andrew Marvell's "To His Coy Mistress" exemplify accentual-syllabic meter:

> Hăd wé bŭt wórld ĕnoúgh, ănd tiḿe,
> Thĭs cóyneşs, ládў, weré nŏ críme.

Each line has four iambic feet—four accented syllables, eight syllables in all.

When you begin reading a poem, it shouldn't take long to recognize its predominate metrical pattern. Usually, after you read a few lines, the pattern will become clear. Sometimes, as in free verse (see pages 150–54), a poem will have no clear pattern. When it does, however, you can identify the pattern by sounding it out in your head, by reading the poem aloud, or by beating out the rhythm with your hands or feet.

Scanning. To indicate metrical patterns visually, you can scan the poem. *Scanning* is a process whereby you mark accented and unaccented syllables with symbols: a breve [ă] for unaccented (unstressed) syllables and an acute accent mark [á] for accented (stressed) syllables:

> Ă blíss ĭn próof; ănd próved, ă vérў wóe.

This line, from Shakespeare's Sonnet 129 (which follows), is iambic pentameter, the traditional accentual-syllabic pattern of sonnets in English: five iambic feet, ten syllables.

Why scan? "To scan only to conclude that a poem is 'written in iambic pentameter,'" Paul Fussell says, "is to do nothing significant. It

is only as a basis for critical perception and ultimately for critical judgment that scansion can justify itself" (28). In other words, the most
valuable use for scanning is to interpret—to explore the meanings of
poems. Scanning allows us to see and show not only the predominate
metrical pattern but also the poet's meaningful variation from it. Poets
achieve such variation by substituting feet for the regular, expected
feet of the pattern. Here, for example, is the first line of Sonnet 129:

> Th' ĕxpeńse/of spiŕ/ĭt iň ă/ waśte/ ŏf sháme.

In the third foot of this line, Shakespeare substitutes a pyrrhic foot
(two unaccented syllables: "ĭt iň") for an iambic foot. The result is
that the line has four stresses, not five.

Poets rarely stick to the predominate metrical pattern of a
poem. As W. K. Wimsatt and Monroe Beardsley say, "It is practically
impossible to write an English line that will not in some way buck
against the meter. Insofar as the line does approximate the condition
of complete submission, it is most likely a tame line, a weak line"
(140). Poets stray from the established meter to avoid a mechanical,
sing-songy rhythm and to make the language sound more colloquial.
Such is the case in "Dover Beach" and "My Last Duchess," both of
which are spoken by fictional characters. Equally important, poets
vary meter to emphasize ideas. By substituting feet, poets catch us by
surprise and call attention to meanings.

Caesura.   Another rhythmic device for emphasizing meaning is the
caesura. A *caesura* is a strong pause somewhere in the line. You mark a
caesura with two vertical lines: ‖. Consider the caesuras in this jump-
rope rhyme:

> Cinderella, dressed in yellow,
> Went upstairs ‖ to kiss a fellow.
> Made a mistake; ‖ kissed a snake.
> How many doctors did it take?
> One, two, three, four . . .

A likely place for a caesura is in the middle of the line. If the meter of the
poem is tetrameter, then a caesura in the middle neatly divides the line
in half. Such is the case in lines 2 and 3 of this poem. A caesura may also
occur near the beginning of a line or near the end. Or there may be no
caesuras in a line, as is probably the case in lines 1, 4, and 5 of this poem.

Caesuras often emphasize meaning. Caesuras in the middle of lines can emphasize strong contrasts or close relationships between ideas. In line 3, both the caesura and the rhyme of "mistake" with "snake" link the abstraction (the mistake) with the action (kissing the snake).

Shakespeare's Sonnet 129 provides a rich example of how caesuras and metrical substitutions convey meaning.

SONNET 129

William Shakespeare

Th' expense of spirit ‖ in a waste of shame
Is lust in action; ‖ and, till action, lust
Is perjured, murderous, bloody, full of blame,
Savage, extreme, rude, cruel, not to trust;
Enjoyed no sooner ‖ but despisèd straight;   5
Past reason hunted; ‖ and no sooner had,
Past reason hated, ‖ as a swallowed bait,
On purpose laid ‖ to make the taker mad;
Mad in pursuit, ‖ and in possession so;
Had, having, and in quest to have, extreme;   10
A bliss in proof; ‖ and proved, a very woe;
Before, a joy proposed; ‖ behind, a dream.
All this the world well knows; ‖ yet none knows well
To shun the heaven ‖ that leads men to this hell.

Here Shakespeare uses caesura and metrical pattern to establish a pattern of contrasts and similarities. Like most sonnets, this one has ten syllables per line and is supposed to be iambic pentameter. But for many of these lines, Shakespeare has only four accents per line, not five. This allows him to make some of his comparisons equal in weight. Line 5, for example, has a strong caesura and four accented syllables:

> Enjóyed no soóner ‖ but despisèd straíght.

The effect is to contrast the two emotional states, pleasure and guilt. Since Shakespeare puts guilt last, he gives it more weight. Lines 11 and 12, however, contain caesuras and five accents each, making the two-part divisions within the lines unequal:

> A blíss in próof; ‖ and próved, a véry wóe;
> Befóre, a jóy propósed; ‖ behínd, a dréam.

The "weaker" sides of the lines contain the pleasure part of the equation and emphasize the brevity and insubstantial quality of pleasure. The "strong" sides emphasize either naïve expectation or guilt.

Shakespeare's metrical substitutions also emphasize stark contrasts: Lust is like

a swallowed bait,	7
On purpose laid to make the taker mad:	8
Mád iň pǔrsuít, aňd iň pǒsséssiǒn só;	9
Hád, háving, aňd iň quést tǒ háve, ěxtréme;	10
A bliss in proof; and proved, a very woe;	11
Before, a joy proposed; behind, a dream.	12

All these lines fit the iambic scheme except 9 and 10. Why? Shakespeare probably wanted to emphasize certain words in these two lines, particularly the first words in each. These words—"mad" and "had"—are prominent because they come first in the line, they are stressed, and they rhyme. The accents in line 10 are especially suggestive. They contrast the past ("had"), the present ("having"), the future ("quest" and "have"). They point out the psychological and moral nature of all three ("extreme").

QUESTIONS ABOUT RHYTHM

Meter has many uses in poetry. It provides a method of ordering material. It creates a hypnotic effect that rivets attention on the poem. Like the beat of music, it is enjoyable for itself. Children take naturally to the pulsing rhythms of nursery rhymes and jump-rope rhymes. But for the purposes of interpretation, the greatest value of meter is the insights it gives us to the meanings of poems.

1. Which metrical pattern does the poem use?

2. What is appealing about the pattern?

3. Where does the poem vary from the established pattern? Why?

4. How and why does the poet use pauses, especially caesuras, within each line?

THINKING ON PAPER ABOUT RHYTHM

1. Count the number of syllables for each line. Write the number at the end of the line.

2. Read the poem aloud, then mark the accented and unaccented syllables of each line.

3. Draw a vertical line between each foot in the line.

4. Identify the metrical pattern (iambic, trochaic, etc.) and the length of the lines (pentameter, hexameter, etc.).

5. Use two vertical lines to mark the caesuras in the poem. Explain how the caesuras relate to the sense of each line.

6. Underline the places where the poet departs from the established metrical pattern of the poem. Explain how these departures relate to the sense of each line.

7. Explain the appropriateness of the metrical pattern to the poem's meaning.

8. Describe how easy or difficult it is to read the poem aloud. Does its metrical pattern slow you down? Or does it allow you to read smoothly? Explain how the difficulty or ease of reading the metrical pattern relates to the poem's meaning and purpose. Line 10 of Shakespeare's Sonnet 116 (pages 144–45), for example, reads more slowly than the other lines:

> Within his bending sickle's compass come

Shakespeare slows the tempo, probably to suggest the slowness of Time, personified here as a man with a scythe (sickle).

Now It's Your Turn

Explore the implications of rhythm in Blake's "The Sick Rose" (page 129). Does it have a dominant metrical pattern? Is the pattern accentual-syllabic? What ideas do caesuras and stressed syllables bring out? Do you have alternatives—choices—for where to place stresses?

Word Sounds

Devices using word sounds. Poets delight in the sound of language and consciously present sounds to be enjoyed for themselves. They also use them to emphasize meaning, action, and emotion, and especially to call the reader's attention to connections between words.

Rhyme, for example, has the effect of linking words together. Important devices using word sounds are the following:

onomatopoeia—The use of words that sound like what they mean ("buzz," "boom," "hiss," "fizz," "pop," "glug").

alliteration—the repetition of consonant sounds at the beginning of words or at the beginning of accented syllables ("the woeful woman went wading Wednesday").

assonance—the repetition of vowel sounds followed by different consonant sounds ("O, the groans that opened to his own ears").

consonance (or *half-rhyme*)—the repetition of final consonant sounds that are preceded by different vowel sounds ("the beast climbed fast to the crest"). Consonance is the opposite of alliteration, which features initial consonant sounds.

rhyme—the repetition of accented vowels and the sounds that follow. There are subcategories of rhyme:

masculine rhyme (the rhymed words end with a stressed syllable: "man-ran," "detect-correct").

feminine rhyme (the rhymed words end with one or more unaccented syllables: "subtle-rebuttal," "deceptively-perceptively").

internal rhyme (the rhymed words are within the line).

end rhyme (the rhymed words appear at the ends of lines).

approximate rhyme (the words are close to rhyming: "book-buck," "watch-match," "man-in").

Edgar Allan Poe's "To Helen" illustrates many of these sound devices:

TO HELEN

EDGAR ALLAN POE

Helen, thy beauty is to me   masculine rhyme/
Like those Nicean barks of yore,   end rhyme
That gently, o'er a perfumed sea,
alliteration   The weary, way-worn wanderer bore
To his own native shore.   5

consonance   On desperate seas long wont to roam
Thy hyacinth hair, thy classic face,
Thy Naiad airs have brought me home   approximate rhyme
To the glory that was Greece,
And the grandeur that was Rome.   10

assonance   Lo! in yon brilliant window-nich
             How statue-like I (see)(thee) stand!   internal rhyme
             The agate lamp within thy hand,
           Ah! Psyche, from the regions which
             Are Holy Land!   15

QUESTIONS ABOUT WORD SOUNDS

It's easy to lose yourself in an analysis of a poem's sound structure and forget why you are making the analysis in the first place. Instead, ask these questions:

1. What sound devices does the poet use?

2. Why does the poet use them?

3. How do they help establish the poem's tone, atmosphere, theme, setting, characterization, and emotional qualities?

4. Above all, what meanings do they suggest?

In Poe's "To Helen," for example, the alliteration in line 4 ("weary, way-worn wanderer") underscores the fatigued state of the wanderer. The consonance of "seas" and "airs" in lines 6 and 8 emphasizes the contrast between them; one is "desperate" but the other assuages despair. And the assonance in line 11 ("in yon brilliant window-nich"), with its emphasis on high, tight, "i" sounds, helps to characterize the luminosity of the place where Helen, statuelike, stands.

Be alert to relationships between ideas established by rhyme, most notably by internal rhyme and end rhyme. Rhyme is a kind of "music" that sounds pretty. But it can be used meaningfully, too. Turn back to Sonnet 129 and examine the complex sound associations Shakespeare creates there. The words sound rough, almost painful, with their harsh consonants, all of which illustrate the frustrated and frenetic emotional state Shakespeare ascribes to lust. Note the variation on "s" sounds in the first line.

Th' expense of spirit in a waste of shame

Line 3 begins a list of qualities. Shakespeare divides and associates them through assonance and alliteration: Lust

Is perjured, murderous, bloody, full of blame.

The words *perjured* and *murderous* are linked by assonance (the "er" sounds) and focus on evil deeds (falsehood, murder), leading to the second half of the line. The words *bloody* and *blame* are linked by alliteration and focus on the results of evil deeds, especially murder: blood and guilt. The linkages signaled by the poem's end rhyme are also meaningful: shame/blame, lust/not to trust, no sooner had/make the taker mad, extreme/dream, yet none knows well/leads men to this hell.

5. We can ask, then, questions like these: In the poem you are analyzing, what linkages of meaning are there to *all* the sound qualities of the words—especially to the obvious ones, such as alliteration, internal rhyme, and end rhyme?

✎ *Thinking on Paper about Word Sounds*

1. Underline instances of alliteration, assonance, and consonance in the poem. Explain the relationship between these devices and the sense of the lines where they occur.

2. Circle rhymed words. Explain similarities and contrasts the rhymed words underscore.

3. Circle words that have meaningful or attractive sound qualities, such as onomatopoetic words. Show how these words add to the poem's sense.

4. When the sounds of a poem are harsh and grating, the effect is called *cacophony.* When they are pleasing and harmonious, the effect is called *euphony.* Underline instances of cacophony or euphony. Explain how they relate to the poem's sense.

5. Describe any sound devices in the poem that catch you by surprise. Say why the poet uses such surprises.

Now It's Your Turn

What sound devices does Robinson employ in "Richard Cory" (pages 357–58)? What effects do they produce? How do they help convey the poem's meanings?

STRUCTURE

Structure is the way the whole poem is organized and put together. Poets give structure to their poems in two overlapping ways: by organizing ideas according to a logical plan and by establishing a pattern of units. Arnold arranges "Dover Beach" in both ways, as do most poets. He divides the poem into four units, each of which has a pattern of end rhyme. And he arranges the whole poem rhetorically—that is, by ideas. Each unit elaborates a single point, and each point follows logically from the preceding one.

Lines. The most immediately visible structural device of poetry is the line. Poetry is organized in lines, prose in paragraphs. The exception is *prose poetry*, which has the verbal texture of poetry (nuanced diction, rhythmical devices, imagery, internal rhyme) but is arranged in paragraphs, not lines. The following passage from Herman Melville's *Moby Dick* (the second paragraph of Chapter 111, "The Pacific"), for example, describes the ship's passage into the mystic waters where dwells the White Whale:

> There is, one knows not what sweet mystery about this sea, whose gently awful stirrings seem to speak of some hidden soul beneath; like those fabled undulations of the Ephesian sod over the buried Evangelist St. John. And meet it is, that over these sea-pastures, wide-rolling watery prairies and Potters' Fields of all four continents, the waves should rise and fall, and ebb and flow unceasingly; for here, millions of mixed shades and shadows, drowned dreams, somnambulisms, reveries; all that we call lives and souls, lie dreaming, dreaming, still; tossing like slumberers in their beds; the ever-rolling waves but made so by their restlessness.

Melville was a sympathetic reader of Shakespeare. Although he does not say that this paragraph is "poetry," it bristles with poetic devices and could justifiably be arranged in lines that would resemble Shakespearean blank verse. As it stands, it is "prose poetry."

Poetry, however, is usually organized in lines. Poets use various criteria for choosing line lengths. The best known criterion is meter—the number of feet per line: monometer, dimeter, trimeter, etc. (See page 133 for the full list.) Pentameter (five feet per line), especially iambic pentameter, has become the most utilized line length in English poetry.

Enjambment. A decision poets face is whether to end-stop or enjamb their lines. *Enjambment* (from the French verb *enjamber,* to straddle, to encroach) is the continuance of a phrase from one line to the next so that there is no pause at the end of the line. An end-stopped line has a definite pause at the end. In Wordsworth's "A Slumber Did My Spirit Seal" (page 110), all the lines are end-stopped:

> A slumber did my spirit seal;
> I had no human fears—
> She seemed a thing that could not feel
> The touch of earthly years.

Other examples are the poems by Brontë (page 108) and Campion (page 125). In contrast, most of the lines in the poems by Millay (page 145), Browning (pages 120–22), Bogan (pages 114–15), and Arnold (page 117–18) are enjambed. In this excerpt from Millay's sonnet, only lines 2 and 5 are end-stopped; the others are enjambed:

> I, being born a woman and distressed   1
> By all the needs and notions of my kind,   2
> Am urged by your propinquity to find   3
> Your person fair, and feel a certain zest   4
> To bear your body's weight upon my breast.   5

Enjambed and end-stopped lines create different effects. Enjambed lines read more naturally, like someone speaking. Even though the poems by Millay, Browning, Bogan, and Arnold feature end-rhyme, when you read these poems aloud, the end rhyme almost disappears. You can see the end rhyme on the page, but you are less likely to hear it. Mary Kinzie says that sentences in poetry are in tension with lines; "sentence tugs against line" (68). When lines are enjambed, "the sentence takes priority over the line" (61). The "more enjambment, or run-on, there is from one line to the next, the less the lines function as individual entities" (68). But when "phrases end at the ends of lines, thus creating pauses, the *lines themselves* are emphasized as rhythmical units and as units of meaning" (68).

Blank verse.   A line form that is almost always enjambed is *blank verse:* iambic pentameter with no end rhyme. Blank verse has been made famous by Shakespeare and many other poets: Christopher Marlowe, John Milton, William Wordsworth, Alfred Tennyson, and Robert Frost, just to name a few. You can see from Frost's "The Death of the Hired Man" (printed on pages 262–66) that blank verse mimics the spoken language. The sentences run from line to line, as if the lines don't exist. Yet they do exist. Blank verse lines provide an underlying rhythmic pattern that listeners feel, even if they cannot hear where the lines end.

Stanza.   A second device for structuring poetry is the *stanza*. Not all poems have stanzas. When they don't, they are *stichic*. When they do, they are *strophic*. Stanzas in a poem typically resemble one another structurally. They have the same number of lines, length of lines, metrical patterns, and rhyme schemes. They are physically separated from other stanzas (by a space inserted between each stanza) and usually present one idea (similar to a paragraph in prose), one happening, or one image.

Rhyme scheme.   *Rhyme scheme*—any pattern of end rhyme—is a traditional method of organizing stanzas. The couplet, the shortest possible stanza, rhymes aa:

> Interred beneath this marble stone,
> Lies sauntering Jack and idle Joan.
> —Matthew Prior, "An Epitaph"

The ballad stanza typically rhymes abcb; that is, the second and fourth lines rhyme:

> It is an ancient Mariner
> And he stoppeth one of three.
> —"By thy long gray beard and glittering eye,
> Now wherefore stopp'st thou me?"
> —Samuel Taylor Coleridge, *The Rime of the Ancient Mariner*

Ottava Rima has eight lines (thus *ottava*, "eight") and rhymes abababcc:

> 'Tis sweet to win, no matter how, one's laurels,
>   By blood or ink; 'tis sweet to put an end
> To strife; 'tis sometimes sweet to have our quarrels,
>   Particularly with a tiresome friend:
> Sweet is old wine in bottles, ale in barrels;
>   Dear is the helpless creature we defend
> Against the world; and dear the schoolboy spot
> We ne'er forget, though there we are forgot.
>   —George Gordon, Lord Byron, *Don Juan*

Spenserian stanza (invented by Edmond Spenser for *The Faerie Queen*) has nine lines and rhymes ababbcbcc. An example is the stanza from John Keats's "The Eve of St. Agnes," printed on page 122.

Fixed and nonce forms. These are but a few of the many shapes stanzas can take. Poets can, of course, create any rhyme scheme or stanza form they choose. But they often work instead within the confines of already established poetic structures. These are called *fixed forms.* Stanzas that conform to no traditional limits, such as those in "Dover Beach," are called *nonce forms.* Fixed forms provide ready-made structural units by which a poet can arrange ideas. But they also challenge poets to mold unwieldy material into an unyielding structure. The result is a tension between material and form that is pleasing to both poet and reader.

To illustrate how poems can be structured, we will look at four well-known poetic forms: the sonnet, the ballad, the haiku, and free verse.

The Sonnet. The sonnet is the most famous fixed form in English. All sonnets consist of fourteen lines of iambic pentameter. The two best known kinds of sonnets are named for their most famous practitioners. A *Shakespearean sonnet* rhymes abab/cdcd/efef/gg and has a structural division of three quatrains (each containing four lines) and a couplet. A *Petrarchan sonnet* rhymes abbaabba in the octave (the first eight lines) and cdecde in the sestet (the last six lines). Poets often vary the pattern of end rhyme in sonnets, especially in Petrarchan sonnets. Each kind of sonnet has a *turn,* a point in the poem at which the poet shifts from one meaning or mood to another. The turn in the Shakespearean sonnet occurs between lines 12 and 13 (just before the couplet). The turn in the Petrarchan sonnet occurs between the octave and the sestet. In both forms, the part of the poem before the turn delineates a problem or tension; the part after the turn offers some resolution to or comment on the problem and releases the tension.

SONNET 116

William Shakespeare

three quatrains		
Let me not to the marriage of true minds	a	
Admit impediments. Love is not love	b	
Which alters when it alteration finds,	a	
Or bends with the remover to remove:	b	4
Oh, no! it is an ever-fixèd mark,	c	
That looks on tempests and is never shaken;	d	
It is the star to every wandering bark,	c	
Whose worth's unknown, although his height be taken,	d	8

three quatrains (cont'd)	Love's not Time's fool, though rosey lips and cheeks	e
	Within his bending sickle's compass come;	f
	Love alters not with his brief hours and weeks,	e
turn →	But bears it out even to the edge of doom.	f 12
couplet	If this be error and upon me proved,	g
	I never writ, nor no man ever loved.	g 14

Shakespeare molds the ideas and images of this poem to fit its form. He states the theme—that love remains constant no matter what—in the first quatrain. In the second, he says that cataclysmic events cannot destroy love. In the third, he says that time cannot destroy love. Finally, in the couplet, he affirms the truth of his theme.

I, BEING BORN A WOMAN

Edna St. Vincent Millay

octave	I, being born a woman and distressed	a
	By all the needs and notions of my kind,	b
	Am urged by your propinquity to find	b
	Your person fair, and feel a certain zest	a
	To bear your body's weight upon my breast:	a
	So subtly is the fume of life designed,	b
	To clarify the pulse and cloud the mind,	b
turn →	And leave me once again undone, possessed.	a 8
sestet	Think not for this, however, the poor treason	c
	Of my stout blood against my staggering brain,	d
	I shall remember you with love, or season	c
	My scorn with pity,—let me make it plain:	d
	I find this frenzy insufficient reason	c
	For conversation when we meet again.	d 14

Millay uses the structure of the Petrarchan sonnet to shape her ideas. The turn occurs between the octave and the sestet. In the octave she tells her lover why she succumbed to his charms. In the sestet, she dismisses him. The ideas in the sestet overthrow those in the octave. Although the last two lines do not rhyme, they are similar to the couplet in a Shakespearean sonnet. They drive home the decisive and climactic point of the poem.

The Ballad. M. H. Abrams defines a ballad as "a song, transmitted orally, which tells a story" (18). He distinguishes between folk ballads, which are anonymous and sung aloud, and literary ballads, which are written for publication by a known author. Literary ballads, like John Keats's "La Belle Dame Sans Merci" and Samuel Taylor Coleridge's *The Rime of the Ancient Mariner,* imitate many of the characteristics of folk ballads. Among these characteristics is the *ballad stanza,* a quatrain that typically has four stresses in lines one and three and three stresses in lines two and four. The rhyme scheme of the ballad stanza is abcb:

He turńed him right and round abóut,	a
And the téar blińded his ée:	b
"I wad néver hae tródden on Írish gróund,	c
If it hád not béen for thée."	a

Other characteristics of ballads include the following: They feature intense conflicts and thus are highly emotional, even melodramatic. Their narratives are so condensed and spare that they leave out whole swatches of the story. Ballads are impersonal; that is, the narrator stands back from the story, taking no sides, making no comments. They often feature a dialogue between two people. These dialogues sometimes proceed by *incremental repetition,* in which lines and even whole stanzas are repeated but with subtle variations that advance the plot. Mary Kenzie claims that the third line of each stanza is the most important because it emphasizes ideas and actions or marks a change (420).

All of these characteristics are subject to alteration. Singers may change them, depending on the ideas or events they want to stress, or the tune they use. Known authors, like Keats and Coleridge, pick and choose the characteristics that suit their purposes. A substantial tradition of folk ballads in English emerged in the Middle Ages along the border of Scotland and England—the Scottish border ballads. When these began to be collected and written down in the eighteenth century, they exerted an enormous influence on English poetry, especially on the Romantic poets. An example of a Scottish border ballad is "The Daemon Lover."

THE DAEMON LOVER

"O where have you been, my long, long love,
 This long seven years and mair?"
"O I'm come to seek my former vows
 Ye granted me before."

"O hold your tongue of your former vows,
 For they will breed sad strife;
O hold your tongue of your former vows
 For I am become a wife."

He turned him right and round about,
  And the tear blinded his ee:
"I wad never hae trodden on Irish ground,
  If it had not been for thee.

"I might hae had a king's daughter,
  Far, far beyond the sea;
I might have had a king's daughter,
  Had it not been for love o thee."

"If ye might have had a king's daughter,
  Yer sel ye had to blame;
Ye might have taken the king's daughter,
  For ye kend that I was nane.

"If I was to leave my husband dear,
  And my two babes also,
O what have you to take me to,
  If with you I should go?"

"I hae seven ships upon the sea—
  And the eighth brought me to land—
With four-and-twenty bold mariners,
  And music on every hand."

She has taken up her two little babes,
  Kissd them baith cheek and chin:
"O fair ye weel, my ain two babes,
  For I'll never see you again."

She set her foot upon the ship,
  No mariners could she behold;
But the sails were o the taffetie,
  And the masts o beaten gold.

She had not sailed a league, a league,
  A league but barely three,
When dismal grew his countenance,
  And drumlie grew his ee.

They had not saild a league, a league,
  A league but barely three,
Until she espied his cloven foot,
  And she wept right bitterlie.

> "O what hills are yon, yon pleasant hills,
>   That the sun shines sweetly on?"
> "O yon are the hills of heaven," he said,
>   "Where you will never win."
>
> "O whaten a mountain is yon," she said,
>   "All so dreary wi frost and snow?"
> "O yon is the mountain of hell," he cried,
>   "Where you and I will go."
>
> He strack the tap-mast wi his hand,
>   The fore-masts wi his knee,
> And he brake that gallant ship in twain,
>   And sank her in the sea.

As with most folk ballads, "The Daemon Lover" exists in numerous versions.

Common meter. *Common meter* is the adaptation of the ballad stanza for hymns. Like the ballad stanza, common meter stanzas have four lines, alternating lines of tetrameter and trimeter, and a rhyme scheme of abcb or abab. A well-known eighteenth-century author of such hymns was Isaac Watts:

> Our God, our Help in Ages past,
> Our Hope for Years to come,
> Our Shelter from the Stormy Blast,
> And our eternal Home.

Emily Dickinson was one of many poets who drew inspiration from the forms and subject matter of hymns. She grew up hearing Watts's hymns and wrote nearly all her poems in common meter. An example is this poem, which exhibits other characteristics of ballads as well:

BECAUSE I COULD NOT STOP FOR DEATH

Emily Dickinson

> Because I could not stop for Death—
> He kindly stopped for me—
> The Carriage held but just Ourselves—
> And Immortality.

We slowly drove—He knew no haste
And I had put away
My labor and my leisure too,
For His Civility—

We passed the School, where Children strove
At Recess—in the Ring—
We passed the Fields of Gazing Grain—
We passed the Setting Sun—

Or rather—He passed Us—
The Dews drew quivering and chill—
For only Gossamer, my Gown—
My Tippet—only Tulle—

We paused before a House that seemed
A Swelling of the Ground—
The Roof was scarcely visible—
The Cornice—in the Ground—

Since then—'tis Centuries—and yet
Feels shorter than the Day
I first surmised the Horses Heads
Were toward Eternity—

The haiku. Like the sonnet, the haiku is an imported form of poetry—the sonnet from Italy, the haiku from Japan. Harold Henderson indicates four "rules" that govern and help define the haiku: (1) It has three lines, with five syllables in the first, seven in the second, and five in the third—a total of seventeen syllables. Since the Japanese language has almost no stresses, haiku meter is syllabic. (2) It makes some reference to nature, especially to the season of the year. (3) It refers to a specific event. (4) The event takes place in the present (14). The following haiku manifests all of these characteristics:

Children play outside
while their parents watch and talk:
summer shadows fall.

In practice, these rules are flexible, both in English and Japanese. Translators of Japanese haiku often cannot maintain the syllable count, because Japanese syllables are sounded differently from English.

Haiku has other characteristics. Its diction is simple. It rarely includes end rhyme. William Howard Cohen says that it presents a "pure image" stripped of extraneous details that suggests rather than directly states meanings. Haiku is charged with emotion (21) and, in keeping with the Zen Buddhist concept of *satori* (sudden realization of one's unity with nature), can "startle us awake to a world in which clarity, mystery, and wonder merge to make the everyday life around us seem as if we have just looked at it for the first time" (28). To achieve this power, haiku will juxtapose seemingly unrelated things to reveal their hidden unity (25). Mary Kinzie claims that a turn occurs "after the fifth syllable or the twelfth" that indicates "a separation between the small and local on one hand, the cosmic, or spiritual, on the other" (327). In the haiku above, for example, the third line "comments" on the other two.

Here are translations of haiku by three of Japan's most renowned writers of haiku: Matsuo Basho (1644–1694), Taniguchi Buson (1715–1783), and Kobayashi Issa (1763–1827).

> How to say goodbye!
> so like a bee who would stay
> all day in one flower.
>> [composed on leaving the house of a friend]
>>> —Basho

> Under the blossoming pear
> a moonlit woman
> reading a faded letter.
>> —Buson

> The old, plump bullfrog
> held his ground and stared at me—
> what a sour face!
>> —Issa

Free verse

The "freedom" of free verse.   In some ways *free verse*—poetry without meter—has the look and feel of metrical poetry. It is arranged in lines, it often has units that look like stanzas (lines grouped together and set apart from other groupings by spaces), and it has the verbal texture of poetry: alliteration, internal rhyme, occasional end rhyme, nuanced diction, rhythmic phrasing). But it is "free" in that it obeys no set metrical patterns.

The first practitioner of free verse in modern times was Walt Whitman (beginning with the 1855 edition of *Leaves of Grass*). Many readers, when they saw Whitman's poetry for the first time, wondered if it was really poetry. They asked why any "prose" writings could not be arranged into lines of varying lengths and be called poetry. Since Whitman's time, so many poets have written in free verse that it has became the predominate form of modern poetry.

Biblical free verse.   Free verse is not really "free." In his book-length treatment of free verse, Charles Hartman says that free verse, like any other poetry, "depends on conventions. Eliminating those of meter merely throws the poet back on those that define verse and govern language in general" (27). There are two broad categories of free verse, each with distinctive conventions. The first is *biblical free verse,* so called because of its antecedents in ancient Hebrew poetry—books from the Hebrew Bible (Old Testament) such as the Psalms, the Song of Solomon, Ecclesiastes, Isaiah, and Jeremiah. The King James translation of the Bible (1611) provided models for Whitman and other authors of free verse.

Here is a well-known example.

PSALM 23

The Lord is my shepherd; I shall not want.

He maketh me to lie down in green pastures; he leadeth me beside the still waters.

He restoreth my soul; he leadeth me in the paths of righteousness for his name's sake.

Yea, though I walk through the valley of the shadow of death, I will fear no evil, for thou art with me; thy rod and thy staff they comfort me.

Thou preparest a table before me in the presence of mine enemies; thou anointest my head with oil; my cup runneth over.

Surely goodness and mercy shall follow me all the days of my life, and I will dwell in the house of the Lord forever.

Characteristics.   Characteristics of biblical free verse include the following: (1) Lines are typically stopped, not enjambed. (2) Lines are often quite long. (3) Rhythms are established by repetitions of phrases that have the same syntactical structure: "He maketh me," "he leadeth me," "he restoreth my soul," "he leadeth me" (Psalm 23). When such phrasal repetitions occur at the beginning of lines, they are called *anaphora*. An example is the first section of Whitman's "Out of the Cradle Endlessly Rocking":

> Out of the cradle endlessly rocking,
> Out of the mockingbird's throat, the musical shuttle,
> Out of the Ninth-month midnight . . .

Whitman's "Cavalry Crossing a Ford" (page 16) features two anaphoric phrases:

> Behold the silvery river . . .
> Behold the brown-faced men . . .

(4) Biblical free verse, like other poetry, includes word sounds—assonance, alliteration, internal rhyme, onomatopoeia, consonance—that make music and highlight ideas. (5) Catalogues (long lists of things) abound:

> The pure contralto sings . . .
> The carpenter dresses his plank . . .
> The married and unmarried children ride home . . .
> The pilot seizes the king-pin . . .
> The mate stands braced in the whaleboat . . .
> The duck-shooter walks by . . .
> The deacons are ordained . . .
> The spinning-girl retreats and advances . . .
> The farmer stops by the bars . . .
> The lunatic is carried at last to the asylum . . .
> —Whitman, "Song of Myself," ll. 257–266

Mary Kinzie says that biblical free verse has a characteristic subject matter and tone: "the sublime setting, the landscape cosmic and majestic, the wonders persisting in time, the emotions elevated and rapturous (or their opposite—desperate and extreme)." It swells with "visionary authority and the massive breath the poet must take to utter it" (338).

Imagist free verse. The second kind of free verse is less oracular, less meant to be spoken aloud. It was created by the Modernist poets of the early twentieth century—Ezra Pound, Amy Lowell, D. H. Lawrence, Carl Sandburg—and continues to hold sway over poetry written in English. Kinzie calls it "imagist free verse." Other names for it are "meditative" or "private" free verse (Paul Fussell) and "conversational" free verse (M. H. Abrams). *Imagist free verse,* Kinzie says, is biblical free verse "condensed into its minim" (340). Its lines are shorter. The poems themselves are shorter. It emphasizes "sharply drawn visual detail," as advocated by the Imagist movement of the early twentieth century (423). It de-emphasizes direct statement of ideas. Lines are enjambed, making the sentences seem more colloquial. Rhythms are more subtle and much less pronounced. Donald Wesling and Eniko Bolloba claim that "more explicitly than the metrical poetry of the period from Chaucer to Tennyson, from Pushkin to Tsvetaeva, free verse claims and thematizes a proximity to lived experience" (427). That is, free verse replicates the activities, concerns, and language of ordinary people.

An example that blends biblical and imagist free verse is this early poem by Ezra Pound:

XENIA

Ezra Pound

And
Unto thine eyes my heart
Sendeth old dreams of the spring-time,
Yea of wood-ways my rime
Found thee and flowers in and of all streams
That sang low burthen, and of roses,
That lost their dew-bowed petals for the dreams
We scattered o'er them passing by.

Here Pound employs the archaic diction and even the syntactical rhythms of the Hebrew Bible, but his lines are so enjambed that they disappear in an out-loud reading. Perhaps because of this, the syntax becomes increasingly obscure toward the end of the poem. We have to reread in order to puzzle out how the sentence fits together.

A simpler example is a poem by Amy Lowell. Like Pound, Lowell was influenced by Japanese and Chinese poetry. This poem is set in Japan and has the spare quality of a haiku. As in haiku, the poem presents an evocative image without comment about its meaning.

ROAD TO THE YOSHIWARA

Amy Lowell

Coming to you along the Nihon Embankment,
Suddenly the road was darkened
By a flock of wild geese
Crossing the moon.

A third example is a poem by Langston Hughes—unusual in its inclusion of end rhyme. This poem invokes the experience and language of ordinary people.

VAGABONDS

Langston Hughes

We are the desperate
Who do not care,
The hungry
Who have nowhere
To eat,
No place to sleep,
The tearless
Who cannot
Weep.

Questions about Structure

Definitions of poetic forms appear in handbooks and encyclopedias of literature, such as *The New Princeton Encyclopedia of Poetry and Poetics* and *A Glossary of Literary Terms* (M. H. Abrams). You can use these definitions as tools to analyze poems—to identify their formal qualities and explore how they convey meanings. Some questions to pose about a poem's structure are these:

1. What devices does the poet use to give the poem structure— rhyme scheme, stanzas, double spaces, indentations, repetition of words and images, varying line lengths, rhetorical organization?

2. How do these devices help communicate the poem's meaning?

An example of the relationship between structure and meaning is the final stanza of "Dover Beach." Here Arnold uses end rhyme to emphasize opposing worldviews:

Ah, love, let us be true	a
To one another! for the world, which seems	b
To lie before us like a land of dreams,	b
So various, so beautiful, so new,	a
Hath really neither joy, nor love, nor light,	c
Nor certitude, nor peace, nor help for pain;	d
And we are here as on a darkling plain	d
Swept with confused alarms of struggle and flight,	c
Where ignorant armies clash by night.	c

The rhyme scheme of the first four lines is almost the same as the next five lines; the only difference is the addition of the fifth line. This similarity divides the stanza in half, and the difference in rhymes corresponds to the difference of the ideas in the two halves (the new, beautiful world versus the war-torn, chaotic, threatening world). The extra line in the second half gives the gloomier view more weight.

Thinking on Paper about Structure

1. Write a sonnet.

2. Write a ballad.

3. Write a haiku.

4. Write a free verse poem.

5. Mark the rhyme scheme of an existing poem.

6. Mark each division or unit of the poem. For a sonnet, for example, indicate divisions between quatrains, couplets, octaves, and sestets. Show structuring devices, like end rhyme.

7. Summarize the meaning of each division of the poem.

8. State relationships between ideas and end rhyme.

9. Account for the different lengths of lines. Why, for example, does Pound make the first line of "Xenia" (page 153) just one word? Why does Hughes make the lines of "Vagabonds" (page 154) increasingly short?

10. Describe the imagery of each unit. Show differences of imagery from unit to unit.

Now It's Your Turn

Elizabeth Bishop's "One Art" is a *villanelle*, a fixed form that originally came from Italy and France. A villanelle has nineteen lines and six stanzas. Each stanza except the last has three lines; the last has four. The first and third lines establish the rhyme scheme: aba, aba, aba, aba, aba, abaa. The first line is repeated at the end of stanzas two and four, the third line at the end of stanzas three and five. These two lines form a couplet at the end of the poem.

Show how Bishop uses the villanelle conventions to convey ideas. What are her ideas? Why would she choose the villanelle to develop them?

ONE ART

Elizabeth Bishop

The art of losing isn't hard to master;
so many things seem filled with the intent
to be lost that their loss is no disaster.

Lose something every day. Accept the fluster
of lost door keys, the hour badly spent.
The art of losing isn't hard to master.

Then practice losing farther, losing faster:
places, and names, and where it was you meant
to travel. None of these will bring disaster.

I lost my mother's watch. And look! my last, or
next-to-last, of three loved houses went.
The art of losing isn't hard to master.

I lost two cities, lovely ones. And, vaster,
some realms I owned, two rivers, a continent.
I miss them, but it wasn't a disaster.

—Even losing you (the joking voice, a gesture
I love) I shan't have lied. It's evident
the art of losing's not too hard to master
though it may look like (*Write* it!) like disaster.

SIGHT:
THE VISUAL QUALITIES OF POETRY

Until the invention of writing, all poetry was oral. But once it was written down, it became visual as well. This was especially true after the invention of the printing press by Johannes Gutenberg in 1450. With the advent of mass printing, poets could assume that large numbers of people would see their poetry. Readers could then see rhyme schemes, punctuation, spelling, stanza sizes, line lengths, the visual shape of the poem.

The visibility of poetry allowed poets to take new liberties with their compositions. They could enjamb lines, knowing that even if people couldn't hear where the lines stopped, they could see where. They could insert approximate or visual rhymes, assuming that even if people couldn't hear them, they could spot the similarities between words. They could block off poems into irregular stanzas, knowing that people could see these units separated by spaces.

Visual poetry.   The printing of poetry led to a kind of poetry called "visual poetry" or "pattern poetry." Eleanor Berry defines *visual poetry* as "poetry composed for the eye as well, or more than, for the ear" (1364). Visual poetry, Dick Higgins says, fulfills the "human wish to combine the visual and literary impulses, to tie together the experience of those two areas into an aesthetic whole" (3).

A famous example of visual poetry is this poem by George Herbert. To see its shape—the angel's wings—you have to turn the page sideways.

EASTER WINGS

George Herbert

Lord, who createdst man in wealth and store,°   °*abundance*
    Though foolishly he lost the same,
       Decaying more and more
          Till he became
           Most poor:
           With thee
        O let me rise
      As larks, harmoniously,
    And sing this day thy victories:
Then shall the fall° further the flight in me.   °*Adam and Eve's sin*

    My tender age in sorrow did begin:
      And still with sicknesses and shame
        Thou didst so punish sin,
          That I became
           Most thin.
           With thee
        Let me combine,
      And feel this day thy victory;
    For, if I imp° my wing on thine,   °*graft*
Affliction shall advance the flight in me.

Typical of visual poetry, the words of Herbert's poem conform to a recognizable shape. The shape, in turn, contributes to the poem's meaning. Higgins, in his history of visual poetry, points out the numerous traditional shapes of visual poetry, including love knots, crosses, animals, pyramids, labyrinths, stars, chalices, hearts, musical instruments, roses, trees.

Modern poetry. Pattern poetry has a limited appeal because there are only so many shapes words will fit into and because it sometimes seems more like a trick than a meaningful device. But for much poetry, especially that written since 1900, the visibility of poetry is crucial. Modernist free verse, with its enjambed lines and conversational style, depends on our ability to see the lines. We can't hear where they end; we have to see. The poet e. e. cummings, for example, built visual elements into his poetry with verve and ingenuity. Unless we can see his quirky punctuation and arrangement of words on the page, we cannot make sense of his poems. Even his name (all lower case) partakes of the visual nature of his poetry.

Examples.   This untitled poem by e. e. cummings comes close to being entirely visual:

l(a

e. e. cummings

l(a

le
af
fa

ll

s)
one
l

iness

Can this poem be read out loud? Perhaps with two readers?

A less radical example of the ingenuity with which Modernist poets include visual elements is "We Real Cool" by Gwendolyn Brooks:

WE REAL COOL

The Pool Players.
Seven at the Golden Shovel.

We real cool. We
Left school. We

Lurk late. We
Strike straight. We

Sing sin. We
Thin gin. We

Jazz June. We
Die soon.

Except for one thing, this poem looks fairly traditional. It has four stanzas. Each stanza is a couplet, rhyming aa. The unusual thing—noticeable only because we see it—is where she places each "we." Syntactically—as subjects of the sentences—they should go at the beginning of the lines. Instead, except for the first one, they appear at the ends.

◯ Questions about the Visual Elements of Poetry

1. What effect does the look of a given poem have on you?
2. What can you see in a poem that is missing from its sound?
3. How do the visual elements of a poem enhance its sound qualities?
4. How crucial to understanding the implications of a poem are its visual features?

◯ Thinking on Paper about the Visual Elements of Poetry

1. Write a pattern poem.
2. Have someone read out loud a poem you have never read or heard. Then read the poem. Write out your reactions to both experiences. What was missing from each experience? Was one experience better—more meaningful, more fun, more interesting—than the other?
3. Mark the visual qualities of a poem. Explain how they contribute to the poem's meaning.

Now It's Your Turn

Show how the visual qualities of "We Real Cool" contribute to its meanings.

Checklist for Interpreting Poetry

Sense in Poems (pages 109–130)

❖ Look up words you don't know.

❖ Locate the normal word order (subject-verb-object) of all sentences.

❖ Inform yourself about all allusions.

❖ Characterize the person or persons speaking—the "I" of the poem.

❖ Construct the story of the poem—what has happened in the past, what is going on now, what is likely to happen in the future.

❖ Establish the temporal, social, and physical context of the poem.

❖ Note all descriptive images and the senses to which they appeal.

❖ Account for tropes and all analogies—metaphors, similes, personifications.

❖ Explore the implications of symbols.

Sound in Poems (pages 130–140)

❖ Establish the predominate metrical pattern or lack of one. Where helpful, scan key passages.

❖ Mark important caesuras.

❖ Note sound devices, such as alliteration, assonance, and end rhyme.

Structure of Poems (pages 140–156)

❖ Track the organization (arrangement, logical development) of ideas.

❖ Note the method of organizing lines—meter and rhyme for metrical poetry; ideas and sound devices for free verse.

❖ Account for variations in line length.

❖ Discern the effect of end-stopped and enjambed lines.

❖ Note how stanzas are organized—rhyme scheme, fixed forms, ideas.

❖ If the poem is a fixed form, learn about its structural conventions.

❖ Show how the poem adheres to or abandons any of these conventions.

❖ For a free verse poem, indicate devices that give it structure.

Sight of Poems (pages 157–160)

❖ Think how the look of the poem—its appearance on the page— affects you.

❖ Explore the connection between the poem's appearance and its meanings.

Works Cited

Abrams, M. H. *A Glossary of Literary Terms.* 7th ed. Fort Worth, TX: Harcourt Brace College Publishers, 1999.

Berry, Eleanor. "Visual Poetry." *The New Princeton Encyclopedia of Poetry and Poetics.* Ed. Alex Preminger and T. V. F. Brogan. Princeton, NJ: Princeton UP, 1993.

Brogan, T. V. F. "Poetry." *The New Princeton Encyclopedia of Poetry and Poetics.* Ed. Alex Preminger and T. V. F. Brogan. Princeton, NJ: Princeton UP, 1993.

Cohen, William Howard. *To Walk in Seasons: An Introduction to Haiku.* Rutland, VT: Charles E. Tuttle, 1972.

Eliot, T. S. "The Three Voices of Poetry." *On Poetry and Poets.* New York: Octagon Books, 1975. 96–112.

Fussell, Paul. *Poetic Meter and Poetic Form.* Rev. ed. New York: Random House, 1979.

Hartman, Charles O. *Free Verse: An Essay on Prosody.* Princeton, NJ: Princeton UP, 1980.

Henderson, Harold G. *Haiku in English.* Rutland, VT: Charles E. Tuttle, 1967.

Higgins, Dick. *Pattern Poetry: Guide to an Unknown Literature.* Albany: State U of New York P, 1987.

Hirsch, Edward. *How to Read a Poem and Fall in Love with Poetry.* San Diego: Harcourt, 1999.

Kinzie, Mary. *A Poet's Guide to Poetry.* Chicago: U of Chicago P, 1999.

Wesling, Donald, and Eniko Bollobaś. "Free Verse." *The New Princeton Encyclopedia of Poetry and Poetics.* Ed. Alex Preminger and T. V. F. Brogan. Princeton, NJ: Princeton UP, 1993.

Wimsatt, W. K., and Monroe C. Beardsley. *Hateful Contraries: Studies in Literature and Criticism.* Louisville: U of Kentucky P, 1965.

6

Specialized Approaches to Interpreting Literature

LITERARY CRITICISM AND THEORY

Criticism before 1900. Before the twentieth century, there was little systematic attempt to interpret works of literature, to probe their meanings. Gerald Graff, in *Professing Literature,* his history of literary studies in higher education, says that before then there was a widespread "assumption that great literature was essentially self-interpreting and needed no elaborate interpretation" (20). Instead, students studied classical works such as *The Aeneid* and *The Odyssey* to learn Latin and Greek grammar. They used bits and pieces of literature in English, such as Mark Antony's funeral speech in *Julius Caesar,* for training in oratory (28, 41). Otherwise, people could not believe that "the literature in one's own language needed to be taught in formal classes instead of being enjoyed as part of the normal experience of the community" (19).

Even so, prior to the twentieth century, the investigation of the nature and value of literature had had a long and distinguished history, beginning with Plato and Aristotle and continuing into modern times with such figures as Sir Philip Sidney, John Dryden, Samuel Johnson, William Wordsworth, Samuel Taylor Coleridge, and Matthew Arnold. But their investigations focused primarily on evaluation, not interpretation. They explored what literature is and praised or condemned works that failed to meet whichever standards they deemed essential. In *The Republic,* to cite one extreme example, Plato condemned *all* literature because it stirs up the passions—lust, desire, pain, anger—rather than nurtures the intellect. At the end of the nineteenth century, however, universities began to include courses in modern literature, and teachers and writers began to give attention to interpreting literature.

Literary theory. Accompanying this shift in attitude was the growth of literary theory. In *Literary Theory: A Very Short Introduction* (1999), Jonathan Culler defines literary theory generally as "the systematic account of the nature of literature and of the methods for analyzing it" (1). Through the first half of the twentieth century, a handful of new theories influenced the interpretation and teaching of literature. The most important of these in the United States was New Criticism, whose methodology was practical and accessible. But with the discovery of French structuralism in the 1960s, new literary theories swamped the old ones and elicited an enormous body of writings. To get a sense of the scale of this output, compare the *MLA International Bibliography of Books and Articles on the Modern Languages and Literatures (MLAIB)* of 1960 to that of today. "MLA" stands for the Modern Language Association, the now huge organization for scholars of modern languages and literatures. Compared to the one-volume *MLAIB* of 1960, the present version consists of five titanic volumes accompanied by expensive and sophisticated computer software.

Resources for theory. This near-obsessive interest in literary interpretation and theory is cause for wonder. Right now there seems to be no end to it. "One of the most dismaying features of theory today," Culler says, "is that it is endless. It is not something that you could learn so as to 'know theory.' It is an unbounded corpus of writings which is always being augmented as the young and the restless, in critiques of the guiding conceptions of their elders, promote the contributions to theory of new thinkers and rediscover the work of older, neglected ones" (15). For those who come new to literary theory, Culler's book is an excellent place to begin. Rather than describe in detail the various theoretical approaches (New Criticism, structuralism, deconstruction, feminism, and so forth), Culler addresses the issues that theory since 1960 has taken up. There are numerous books that survey theories. Very readable are Raman Selden and Peter Widdowson's *A Reader's Guide to Contemporary Literary Theory* (1997) and Hans Bertens's *Literary Theory: The Basics* (2001). One that examines the usefulness of recent theories to interpretation is K. M. Newton's *Interpreting the Text: A Critical Introduction to the Theory and Practice of Literary Interpretation* (1990).

PLACES FOR INTERPRETATION

Taking our cue from Culler, we will briefly report on some of the influential theoretical approaches to highlight the "places" interpreters can look to find meaning in works of literature. So far, we have concentrated on the work itself—how we can use properties of literature and genres as avenues to meaning in individual works. An expanded version of the author/work/reader pattern, introduced in Chapter 1, provides a comprehensive diagram of all the places to look for meaning in literature.

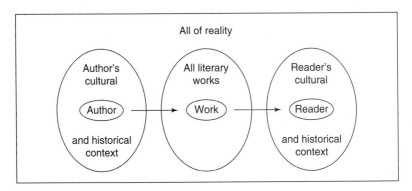

This diagram highlights four general sites of meaning. The first centers on the author, who begins the process of creation and communication. It includes the circumstances of the author's life (biography); the author's values, intentions, and methods of composition (the author as artist); and the events, patterns of life, and beliefs of the author's time (history). The second centers on the work. It encompasses the artistry and elements of the work (its form), the language of the work (its linguistic makeup), and the work's relationship to other works and literary practices (its intertextuality). The third centers on the reader. It includes the individual reader: his or her interests, reading skills, and knowledge. Included also are groups of readers, such as those who first read the work as well as those who read the work now. And, as with authors, it focuses on the influence of environment on readers. The final place is all of reality. This includes the work's connection to the world outside it, its "truth." Just as the work is surrounded by all of reality, so too are authors and readers, all of whom have their own understanding of "reality." Using what they know, authors incorporate aspects of reality in their works. In turn, readers, based on what they know, try to ascertain reality in works of literature.

Interpreters of literature typically deal with more than one of these sites of meaning. When we interpret a work of literature, for example, we may focus largely on the work itself, but we may also draw upon information about an author's life or about philosophical concepts of reality. M. H. Abrams, who in *The Mirror and the Lamp* (1953) originated the concept of sites of meaning, says that theoretical approaches almost always touch on more than one of these places, but most "exhibit a discernible orientation toward one only" (6). We will discuss theoretical approaches here according to which place they mainly illuminate. Since the work of literature is central to all attempts to interpret it, we will start with it.

THE WORK

Three theoretical approaches—New Criticism, structuralism, and deconstruction—demand concentrated study of the work of literature itself. Although all three insist that interpreters pay close attention to the details of individual works, structuralism and especially deconstruction are strong reactions against many of the assumptions of New Criticism. Closely related to the study of individual works is the study of how a work relates to other works, its *intertextuality*. In Chapter 2, we looked at one kind of intertextuality—authors' reliance on conventions and genres to create their own works. In this chapter, we will examine another approach to intertextuality: archetypal criticism.

Basic questions about meaning in individual works include the following:

❖ What meanings do elements within the work—characterization, plot, irony, setting, and so forth—suggest?
❖ What works are alluded to within the work? What meanings do those works suggest for this one?
❖ To what genre(s) does this work belong? What meanings associated with the genre(s) are present in this work?
❖ What meanings do repeated patterns—archetypes—convey in this work?

New Criticism

A product of the rise of Modernism, New Criticism was one of the twentieth century's first theories about interpreting literature. Although New Criticism began well before World War II, with the criticism of T. S. Eliot and I. A. Richards, it received its fullest expression after the war by such critics as John Crowe Ransom, W. K. Wimsatt, Allen Tate, Cleanth Brooks, and Robert Penn Warren. These and other New Critics published best-selling textbooks that established practical and easily understood ways of teaching and studying literature. These ways continue to influence the study of literature in higher education.

Definition of New Criticism.   The term *New Criticism* comes from the title of a book published by John Crowe Ransom in 1941, *The New Criticism*. Ransom surveyed the work of recent ("new") critics and thereby made clear some of his own critical principles. Other critics who agreed with Ransom came to be called the New Critics. The New Critics broke dramatically with the nineteenth-century emphasis on historical and biographical background. They held that understanding and appreciating a work of literature need have little or no connection with the author's intended meanings, with the author's life, or with the social and historical circumstances that may have influenced the author. Everything the reader needs to understand and appreciate a work is contained within the work itself.

Irony and unity.   The New Critics saw their method as "scientific." The work is a self-contained phenomenon made up of "physical" qualities—language and literary conventions (rhyme, meter, alliteration, plot, point of view, and so forth). These qualities can be studied in the same way a geologist studies a rock formation or a physicist the fragmentation of light particles. But some New Critics, like Cleanth Brooks, claimed that because of the metaphorical nature of literature, ideas in literature cannot be paraphrased, cannot be separated from the work's form. One can state what a work is "about" or summarize a work's themes, but a work's meaning is far more complex than such statements alone. Brooks argued that a work's complexity lies in its "irony"—its inclusion of "discordant" elements that clash and cause tension within the poem. Meaningful poetry "does not leave out what is apparently hostile to its dominant tone, and which, because it is able to fuse the irrelevant and discordant, has come to terms with itself and is invulnerable to irony." By "invulnerable to irony" he means "the stability of a context in which the internal pressures balance and mutually support each other" (732). Such a hard won stability and balance gives poems unity: The "poem is like a little drama. The total effect proceeds from all elements in the drama, and in a good poem, as in a good drama, there is no wasted motion and there are no superfluous parts" (730).

Evaluation of works. The New Critics used their theories to judge the quality of works of literature. Because they favored complex yet unified works, they downgraded works that seemed simple or those that lacked unity. They preferred "difficult" works that contained apparently illogical and troubling material. They approved of works that stayed away from social and historical subject matter and that dealt rather with private, personal, and emotional experience.

Influence of New Criticism. As a method for teaching and interpretation, New Criticism was highly appealing. The New Critics believed that the language of great works of literature was accessible to modern readers. They were confident that well-trained interpreters could analyze, understand, and evaluate works of literature. Since to them great literature was one of civilization's proudest achievements, they imbued literary criticism with a noble, even priestly quality. Their method of analyzing literature—using literary elements to reveal artistry and meaning—was easy to understand and even "democratic"; anyone could appreciate and interpret great literature once they learned how. Finally, their method excused interpreters from having to master biographical and historical background. They believed that all that was needed was a careful and thorough scrutiny of the works themselves.

Resources. Two influential New Critical essays are "The Intentional Fallacy" and "The Affective Fallacy," both by W. K. Wimsatt and Monroe Beardsley, contained in Wimsatt's *The Verbal Icon* (1954). A stimulating work of New Criticism is Cleanth Brooks's *The Well Wrought Urn* (1947). See especially Chapter 1 ("The Language of Paradox") and Chapter 11 ("The Heresy of Paraphrase").

Structuralism

A new approach. By the 1950s and 1960s, New Criticism had become the dominant theoretical approach that guided teaching and interpretation. New Critical textbooks, like those written by Cleanth Brooks and Robert Penn Warren, pervaded the classrooms. New Critical interpretations of literature filled the scholarly journals. College students who took introductory courses in literature were asked to learn the characteristics of fiction, drama, and poetry and tease out their implications from works published in anthologies. But at the peak of this dominance, a new generation of graduate students and teachers discovered structuralism, which had existed since the 1930s in Europe but whose theorists' works were not translated into English until the 1960s. Although structuralism shared some of the methods of New Criticism—notably an emphasis on close reading and attention to the particularities of the text—it was diametrically opposed to it in fundamental ways and took the teaching and inter- pretation of literature in new directions.

Saussure's theories of language.   Like New Criticism, *structural- ism* denied the value of historical, social, and biographical informa- tion, and concentrated on identifiable elements in works of literature. Unlike New Criticism, its theory and methodology were grounded in linguistics. Although some nineteenth-century thinkers anticipated structuralist principles, structuralism originated from the work of the Swiss linguist Ferdinand de Saussure (1857–1913). Early in the twen- tieth century, Saussure taught three innovative courses in linguistics. Because he left no notes on the content of these courses, his students pooled their notes and published a reconstruction of the courses called *Course in General Linguistics* (1916). This work is the basis of Saussure's fame and provides the theoretical underpinning of both structuralism and post-structuralism.

Saussure's key points about the nature of language broke new ground for studying literature. First, a language is a complete, self- contained system and deserves to be studied as such. Before Saussure, linguists investigated the history of languages (how lan- guages evolved and changed through time) and the differences among languages; for this kind of study, Saussure coined the word *diachronic* (literally "through time"). Saussure argued that, instead of the history of a language, linguists should also study how it functions in the pres- ent, how its parts interrelate to make up a whole system of communi- cation. This kind of study Saussure called *synchronic* ("at the same time"). Second, Saussure claimed that a language is a system of signs. He defined a *sign* as consisting of two things—a *signified* and *signifier.* The concept of an object—"tree"—is the signified. The word sound for the concept—*tree*—is the signifier. Third, Saussure held that the basic structure of language rests on differences between the sounds of words. The difference between the initial consonants of *path* and *math* gives both words meaning. The structure of language rests on binary oppositions like this one—sets of two words that have meaningful differences of sound.

Fourth, Saussure said that the connection between the sounds of a language system and the concepts they represent is completely arbitrary. Any sound, it does not matter which one, could represent the concept of a given thing. The sound for the concept "tree" varies from language to language, yet users of each language know that the sound represents (signifies) "tree." Fifth, any given language is self-contained. The signs that make up a language have no meaning outside the system of that language. Finally, Saussure distinguished between the whole system, which he called *langue* (French for "language"), and one person's use of the system, which he called *parole* (French for "word" or "speech"). *Langue* consists of everything that makes the system work, such as binary oppositions, words, syntax, and inflections. *Parole* consists of these same elements but with variations from user to user. Each speaker of a language uses the same system but does so in a slightly different way.

Structuralist literary criticism.   In the 1930s and 1940s, literary critics in Europe began applying Saussure's ideas and methods to the study of literature. This application took two different but often merging paths: literary criticism and cultural criticism. A term that describes both kinds of criticism is *semiotics,* the systematic study of signs. In most ways, the terms *structuralism* and *semiotics* are synonymous.

Structuralist literary critics attempt to show that literature is a form of language or that it functions like language. These critics saw the individual work of literature as similar to *parole,* and literary genres or literature in general as similar to *langue.* Just as linguists studied instances of *parole* in order to understand *langue,* literary critics studied works of literature in order to understand the system of signs that make up a genre or literature as a whole. They might study a Sherlock Holmes story in order to understand detective fiction, a specific poem in order to understand lyric poetry, a Shakespeare play in order to understand drama, a Louis L'Amour novel in order to understand westerns.

Stylistics.   One kind of structuralist literary criticism is *stylistics,* the study of the linguistic form of texts. Stylistics can deal with both prose and poetry, but has dealt mainly with poetry, particularly with the qualities of language that distinguish poetry from prose. Some stylistic critics claim that it is *only* qualities of language that distinguish poetry from prose. By analyzing individual poems, these critics attempt to identify those qualities.

Semiotics. Structuralists who study entire cultures attempt to understand a culture's sign systems. The study of signs is called *semiotics.* The most prominent practitioner of this kind of criticism is the French anthropologist Claude Lévi-Strauss. Lévi-Strauss claims that a culture is bound together by systems of signs and that these systems are like language. He uses Saussurian linguistics as a way of describing the "grammar" of these systems. All aspects of a culture—technology, religion, tools, industry, food, ornaments, rituals—form sign systems. The people of the culture are unaware of these systems, so the structural anthropologist's task is to bring them to light. Lévi-Strauss is perhaps best known for his study of myth. He examines multiple versions of individual myths in order to isolate their essential structural units. Although Lévi-Strauss applies his theories to the study of tribal cultures, other critics, like the Frenchman Roland Barthes, use Lévi-Strauss's approach to "psychoanalyze" modern society. They look for the unconscious sign systems that underlie all aspects of Western culture, including food, furniture, cars, buildings, clothing fashions, business, advertising, and popular entertainment.

Structuralist analysis of culture and literature often merges because literature can be considered an artifact of culture. Literature is a system of signs that can be studied for itself and for its place in a given culture. As a result, structuralist critics often shy away from complex and classic works and focus instead on popular literature. The Italian critic Umberto Eco writes essays on spy thrillers and comic book stories. He has even written a "semiotic" detective novel, *The Name of the Rose* (1983). Structuralist critics are also usually more interested in fitting a work within a culture or a tradition than in understanding the work itself.

Resources. Two readable book-length treatments of structuralism are Robert Scholes's *Structuralism in Literature: An Introduction* (1974) and Terence Hawkes's *Structuralism and Semiotics* (1977). Tzvetan Todorov's "The Grammar of Narrative" in *The Poetics of Prose* (1977) equates narrative structure to sentence structure. Umberto Eco's *The Role of the Reader: Explorations in the Semiotics of Texts* (1979) includes essays on Superman and James Bond. A collection of stylistic studies is *Linguistics and Literary Style,* edited by Donald C. Freeman (1970); see, for example, J. M. Sinclair's "Taking a Poem to Pieces."

Deconstruction

Deconstruction, the most influential form of post-structuralism, evolved from Saussure's theories of language. It became the most influential and eye-opening application of structuralism to the interpretation of literature. It accepts Saussure's analysis of language and uses his methodology to examine the language of literary works, but it concerns itself with the relationship between language and meaning. Deconstruction, in fact, offers a radical theory of reading that altogether rejects the certainty of meaning. The philosopher-critic who invented deconstruction is the Frenchman Jacques Derrida.

Deconstruction and structuralism. The basis of Derrida's radical skepticism is Saussure's distinction between signifier and signified. Before Saussure theorists of language maintained that words represent concrete objects. The word *tree* represents the object "tree." But Saussure questioned the pervasiveness of such one-to-one correspondences. Words, he said, refer not to objects but to "concepts," which are expressed by other words. It seems possible, then, that language, or at least parts of language, may not refer to anything in the sensuously apprehensible world. Saussure said that language is a self-contained system and that to function it does not need to reflect reality, it needs only to reflect itself. Signs gain meaning from other signs in the system, not necessarily from the real world. This possible separation between language and the world outside language (the "real" world) suggests that language molds human thought. Language, Terence Hawks says, possibly "constitutes the characteristic structure of human reality" (28).

Derrida concludes from Saussure's theories that there is a "gap" between signifier and signified. This gap blurs the meaning of the signifier so that we cannot know exactly what it refers to. Derrida coined the term *différance* to represent this ambiguity of language. The French verb *différer* means "to differ" and "to defer." Saussure based his concept of the structure of language on sound differences—binary oppositions—between words. The French term is *différence*. Derrida, however, seizes upon the other meaning of *différer* to show that certainty of meaning, certainty of connection between signified and signifier, is constantly deferred. His coinage is *différance*.

These two words, *différence* and *différance,* sound the same in French, which points to another of Derrida's concepts. Saussure emphasized the sound of language in his concept of its structure. Derrida, however, believes that the presence of people speaking a language creates the false illusion that secure connections exist between signified and signifier. This emphasis on the sound of language Derrida calls *phonocentrism.* Only in writing can the endless displacement of meaning, the "undecideability" and "free play" of meaning, be exposed. Derrida thus favors writing as a more revealing representation of language.

Implications of deconstruction.   Derrida's claim that meaning is constantly deferred in language has broad implications. He rejects, as Terence Hawkes says, the belief "that, in spite of our always fragmentary experience, somewhere there must exist a redeeming and justifying *wholeness,* which we can objectify in ourselves as the notion of Man, and beyond ourselves as the notion of Reality. This yearning underwrites and guarantees the belief that *necessary* connections exist between signifier and signified, and that these are ultimately locked in a 'meaningful,' wholly unbreakable, real-world-generating union" (146). Derrida claims that because language is our only means of knowing anything and because language is ambiguous, no such comforting notions exist.

Deconstruction and literary criticism.   Literary critics who utilize Derrida's ideas see literature as like language, a "text" that consists of an infinite chain of postponed connection between signified and signifier. A work of literature is a self-contained system that exists independently from the real world. As we read, we absorb this system with our consciousness, which Derrida maintains is itself made up of language. Reading is the confrontation of one language system (our consciousness) with another (the text). Recovering meaning from texts, then, is impossible because interpretations of a text never point to the real world but only to more language. Our interaction with the text makes us *think* we are moving toward meaning, but we never get there.

The purpose of deconstructive criticism is to expose the indeterminancy of meaning in texts. Derrida calls his critical method *deconstruction.* To "deconstruct" a work, the critic analyzes the text—especially its language—to show that whatever connection may seem to exist between the text and the real world is an illusion created by the author's clever manipulation of language. Whatever the author may have intended the work to mean or whatever a reader may think it means is always undercut by the ambiguity of the work's language. The gap between signifier and signified is symptomatic of a "space" of emptiness, nothingness, nonmeaning that lies at the heart of every text. The critic attempts to demonstrate that the presence of this space makes the text an "abyss" of limitless and contradictory meanings.

The appeal of deconstruction.   Deconstruction may seem disquieting for those who want to understand the meaning of literature. Without question, nihilism pervades Derrida's theory of language and literature. But when deconstruction became known in the United States and Great Britain in the 1970s, it seemed like a breath of fresh air to those who felt excluded by New Criticism. The New Critics' certainty about interpreting literature led them to downgrade many works and authors. Most of the New Critics—Brooks, Warren, Ransom, Tate—were from the American South and espoused traditional political and social values. But the next generation of critics came of age in the 1960s, a time of radical rethinking of social and political practices. They embraced deconstruction as a means of expanding the literary canon to include previously "marginalized" groups of authors, especially women and persons of color, as well as genres the New Critics denigrated or ignored. Semiotics further made interpreting popular culture, not just "high" culture, appealing.

Resources.   An accessible book-length study is Christopher Norris's *Deconstruction: Theory and Practice* (1982). The seminal text on deconstruction is Derrida's *Of Grammatology* (1976).

Archetypal Criticism

Archetypes.   Although the post-structuralists may seem extreme in claiming that works never connect with the real world, only with other works, they made critics aware of how reliant authors are on the conventions and genres of all literature. We have already discussed this kind of intertextuality in Chapter 2. Another approach to intertextuality is *archetypal criticism*. Northrop Frye, the preeminent advocate of archetypal criticism, defined *archetype* as "the recurring use of certain images or image clusters" in literature (*Critical Path,* 23). But, more broadly, archetypes can be defined as any repeated patterns in literature, whether of plot, character, themes, settings, or images.

The hero as archetype. An example of a literary archetype is the hero. As outlined by Joseph Campbell in *The Hero with a Thousand Faces* (1949), the hero's career has three main parts. In the first, the "Departure," heroes receive a "call to adventure." By a seeming accident, someone or something invites the hero into "an unsuspected world," into "a relationship with forces that are not rightly understood" (51). Often heroes receive supernatural aid from a "protective figure" who helps them in their adventures (69). In the second part of the hero's story, the "Initiation," heroes cross a dangerous "threshold" into a strange, fluid, dreamlike world where they undergo a succession of trials (77, 97). The climax of these trials is the hero's victory over all opposition. Sometimes this victory is accompanied by a mystical vision that exposes the life-creating energy of all existence (40–41). The third part of the hero's story is the "Return." Because of their victory, heroes now have a boon to bestow upon those left behind (30). The trip back to their homeland can be arduous, but once back they have a choice: they can withhold or bestow the boon. They also face the problem of integrating their transcendent experiences with the "banalities and noisy obscenities" of their old world (218).

The hero is one of numerous archetypal characters. Others include such figures as the scapegoat, the outcast, the earth mother, the femme fatale, the rebel, the cruel stepmother, the "spiritual" woman, the tyrannical father, the star-crossed lovers. These characters often find themselves in archetypal situations such as the quest, the initiation, the fall from innocence, death and rebirth, and the task. The more archetypal a work, the more it seems dominated by polarities, such as good versus evil, light versus darkness, water versus desert, heights versus depths.

Sources of archetypes. What is the source of archetypes? Where do they come from? Some critics say that archetypes are merely structural elements in literature. They do not come from anywhere except literature itself. Other critics, like Northrop Frye, agree that this might be so, but suggest also that archetypes exist in real life and are incorporated into literature as part of its meaning. In his best-known work, *Anatomy of Criticism* (1957), Frye attempts to show that all of literature is bound together by a structure of archetypes, which arise from human experiences, wishes, and needs. Another possible source of archetypes is the human psyche. The Swiss psychologist Carl Jung argued that archetypes exist in the human "collective unconscious." Jung accepted Freud's concept of the unconscious mind, but, whereas Freud held that each person's unconscious is unique, Jung argued that a part of the unconscious is linked by historical associations and communal "memories" to the unconscious minds of all people. To represent this phenomenon, he coined the phrase "collective unconscious." He believed that certain human products and activities—myth, symbols, ritual, literature—reproduced these memories in the form of "archetypes." Jung defined an *archetype* as any figure or pattern that recurred in works of the imagination from generation to generation. Still another source of archetypes is culture. Richard Slotkin, in his mammoth three-volume investigation of the influence of the frontier on American culture—*Regeneration Through Violence* (1973), *The Fatal Environment* (1985), and *Gunfighter Nation* (1992)—claims that numerous archetypes that influence American culture arose from the frontier experience. The most important of these, he says, is regeneration through violence, the concept that as a nation and as individuals, Americans must undergo violence in order to gain psychic wholeness and take possession of their rightful heritage. The "artifacts" of American culture—novels, films, legends, paintings, comic books, television shows—bear witness to this archetype's influence on American life. The title of the third volume—*Gunfighter Nation*—sums up Slotkin's belief about how this archetype continues to shape the American consciousness.

Literary criticism. What meanings do archetypes impart to works of literature? The task of the archetypal critic, Frye says, is to help readers see the "structures" of what they read by identifying literature's "organizing patterns of convention, genre and archetype" (*Critical Path* 24). Like any other structural element, archetypes are potential but not inevitable places of meaning. But those critics who see archetypes as linked to real life—to universal human experience, the human psyche, or culture—claim that archetypes import powerful ideas to works of literature, ideas that resonate subliminally and emotionally with readers. Archetypes are thus equivalent to *myth,* as defined here by Alan Watts: "Myth is to be defined as a complex of stories—some no doubt fact, and some fantasy—which, for various reasons, human beings regard as demonstrations of the inner meaning of the universe and of human life" (7). "A mythology," Slotkin says, "is a complex of narratives that dramatizes the world vision and historical sense of a people or culture, reducing centuries of experience into a constellation of compelling metaphors" (*Regeneration* 6). Archetypal criticism—sometimes called myth criticism—strives to locate those larger meanings in works of literature.

THE AUTHOR

Although not the only determiner of meaning in a literary work, authors are the most important. They choose the genres and conventions of their works. They craft their works to embody ideas. As readers, we are drawn to certain works because we like the way authors write—their style, values, and artistic techniques. Most theoretical approaches to literature manifest at least some interest in the author. Three that focus largely on either the author or the author's period are historical criticism, biographical criticism, and new historicism.

Basic questions about how an author's life and times affect the meaning of a work include the following:

❖ What facts about the author's life suggest ideas in the work? Did anything that happened to the author affect his or her themes or choice of subject matter?
❖ What was the author's worldview? Which of the author's beliefs seem reflected in this work?
❖ What commentary on the work did the author make? Does it point to ideas in the work?
❖ What worldview was typical of the author's time? What aspects of this worldview seem prevalent in this work? Does the author seem to accept or rebel against this worldview?
❖ How did people respond to the author's work? What ideas did they find in it?

Historical and Biographical Criticism

Historical criticism.   *Historical* and *biographical criticism* are closely related and received their intellectual impetus from nineteenth-century ideas about science. Historical critics believed they could illuminate works of literature by studying what gave birth to them: the intellectual and cultural environment from which they came, their sources and antecedents, authors' lives, authors' intentions, and authors' language. They believed that their approach was "scientific" because they were dealing with objective reality—historically verifiable facts—and were using a scientific method for collecting such facts.

Two French philosophers influenced historical and biographical criticism: Auguste Comte and especially Hippolyte Taine. Taine, in his *History of English Literature* (1863), held that all art is an expression of the environment and time in which the artist lived. Historical critics concentrated on authors they assumed were "great," not worrying much about why or what the works meant. A major emphasis of historical criticism was the historical periods and intellectual movements to which works belonged. Critics studied the conventions and ideas that characterized movements, such as blank verse during the Renaissance and an emphasis on free will during the Romantic period. They placed works within evolving traditions (the novel, Christian literature, allegory, political fiction, the epic) and compared them to the literature of other countries.

In higher education today, a prevalent manifestation of historical criticism is the literature survey course, which links literature to authors' lives, historical periods, and intellectual movements. Literary histories, such as the *Columbia Literary History of the United States* (1988) and *The Literary History of England* (1967), owe their methodology and format to historical criticism. Although the meaning of individual works of literature was not explicit in such venerable historical studies as E. M. W. Tillyard's *The Elizabethan World Picture* (1943), M. I. Finley's *The World of Odysseus* (1978), and A. O. Lovejoy's *The Great Chain of Being* (1936), meaning was implicit. These historical critics assumed that the ideas associated with a particular age were manifested in the works of the age.

Biographical criticism. Samuel Johnson was the first great biographical critic. His *Lives of the Poets* (1779, 1781) provided truthful accounts of authors' lives and astute assessments of their literary achievements. Biographical criticism became increasingly popular during the nineteenth and twentieth centuries and is still very much practiced. The assumption lying behind all literary biography is that the facts of authors' lives are important to their works. Some literary biographers make little overt connection between authors' lives and their works. But others, like the following, integrate facts about authors' lives with interpretations of their works: K. J. Fielding's *Charles Dickens: A Critical Introduction* (1964); F. W. Dupee's *Henry James: His Life and Writings* (1956); and Arthur Mizener's *The Far Side of Paradise: A Biography of F. Scott Fitzgerald* (1965).

Goals of historical and biographical criticism. The purpose of historical and biographical criticism is well summed up by Douglass Bush, himself the author of outstanding examples of historical criticism: "Since the great mass of great literature belongs to the past, adequate criticism must grow out of historical knowledge, cultural and linguistic, as well as out of intuitive insight. Every work must be understood on its own terms as the product of a particular mind in a particular setting, and that mind and setting must be re-created through all the resources that learning and the historical imagination can muster—not excluding the author's intention, if that is known. The very pastness of a work . . . is part of its meaning for us and must be realized to the best of our power" (8). If we do not pay attention to authors and their historical context, Bush says, we run the risk of anachronistic misreadings and misunderstandings. We may be limited in our ability to "re-create the outward and inward conditions in which a work of art was engendered, but unless we try, we cannot distinguish between its local and temporal and its universal and timeless elements, indeed we may not be able to understand some works at all" (8).

New Historicist Criticism

New versus "old" historicism.   New historicism emerged in the late 1970s as a "new" way to use history to understand and evaluate works of literature. It shares "old" historicism's belief that the historical culture from which a work comes helps us understand the work. It differs drastically from the older historicism in its beliefs about the nature of literature, the nature of history, the ability of people to perceive "reality," and the purpose of literary studies. Its sympathy for disadvantaged—"marginalized"—peoples gives it a political slant lacking in older historicism. This sympathy, along with its other beliefs and methods, has profoundly influenced other, more narrowly focused theoretical approaches such as feminist, Marxist, and ethnic criticism. Its breadth of inclusion has made new historicism highly visible today in the teaching and study of literature. The term *new historicism* applies to the American version of "cultural studies." The British version, called cultural materialism, is more overtly Marxist than new historicism, but both are heavily influenced by the French historian and philosopher Michel Foucault.

Cultures.   The key assumptions of new historicism are embedded in its understanding of several related concepts: culture, text, discourse, ideology, the self, and history. These concepts, in turn, establish the new historicist approach to the study of literature and are based on structuralist and deconstructionist theories of language. The first term, *culture,* is the most important. In an anthropological sense, "culture" is the total way of life of a particular society—its language, economy, art, religion, and attachment to a location. For new historicists, culture is also a collection of codes that everyone in a society shares and that allows them to communicate, create artifacts, and act. These codes include not just language but every element of a culture—literature, dress, food, rituals, and games.

Text. As a web of sign systems, culture is thus "textual." A *text*, traditionally defined, is a written document that employs a symbolic system (words, mathematical symbols, images, musical notation). The structuralists expand "text" to mean any system of codes. The poststructuralists go further by claiming that because everything we know is filtered through "language," *everything* is text. "There is nothing outside the text," Derrida says. New historicists accept the structuralist concept of text but reject the deconstructionist concept that people cannot see the texts that surround them. Yes, they say, cultures consist of "texts," "discourses," and "ideologies," but people can analyze these texts and expose their weaknesses.

Discourse. By *discourse*, the structuralists mean any system of signs, whether verbal or nonverbal. "Discourse," then, is analogous to language (Saussure's *langue*) and "text" to specific uses of language *(parole)*. Foucault claims that groups of people, such as doctors, lawyers, priests, and athletes, create their own discourses. Each discourse has its own unique "discursive practice"—word choice, sentence structure, bodily movements, prejudices, rhetorical forms, and "rules" about where and when to use the discourse. Foucault claims that discourses are "political": People with power—social, economic, political, or artistic—use discourse to manipulate other people and maintain their own power.

Ideology. *Ideology* is a system of beliefs that governs a group's actions, its view of reality, and its assumptions about what is "normal" and "natural." Ideology is communicated by discourse and represented by texts. New historicists typically see ideology in political terms. One group of people unfairly imposes its ideology upon others, devaluing and exploiting those who fail to fit its definitions of the "normal" and "natural." Power elites can be persons within a society—wealthy persons, politicians, white people, males—or whole societies, such as countries that colonize and impose their ideology upon other regions. When an ideology becomes so pervasive that most people are unaware of its influence, it becomes "hegemonic." People assume that it represents the way things really are. However, no ideology is comprehensive enough to extend fair and equal treatment to all people. Thus, some people are "marginalized" and made vulnerable to exploitation.

The self. If texts, discourse, and ideology are so dominant in society, how does the individual, the "self," fit in? New historicists see the *self* as controlled by cultural codes and nearly blind to their existence. The self is a "subject." Like the subject of a sentence, it performs actions and relates to "objects" (physical things, other people, literary texts). But the self is also passive, "subject to" culture, discourse, and ideology. For this reason, people's ability to understand history is limited. They cannot see that *history*—the study and recounting of the past—is a social construct. Historians, Foucault says, can never know with certainty which events caused other events or which events are important. Human events are filled with inconsistencies, irregularities, and singularities that resist rational understanding. Historians may believe they are telling coherent stories about past events, but such constructs are always false. Even worse, to enhance their power, power elites create "official" histories, such as those taught in school and recounted in textbooks.

Concept of "literature." The new historicist approach to literary study emerges from all of these concepts. Its beliefs about three things—literature, the author, and the reader—help distinguish it from other theoretical approaches. New historicists claim that *literature* is merely a "text" indistinguishable in nature from all the other texts that constitute a culture. The concept "literature" is "socially constructed"; every society decides what "literature" is and what its conventions are, and these definitions always vary from society to society and age to age. Equally relative are judgments about literary value. No single author's works are better than those of other authors, no single work is better than others, no one culture's works are better than those of other cultures. Rather, *all* texts, literary and otherwise (including "popular" texts such as television shows, advertisements, and drugstore romances), are worthy of study.

Author and reader. The *author*, for the new historicists, is far less noble and autonomous than in other approaches. Like everyone else, authors are "subjects" manufactured by culture. A culture "writes" an author who, in turn, transcribes cultural codes and discourses into literary texts. Authors' intentions about the form and meaning of their work merely reflect cultural codes and values. Likewise, culture "programs" the *reader* to respond to its codes and forms of discourse.

When readers read works of literature, they respond automatically to the codes embodied by them.

Literary criticism.   Not all new historicists are so deterministic and relativistic as this description would indicate. Some reject Foucault's pessimism about a person's ability to understand historical reality, to read texts objectively, and to make changes in society. However, new historicists do tend to share beliefs about the purposes of literary study. First, they believe that literature must be studied within a cultural context. Old-style historicists see historical facts mainly as a means to clarify ideas, allusions, language, and details in literature. New historicists believe that literature *is* history, is "enmeshed" in history. When new historicists study literature, they examine such things as how the work was composed, what the author's intentions were, what events and ideas the work refers to, how readers have responded to the work, and what the work means for people today. They draw upon many disciplines—anthropology, sociology, law, psychology, history—to show what role literature has played in history, from the author's time to the present.

Second, new historicists focus on literature as cultural text. They study the relationship between literature and other texts, including nonliterary and popular texts. They identify the codes that constitute literary discourse and ascertain how people use such discourse to communicate with one another and to comment on society.

Third, new historicists scrutinize the relationship of literature to the power structures of society. They want to show how literature serves, opposes, and changes the wishes of the power elites and therefore what ideologies literature supports or undermines. Finally, many new historicists see criticism itself as an "intervention" in society. By marking literature's cultural roles, its ideologies, its effects, and the biases readers have brought to it, new historicists aspire to diminish the injustices of race, class, and gender.

Resources.   Since new historicism is a fairly new critical approach to literature, its concepts and methods continue to evolve. Some general studies include Jerome McGann's *Historical Studies and Literary Criticism* (1985) and Harold Veeser's *The New Historicism* (1989). Some of the best-known new historicist criticism has focused on Renaissance literature, such as *Political Shakespeare: New Essays in Cultural Materialism* (1985), edited by Jonathan Dollimore and Alan Sinfield, and Stephen Greenblatt's *Renaissance Self-fashioning from More to Shakespeare* (1980).

In *Orientalism* (1978), Edward Said offers a "post-colonial" version of new historicism. He argues that Western culture has fabricated a distorted and unfair discourse about the East, manifested in countless works of literature and popular culture. Another post-colonial author is the Nigerian Chinua Achebe, who eloquently attacks the racism in Joseph Conrad's *Heart of Darkness* in "An Image of Africa: Racism in Conrad's *Heart of Darkness.*" As for Michel Foucault, many of his works are excerpted in *The Foucault Reader* (1985). David R. Shumway's *Michel Foucault* (1989) and Lois McNay's *Foucault: A Critical Introduction* (1994) are succinct critical overviews of Foucault's work and thought.

THE READER

As the "receiver" of works of literature, readers complete them. Their task is to make sense of them—to determine why they like the works and what ideas rest in them. Many theoretical approaches—historical criticism, New Criticism, structuralism, deconstruction—assume that readers are the same in their ability to understand literature. Any well-trained reader, they maintain, can perceive the properties of literature. But other approaches suggest that readers actually contribute to the meaning of works. In this section, we will look at the most notable of these approaches, reader-response criticism.

Basic questions about how readers find meaning in a work include the following:

❖ How do interpretations of the work vary from reader to reader? What beliefs and experiences lead readers to their interpretations?
❖ How have your own interpretations of the work varied from different times you have read it? What accounts for the difference?
❖ How have interpretations of the work differed from one historical period to another?
❖ What do you find appealing or unappealing about the work?
❖ What in your own life leads you to your interpretations of the work?

Reader-Response Criticism

Importance of the reader. *Reader-response criticism* studies the interaction of reader with text. Reader-response critics hold that the text is incomplete until it is read. Each reader brings something to the text that completes it and that makes each reading different. Reader-response critics vary on what that "something" is. Recent psychoanalytic critics, such as Jacques Lacan and Norman Holland, say that the something is the unconscious. Deconstructionist critics say that it is the "language" that constitutes the conscious mind. New historicist critics say that it is the ideology of the dominant culture. All agree that the text has no life of its own without the reader.

Of all the post–World War II movements in literary theory, reader-response criticism perhaps most successfully challenges the dominance of New Criticism in the university classroom. It borrows methodology from New Criticism, structuralism, and post-structuralism, but rejects their contention that the work must be studied in isolation from its context. Context—historical, biographical, cultural, psychoanalytic—is relevant to the understanding of the text. Reader-response criticism furthermore rejects the deconstructionist claim that texts are meaningless. Texts may be incomplete in themselves, but the reading of them makes them potentially reflective of the real world—or at least the reader's experience of the real world.

Gaps in works of literature. Some reader-response critics, most notably the German critic Wolfgang Iser, argue that works contain "gaps"—not because of the slippage between signifier and signified but because of the incompleteness of works. Authors always leave something unsaid or unexplained and thus invite readers to fill the resulting spaces with their own imaginative constructs. Iser claims, therefore, that many equally valid interpretations of a work are possible. Interpretations of a work will vary from person to person and even from reading to reading. Critics who agree with Iser often attempt to study how readers fill the gaps in works. These critics are more interested in mapping the process of reading than in explaining individual works.

Interpretive communities. Perhaps the most prominent group of reader-response critics focuses on how biographical and cultural contexts influence the interpretation of texts. These critics argue that reading is a collective enterprise. The American critic Stanley Fish states that a reader's understanding of what "literature" is and what works of literature mean is formed by "interpretive communities"—groups to which readers belong. These groups could be small (a circle of friends) or large (a region or cultural entity like "Western civilization"). Fish rejects the idea that a text has a core of meaning that everyone in any age would accept. Rather, shared understandings of a text's meaning come from the beliefs of a community of readers, not from the text. Each reader's preconceptions actually "create" the text. If, for example, a reader believes that a miscellaneous collection of words is a religious poem, the reader will perceive it as a religious poem. If a reader believes that the work fits a particular theory, the reader will find facts in the work to support that theory. The theory, in a sense, "creates" the facts.

Resources. Because of the influence and provocative nature of reader-response criticism, writings about it abound. *The Reader in the Text: Essays on Audience and Interpretation,* edited by Susan R. Suleiman and Inge Crosman (1980) provides an introduction to reader-response criticism as well as essays by prominent critics. Stanley Fish's *Is There a Text in This Class?: The Authority of Interpretive Communities* (1980) is a collection of lively essays.

ALL OF REALITY

As we said in Chapter 2, one of the pleasures of reading literature is noticing its reflection of reality, its claims to truth. Literary theorists vary in their faith that human beings can do this. The New Critics and traditional historicists were strongly confident that readers can do so. The deconstructionists are so skeptical about "truth" that, for them, all knowledge seems uncertain and relative. Most theoretical approaches make at least minimal claims about the nature of reality and urge readers to rely on those claims to interpret literature. But some approaches make their understanding of truth the sole or major basis for reading literature. No matter what the author may have intended, they examine works of literature for signs of their own version of truth. Three examples of such reality-based approaches are Marxist criticism, psychological criticism, and feminist and gender criticism.

Basic questions about making a connection between a work and the real world include the following:

❖ How would different theories about the nature of reality change the interpretation of the work? For example, would one's religious beliefs—Muslim, Christian, Jewish, Buddhist—cause one to interpret the work differently?

❖ What have you learned about "reality" from the work—things you did not know before you read it?

❖ What are your own standards for assessing the "truth" in a work?
❖ What direct statements about reality does the work make?

Marxist Criticism

Early Marxist critics. Fully developed *Marxist criticism* appeared early in the twentieth century, especially in the 1930s during the Great Depression. This "socialist" criticism applauded literature that depicted the difficulties of the poor and downtrodden, especially when they struggled against oppressive capitalist bosses. Examples of literature with such strong "proletarian" elements are works by Carl Sandburg, Émile Zola, Maxim Gorky, Charles Dickens, Richard Wright, John Steinbeck, Theodore Dreiser, and John Dos Passos. Early Marxist critics approved of a socialist solution to the problems of the oppressed and judged the quality of works on the basis of their Marxist orientation. Granville Hicks's *The Great Tradition: An Interpretation of American Literature Since the Civil War* (1935) is a still-readable example of early Marxist criticism.

Recent critics. Since World War II, a new generation of critics has infused Marxist criticism with renewed vigor. An example is the Hungarian critic Georg Lukacs, who argues that literature should re-flect the real world. Lukacs does not mean that literature should be a mirror image of society by, for example, giving detailed descriptions of its physical contents or its patterns of behavior. Rather, literature should represent the economic tensions in society as described in Marx's writings. Ironically, for Lukacs, works that accurately repre-sent the real world may be less "real" than works that emphasize themes (ideas) over description. Lukacs believes that literature might even have to distort reality in order to represent the "truth" about so-ciety. To show the economic struggles caused by capitalism, for exam-ple, an author might have to create character types one would never meet in real life. Lukacs, therefore, prefers the novels of Balzac to those of Flaubert because, even though Balzac's plots and characters are less plausible than Flaubert's, Balzac reveals the economic pitfalls of capitalism as Marx saw them.

Most recently, Marxist criticism, like much late-twentieth-century literary theories, have been strongly influenced by structural-ism. Structuralist Marxism overlaps with new historicism (described above) and is often indistinguishable from it. Structuralist Marxists see authors and readers as enmeshed in a system of signifying codes.

Authors and readers are shaped and determined by these codes. Although taken together the codes have no overall coherence, all are connected in some way to economic forces. Most people living in a society ascribe to its *ideology,* the false ideas about society's purposes and coherence promulgated by the power elites. Even though people are molded by society, they can nonetheless critique its ideology and change society for the better.

Resources. The purpose of Marxist's literary criticism is to expose how works of literature represent dominant ideologies. Some Marxist critics, like Louis Althusser, believe that literature helps readers see the contradictions and fault lines in ideology. Others, like Terry Eagleton, hold that literature furthers ideology by making it seem attractive and "natural." Eagleton's *Marxism and Literary Criticism* (1976) provides an overview of recent Marxist criticism. His *Literary Theory: An Introduction* (1983) surveys modern critical theory from a Marxist point of view. See also Althusser's essay "A Letter on Art."

Psychological Criticism

Freud's influence. *Psychological criticism* applies modern psychological theories to authors and their works. Because Sigmund Freud's psychoanalytic theories dominated the field of psychology during the first half of the twentieth century, psychological critics found his ideas especially fruitful for interpreting literature. Although not all of Freud's ideas relate to literature, three seemed pertinent to early Freudian critics: the dominance of the unconscious mind over the conscious, the expression of the unconscious mind through symbols (most notably in dreams), and the primacy of sexuality as a motivating force in human behavior. These three ideas are related. Freud believed that sexual drives reside in the unconscious, that the conscious mind represses them, and that unconscious symbols usually represent this repressed sexual energy.

Early Freudian critics saw literature as a kind of "dream" and thus a source of insight into the authors themselves. Using works of literature as symbolic representations of an author's subconscious, Freudian critics created psychological portraits of authors. An example is Marie Bonaparte's *The Life and Works of Edgar Allan Poe: A Psychoanalytic Interpretation* (1949). Early Freudian critics also used psychoanalytic principles to analyze characters in works of literature. They looked upon characters as having motivations, conflicts, desires, and inclinations similar to those of real people. They sought psychological clues to the makeup of literary characters, especially the unconscious symbolic expressions found in dreams and repeated patterns of behavior. In Eugene O'Neill's *Long Day's Journey Into Night,* for example, whenever Mary Tyrone raises her hands to her hair, she unconsciously expresses anxiety about her wrecked youth, health, and innocence. Psychological critics were also drawn to works that are themselves dreamlike, such as Lewis Carroll's *Alice in Wonderland,* or that contain accounts of characters' dreams.

Authors themselves often imported psychological ideas to their works. Eugene O'Neill, D. H. Lawrence, Tennessee Williams, and many others were well-read in Freudian psychology. Some writers employed structural devices based on psychological theories. Examples are the *stream of consciousness* technique, which conforms to William James's ideas about the workings of the conscious mind, and the surrealistic technique, which conforms to Freud's ideas about the undisciplined unconscious. Examples of stream-of-consciousness narration are James Joyce's *Portrait of the Artist as a Young Man* and *Ulysses,* William Faulkner's *The Sound and the Fury,* T. S. Eliot's "The Love Song of J. Alfred Prufrock," Virginia Woolf's *To the Lighthouse,* and Eugene O'Neill's *Strange Interlude.* Examples of surrealism are James Joyce's *Finnegans Wake* and the fiction of Franz Kafka.

Recent criticism. Recent psychological critics continue to find Freud's theories a rich source of ideas about literature but, whereas earlier critics focused on authors and characters, recent critics have turned their attention to readers and texts. The critic Norman Holland, for example, argues that readers' psyches respond subconsciously to certain aspects of works of literature. The reader in effect "makes" the text, so that the text is different for every reader. Like Holland, the French critic Jacques Lacan posits ideas about how readers respond to literary texts. Lacan combines Freud's theories of the unconscious with Saussurian linguistics. He holds that the human psyche is made up of language. Our conscious and subconscious minds are born into language, a system of signifiers. From infancy to adulthood, we grow toward what we think is a secure and coherent identity. But at the heart of the psyche is an unbridgeable gap between signifier and signified. As a result, our psyche is never fully coherent, our identity never stable. His most famous application of this theory to literature is a long essay on Edgar Allan Poe's "The Purloined Letter." Lacan claims that the missing letter, which the detective Dupin has been commissioned to find, is equivalent to the signifier. But because it is missing it is a "symbol only of an absence" (Lacan, 38). It stands for the "lack" or emptiness that lies within all of us.

Resources.   A well-known work of early psychological criticism is Ernest Jones's *Hamlet and Oedipus* (1949), in which Jones, a psychiatrist, argues that Hamlet's problems stem from Oedipal conflicts. An anthology of psychological criticism is *Literature and Psychoanalysis,* edited by Edith Kurzweil and William Phillips (1983). *The Purloined Poe,* cited in the previous paragraph, features psychoanalytic readings of Poe's story "The Purloined Letter."

Feminist and Gender Criticism

Influence of feminist criticism.   Feminist and gender criticism have much in common with reader-response and new historicist criticism, especially with critics who, like Stanley Fish, believe that interpretations of literature are influenced by communities of readers. We include it here under "All of Reality" because it bases its interpretations on ideas about the nature of females and female experience. With the rise of feminism in the 1950s and 1960s, feminist critics claimed that, over the years, men had controlled the most influential interpretive communities. Men decided which conventions made up "literature" and judged the quality of works. Men wrote the literary histories and drew up the lists of "great" works—the literary canon. Because works by and about women were omitted from the canon, female authors were ignored, and female characters misconstrued.

Since the 1960s, feminist literary critics have successfully challenged these circumstances. Far more women now teach, interpret, evaluate, and theorize about literature than ever before. Previously neglected works such as Zora Neale Hurston's *Their Eyes Were Watching God* (1937), Kate Chopin's *The Awakening* (1899), Charlotte Perkins Gilman's "The Yellow Wallpaper" (1892), and Rebecca Harding Davis's *Life in the Iron-Mills* (1861) are now widely read. Certain literary genres practiced by women, such as diaries, journals, and letters, have gained more respect. Numerous anthologies, literary histories, and interpretive studies explore women's contributions to literature. Recently, however, a new movement, "gender studies," has evolved out of feminist studies in order to address broader issues; notably, the nature of both femininity and masculinity, the differences within each sex, and the literary treatment of men and homosexuals. Gender studies "complicate" feminist studies because, although they share many interests, they are not exactly the same. Both, however, are political in that they argue for the fair representation and treatment of persons of all "genders."

First stage. A survey of the history of feminist and gender criticism helps spotlight their concerns. The first stage of feminist criticism began with two influential books: Simone de Beauvoir's *The Second Sex* (1949) and Kate Millet's *Sexual Politics* (1970). Both authors criticized the distorted representation of women by well-known male authors. Their work laid the foundation for the most prevalent approach of this stage, the "images of women" approach. Following de Beauvoir and Millet, feminist critics called attention to the unjust, distorted, and limited representation ("images") of females in works of literature, especially works authored by males. They celebrated realistic representations of women and brought to light neglected works by and about women. They sought to expose the "politics" of self-interest that led people to create stereotypical and false images of women.

Second stage. In the second stage of feminist criticism, beginning in the early 1970s, critics shifted away from works by males to concentrate on works by females. Elaine Showalter, a prominent critic from this period, called this approach "gynocriticism." Especially influential was the work of French critics such as Luce Irigaray, Julia Kristeva, and Hélène Cixous. Their criticism, called *écriture féminine* (female writing), argued for an "essential" (biological, genetic, psychological) difference between men and women that causes women to think and write differently from men. Gynocritics urged women to become familiar with female authors and to discover their own female "language," a language that supposedly enters the subconscious before the "patriarchal" language of the dominant culture. They tried to delineate a female poetics, a use of literary conventions and genres that seems typically "female." Some critics based feminist poetics on the possible connection between writing and the female body. Because women's bodies have more fluids than men's, they argued, women's writing is more "fluid." It is less structured, less unified, more inclusive of many points of view, less given to neat endings, and more open to fantasy than writing by men. It rejects or undermines the "marriage plot" and the "happy ending," in which a strong female protagonist "capitulates" to a male by marrying him. Female poetics seeks to understand why female authors tend to favor certain genres (lyric poetry, novel, short story, tale, letters, diaries, memoirs) over others (epic, martial romance, drama, satire).

Third stage.   The third stage of feminist criticism rebelled against the "essentialist" assumptions of gynocriticism and is closely allied with new historicism in its focus on the cultural creation of identity. Gayle Rubin, in two influential essays—"The Traffic in Women" (1975) and "Thinking Sex" (1984)—distinguishes between "sex" and "gender." Whereas *sex* is the biological difference between males and females, *gender* is the cultural difference. Culture determines the traits and behavior that set masculinity apart from femininity and rules on "normal" and "natural" gender distinctions. Western culture, for example, has seen women as passive rather than active, irrational rather than rational, subjective rather than objective, at home rather than at "work," spiritual rather than material, and impractical rather than practical. It has ruled that certain kinds of behavior are "abnormal" and "unnatural" for females to practice, such as pursuing careers, doing construction work, being pastors or priests, wearing "male" clothes, or being assertive. Such gender distinctions, feminist critics claim, are arbitrary and almost always give women less power, status, and respect than men. In one sense, the feminist focus on gender is deterministic: Many women are "trapped" by the gender traits assigned to them by culture. In another sense, however, it offers hope. Culture, unlike biology, can be changed—through education, social action, and politics.

Gender criticism.   All three of these "stages" of feminist criticism have overlapped and coexisted. They continue to be practiced. But the focus on gender in the third stage led not only to a new stage of feminist criticism, it also helped to establish the broader movement of gender criticism. Until the mid-1980s, many feminist critics assumed that all women were the same in their biological nature, their gender traits, their shared history of oppression, and their aspirations. Most feminist critics, furthermore, wrote from the perspective of an elite group of people: women who were Western, politically liberal, middle class, and highly educated. Beginning around 1985, some feminist critics challenged these assumptions and this perspective. Feminist critics, they said, should look at the many ways in which women differ from one another. Factors other than gender, they said, give females identity. These factors include such things as race, ethnic background, and socioeconomic circumstances. Critics began studying the literary representation of women in minority cultures, in non-Western cultures, at various economic levels, and in different work situations.

They began examining ways females themselves marginalize or "erase" other females. Perhaps most important, they began to pay attention to sex and gender differences among women, especially between heterosexuals and homosexuals.

Foucault. Gender criticism, perhaps because it is so new, remains a nebulous, difficult-to-define approach to the study of literature. It covers almost anything having to do with "gender," including feminist criticism, theories of cultural influence, and crimes such as sexual abuse. One of the most important aspects of gender criticism is its exploration of the literary treatment of homosexuality. As with new historicism, the theorist who most influences gender studies is Michel Foucault. The first volume of his three-volume study *The History of Sexuality* (1976) states his basic ideas about sexuality. The Western concept of "sexuality," Foucault maintains, is not a universal category but was invented in the late nineteenth century. Sexuality in the modern West is not innate or biological but is instead a matrix of concepts created by society. Society, in other words, "constructs" sexuality. These concepts constitute an "ideology" that benefits people in power, most notably bourgeois capitalists. Like all ideologies, this one is manifested in discourses such as religion, science, politics, medicine, and literature.

Some gender critics disagree with Foucault's heavy emphasis on cultural determinism. They believe that sexual identity, including homosexuality, results from biological rather than cultural causes. Gay criticism (which deals with men) and lesbian criticism (which focuses on females) at first espoused homosexuality as no less "natural" and "normal" than heterosexuality. Gay and lesbian "pride" meant coming out of the closet, accepting a common identity, and joining the struggle against homophobia. Gay and lesbian critics studied the works and lives of authors who were admitted homosexuals and bisexuals or who seemed to have suppressed homosexual tendencies. They sought to expose the politics of gender in society and literature—how certain groups manipulate concepts of gender for their own benefit.

Queer theory. But queer theory, a new and still evolving branch of gay and lesbian criticism, calls into question the "essentialist" concepts of gender held by earlier gay and lesbian critics. As Annamarie Jagose (in *Queer Theory: An Introduction*) says, instead of holding that homosexuality, or any sexuality, is the same for everyone, queer theory embraces the post-structuralist notion that all meanings, including sexual identity, are unstable: "within poststructuralism, the very notion of identity as a coherent and abiding sense of self is perceived as a cultural fantasy rather than a demonstrable fact" (82). Foucault's belief that sexuality is "not an essentially personal attribute but an available cultural category" (79) has greatly influenced queer theory. But perhaps even more influential is Judith Butler's argument (in *Gender Trouble*) that sexuality is "performitive," is based on behaviors we learn from culture. "Performing" these behaviors constructs our sexual identity. The main goals of queer theory seem to be to describe such "performances" and to challenge the validity of all "normal" identities, not just sexual but racial, ethnic, and national (99).

Resources.   Perhaps the best place to begin reading feminist criticism is with an anthology of essays such as *The New Feminist Criticism: Essays on Women, Literature, and Theory* (1985), edited by Elaine Showalter. Ellen Moers's *Literary Women* (1976); Sandra Gilbert and Susan Gubar's *The Madwoman in the Attic: The Woman Writer and the Nineteenth-Century Literary Imagination* (1979); and Kate Millett's *Sexual Politics* (1970), mentioned above, are among the best examples of "images of women" criticism. Virginia Woolf's *A Room of One's Own* (1929) and Hélène Cixous's "The Laugh of the Medusa" (1976) are well-known examples of gynocriticism. Gayle Rubin's essays, mentioned above, and Elaine Showalter's edited collection, *Speaking of Gender* (1989), represent the shift of interest toward gender. Two texts that deal with the broadening of feminist criticism are Barbara Smith's "Toward a Black Feminist Criticism" (1975) and *Wild Women in the Whirlwind: Afra-American Culture and the Contemporary Literary Renaissance,* edited by Joanne Braxton and Andree Nicola McLaughlin (1989). *The Gay and Lesbian Literary Heritage* (1995), edited by Claude J. Summers, is a one-volume encyclopedia featuring articles on authors, terms, and theoretical approaches. *The Gay and Lesbian Studies Reader,* edited by Henry Abelove (1993), is an anthology of essays. Eve Kosofsky Sedgwick's *Between Men: English Literature and Male Homosocial Desire* (1985) deals with heterosexuality and homosexuality in literature before the twentieth century. Judith Butler's *Gender Trouble: Feminism and Popular Culture* (1990) develops her concept of sexual identity as "performitive." For works by and about Michel Foucault, see the discussion of new historicism.

Works Cited

Abrams, M. H. *The Mirror and the Lamp: Romantic Theory and the Critical Tradition.* New York: Norton, 1958.

Brooks, Cleanth. "Irony as a Principle of Structure." *Literary Opinion in America.* Ed. Morton Zabel. Vol. II. Gloucester, MA: Peter Smith, 1968. 729–41.

Bush, Douglass. "Literary History and Literary Criticism." *Literary History and Literary Criticism,* Ed. Leon Edel. New York: New York UP, 1965.

Campbell, Joseph. *The Hero with a Thousand Faces.* New York: World, 1949.

Culler, Jonathan. *Literary Theory: A Very Short Introduction.* New York: Oxford UP, 1999.

Frye, Northrop. *The Critical Path.* Bloomington: Indiana UP, 1971.

Graff, Gerald. *Professing Literature: An Institutional History.* Chicago: U of Chicago P, 1987.

Hawkes, Terence. *Structuralism and Semiotics.* Berkeley: U California P, 1977.

Jagose, Annamarie. *Queer Theory: An Introduction.* New York: New York UP, 1996.

Lacan, Jacques. "Seminar on 'The Purloined Letter.'" *The Purloined Poe: Lacan, Derrida, and Psychoanalytic Reading.* Ed. John P. Muller and William J. Richardson. Baltimore: Johns Hopkins UP, 1988.

Slotkin, Richard. *Regeneration Through Violence.* Hanover, MA: Wesleyan UP, 1973.

Watts, Alan. *Myth and Ritual in Christianity.* New York: Vanguard, 1954.

PART TWO

Writing about Literature

7

Writing about Literature

WHY WRITE ABOUT LITERATURE?

The answer to this question rests upon two considerations: your purpose and your audience. You may be so enthusiastic about a work that you e-mail friends, urging them to read it. Or you may be so confused by a work that you write down your thoughts just to clarify them for yourself. Or you may be so excited about your insights into a work that you want to share them with others. The common characteristic of such writings is that they require interpretation. Whoever your audience may be, they want to understand the works you write about. As a writer, your aim is to help them do so.

HOW CAN YOU WRITE ABOUT LITERATURE?

The essay. Writing about literature can take many forms, such as informal jottings, meant only for yourself; effusions of praise or condemnation; and even book-length studies of complex interpretive problems. The kind of writing we emphasize in this book is the essay about literature. An *essay* is a piece of writing that has the following characteristics:

1. Relative brevity—from about two to fifty pages.

2. Formality. It does not have to be stuffy and stilted, but it follows certain forms that have become conventional. It adheres, for ex-

ample, to rules of usage—punctuation, spelling, syntax, diction—characteristic of mainstream publications (newspapers, magazines, and books). It has a thesis that unifies the whole essay. It follows an organizational pattern that emphasizes intellectual coherence.

3. A "serious" audience, persons who care about the subject and will take time to consider what the author has to say.

4. Persuasiveness. Its purpose is to persuade readers that the author's ideas are worthy of consideration.

5. Give and take between author and readers. It usually responds to others who have written or spoken on the topic and assumes that its readers can talk back.

6. Argumentation. Although in common usage *argument* means a heated exchange between angry people, for writing it means reasoned discussion. Essays are "argumentative." They develop a line of thought (a logically related series of claims), they support a thesis and related claims with evidence, and they organize claims and evidence coherently and logically.

The essay is a versatile and elastic genre, applicable not just to literature but to all kinds of subject matter and circumstances. Take, for example, the crime scene we mentioned in Chapter 1. You, the detective, have examined the scene, sifted through the evidence, and decided who is guilty. Now you have to tell people your conclusions. Your "telling" could, of course, be aloud, but if you are like most police detectives, you will have to write it out as an essay. It may be called something else—a report, say—but it will have the characteristics of an essay: a thesis (so-and-so did the deed) and an orderly presentation of claims and evidence that support the thesis (*because* of what I learned at the crime scene and elsewhere, I conclude that so-and-so is guilty). Your essay's audience will be all those who must rely on it to render justice: other police officers, the district attorney, the defending attorney, the judge, the jury.

Or consider another scenario. For a year, you have worked amazingly well in a new job, but your immediate supervisor threatens to fire you. To keep your job, you write a letter to your supervisor's boss. Although this will not be called an essay, it really is. It will argue a thesis—that you have done outstanding work and should retain your job. You will defend your thesis with claims about your successes and with specific evidence to support your claims. The outcome, we can hope, is that your supervisor will be fired, not you.

The essay as communication. In both of these examples, we can see a pattern of communication similar to that introduced in Chapter 1: author-work-reader. The same pattern applies to writing about literature, only this time, you are the author. Its complete representation looks like this:

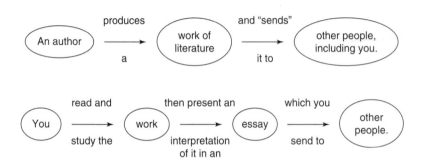

The purpose of your essay is to explain your interpretation to readers and persuade them that your interpretation is worthy of serious consideration. As a reader you were the receiver of an author's work of literature. Now you turn that situation around. You become an author *about* that same work of literature.

THE WRITING PROCESS

When we write essays, we typically think and write in stages. Writers rarely follow this process rigidly—first one step, then another, then another. Rather, they go back and forth among stages and do many tasks simultaneously. But as they write essays, they inevitably follow the general outline of a process. Understanding this process—the writing process—helps us plan the task of writing. It also helps reduce "writer's anxiety," that dreadful feeling that we must come up with an essay all at once, produce it seemingly out of thin air. Like building a house, writing gets done in small steps. Knowing what the usual process is helps us relax and take steps one at a time. Even when we have to go back to earlier steps, as most writers do, we can feel sure we are moving toward completion. The writing process consists of four main sets of activities.

❖ First Stage: Inventing

1. Studying the subject. The "subject" of essays about literature is the work of literature.

2. Identifying your audience (its needs and interests).

3. Recognizing any limitations placed on your essay (length, time in which you have to write it, specifics of an assignment).

4. Generating topics. (See Chapter 8.)

❖ Second Stage: Drafting

1. Determining a thesis and supporting claims.

2. Gathering facts from the work and, if helpful, from secondary sources to support claims.

3. Creating a plan of organization for a first draft.

4. Writing the first draft.

❖ Third Stage: Revising

1. Reading your draft critically. If possible, getting others to read and comment on it.

2. Rethinking the topic, plan of organization, and line of reasoning.

3. Gathering more support for claims.

4. Writing further drafts.

❖ Fourth Stage: Editing

1. Producing a final draft in the format expected by your audience.

2. "Publishing" the essay (by turning it in to your professor, by sending it to a circle of readers, by submitting it to a real publication such as a magazine or newspaper).

The next chapter, Chapter 8, takes up the first stage of the writing process: inventing.

8

Choosing Topics

The most challenging question of the invention stage of the writing process is, "What can I write about?" For writers about literature, the answers are as varying as the people who write. People respond so differently to works of literature that it is hard to predict what they—and you—might choose to write about. For each of us, the most fruitful question for raising topics is probably, "What connections within the work or to the world outside the work do I find?" Answer that for yourself and then write about one of those meanings. This chapter offers a number of more specific suggestions about how to search for topics and how to state them so that they are interesting and easy to discuss.

PRELIMINARY STEPS

Be an Active Reader

We discussed this topic in Chapter 1 and throughout the first half of the book. Read actively rather than passively. Rather than just process works of literature, think about them as you read. Ask questions like the following:

❖ What don't I understand?
❖ Why is the author using this convention over other conventions?

❖ What ideas do the characters espouse?
❖ Can I detect the author's bias in favor of certain ideas?
❖ What interests me about the work?
❖ What do I dislike? What do I like?
❖ What experiences in my own life does the work reflect?

If it helps to skim parts of a work—even the whole work—and then reread, so as to get the whole picture, then do that. Consider the "places" to look for meaning we surveyed in Part One. Choose one or more of them to concentrate on as you read. Rather than let the work control you, use strategies of investigation and analysis to control it. You might object that such an "intellectual" approach to reading literature takes the fun out of it. Yes, there are times when we want to relax and not think much about what we are reading. But analyzing and interpreting works of literature is pleasurable, too. In the long run, it is the most satisfying way of reading literature.

Identify Your Audience

This one is tricky.

Writing as dialogue. A handy way to think about audiences for essays, no matter what the subject matter, is to imagine yourself in conversation with a friend. This person likes you and is interested in your ideas. You are having coffee with her at an outdoor café. You say, "The other day I was reading this strange story by Edgar Allan Poe, 'The Cask of Amontillado.' What puzzles me is that the narrator, Montresor, is not telling the story to us but to somebody else, someone in the story. But we never learn who it is. I think, though, that I can make a good guess." Your friend asks, "Who do you think it is?" You tell her. She then asks, "Why do you think so?" You explain, giving reasons and details from the story. She may disagree with some of our claims, maybe all of them. You respond to her challenges until you both come to agreement or get tired of the topic. Throughout your conversation with her, you tailor your comments for her—explaining what you think she needs to know, using language she can understand, anticipating questions she might ask. Different friends would elicit different approaches from you. If your friend were eighty years old, you might speak to her differently than if she were twelve.

Such a dialogue between people who care about the topic under discussion and who respect one another is the basis of all essays. It is what makes them meaningful, productive, and enjoyable. When you write essays, your readers will not be right there in front of you, ready to speak back about every nuance of your argument. But readers will respond to your surrogate, the words on the page. Inwardly, they will ask the same questions that they would ask if you were there with them. Write, then, as if your readers are in a conversation with you and are eager to learn your ideas. Determine who they might be—their values, level of knowledge, facility with language, and so on, and adjust your writing for them accordingly. Sometimes, readers may not be friendly toward you. They might be skeptical about your subject, your ideas, or even your ability. If so, anticipate their questions. Ask yourself questions like these: To whom are you writing? What do they want from you? What information and explanation do they need from you in order to understand you? What effect do you want to have on them?

Professors as audience. When you write for courses, however, identifying your audience becomes tricky. In such a case, isn't your professor your audience? Yes, of course. You want him or her to think well of your essay and to give it a high grade. It behooves you to learn the professor's criteria for judging essays. Most professors want a well-crafted essay—such qualities as a clear statement of thesis, logical and coherent organization, fluent and correct prose, convincingly supported claims, thorough development of the topic. So far, so good. But professors often have a second audience in mind when they evaluate your essays—not just themselves but a "general" audience, one that is larger than the professor, one that includes the professor.

A general audience. Who belongs to this audience? Two groups who do *not* belong are (1) experts on your subject and (2) people incapable of grasping your reasoning (children, for example). You could write for both of these audiences, but if you wrote for an audience of experts, you would have to be an expert yourself and have something to tell them that they do not already know. Most students do not have enough time to master subjects that thoroughly. This, by the way, is another reason for not writing solely for your instructor. The instructor is an "expert" who, fortunately, rarely expects students to meet the needs of an audience of experts. On the other hand, if you wrote for the mentally immature, your essay would be too simpleminded for college courses.

Rather, a general audience consists of persons who are intelligent, who have read or can read the work you want to discuss, and who want to understand it better. It consists of individuals who are your equals, who form a community of which you are a part, to whom you can talk with equal authority. They share your interests and eagerly await your comments. If it will help, visualize people you know—classmates, friends, relatives, students at other campuses—as belonging to this audience. As with our conversation-over-coffee scenario, imagine yourself in a dialogue with them, saying things that would interest them, responding to their questions and comments. Project an image of yourself as the conscientious searcher for truth. Let your audience know that you are doing everything possible, within the limits of your time and ability, to answer the questions you have raised.

One reason professors may prefer you to write for a general audience is that you are more likely to include the facts and reasoning needed by *both* a general audience and your professors to understand and be convinced by you. When writing solely for professors, students often think, "The professor already knows this, so I won't include it." The professor usually *does* want you to include it. Professors cannot read your mind. In order to think well of your work, they need to see how you arrived at the claims you make. Professors know, furthermore, that writing for a general audience is the kind of writing you are most likely to do once you leave college. Your writing in the "real world" will usually be for groups of people, not just one person. Writing college essays for a general audience gives you practice in this kind of writing.

Yourself as audience.   A third audience to write for is yourself. Writing essays is one way of satisfying your own intellectual needs and desires. Writing is not simply the product of thinking; it is a *way* of thinking. Some theorists argue that only when you write your ideas can you be sure you have thought them through carefully. The process of writing essays, for example, underscores the need to use sound logic, to include all the steps in your reasoning, to state ideas precisely so your arguments will withstand scrutiny. It is easy *not* to do these things when you are just thinking to yourself or speaking to other people. Francis Bacon's maxim sums this point up well: "Reading maketh a full man, conference a ready man, and writing an exact man."

Perhaps the most important aspect of writing is its ability to draw forth your ideas. One kind of essay about literature is the essay examination (discussed in Chapter 12). In writing essay examinations, students often discover ideas they never knew they had. Writing mates your knowledge of literature with the instructor's questions to give birth to new ideas. Essays about literature, then, can be journeys of self-discovery that lead you to new intellectual vistas. In this sense, you are part of your audience. You share your readers' curiosity and their desire to have puzzling questions answered. You write to convince them. You write also to discover and clarify your own ideas and to convince yourself of their validity.

Raise Questions about the Work

Related to the identity and needs of your audience is the nature of your topic. Your audience wants to understand the work you wish to discuss. They want to know your interpretations of it. But what will you interpret—everything in the work or just some part of it? Since essays are relatively short, rarely can you interpret everything in a work. Instead, limit yourself to some part of it. But which part?

The answer: Write about a specific problem of interpretation. The "problem" should be a question about how the work holds together, how it "works." Your question could focus on the motivation of characters, the effect of physical surroundings on characters, the arrangement of events in the plot, the sound devices in a poem, a theme in the work—anything that demands interpretation. Your essay should identify that question and provide an answer to it. The topics of interpretive essays always refer to questions. You might announce your topic as "Hamlet's Indecision" or "Macbeth's Hunger for Power," but the audience knows that behind topics like these lie questions: Why does Hamlet hesitate to act? What propels Macbeth to seek power and to continue seeking it? The purpose of taking up such topics is to answer the questions that give rise to them. When you state your topic, you do not have to phrase it as a question, yet good topics always imply questions of interpretation.

Narrow Your Topic

Topic as thought-provoking. What makes a topic good? One way to judge the quality of an essay topic is to ask yourself how easily your audience could answer the question that lies behind it. A useful criterion is that a topic is "good" if your readers could readily *not* answer the question after reading the work once. They could not answer it convincingly, either for themselves or for others, without reviewing and studying the work. The topic, in short, must be genuinely thought provoking.

Topic as interesting. A second consideration is the meaningfulness of your topic. As the author, you should care about the topic, and your audience should be interested in it. To assess your audience's interest, imagine yourself as part of your audience. What would you want to know if you were reading your own essay? One of the *least* interesting questions is: What happened in the work? True, the events and details of works are sometimes hard to understand and need clarification, but usually readers can understand a work's details after reading it one time. You do not need to provide information your audience already knows.

Topic as focused. A third way to assess the quality of a topic is to ask if it is focused narrowly enough for the confines of your essay. Most of the essays you write for college literature classes will run from three to ten printed pages (900 to 3,000 words). Your topic is good if you can deal with it thoroughly within those limits. For example, "Comedy in *Romeo and Juliet*" would probably be too broad for an essay topic; "The Nurse As Comic Figure" would be more specific and manageable. "Love in *Romeo and Juliet*" would be too broad; "Juliet's Mature Love versus Romeo's Adolescent Love" would be better. "Values in *Romeo and Juliet*"—too broad; "Shakespeare's Attitude Toward Suicide"—better. "Juliet as Character"—too broad; "Juliet's Change from Child to Young Woman"—better.

Charlotte Brontë's novel *Jane Eyre* provides an example of an essay topic that meets these three criteria. Brontë grew up absorbing the superstitions of the English north country. These superstitions included beliefs in fairies, elves, and demons. We do not have to read far into *Jane Eyre* before encountering references to them. Jane, the narrator and main character, says that as a child she looked in vain for elves "under mushrooms and beneath the ground-ivy" and concluded that "they were all gone out of England to some savage country where the woods were wilder and thicker, and the population more scant" (53). After her first encounter with Mr. Rochester, he accuses her of being a fairy who "bewitched" his horse and caused it to fall. Her reply is that the fairies "all forsook England a hundred years ago" (153–54). Throughout her relationship, he calls her "elf," "fairy," "dream," "changeling," "sprite" (272, 302). After she returns at the end of the novel, he reverts to his epithets, once again calling her "fairy," "ghost," "changeling," "fairyborn and humanbred" (457–63).

If you spot this fairy lore motif in *Jane Eyre* you might think, "Aha, why not write an essay on that?" You could title the essay "Charlotte Brontë's Use of Fairy Lore in *Jane Eyre*." The question underlying the topic would be: What significance does this lore have in the novel? The purpose of the essay would be (1) to raise this question, (2) to show that the fairy lore actually does exist in the novel, and (3) to provide an answer to the question. This answer would be the "thesis" of the essay. The topic is meaningful because fairy lore is prominent in the work and is consistently associated with the main character; the topic promises to lead to an interpretation of the novel. Furthermore, the topic is complex enough so that most readers could not convincingly answer its implicit question without rereading and studying the novel. And the topic is specific enough to be dealt with thoroughly in an essay of about six or so double-spaced pages. The topic, in short, is "good."

For some individuals, finding a good topic is easy and automatic. One person might happen to notice the references to fairies in *Jane Eyre,* and think, "Hey, that would be interesting to write about." For others, however, discovering good topics is difficult and frustrating, capable of inducing writer's block. You or any writer can experience both situations. You might find that one work suggests all kinds of topics, whereas another leaves you at a total loss. If you ever find yourself in the latter situation, try a search strategy.

SEARCH STRATEGIES

A *search strategy* is a procedure for locating and examining important aspects of a work. It is a self-teaching device that helps you think about the work. As you examine the work, you become aware of areas you can raise questions about, questions that may lead to good topics. The following are brief descriptions of some well-known search strategies.

Focus on the Work's Conventions (Its Formal Qualities)

As we say in Part One of the book, the conventions (elements) of a work—such things as characterization, setting, plot, poetic style—make up its form and are "places" to locate meaning in works of literature. In your search for a topic, you may not want to examine *every* component of a work, but you can think about various ones until you hit on ideas that interest you. Systematically examining conventions in a work, in other words, is a process of discovery, rather like shining a flashlight on different parts of a darkened room. You could even turn conventions of a work into essay topics: "Setting in Austen's *Pride and Prejudice*," "Meter and Rhyme in Shakespeare's Sonnet 116," "Characterization in O'Neill's *The Hairy Ape*," "Irony in Poe's 'The Cask of Amontillado.'" Your purpose would be to show how the author uses these conventions and how they are important to the overall scheme of the work. See, for example, the essay in Chapter 13 on the poem "Richard Cory."

Use Topoi (Traditional Patterns of Thinking)

Generations of communicators have recognized that certain ways of thinking—patterns of thought—are helpful tools for examining subjects and developing ideas about them. In his *Rhetoric*, perhaps the greatest book about writing, Aristotle called these patterns *topoi*, which means "places." Aristotle seems to have meant that these patterns are "places" to look when you need to find ideas. Several of the traditional patterns are especially useful—at times inevitable—for coming up with ideas about literature and for explaining it. The following are descriptions of well-known *topoi*.

Definition.   Definition is unavoidable in arguments because premises often contain terms that must be defined. Quite often, these terms are not controversial or ambiguous and therefore need no formal definitions. However, when you have controversial terms, you must define them, and you must use all key terms in a such a way that your readers know what you mean by them.

Apart from the necessity of defining terms in your thesis, definition can be useful in two other ways. First, your claims about the facts may rest upon the definition of a particular word within the work. Second, you may want to focus your whole essay on a definition. You might, for example, show that "imagination" is Isabel Archer's most admirable trait in Henry James's novel *The Portrait of a Lady*. Your essay would attempt to explain what James means by the term. Or you might argue that Jane Austen in *Pride and Prejudice* distinguishes between "good pride" and "bad pride." Again, you would discuss the novel in order to define these terms. Finally, you might claim that Emily Brontë uses "gothic" elements in *Wuthering Heights*. You would need a reliable definition of *gothic* to make your case convincing, and to apply all parts of the definition to the work, showing which ones fit and which do not. A handbook of literary terms, such as M. H.

Abrams's *A Glossary of Literary Terms* (1999) and the articles in encyclopedias such as *The Encyclopaedia Britannica* are helpful starting points for finding definitions of literary and philosophical concepts.

Structure. Focus on structure helps identify an object's parts and how they contribute to the coherence and meaning of the whole. A structure is something that has a definite pattern of organization. Works of literature always have a structure, sometimes more than one structure. Some works conform to established structures like the sonnet form; other works invent their own structures. Your purpose in writing about a work's structure is to identify the structure and explain its relationship to other elements such as theme and characterization. You might, for example, claim that the passage of the seasons provides the structure of William Wordsworth's poem "The Ruined Cottage"; or that the rhyme scheme of his "I Wandered Lonely as a Cloud" emphasizes the narrator's shift from feeling isolated to feeling connected to nature. The less obvious the structure or its effect on the work, the more revealing your essay would be. You might even argue that the work has several structures—an obvious structure and a less-obvious structure.

Process. Tracking process identifies the stages in which things change—characters, states of mind, societies, settings, situations, conditions. Because literature often represents events occurring in time, it lends itself to process analysis: Characters change from weak to strong, societies from coherent to incoherent, settings from beautiful to ugly.

When describing a process, avoid simply retelling the plot. Instead, explain and illustrate clear *steps* in the overall process. Present them in the order in which they occur in time. Each step would be a unit—probably a paragraph—of your paper. The claim of each unit would be your proposition about what characterizes the step.

Cause and effect. Examining cause and effect helps you investigate the causes and effects of things. When you investigate *causes,* you are always dealing with things in the past. Why does Goodman Brown go into the forest? Why does Hedda Gabler act the way she does? What causes Pip to change? Two kinds of causes usually figure in works of literature, the immediate or surface cause and the remote or deep cause. In Theodore Dreiser's *An American Tragedy,* the immediate cause of Roberta Alden's death is that she is pregnant. Clyde Griffiths kills her because he wants her out of the way so he can marry Sondra Finchley. The remote cause, however, is all those forces—childhood experiences, parental models, heredity, financial situation, cultural values, religious background, and accident—that have molded Clyde and that make the reasons he kills Roberta complex.

When you investigate *effects,* you may deal with things in either the past or the future. In William Faulkner's fiction, you might examine the effect of slavery on Southern society and on his characters. These effects are part of the historical past in his work. You might also predict what the South will be like in the future, given the way he depicts it.

Because literature often deals with the actions of complex characters and societies, analyzing cause and effect is a fruitful source of essay topics. We constantly wonder why characters do what they do and what effects their actions have had or will have. Just as in real life, cause and effect in literature can be subtle. Your task is to discover and communicate those subtleties.

Comparison. Comparison means indicating both similarities and differences between two or more subjects. One use of comparison is to establish the value of something. You might argue that one of Shakespeare's comedies is not as good as the others because it lacks some of the qualities the others have. Another use of comparison is to explain your insights about aspects of a work. A comparison of the two sets of lovers in Tolstoy's *Anna Karenina,* for example, helps us understand his distinction between sacred love and profane love. Comparing the themes of one work to another is also revealing. Sir Walter Raleigh's poem "The Nymph's Reply to the Shepherd" is a response to Christopher Marlowe's poem "The Passionate Shepherd to His Love." (See Chapter 2, pages 24–25, for the texts of these poems.) Raleigh not only disagrees in general with the premise of Marlowe's poem, he also makes nearly every line of the poem respond to the parallel line in Marlowe's poem. A line-by-line comparison of the two poems helps make Raleigh's themes clear.

Comparison is revealing also when the author of a work contains allusions. An *allusion* is a reference to another work, a historical event, a myth, or an author. An allusion is always an invitation to compare the work at hand to the thing alluded to. Wordsworth, for example, in his long autobiographical poem *The Prelude* often alludes to Milton's *Paradise Lost.* One could compare *The Prelude* and *Paradise Lost* to clarify Wordsworth's methods and themes.

Respond to Comments By Critics

Comments by literary critics are often a fruitful source of topics. Critics write about individual works, about an author's entire work, about the nature of literature itself, about a work's connection to society. Your purpose would be to make a critic's whole approach or an isolated comment by a critic the starting point of your essay. Chapter 6 outlines several well-known critical approaches to literature, but consider for the moment how you might use the following observation made by Terry Eagleton in *Literary Theory: An Introduction* (1983):

> Watching his grandson playing in his pram one day, Freud observed him throwing a toy out of the pram and exclaiming *fort!* (gone away), then hauling it in again on a string to the cry of *da!* (here). This, the famous *fort-da* game, Freud interpreted in *Beyond the Pleasure Principle* (1920) as the infant's symbolic mastery of its mother's absence; but it can also be read as the first glimmerings of narrative. *Fort da* is perhaps the shortest story we can imagine: an object is lost, and then recovered. But even the most complex narratives can be read as variants on this model: the pattern of classical narrative is that an original settlement is disrupted and ultimately restored (185).

Here, Eagleton states an aspect of narratives that most people have probably not thought about: that there is a lost-and-found pattern and variations on it in many narratives. Examples abound: Homer's *Odyssey,* Milton's *Paradise Lost,* Melville's *Moby-Dick,* Coleridge's *The Rime of the Ancient Mariner,* Keats's "La Belle Dame sans Merci," Shakespeare's *King Lear,* Jane Austen's *Pride and Prejudice.* You could make Eagleton's comment the basis for an essay about a narrative—a novel, a short story, a poem, a play. You would try to explain how the pattern or a variation on it operates in your work. You would begin your essay by explaining Eagleton's idea, giving proper credit to him. (For when and how to give credit in your essays, see Chapter 11.) Then you would answer questions such as: What has been lost? How was it lost? How are the protagonists trying to recover it? Do they succeed? What qualities allow them to succeed or cause them to fail?

Eagleton's comment covers many works of literature, but critics also write extensively about individual works. You could use a critic's idea about a specific work as a starting point for an essay. Your essay could support or disagree with it. For an explanation of how to find critical interpretations of individual works, see the treatment of sources in Chapter 11, pages 279–81.

When you think of literary criticism, you may think only of published works, but do not forget your instructor and the other students in your class. Your instructor is a critic who "publishes" comments in class, aloud to you, and students often give interesting responses to the instructor and to one another. All of these comments can provide excellent starting points for essays.

Draw from Your Own Knowledge

Specialized knowledge.   People at all levels of achievement know a great deal and are learning all the time. If you are a student, you are most likely taking courses in a wide range of disciplines. All of this knowledge interconnects. You can bring it to bear on works of literature. Subject areas such as psychology, sociology, philosophy, design, art history, history of science, religious studies, cultural history, political history, even landscape gardening illuminate literature. Ibsen's Hedda Gabler (in the play *Hedda Gabler*) is a deeply troubled person. Can you find in your psychology textbooks theories that would help explain her problems? Ernest Hemingway said in an early version of "Big Two-Hearted River" that he wanted to write the way Paul Cézanne painted. Can you explain Hemingway's themes and methods by comparing his writing to Cézanne's pictures and theories of art? In the poem "Heritage," Countee Cullen conveys an ambivalent attitude toward Africa. How does the American understanding (or misunderstanding) of Africa when he wrote the poem (1925) explain his frustration? Anton Chekhov wrote plays at the turn of the twentieth century. What was happening in Russia then that his plays reflect?

Personal experience.   Another kind of knowledge writers often overlook is their own experience. Most students have expertise outside the academic world—through work, travel, family, and other activities. This expertise can illuminate works of literature. Have you done some sailing? If so, explain the complex maneuvers the young captain makes at the end of Joseph Conrad's "The Secret Sharer" and suggest what this knowledge tells us about the captain. (Is he taking a foolish, irresponsible risk?) Speaking of Conrad, have you been to the Congo River, the setting of *Heart of Darkness?* If so, are vestiges of the colonialism he condemns still there? What can you tell us about the landscape and atmosphere that would help us better understand this puzzling novel? Have you seen any bullfights? If so, help us understand the symbolic meaning of bullfighting in Hemingway's fiction. Have you been the victim of prejudice? If so, provide insights into the dynamics of bigotry dramatized in Bernard Malamud's *The Assistant* or Richard Wright's *Black Boy*.

TALKING AND WRITING STRATEGIES

Talking and writing are themselves ways of generating ideas. When you talk with someone—even to yourself—about a work, or when you write about it, you often come up with ideas you never knew you had. This is why the writing process often involves going back and forth among stages. As you write a first draft, you discover ideas that lead you to rethink your topic and major claims.

Talk Out Loud

Imagine yourself talking to a friend about a work you want to write about. Or, better, find a real person to talk to. Talk out loud. Keep your partner in mind. You really want to explain this work to her. Say anything you want about the work—what you like and dislike, what interests you or does not interest you. Make claims about the work—what it means, what motivates the characters, what the setting is like. Support your claims with evidence. Ask your listener to respond. Does she agree or disagree? Listen to her counterclaims and reasons. At least summarize the work for her. Ask if she understands and agrees with your summary. As you exchange ideas—or imagine that you are exchanging ideas—focus on themes of the work. What points does the writer seem to be making? By talking out loud, you get your mind working and push yourself toward developing interpretations of your own.

Make Outlines

Outline the work. The outline need not be formal (complete sentences, Roman and Arabic numerals, and so forth). Rather, it can be a list or a series of statements that indicate key aspects of the work. Write down the outline, so you can remember everything you put in it. Focus the outline on the whole work or one element of the work.

Possibilities for organizing outlines abound. It can follow the spatial order of the work; that is, it can show events in the order they appear in the work. It can follow a chronological organization, the order in which the events occur in time. Or it can be arranged according to journalist's questions: who, what, when, where, why, how. The first four questions get the facts straight. The last two get you thinking about relationships among the facts. Who are the important characters in the work? What are they like? What has happened before the work begins? During what period is the action set? Where does the action occur? Why does the action happen? The journalist' questions often lead to others and finally to a careful consideration of the work.

Freewrite

Choose a work or some aspect of a work and begin writing about it. Keep writing for five or ten minutes. If you can't think of anything new to say, repeat the last sentence over and over until something new occurs to you. While doing this forget about sentence structure and correct usage. Freewriting generates thought, even if you repeat ideas or write nonsense. Freewriting may provide you a topic and a rough outline for a full-blown essay.

Brainstorm

Brainstorm—think and write without restraint—about a work of literature. Let your mind flow where it will, but maintain focus on the work or some aspect of the work. Brainstorming requires pen and paper—lots of paper. As ideas come to you, jot them down. Make a game of this—creative play. Don't worry about spelling, complete sentences, and orderly arrangements of ideas. Include even crazy ideas. Channel thought with questions like these: Which works do I like best? (Jot down the possibilities.) What interests me most about the work? (Jot these down.) What do I dislike? (Jot these down.) Why do I like or dislike these things? (Jot down your reasons.) What do I want to write about? (Jot these down.) If characters interest you, brainstorm about them. If you tire of characters, shift to something else.

When you stop brainstorming, sort out, make connections, arrange your jottings into groups, and eliminate the unusable. Try different arrangements and relationships. Try even the strangest, most unlikely connections. If you have a list of ten items, group them. If you see connections between some but not others, keep the ones that connect and cross out the others. Then brainstorm about the qualities linking the remaining items. These could be the basis for your essay.

Make Notes

Notes are bits of writing you do for yourself. Write them wherever it is most convenient and helpful: in the margins of books you own, on little slips of paper, in a notebook. Since they are for yourself only, you need not worry about spelling, punctuation, or even coherence. Notes are almost always short and pithy. Jotting down notes *as* you read stimulates interaction between you and the text. Writing notes *after* you read helps you think about the whole work, raise questions, state interpretations, and call attention to intriguing passages and details. The following are notes made by a student after she read Homer's *Odyssey:*

Notes on the <u>Odyssey</u>

Why does Odysseus want to leave Calypso's island?
He's got such a good deal there.

If he loves Penelope, why does he sleep with
Calypso? And Circe? Is this being "faithful"? I wonder what Penelope will think when he "confesses" (if
he ever does). Could she do the same thing--sleep
around--and get away with it? Double standard.

Athene: Obsessed with tying up loose ends.
Although a goddess, power limited. Poseidon. Are
they rivals?

Nausicaa: my favorite. "There slept a girl who
in form and feature was like the immortal goddesses" (86). The "handsome girl" who, like Leto's
daughter, is "the loveliest amid a whole bevy of
beauties" (89). Innocent but spunky.

Zeus is patron of "strangers and foreigners in
distress" (92). Why doesn't Zeus just zap the suitors?

> Odysseus: A Greek Woody Allen (always worrying
> and down on himself).
>
> At the end, Odysseus's treatment of the ser-
> vant girls: horrible. Bloody and excessive. Sexist?

Keep a Journal

Journals are more coherent, more polished, and more developed than notes. You may be the sole audience for your own journals, but sometimes they are for others as well. The journals of authors like Ralph Waldo Emerson, Henry James, and F. Scott Fitzgerald provide fascinating insights into their lives and works. Like these authors, writers often use journals not only to try out lines of thought, but also to get other peoples' reactions to them. The root word for journal—*jour,* the French word for "day"—suggests that they are more systematic and regular than notes. Write in your journal, if not daily, then regularly. Take more time developing your ideas than for notes. The journal below is by the same student who wrote the previous notes on the *Odyssey.* Notice how her journal entry is more developed than her notes and less developed than her essay (which immediately follows the journal entry).

> Journal Entry on the <u>Odyssey</u>
>
> Two things bother me about the <u>Odyssey</u>. One is the
> way Homer presents women. Women are almost always
> more limited in what they can do than men and are
> treated as inferiors by the male characters. As a
> female I resent this attitude. I will admit that
> females in the <u>Odyssey</u> are stronger--more admirable
> and influential--than in some of the other things we
> have read this semester. If Athene weren't always

helping Telemachus and Odysseus, where would they
be? But Athene's femaleness seems unimportant. She
isn't human, for one thing. And for another, when
she takes human form, she almost always appears as
a male. Penelope is admirable, I suppose, for being
so loyal and patient, but she has to stay home and
do domestic duties (for twenty years!) while her
husband gets to roam the world, have adventures,
and sleep with beautiful goddesses. What would the
men of Ithaca have thought had Penelope had similar
adventures? Probably lynched her. Finally, at the
end, I think that Odysseus's treatment of the dis-
loyal female servants is excessive. They are sen-
tenced without a trial. Who knows, they might have
been coerced by the piglike suitors. They don't deserve to die, especially in such a gruesome way.
What threat to Odysseus and Ithaca could they be if
left alive?

The other thing is Odysseus's attitude toward
Ogygia, Calypso's island. I keep wondering why he
wants to leave. Ogygia seems like paradise.
Odysseus says he loves Penelope and wants to return
to her, but is that the real reason? Ogygia strikes
me as being similar to Eden in the Bible. It even
has four rivers, just like Eden. In the Bible, Adam
and Eve are kicked out of Eden as punishment for
eating the apple. Yet, in the <u>Odyssey</u>, Odysseus
<u>wants</u> to leave. Why? I think I might want to stay.
Look at what he's got. He has a beautiful woman who
loves him and takes care of him. He could have im-

mortality. (Calypso promises to make him immortal
if he will stay.) Ogygia is beautiful. All my life
I have thought that losing paradise, as Adam and
Eve did, would be terrible. Why would someone wish
to lose it? As a person (character), Odysseus seems
very restless. Maybe that's the reason. Once he returns home, you wonder if he will stay long.

SAMPLE ESSAY ABOUT LITERATURE

The following essay is by the student whose notes and journal immediately precede this text. It is a response to her reading of the *Odyssey*.
Notice how her essay evolves out of her informal writing. In her notes
she comments briefly on the "paradise" theme. She returns to it for
more extended comment in her journal. She decides, finally, to focus
an entire essay on this one theme. You can see from her notes and
journal entry that she could have also written on other topics—the
nature of the gods, Nausicaa, Athene, and gender equity. But she instead chose to write on this one.

Henderson 1

Michelle Henderson
Professor Elliott
English 251-03
2 September 20--

Paradise Rejected in Homer's Odyssey
For centuries, people have considered the biblical Garden of Eden as a model for "paradise."
Surprisingly, a work of literature nearly as ancient as the Bible, Homer's Odyssey, contains a

place so similar to Eden that it, too, qualifies as
a paradise. This place is Calypso's island, Ogygia.
Yet as alike as Eden and Ogygia are, the mortals
who dwell there react to them very differently.
Adam and Eve want to remain in Eden, but because of
their disobedience they are expelled. In contrast,
Odysseus chooses to leave Ogygia. This choice is
puzzling. Why would he want to leave paradise?

Ogygia is similar to Eden in at least four
ways. First, it looks and feels the same. The
Genesis account says that God caused trees to
"spring from the ground," trees that were "pleasant
to look at and good for food" (2:9). A river flows
"from Eden to water the garden" and branches into
four "streams," called Pishon, Gihon, Tigris, and
Euphrates (2:10-14). Eden is a "garden," a pleasant
place where all forms of vegetation and animal life
exist together in harmony (2:19-25). Homer's description of Calypso's Ogygia is almost the same,
complete with the four springs:

> Round her cave there was a thick wood of
> alder, poplar, and sweet smelling cypress
> trees, wherein all kinds of great birds
> had built their nests--owls, hawks, and
> chattering sea-crows that occupy their
> business in the waters. A vine loaded with
> grapes was trained and grew luxuriantly
> about the mouth of the cave; there were
> also four running rills of water in chan-
> nels cut pretty close together, and turned

hither and thither so as to irrigate the
beds of violets and luscious herbage over
which they flowed. Even a god could not
help being charmed with such a lovely
spot . . . (73-74).

Ogygia, furthermore, is fragrant: "There was a
large fire burning on the hearth, and one could
smell from far the fragrant reek of burning cedar
and sandal wood" (73).

Ogygia is like Eden in a second way: its inhabitants live in comfort and without pain. Adam,
Eve, and Odysseus hardly have to lift a finger to
get the necessities of life. Although God puts Adam
"in the garden of Eden to till it and care for it"
(2:15), Adam doesn't work. "Work" is what he has to
do after he is cast out of the garden: "You shall
gain your bread by the sweat of your brow until you
return to the ground" (3:17). Adam and Eve are free
from pain in Eden. Only after they eat the apple
does God give them pain. He tells Eve that he "will
increase your labor and your groaning, and in labor
you shall bear children" (3:16). He says that Adam
will have to overcome the "thorns and thistles" of
the earth (3:17). As for Odysseus, Calypso seems to
provide all the food he could want: "Calypso set
meat and drink before him of the food that mortals
eat; but her maids brought ambrosia and nectar for
herself, and they laid their hands on the good
things that were before them" (77). We get the impression that, just as she provides food for

Odysseus, she can protect him from pain. "Good luck
go with you," she tells him, "but if you could only
know how much suffering is in store for you before
you get back to your own country, you would stay
where you are, keep house along with me, and let me
make you immortal . . ." (77).

   Third, like Eden, Ogygia provides loving companionship. After creating Adam, God worries that
Adam will be lonely, so God first creates the animals and then Eve to keep him company. Adam and Eve
are the first married couple, becoming "one flesh"
(2:18-25). Odysseus, of course, yearns to be with
his wife, Penelope, but he has a loving companion
in Calypso and seems to enjoy her company:
"Presently the sun set and it became dark, whereon
the pair retired into the inner part of the cave
and went to bed" (78).

   Finally, in Ogygia as in Eden, there is no
death. God tells Adam and Eve that if they eat of
the tree of knowledge they will die (2:16-18). And,
sure enough, after they eat the apple God tells
them, "Dust you are, to dust you shall return"
(3:19). We can infer, then, that before they eat the
apple, they have eternal life. Odysseus is mortal,
but he, too, has the promise of immortality. Calypso
tells Hermes, "I got fond of him and cherished him,
and had set my heart on making him immortal, so that
he should never grow old all his days" (75).

   In sum, Adam, Eve, and Odysseus possess the
benefits of paradise: a beautiful environment, an

easy and painless life, loving companionship, and eternal life.

Yet Odysseus rejects this paradise. Why?

The answer Odysseus himself gives is that he loves Penelope and wants to be with her. His actions support this statement. When we first see him, he is "on the sea-shore as usual, looking out upon the barren ocean with tears in his eyes, groaning and breaking his heart for sorrow" (74). Odysseus admits that Calypso is far more beautiful than Penelope. He tells Calypso, "I am quite aware that my wife Penelope is nothing like so tall or so beautiful as yourself. She is only a woman, whereas you are an immortal. Nevertheless, I want to get home, and can think of nothing else" (77). At the end of the Odyssey, after many hardships, he does just that. The climax of the story occurs when Odysseus and Penelope at last retire to bed to consummate their long-awaited reunion.

A less obvious explanation for Odysseus's rejection of paradise, however, springs from his nature. He is incredibly creative and energetic and thrives on meeting challenges and devising stratagems. Early in the epic (52-53) Helen of Troy recounts the story of Odysseus's most famous stratagem, the Trojan Horse. Odysseus later tells with loving detail how he crafted his marriage bed:

> [The bed] is a marvelous curiosity which I made with my very own hands. There was a young olive growing within the precincts

of the house, in full vigor, and about as
thick as a bearing-post. I built my room
round this with strong walls of stone and
a roof to cover them, and I made the doors
strong and well-fitting. Then I cut off the
top boughs of the olive tree and left the
stump standing. This I dressed roughly
from the root upwards and then worked with
carpenter's tools well and skillfully,
straightening my work by drawing a line on
the wood, and making it into a bed-prop. I
then bored a hole down the middle, and
made it the center-post of my bed, at
which I worked till I had finished it, in-
laying it with gold and silver; after this
I stretched a hide of crimson leather from
one side of it to the other. (354-55)

Homer gives a similarly detailed and admiring account of how Odysseus constructs the raft on which
he escapes from Ogygia (78-79).

Odysseus, in short, is a craftsman, a maker, a
builder. He crafts the stratagem of the Trojan
Horse. He crafts his escape from Polyphemus, the
Cyclops (135). He crafts his way past Scylla and
Charybdis (188-89). He crafts his artful speech to
Nausicaa that wins her help (90-91). He tells the
story of his adventures, Alcinous says, "as though
you were a practiced bard" (172). Finally, he
crafts the defeat of the suitors. He loves stratagems so much that he invents them for the sheer

pleasure of it. After telling Athene one of his
elaborate lies, she says,

> He must be indeed a shifty lying fellow
> who could surpass you in all manner of
> craft even though you had a god for your
> antagonist. Dare-devil that you are, full
> of guile, unwearying in deceit, can you
> not drop your tricks and your instinctive
> falsehood, even now that you are in your
> own country again? (205)

How satisfied would Odysseus be in a place like
Ogygia? He would hate it. Ogygia, like the Garden of
Eden, provides everything one could possibly want.
That's the trouble with it. There are no challenges,
no obstacles to overcome. People whose love for overcoming obstacles is "instinctive" would be so bored
and so restless they would go crazy. That is the real
reason Odysseus chooses to leave Ogygia. He loves
Penelope. But he loves, also, the very things we usually think of as bad--the difficulty and pain of life.
Athene tells Zeus at the beginning that Odysseus "is
tired of life" (2). Odysseus would rather die than
live forever in the static eternity of "paradise."

Works Cited

Homer. <u>The Odyssey</u>. Trans. Samuel Butler. New York:
      E. P. Dutton, 1925.

<u>The New English Bible</u>. New York: Oxford UP, 1971.

Note: Normally, the Works Cited list would appear on a separate page, but we print it here, right
after the essay, to save space.

Comments on the Essay

This essay represents the interpretive and argumentative nature of essays about literature. The author begins by raising a question: Why does Odysseus leave Ogygia? This is her *topic*. She follows the question with claims about the nature of paradise and about Odysseus's motivation for leaving. She supports her claims with evidence. In her conclusion (final paragraph), she answers her question. This answer is her *thesis*. The essay deals with a serious issue that would interest thoughtful readers of the *Odyssey*. She shows them that the paradise theme is *meaningful* because of the light it sheds on Odysseus's values and motivations.

Checklist for Choosing Topics

- ❖ Be an active reader.
- ❖ Write for a general audience (not just your professor).
- ❖ Identify questions that underlie your topics.
- ❖ Choose topics that are
  - thought-provoking
  - interesting
  - focused enough to develop thoroughly in an essay.
- ❖ Use search strategies to generate topics:
  - analysis of the work's conventions
  - *topoi*
  - comments by critics
  - your knowledge
  - talking out loud
  - outlining
  - freewriting
  - brainstorming.
- ❖ Make notes on the work.
- ❖ Keep a journal.

Works Cited

Brontë, Charlotte. *Jane Eyre*. New York: Penguin, 1966.

Eagleton, Terry. *Literary Theory: An Introduction*. Minneapolis: U of Minnesota P, 1983.

9

Drafting the Essay

This chapter deals with the second stage of the writing process, drafting the essay. By the time you reach this stage, you should have chosen a topic and thought about what you want to say about it. Now your task is to draft the essay. How do you do this? To help you answer this question, we discuss the basic aspects of the interpretive essay and offer some guidelines for writing a first draft.

THE ARGUMENTATIVE NATURE
OF INTERPRETIVE ESSAYS

Qualities of essays. Essays about literature are almost always argumentative. Although writings about literature can be purely informational (that is, just give information) or be purely expressive (that is, just state opinions), essays are argumentative. An *essay* has three main qualities. First, it persuades an audience of the validity of its ideas. Second, it uses evidence (facts, reasoning, and, when necessary, testimony) to explain and support its ideas. And third, it has a *thesis*, an overall claim supported by specific claims.

Essays as argumentative. The argumentative nature of essays about literature emerges from the relationship between the work and its reader. Good literature is complex. It communicates on many levels of meaning and by many methods. A single work may exist as a system of sounds, of symbols, of ideas, of images, of analogies, of actions, of psychological portrayals, of moods, of grammatical structures—all of which are separate entities, yet all of which interrelate. Furthermore, literature also invites readers to participate in creating the work. A work is not complete until it is read. The author leaves "gaps" in the work for readers to fill with their imagination. The completed work—the work that is read—is something more than the words on the page. It is a collaboration between text and reader. As a result, perceptions of a work vary from age to age, reader to reader, even reading to reading. This variability of perception occurs because no single reading, however careful, can take in all the elements of most works, or synthesize them into all their structural relationships, or include all the vantage points from which even one reader might experience a work.

Consequently, no single view of a work, whether your own or someone else's, can be the all-encompassing or final view. Cultures change, people change and, as a result, perception changes. It is a common experience for children to enjoy works—*Huckleberry Finn, Gulliver's Travels,* "Rip Van Winkle," *Alice in Wonderland*—and as adults to enjoy them again, but for very different reasons and with entirely new understandings of them. This does not mean that all interpretations of a work are equally valid. Interpretations of literature are subject to the same rules of human thought—accurate observation, sound reasoning, systematic procedure, thoroughness of treatment—as any other interpretive discourse. But no single interpretation can encompass the whole work.

Because literature is complex and can be perceived variously, essays about literature are arguments. You, the writer of the essay, cannot take for granted that your interpretation of the work is the same as your reader's. Your reader may have missed the very facts in the work you have found most compelling or most "obvious." Your reader may have a totally different understanding of the work than you do. If you want your reader to grasp your interpretation or accept it as valid, you must explain and persuade. You must write an argument.

THE STRUCTURE OF ESSAYS ABOUT LITERATURE

Argumentative essays have two interrelated structures: an *argumentative structure* based on logic and a *rhetorical structure* based on persuasion. Because argumentation is a means of persuasion, the argumentative structure is really part of the rhetorical structure. But the two structures are not exactly the same, so we will talk about them separately.

The Argumentative Structure

Inductive reasoning. The argumentative structure of an essay consists of two kinds of reasoning: inductive and deductive. *Inductive reasoning* is the "scientific method." It consists of observing specific instances of something and drawing conclusions about them. You notice, for example, that in Act One of *Hamlet,* Hamlet exhibits melancholy behavior once. Then in Act Two, he is melancholy twice. In Act Three, he is melancholy four times. In Act Four, six times. And in Act Five, all the time. Having observed these instances of Hamlet's behavior, you can legitimately conclude that Hamlet is a melancholy fellow and that his melancholia increases throughout the play.

Inductive reasoning is essential for interpreting literature, but in itself it can seem like a dead end. So what if Hamlet is melancholy? To get beyond the "so what" question, you need a second kind of reasoning, deduction. What if, for example, you want to claim that Hamlet's melancholia is the cause of something or, that by Act Five, it reaches crisis proportions? *Deductive reasoning* allows you to support such claims, to *do* something with your inductive conclusions.

Deductive reasoning. Syllogisms are the basis of deductive reasoning. A *syllogism* is a unit of reasoning that consists of two claims that support a third claim. The two supporting claims are called *premises* and the third claim is called a *conclusion.* The *major premise* states a general concept. The *minor premise* is a specific instance of that concept. The *conclusion* connects the specific instance to the general concept:

MAJOR PREMISE: All complex characters are fascinating.

MINOR PREMISE: Anna Karenina is a complex character.

CONCLUSION: Therefore, Anna Karenina is fascinating.

Although in formal logic all three parts of a syllogism are stated, in argumentative essays parts of syllogisms are usually left unstated. The above syllogism would probably be stated something like this: "Anna Karenina is fascinating because she is so complex." Here, the major premise has been left out and is present only as an assumption. Such incompletely stated syllogisms are called *enthymemes.* Authors use enthymemes when they believe the unstated premises would seem obvious or readily acceptable to their readers. But just because an author uses enthymemes does not mean that the syllogisms are not present in the author's reasoning. Readers can recover all the parts of the syllogisms to examine critically an essay's reasoning.

The deductive reasoning of an essay consists of a series of syllogisms that support a thesis. Consider, for example, the deductive reasoning of the student essay on the *Odyssey* in the previous chapter (pages 218–24). The student's thesis is that although Ogygia might seem like paradise to most people, Odysseus leaves it because to him it is not. She supports this thesis with two sets of syllogisms. In the first set she reasons why Ogygia seems like a paradise:

Many people believe that all places like Eden are paradises.

Ogygia is like Eden.

Therefore, many people would believe that Ogygia is a paradise.

In the second set of syllogisms, she reasons why Odysseus fails to find Ogygia a paradise.

1. All people who constantly scheme and love to overcome challenges are creative.

   Odysseus constantly schemes and loves to overcome challenges.

   Therefore, Odysseus is creative.

2. All creative people would hate living in a place that demands no creativity.

   Odysseus is a creative person.

   Therefore, Odysseus would hate living in a place that demands no creativity.

3. All places that anyone would hate are not paradise.

   Places that demand no creativity, like Ogygia and Eden, are places that some people (namely, Odysseus) would hate.

   Therefore, Ogygia is not, for Odysseus, a paradise.

These two sets of syllogisms—the syllogism about the nature of paradise and the ones about Odysseus—form the deductive framework of this student's essay. If you read her essay carefully, you will see that she leaves parts of her syllogisms unstated. She uses enthymemes. Such incompleteness is typical of essays. The point, however, is that the deductive reasoning of all essays consists of a chain of syllogisms, whether fully stated or not, that lead to and support a thesis.

But what about the inductive reasoning in her essay? We see inductive reasoning in two crucial places: (1) her claim that Ogygia is like Eden and (2) her claim that Odysseus is a craftsman. She arrived at these claims by noticing numerous related facts about Ogygia and Odysseus's behavior. Now, in her essay, she supports her claims with some of these facts. But had she done no more than this, we might be tempted to ask, "So what?" So what if Ogygia is like Eden? So what if Odysseus is crafty? She anticipates our "so what" questions by positioning her claims as minor premises in two key syllogisms. She thus joins inductive reasoning and deductive reasoning to establish the argumentative structure of her essay.

The Rhetorical Structure

Rhetoric defined.   *Rhetoric,* simply put, is the art of persuasion. It consists of all the devices writers use to make their claims attractive and convincing. For essays, the most important rhetorical device is argumentation—the reasoning that supports your thesis. Reasoning, however, is not the only rhetorical device you can use in an essay. Other rhetorical choices include how you organize the essay, where you put your thesis, what parts of your syllogisms you leave unstated, and which parts you emphasize and support with evidence from the text. All of these choices help create the rhetorical structure of the essay.

How to organize your essay.   The organization of any essay depends in part on the line of reasoning you develop, and this will vary from topic to topic. But the general structure of an argumentative essay is fairly standard and almost always contains the following units:

1. **Title.** The *title* should tell enough about the topic of the essay to capture the interest of readers and let them know the focus of the essay. It helps to include the author's name and the title of the work you are discussing: "The Jungle as Symbol in Joseph Conrad's *Heart of Darkness.*"

2. **Introduction.** The *introduction* should state the topic of the essay and should be interesting enough to make the reader want to keep on reading. You may want to spell out your thesis here, but you

could also announce it later in the essay. The introduction should be relatively short—one to three paragraphs.

3. **Body.** The *body* is the place where you develop your line of reasoning. It consists of a series of paragraphs that contain claims (usually one claim per paragraph) along with supporting evidence. The body should contain as many paragraphs and be long enough to make your argument convincing.

4. **Conclusion.** The *conclusion* signals that the essay has come to an end. It should remind the reader of the problem posed at the beginning of the essay (the topic) and briefly summarize the solutions. It should state or restate the thesis. The conclusion should be brief, a paragraph or so.

The student essay on the *Odyssey* illustrates these structural principles. The title—"Paradise Rejected in Homer's *Odyssey*"—gives enough information about the topic for readers to know, and be intrigued by, the focus of the essay. The introduction (the first paragraph) presents the topic as a problem to be solved: Why does Odysseus leave "paradise"? The body of the essay consists of a series of paragraphs spelling out the chain of syllogisms that make up the author's reasoning. The conclusion—the last paragraph—answers the question raised in the beginning.

Where to put the thesis.   You have three choices: You can put it in the introduction, you can put it in the conclusion, or you can leave it unstated but implicit. You have to decide which is rhetorically most effective for your topic. If you state the thesis at the beginning, readers have the comfort of knowing what to look for as they read the rest of the essay. If you withhold it until the end, you create a sense of suspense that is climaxed by the revelation of thesis. If you leave the thesis implicit, you allow readers to infer it for themselves and to participate with you in the process of discovery.

The author of the essay on the *Odyssey* puts her thesis at the end of the essay rather than at the beginning. Her rhetorical strategy is to open the essay with an intriguing question, then lead us toward an answer—her thesis—at the end.

Which premises to support with evidence from the text.   Your syllogisms, and ultimately your thesis, are believable only if your audience accepts the premises of the syllogisms. You do not have time to support all your premises with evidence, and you do not really need to. Your audience will accept most of them as true, but you will have to support some of them to make your argument believable. Which ones? This, too, is a question about rhetorical strategy. You have to decide which premises your audience will accept as true and which ones they will want supported with evidence. For essays about literature, "evidence" consists of anything inside or outside the text that bears on your topic.

The author of the student essay on the *Odyssey* leaves many of her premises and conclusions unstated. The ones she emphasizes and supports with evidence are (1) that Eden and Ogygia are similar and (2) that Odysseus is creative. Is she right to have supported these claims and not some others? Only she and her readers can answer that question for sure. Some readers might say no, that she needs to support other claims as well. Others may say yes, that these are the key claims needing support. Arguing effectively depends on your ability to choose for the benefit of your audience which claims to state and support. Where you present them—and how—becomes part of the rhetorical structure of your essay.

GUIDELINES FOR WRITING FIRST DRAFTS

You are now about to begin writing. The following guidelines are suggestions about what to think about and do as you write.

Keep in Mind the Needs of Your Audience

As you write the drafts of your essay, think of your audience and its needs. You will write better essays if you write for an audience that includes not just your instructor but anyone who enjoys literature and has ideas about it. Your goal is to convince them that your ideas have merit. Imagine yourself in conversation with your audience. In order to follow your line of thought, they will want to know certain things. Try to anticipate and supply their needs, just as you would if you were talking with them in person.

One of their needs is for clarity. They deserve a full and clear explanation of the points you are making. Your readers—including your instructor—cannot read your mind. Assume that they have already read the work or can read it. This means that you need only summarize and paraphrase those parts of the work that illustrate your points. But if you do not spell out your ideas, your readers may miss them altogether. In being fully clear, you may feel that you are being childishly obvious, but it is better to be obvious than risk having readers miss your points.

Your readers also need to be convinced. Assume that they want to learn from you, but do not expect them to surrender their views of the work just because you tell them to. Think of them as constantly asking, Why should we believe what you say? Your task is to explain and show them why.

Avoid Extreme Subjectivity (Overuse of "I")

Should you use "I" in essays about literature? Some teachers insist that students not use "I." One reason is that teachers want students to avoid stating their opinions without supporting them with facts and reasoning. We are used to asserting opinions in casual conversation: "The Harry Potter books are wonderful!" But the essay form demands proof and reasoning. Another reason is that if you fill your essays with phrases like "I feel," "I think," "I believe," "It seems to me," your essay, no matter how thorough and well reasoned, will sound overly opinionated. Notice how the author of the essay on the *Odyssey* uses "I" frequently in her notes and journal but eliminates it entirely from her essay.

Having said this, however, essays about literature are inevitably "subjective." Yes, you have to pay careful attention to details in the text. These are the basis for all your claims about it. Yes, you have to use sound logic to support claims. Yes, you have to be objective—willing to entertain understandings of a work other than your own. But nearly all works of literature are open to interpretation. That is why we write about them. Your interpretations are likely to be different from other people's. For this reason, it is standard practice for critics to use "I" when writing interpretations of literature, even in the most scholarly writing. Many essays, in fact, would sound stilted and strange if their authors did not use "I." An example is the student essay on George Eliot's *Adam Bede*, reprinted in Chapter 13. The author compares her own experiences to those of a character in the novel. Even in essays that do not, like this one, take a reader-response approach to literature, the inclusion of an occasional "I believe" makes rhetorical sense. It emphasizes where the author departs from others' opinions: "Scores of critics see Hetty as selfish and thoughtless, but I see her more sympathetically."

Two suggestions, then, pertain to the use of "I" in your essays. First, use "I" helpfully but sparingly. Second, find out your teacher's preference about the use of "I" and write accordingly.

Draw Up a Rough Outline

Many people find rough outlines indispensable for drafting essays. A rough outline consists of the main points you want to make, including the thesis. If the author of the essay about the *Odyssey* had made a rough outline, it would look something like this:

```
                    Introduction
Raise this question: Why does Odysseus leave
Ogygia, which seems like paradise?


                       Body
Claim #1: Ogygia is a paradise.
Support this claim by comparing Ogygia to Eden (my
standard for what paradise is). Give facts from the
two texts.
Claim #2: Odysseus leaves Ogygia because he wants
to be with Penelope and because he is too creative
to be happy there.
Support these claims with facts from the Odyssey.


                    Conclusion
Claim #2 is the answer to my question and therefore
my thesis. I will make it my conclusion as well.
```

Rough outlines are just that—*rough*. They include only the main points of your draft, not all the nuances. Their usefulness is to give you a general sense of your line of thought and rhetorical strategy and to help you make sure that all claims relate to your topic. When you start writing, you may discover new ideas or run into dead ends. If so, redo your rough outline and go on from there.

Begin Writing

Don't bog down. If you have trouble with the introduction (as many people do), move on to the body of the paper. Work on stating your claims clearly and supporting the key ones with evidence. Tackle the claims that seem easiest to support first. Once you get a draft written, it is easier to rearrange claims, to fill in gaps, and to decide for sure what your thesis is.

Use Sound Deductive Reasoning

The deductive logic of your essay is made up of the syllogisms and chains of syllogisms that constitute your reasoning. If one or more of your syllogisms is invalid, the whole of your argument is undermined. Logic is a complex topic we do not have the space to discuss thoroughly here. But a general rule is to avoid *non sequiturs*. The Latin term *non sequitur* means, "It does not follow." A *non sequitur* results from the improper—that is, illogical—statement of a syllogism. For example, the conclusion of the following syllogism "does not follow" from the premises:

MAJOR PREMISE: All complex characters are fascinating.

MINOR PREMISE: Anna Karenina is fascinating.

CONCLUSION: Anna Karenina is complex.

Just because Anna is fascinating does not mean she is complex. She may be fascinating for many other reasons. The correct statement of this syllogism is as follows:

MAJOR PREMISE: All complex characters are fascinating.

MINOR PREMISE: Anna Karenina is a complex character.

CONCLUSION: Therefore, Anna is fascinating.

When you plan and write your essay, think about the validity of your most important syllogisms. After you finish the first draft, go back over it to make sure your syllogisms are valid. For practice, identify some of the key syllogisms in one of the essays in Chapter 13 or in an argumentative essay in a newspaper or news magazine. Write down the syllogisms and see if they are properly stated.

Support Key Claims with Facts

The believability of your argument rests not only on the validity of your reasoning but on the truth of your premises. The logic of your syllogisms may be perfectly valid, but if readers do not accept your premises as true, they will reject your conclusions, including your thesis:

MAJOR PREMISE: All healthy people eat spinach.

MINOR PREMISE: Hugo is a healthy person.

CONCLUSION: Hugo eats spinach.

This syllogism is stated correctly, but the major premise is highly questionable. Or look again at the correctly stated syllogism about Anna Karenina above. Is it true that "all complex characters are fascinating"? If not, the conclusion that Anna is fascinating is dubious.

Establish the truth of premises by supporting them with facts. Anything in the work is a "fact." Facts can be quotations, words, incidents, details of setting, descriptions of characters, conflicts within the plot, word sounds, punctuation—anything in the work. Facts need not be just quotations; they can be your summaries of scenes and events.

Notice, for example, how the author of the essay on the *Odyssey* combines summary and quotation to support her claim that Odysseus is a craftsman:

> Odysseus is a craftsman, a maker, a builder. He crafts the stratagem of the Trojan Horse. He crafts his escape from Polyphemus, the Cyclops (135). He crafts his way past Scylla and Charybdis (188–89). He crafts his artful speech to Nausicaa that wins her help (90–91). He tells the story of his adventures, Alcinous says, "as though you were a practiced bard" (172). Finally, he crafts the defeat of the suitors. He loves stratagems so much that he invents them for the sheer pleasure of it. After telling Athene one of his elaborate lies, she says,

> He must be indeed a shifty lying fellow who
> could surpass you in all manner of craft even
> though you had a god for your antagonist. Dare-
> devil that you are, full of guile, unwearying
> in deceit, can you not drop your tricks and
> your instinctive falsehood, even now that you
> are in your own country again? (205)

The only "long" quotation in this paragraph is the one at the end. Otherwise, the paragraph consists of the author's summary of relevant facts as well as brief quotations she weaves into her own sentences. She also gives page references, so readers can check her facts or get a sense of their context. Page references have a rhetorical function as well. They say, in effect, "Reader, I know what I'm talking about. If you don't believe me, go check my references."

Use Sound Inductive Reasoning

When you reason inductively, you draw conclusions from facts in the work. Instances of Hamlet's melancholia, for example, lead you to conclude that he is melancholy. When you include inductive reasoning in an essay, you usually reverse this order. You state a claim (the conclusion of your inductive reasoning). Then you present facts that led you to it.

To make your inductive reasoning convincing, keep in mind three rules of evidence. First, you need not report every fact that supports your claim, but give enough facts so readers can see for themselves that your claim is reasonable. Second, report facts that are representative of all the facts, not just isolated, atypical facts (the one and only time that Hamlet is melancholy). Third, account for facts that contradict your thesis. If there are incidents in which Hamlet is not melancholy, you need to explain why these do not nullify your claim that he is melancholy. Often, when you explain away negative examples of your claims, you make your overall argument more subtle and convincing. Hamlet's gaiety, you might argue, does not contradict his melancholia; rather, it is a cover for it, a mask he wears.

Define Key Terms

Learn the meaning of important words in primary sources. Look up words in a good dictionary when you have any doubts about their meaning. Doing so is especially necessary for poetry and earlier authors such as Shakespeare and Chaucer. For definitions of terms, the two most authoritative dictionaries are *The Oxford English Dictionary* (1989); and *Webster's Third New International Dictionary of the English Language* (1966). *The Oxford English Dictionary (OED)* is based on "historical principles"; it describes and gives examples of a word's use over the years. If you want to know what a word meant to Shakespeare or Chaucer, look it up in the *OED*. The *Merriam-Webster's Third International* is a "descriptive" dictionary; it describes how the word is used and spelled today. The college edition of the Merriam, abridged from the *Third New International,* is adequate for nearly all your needs, as are most hardcover "desk" dictionaries on the market. As of this writing, you can search *The American Heritage Dictionary* (3rd edition, 1996) online at http://www.bartleby.com/61. Also, your library may subscribe to the online version of the *OED*. A website that includes a dictionary, a thesaurus, and other materials related to languages is http://www.yourdictionary.com. For definitions of specialized literary terms, such as *gothic* and *Naturalism,* see M. H. Abrams's *A Glossary of Literary Terms* (1999).

Organize Evidence According to a Coherent Plan

Evidence consists of everything you offer in support of your claims and thesis. It includes both your reasoning and whatever facts you use to buttress your reasoning. The most important "coherent plan" for presenting evidence is your line of thought, the chain of enthymemes that lead to your thesis. These will vary from topic to topic. You will have to work out a different plan of reasoning for each essay.

Nonetheless, there are several ways of presenting facts from literature that make evidence easy to follow.

1. *Spatial organization* presents the facts as they appear in the work, from beginning to end.

2. *Chronological organization* takes up the facts in the order in which they occur in time. Often, spatial order is the same as chronological but not always. Many works employ devices such as stream of

consciousness and flashbacks that make spatial sequence different from chronological. Detective fiction, for example, depends on a gradual revelation of past events. Not until you finish reading a detective novel can you know the chronological order of events. One advantage of either organization is that you give the reader the sense that you are covering all the important details of the work.

3. *Organization by ascending order of importance* moves from the least important facts or claims to the most important. The advantage of this method is that it gives your essay suspense by ushering readers toward a climax. Organizing from the least controversial claims to the most controversial is a variation on this plan.

The paragraph about Odysseus's craftsmanship (pages 237–38) combines two of these plans of organization. The author arranges her facts *chronologically* by starting with the Trojan Horse and ending with the defeat of the suitors. Had she arranged them spatially—as they appear in the text—they would be out of chronological sequence. She also arranges her facts, at least roughly, in *ascending order of importance*. She ends with Odysseus's most important stratagem, the defeat of the suitors, and with his most surprising trait, his love of stratagems. This plan provides an orderly review of Odysseus's career, makes her facts easy to follow, and gives her presentation a measure of suspense.

Make Comparisons Complete and Easy to Follow

When you make extended comparisons, organize them so they are easy to follow. Cover the *same aspects* of all the things compared. If you talk about metaphor, symbolism, and imagery in one work, you need to talk about these same things in the other work. Also, discuss items *in the same order.* If you talk about metaphor, symbolism, and imagery in one work, keep this same order when you discuss the other work: metaphor first, symbolism second, imagery last. The outline for such a comparison would look like this:

Work #1
   Metaphor
   Symbolism
   Imagery

Work #2
  Metaphor
  Symbolism
  Imagery

For comparisons of more than two things or for long, complex comparisons, another method of organization may be easier for readers to follow:

Metaphor
  Work #1
  Work #2
  Work #3
Symbolism
  Work #1
  Work #2
  Work #3
Imagery
  Work #1
  Work #2
  Work #3

The student essay on the *Odyssey* uses this second plan of comparison:

Claim: Eden and Ogygia are similar.
  Reason #1: Their physical features are similar.
        A. Eden has certain physical features (described).
        B. Ogygia's physical features (described) are almost exactly the same.
  Reason #2: Their inhabitants live comfortable and painfree lives.
        A. Eden
        B. Ogygia
  Reason #3: The inhabitants have companionship.
        A. Eden
        B. Ogygia
  Reason #4: Both places are free from death.
        A. Eden
        B. Ogygia

There are other ways to organize comparisons. You could, for example, discuss all the similarities together, then all the differences. The general rule is to make the comparison thorough and orderly, so readers can see all the lines of similarity and difference. Doing this usually requires ample revisions of your outlines and drafts. The next chapter, Chapter 10, deals with the revision and editing stages of the writing process. It concludes with two drafts of a comparison essay, illustrating how revision can improve the organizational structure of an extended comparison.

Checklist for Drafting the Essay

- ❖ Plan the rhetorical structure of your essay.
- ❖ Make a rough outline of the essay.
- ❖ Compose a title that signals the focus of the essay.
- ❖ Decide where you will state your thesis.
- ❖ Write an introduction that explains the problem(s) you plan to solve.
- ❖ Lay out the organization of the body of the essay.
- ❖ Write out your key syllogisms. State them so they make logical sense.
- ❖ Decide which premises you will support with evidence.
- ❖ Make sure your premises follow convincingly from the evidence.
- ❖ Define important terms.
- ❖ Organize comparisons so they are easy to follow.
- ❖ Write a conclusion that announces how the problem is solved.

Works Cited

Abrams, M.H. *A Glossary of Literary Terms.* 7th ed. Fort Worth: Harcourt, 1999.

The American Heritage Dictionary. 3rd ed. Boston: Houghton Mifflin, 2000. <http://www.bartleby.com/61>.

Gove, Philip Babcock, ed. *Webster's Third New International Dictionary of the English Language.* Unabridged. Springfield: Merriam, 1966.

Simpson, J.A., and E.S.C. Weiner. *Oxford English Dictionary.* 2nd ed. 20 vols. Oxford: Oxford UP, 1989.

yourDictionary.com. 2000. 24 October 2000 <http://www.yourdictionary.com>.

10

Revising and Editing

REVISE THROUGHOUT THE WRITING PROCESS

The third stage of the writing process is revision. The word *revision* means "to see again." Revision takes place throughout the writing process. You constantly see your work anew, and act upon that fresh understanding by rewriting. Assume that you will make several drafts of the essay, from scribbled lists to finished product—say, three to five drafts. Give yourself time—a week or so—to write the essay. You may be able to bring off an "all-nighter" every now and then, but few people can do so consistently. Work hard for a while, put your essay aside, let the ideas percolate, then come back to the essay fresh.

REVISE FOR THE FINAL DRAFT

Some people could go on revising forever, but most need to move quickly toward a final draft. The final draft differs from the earlier drafts because readers expect it to conform to "formal" rules that govern a particular format. To help yourself prepare the final draft, think about what your audience will expect from it. They will, of course, want the qualities of a good argument we have discussed: interesting topic, sound logic, thorough discussion of the works, easy-to-follow organization. But readers want also to feel that your writing is worth reading, that you are competent to talk about your topic, and that you can teach them something. Rhetoricians call this personal quality ethos. *Ethos* is the image that writers project of themselves. You cannot help projecting a "self" when you write. Create, therefore, a compelling, trustworthy ethos.

The content and organization of the essay are the most important indicators of your ethos. By reasoning well and supporting claims with evidence, you make readers feel that you are conscientious and that your essay is intellectually sound. Other aspects of the final draft also help create a persuasive ethos. They are prose style, rules of usage, and physical format (the appearance of the essay). We treat these aspects in this chapter.

WRITE A CLEAR AND READABLE PROSE STYLE

Style is the way writers put words together in units of thought—sentences—and the way they link sentences to make larger units—paragraphs, essays, books. Closely related to style is tone. *Tone* is a writer's attitude toward the material and the readers. You convey tone through style.

Adjust your style and tone to fit the occasion and audience. Sometimes the occasion and audience call for informal and humorous writing, such as for speeches made at parties or essays written for satirical magazines. At other times, they call for gravity and formality, such as for newspaper editorials and letters of application. The occasion and audience for essays about literature almost always require a measure of formality. Your audience is usually intelligent, literate, and serious. They take the trouble to read your essay because they want to learn. They might welcome some levity, some lightheartedness, but they mostly want you to get down to business and not waste their time. They want to learn from you economically, to get through your essay with pleasure but as effortlessly as possible.

Your style for this audience should meet these needs. Make your style clear, interesting, and readable: vary sentence structure, avoid the passive voice, emphasize active and concrete verbs, eliminate wordiness and unnecessary repetition, use words with precision, and base syntax on the natural rhythms of spoken English. Give your tone seriousness of purpose but avoid stiff formality: Stay away from incomprehensible words and long complex sentences. Because essays about literature involve personal judgment, use "I" to distinguish your ideas from those of others and to stress the individuality of your views. But use "I" sparingly, so you do not give the impression of being subjective and egotistical.

A well-known guide to writing graceful and clear prose is *The Elements of Style* by William Strunk, Jr., available at no charge on the Internet at http://www.bartleby.com/141/index.html.

HAVE OTHER PEOPLE READ AND RESPOND TO YOUR DRAFT

In one sense, writing is an isolated, individualized task. We have to do it alone. In another sense, however, it can be collaborative. Other people's reactions to your writing can help you to improve. After all, your writing is *for* an audience. So, before you draw up a final draft, you might get someone else to read your essay. Ask them to answer such questions as these: Can you follow my line of thought? Do you agree with my reasoning? Can I support my claims more convincingly? Is my writing clear and fluent? Should I use different strategies of persuasion? Will my audience understand me? You may disagree with the answers you get, but even "wrong" answers can help you see "right" strategies. Your goal is to get fresh perceptions of your essay so you can make your final draft as good as it can be.

EDIT THE FINAL DRAFT

The final draft of your essay is the one you will "publish." Publishing can mean printing the essay in a journal, newspaper, magazine, or book. It can also mean distributing it yourself to a group of people. For university courses, it means turning in the essay to the professor or to the rest of the class. The "published" draft of the essay should follow a certain format. What should that format be? The format described in the following sections is typical of the writing done in a university setting and is based on the guidelines in the *MLA Handbook for Writers of Research Papers* (6th ed., 2003).

Rules of Usage

Usage refers to the way English is applied in most published writing: in newspapers, magazines, books, advertisements, brochures, financial reports, and scholarly journals. Although some rules of usage are arbitrary and seem to serve no purpose other than convention, most serve important purposes. First, they often aid clarity. Punctuation, for example, represents parts of the sentence—pauses and inflections—that words do not. Marks of punctuation can be as important as the words. Misplace a comma, and you can change the meaning of a sentence. A hilarious treatment of punctuation gone astray is Lynne Truss's *Eats, Shoots and Leaves: The Zero Tolerance Approach to Punctuation* (2004). Second, rules of usage help communicate your ethos. Rules of usage are a form of etiquette; educated people are expected to follow them. By doing so, you communicate an image of competence and respect for your readers.

If you are unfamiliar with basic rules of usage, they are not difficult to learn. Study and practice using them, and you will learn them quickly. Get a handbook of usage, such as *Hodge's Harbrace Handbook,* and refer to it when you write. An online resource is *Guide to Grammar and Writing* at http://www.ccc.commnet.edu/grammar.

Although all rules of usage are important for your writing, in this book we concentrate on rules common to essays about literature. These include rules that govern documentary procedure, which we discuss in Chapter 11, as well as those that apply to such things as quotations, punctuation, capitalization, underlining, and the physical format of papers. In the following sections, we describe basic rules of usage. For a more thorough treatment of such rules, see the *MLA Handbook for Writers of Research Papers.* See, also, the sample essays in Chapters 8, 11, 13, and at the end of this chapter for examples of how these rules are used in practice.

Citations of Sources

Give credit for the sources you draw upon. These include primary sources (the works of literature you discuss) and secondary sources (works by critics and historians that bear upon the primary sources). You give credit in two ways: by means of parenthetical citations within your text and a Works Cited list, located at the end. You can find guidelines for setting up and punctuating parenthetical citations on pages 304–10 and for Works Cited lists on pages 312–13. The sample essays throughout the book, including the one at the end of this chapter, illustrate both kinds of citation. Many of the illustrations under "Quotations" in this chapter include parenthetical citations.

Quotations

Quotations serve two key purposes in essays about literature: They help exemplify claims, and they reproduce the language of the source.

1. **Identify quotations in your text.**
   a. For primary sources, identify the author, the work, and the context of quotations.

   Incomplete Information

   The woman tells her lover that the world "isn't ours anymore."

   Complete Information

   Near the climax of the lovers' conversation in Hemingway's "Hills Like White Elephants," the woman tells the man that the world "isn't ours anymore."

   Readers need to know *where* in the text quotations occur. Otherwise, the quotation could seem meaningless.

   b. Identify quotations from secondary sources by giving the author's name or claim to authority.

   Name Missing

   "A fully articulated pastoral idea of America did not emerge until the end of the eighteenth century."

   Name Included

   Leo Marx claims that a "fully articulated pastoral idea of America did not emerge until the end of the eighteenth century."

   Claim to Authority Included (Instead of Name)

   A prominent American critic claims that a "fully articulated pastoral idea of America did not emerge until the end of the eighteenth century."

There are several reasons for introducing quotations: First, giving the critic's name or claim to authority clearly distinguishes your ideas from the other writer's. Quotation marks can of course help to make this distinction, but introducing the quote by author makes the distinction emphatic. Second, when readers see quotation marks, they are naturally curious about who said the quoted passage. As they read your essay, they want also to note the different approaches of the critics you cite. Third, by giving the author's name, you distinguish between secondary and primary sources, a distinction that may not be clear from the quotation alone. Finally, it is a matter of courtesy to give credit in your text to the words and ideas of other people. You are, in a way, thanking them for their help.

2. **Introduce quotations with your words and with correct punctuation.**

Although quotation marks provide visual evidence of a quotation, you need to indicate who speaks and, if relevant, the nature and context of the speech. You do this in your own words and with proper punctuation.

a. When you introduce a quotation with a complete sentence, end the sentence with a colon.

```
Warren is impatient with Silas's shortcomings and unfor-

givingly judgmental:

     "I told him so last haying, didn't I?

     'If he left then,' I said, 'that ended it.'" (13-14)
```

b. When you introduce a quotation with an incomplete sentence, end the phrase with a comma. Such phrases are usually "tags" that indicate who speaks: "he says," "she states," "they shout out," etc.

```
The monster tells Victor, "I was benevolent and good;

misery made me a fiend" (95-96).

As Sterrenburg states, "The Monster proves a very philo-

sophical rebel" (161).
```

If you put the tag inside the quotation, separate it from the quotation with commas.

```
"I am malicious," he says, "because I am miserable"
(138).
```

c. When you blend quotations into your own sentences, so that the quotations are part of the grammatical structure of your sentences, you don't need to separate the quotation from your words with punctuation.

```
She realizes that "he has come home to die" (111).
His physical weakness
     hurt my heart the way he lay
     And rolled his old head on that sharp-edged
        chair-back. (147-48)
```

Note that even though the second example is an indented quotation, it is nonetheless a grammatical part of the author's sentence and thus needs no punctuation.

3. **Integrate quotations into your own sentences.**

```
Because of this increasing darkness, Brown cannot be
quite sure of what he does or hears. The devil's walking
stick, for example, seems to turn into a snake, but this
may be "an ocular deception, assisted by the uncertain
light" (76). He thinks he hears the voices of Deacon
Gookin and the minister, but "owing doubtless to the
depth of the gloom of that particular spot, neither the
travellers nor their steeds were visible" (81).
```

Once you introduce your source, you may want to integrate short quotations—words or phrases—into your own sentences, as in the above example. The quotations become part of your own thoughts rather than thoughts separate from yours. This technique allows you to summarize a source concisely and yet retain the language and authenticity of the source. If you use this method, you should obey several rules.

a. As much as possible, make the tenses in the quotation correspond to the tenses of your sentences.

Awkward

```
While the legislators cringe at the sudden darkness,
"all eyes were turned to Abraham Davenport." [Cringe is
present tense; turned is past tense.]
```

Better

```
While the legislators cringe at the sudden darkness,
"all eyes [turn] to Abraham Davenport."
While the legislators cringe at the sudden darkness,
"all eyes" turn to Abraham Davenport.
```

b. Be sure that sentences are complete.

Incomplete

```
Yeats asks if "before the indifferent beak." [Incomplete
sentence; makes no sense.]
```

Complete

```
Yeats asks if Leda "put on [the swan's] knowledge" be-
fore his "indifferent beak could let her drop."
```

c. Clarify pronouns that have no clear antecedents.

Unclear

```
Captain Wentworth says, "It had been my doing--solely
mine. She would not have been obstinate if I had not
been weak." [The antecedent of "she" is unclear.]
```

Clear

```
Captain Wentworth says, "It had been my doing--solely
mine. [Louisa] would not have been obstinate if I had
not been weak."
```

d. Be sure that subject and verb agree.

Disagreement

```
Wilfred Owen says that the only prayer said for those
who die in battle is war's noise, which "patter out
their hasty orisons." [Subject: noise; verb: patter. The
subject is singular, the verb plural.]
```

Agreement

```
Wilfred Owen says that the only prayer said for those
who die in battle is the "rapid rattle" of guns, which
"patter out their hasty orisons." [Subject: guns; verb:
patter. Both subject and verb are now plural.]
```

When you integrate a quotation into your sentence, make it a grammatical part of the sentence. The entire sentence, including the quotation, must conform to the standard rules of usage. See item 5 below for methods of altering (interpolating) quotations.

4. **Quote accurately.** Copy exactly what the author has written.

5. **Make editorial changes in quotations clearly and correctly.** You may legitimately change the quotation in two ways:
   a. By using *ellipses.* An ellipsis (three spaced periods) indicates omitted material. Writers often leave out sections of quotations for the sake of brevity or clarity. To indicate omitted material in the middle of a sentence, use three periods. Put spaces before each period and after the last one. Here, for example, is a quoted sentence with omitted material *within* the sentence.

   ```
   As one critic says, "Oedipus is guilty for two reasons:
   because of the deeds he actually committed . . . and be-
   cause of his desire to commit them."
   ```

   To indicate omitted material from the *end* of a sentence, follow this sequence: space after the last word, then three spaced periods, and finally the quotation mark right after the last period.

```
In certain moods, Wordsworth confessed, he "was often
unable to believe that material things can live for-
ever . . . ."
```

If your *parenthetical reference* comes at the end of a quotation like the preceding one, put a space after the last word, then the three spaced periods, then the quotation mark, then the parenthetical reference, then the final period.

```
In certain moods, Wordsworth confessed, he "was often
unable to believe that material things can live for-
ever . . ." (175).
```

You can also use an ellipsis to indicate the omission of whole sentences, a paragraph, or several paragraphs. The following example omits part of a long paragraph.

```
Ruskin gives two reasons for his belief that to demand
perfection of art is to misunderstand it: "The first is
that no great man ever stops working till he has reached
his point of failure. . . . The second reason is that im-
perfection is in some sort essential to all that we know
of life."
```

In this example the period goes immediately after the final word of the sentence ("failure"), then a space, then the three spaced periods.

There is no need to place ellipses at the *beginning* of quotations:

```
Even the commonest people, the duke says, would elicit
from her "the approving speech, / Or blush, at least."
```

b. By using *brackets*. Brackets indicate editorial changes that *you,* not the author, make to clarify the quotation or to make it fit the grammatical structure of your sentence. Use brackets for *your* changes, not parentheses. Otherwise, your reader will construe them as part of the original quote.

Unclear

```
Alceste says that "sins which cause the blood to freeze /
Look innocent beside (Célimène's) treacheries."
```

Clear

```
Alceste says that "sins which cause the blood to freeze /
Look innocent beside [Célimène's] treacheries."
```

```
Flaubert says that "she [has] an excess of energy."
```

6. **Indent long quotations.** A *long quotation* consists of more than four lines of poetry or prose. Usually, your introduction to a long quotation will be a complete sentence. Conclude your sentence, then, with a *colon* (not a comma or a period). Indent the quotation ten spaces (one inch) from the left margin. Do not use quotation marks for indented quotations.

```
The duke is chagrined that his own name and presence were
not the sole sources of her joy:
                                                        She had
       A heart--how shall I say?--too soon made glad,
       Too easily impressed; she liked whate'er
       She looked on, and her looks went everywhere.
       Sir, 'twas all one! My favour at her breast,
       The dropping of the daylight in the West,
       The bough of cherries some officious fool
       Broke in the orchard for her, the white mule
       She rode with round the terrace—all and each
       Would draw from her alike the approving speech,
       Or blush, at least.
```

As in this example, position the words of a quoted poem, especially in the first line, exactly where they appear in the line. If you are quoting a whole paragraph of prose, do not indent the first line. Instead, place it flush to the left margin of the quotation. If you quote more than one paragraph, indent the first line of each as you normally would.

7. **Punctuate quotations from prose correctly.**
   a. Use *double quotation* marks (" ") for quotations. For quotations within quotations, use double quotation marks for the main quote and single quotation marks (the apostrophe mark) for the inner quote.

   ```
   After his interview with Hester, Dimmesdale sinks into
   self-doubt: "'Have I then sold myself,' thought the min-
   ister, 'to the fiend whom, if men say true, this yellow-
   starched and velveted old hag has chosen for her prince
   and master!'"
   ```

   b. Put *periods* and *commas* inside quotation marks.

   ```
   After performing her "duties to God," as she called
   them, she was ready for her "duty to man."
   ```

   c. Put *colons* and *semicolons* outside of quotation marks, unless they are part of the original text being quoted.

   ```
   She had the "exquisite pleasure of art"; her husband had
   only envy and hatred.
   ```

   d. Put *other marks of punctuation* (question marks, dashes, exclamation points) inside quotation marks when they are part of the quoted material, outside when they are not.

   ```
   One critic asked, "Could the Pearl Poet really be the
   author of Sir Gawain and the Green Knight?"
   But can it be, as one critic claims, that "the Pearl
   Poet really [is] the author of Sir Gawain and the Green
   Knight"?
   ```

8. **Punctuate quotations from poetry correctly**
   a. *When quoting one line of poetry or less,* you can make the quotation part of your sentence. Use a slash mark, with a space before and after it, to indicate line divisions.

```
Hopkins describes God's grandeur as gathering "to a
greatness, like the ooze of oil / crushed" (3-4).
```

b. *When quoting more than three lines of poetry (or, if you prefer not to use slash marks),* indent the quotation ten spaces (one inch) from the left margin. Indented quotations of poetry do not need quotation marks, nor do they need slashes to mark line divisions. Double space between lines.

```
Frost describes nature in metaphoric terms:
            Part of a moon was falling down the west,
            Dragging the whole sky with it to the hills.
            Its light poured softly in her lap. (103-05)
```

Some people prefer not to use slash marks when quoting poetry. Instead, they indent quotations even if they are short.

```
Hopkins describes God's grandeur as gathering
            to a greatness, like the ooze of oil
    Crushed. (3-4)
```

c. *When you indent quotations from poems,* place the lines exactly where they appear in the poem.

```
Mary offers a counter definition of home:
                    I should have called it
    Something you somehow haven't to deserve. (119-20)
```

In this example, part of the first line is omitted. The rest of the line—quoted here—is printed where it appears in the original.

d. *If a line of poetry extends past the right margin,* continue it on the next line. Indent the continued line three spaces.

```
They take a serpentine course, their arms flash in the
    sun--hark to the musical clank,
```

This example is from Whitman's "Cavalry Crossing a Ford" (page 16). Many of his long lines turn over to a second line.

Other Rules of Usage Related to Essays about Literature

Essays about literature obey the same rules of usage as other essays. Several rules deserve special mention.

1. **Tense.** Describe fictional events, whether in drama, poetry, or prose fiction, in the present tense. For examples of this practice, see the student essays in this and other chapters.

2. **Authors' names.** When you mention an author the first time, use the full name (Charles Dickens). For subsequent references, use the last name (Dickens).

3. **Underlining versus italicizing.** For student papers, the *MLA Handbook* recommends underlining instead of italicizing because underlining is easier to see.

4. **Words used as words.** Underline words used as words.

   In England the word <u>honor</u> is spelled with a <u>u</u>: <u>honour</u>.

5. **Titles**
   a. Capitalize the first letter of the title, plus the first letter of all words except articles, short prepositions, conjunctions, and the preposition *to* in infinitives ("First to Go"). Capitalize the first letter after a colon.

      "How I Won the World but Lost My Soul to the Devil's Wiles"

      In the following example, the colon indicates the subtitle of the book.

      <u>Exile's Return: A Narrative of Ideas</u>

   b. Use quotation marks for titles of works included within larger works. Examples are short stories; short poems; songs; chapter titles; articles in journals, magazines, and newspapers; and unpublished works such as dissertations and master's theses.
   c. Underline the titles of works published independently, such as books, plays, long poems published as books, periodicals, pam-

phlets, novels, movies, compact discs, works of art, works of music, and radio and television programs. An exception is sacred writings such as the Bible, books of the Bible, the Koran, and the Talmud.

d. Do not underline, italicize, or put in quotation marks the titles of your own essays.

e. Many instructors prefer that your essay titles include full names of authors and works.

Incomplete

```
The Four Stages of Knowledge in Huck Finn
```

Complete

```
The Four Stages of Knowledge in Mark Twain's The
Adventures of Huckleberry Finn
```

f. Shortened titles. If your instructor approves, in the text of your essay you may use shortened titles for works you frequently cite: "Prufrock" for "The Love Song of J. Alfred Prufrock" or *Huck Finn* for *The Adventures of Huckleberry Finn.*

6. Foreign language terms

a. Underline foreign words used in an English text, such as *sans doute, et tu Brute, amor vincit omnia.*

```
She objected to her son-in-law's behavior because it was
not comme il faut.
```

Reproduce, either by hand or in type, all marks and accents as they appear in the original language: *étude, à propos, même, übermensch, año, leçon.*

b. Some foreign words, like *cliché, laissez-faire,* and *genre,* have been naturalized—that is incorporated into—English usage and need not be underlined. Use your dictionary to determine whether the word or phrase needs underlining. Foreign words in dictionaries are either italicized or placed at the back of the book in a separate section.

```
Adam Smith advocated a laissez-faire economic policy.
```

c. Do not underline quotations that are entirely in another language.

```
Louis XIV once said, "L'état, c'est moi."
```

PHYSICAL FORMAT

As with rules of usage, the appearance of your essay also affects your argument. Readers want an essay that is easy to read, pleasant to hold, and attractive to view. The more care you take with the appearance of the essay, the more competent your readers will think you are. Although your instructor may have specific preferences, the following are standard guidelines.

1. **Typewritten and handwritten essays.** Most instructors prefer that you type or print all your work. Some may allow you to handwrite college essays. Before you do, however, check with your instructor. Whether you handwrite, type, or print your essay, use only one side of each sheet of paper. For *handwritten* essays, use black or blue ink. (Pencil smears and rubs off). Use lined paper. Write on every other line. Write legibly.

2. **Paper.** Use standard-size paper (8 1/2 × 11″), not legal-pad size or notepad size. Use a sturdy weight of paper. Avoid paper that has been ripped out of a spiral-bound notebook.

3. **Spacing.** Double-space everything, including indented quotations and works cited entries.

4. **Pagination.** Number *all* pages, beginning with the first page. Number pages consecutively, including pages for endnotes and works cited. Put the page numbers in the upper right-hand corner of each page. To avoid having pages misplaced, put your last name before each page number, with a space between the two. Example:

```
                                         Caraway 16
```

5. **Margins.** For typewritten essays, leave one-inch margins at the top, bottom, and sides. This gives the page a "frame" and a place for corrections and comments. For handwritten essays, leave margins at the top, bottom, and left side.

6. **First page.** One inch from the top of the first page, on the left-hand side, put your name, the instructor's name, the course title, and the date, each on a separate line. Double-space between the lines. After the last line (the date), double-space again and center your title. If your title has more than one line, double-space between lines. Double-space between the title and the first line of text. Do not underline your own title or put it in quotation marks.

Title pages for college essays—even research essays—are unnecessary. But if your instructor expects a title page, check with him or her for its content and form. For examples of first pages, see the sample essay at the end of this chapter and those in the last chapter of this book.

7. **Corrections.** You may write corrections on final copies of essays—if the corrections are few and inconspicuous. In typed essays, white out incorrect letters and write or type in the correct letters. In hand-written essays, draw a horizontal line through unwanted words and write the correct words just *above* the line. Separate run-together words with vertical lines (for example, made│a│mistake). To delete words, phrases, and clauses, draw a single horizontal line through them. Add words, phrases, and clauses by writing them in above the line. Use a caret (∧) below the line to show where inserted material should go.

8. **Putting the essay pages together.** Avoid covers or binders. Join the pages of your essay with a paperclip, unless your instructor specifies some other method.

9. **Copies.** Make a photocopy of your essay or backup a copy on a disc. If your instructor loses your essay, you can immediately present him or her with a copy. If your instructor keeps your essay indefinitely, you will have a copy for your files.

10. **To fold or not to fold.** Leave your essay unfolded unless your instructor specifies otherwise.

SAMPLE ESSAY IN TWO DRAFTS

The student essay that follows the poem below gives a brief idea of how the revising process works. Nearly all writers, no matter how experienced, go through several drafts of an essay before they produce the final draft. Printed here are an early draft of the essay and, after considerable revision, a final draft. Since the essay is about a poem by

Robert Frost, we reprint the poem here. The poem first appeared in
North of Boston, published by Henry Holt in 1914.

THE DEATH OF THE HIRED MAN

Robert Frost

Mary sat musing on the lamp-flame at the table
Waiting for Warren. When she heard his step,
She ran on tip-toe down the darkened passage
To meet him in the doorway with the news
And put him on his guard. "Silas is back."
She pushed him outward with her through the door
And shut it after her. "Be kind," she said.
She took the market things from Warren's arms
And set them on the porch, then drew him down
To sit beside her on the wooden steps. 10

"When was I ever anything but kind to him?
But I'll not have the fellow back," he said.
"I told him so last haying, didn't I?
'If he left then,' I said, 'that ended it.'
What good is he? Who else will harbor him
At his age for the little he can do?
What help he is there's no depending on.
Off he goes always when I need him most.
'He thinks he ought to earn a little pay,
Enough at least to buy tobacco with, 20
So he won't have to beg and be beholden.'
'All right,' I say, 'I can't afford to pay
Any fixed wages, though I wish I could.'
'Someone else can.' 'Then someone else will have to.'
I shouldn't mind his bettering himself
If that was what it was. You can be certain,
When he begins like that, there's someone at him
Trying to coax him off with pocket-money,—
In haying time, when any help is scarce.
In winter he comes back to us. I'm done." 30

"Sh! not so loud: he'll hear you," Mary said.

"I want him to: he'll have to soon or late."

"He's worn out. He's asleep beside the stove.
When I came up from Rowe's I found him here,
Huddled against the barn-door fast asleep,
A miserable sight, and frightening, too—
You needn't smile—I didn't recognize him—

I wasn't looking for him—and he's changed.
Wait till you see."

        "Where did you say he'd been?"

"He didn't say. I dragged him to the house,   40
And gave him tea and tried to make him smoke.
I tried to make him talk about his travels.
Nothing would do: he just kept nodding off."

"What did he say? Did he say anything?"

"But little."

        "Anything? Mary, confess
He said he'd come to ditch the meadow for me."

"Warren?"

        "But did he? I just want to know."

"Of course he did. What would you have him say?
Surely you wouldn't grudge the poor old man
Some humble way to save his self-respect.   50
He added, if you really care to know,
He meant to clear the upper pasture, too.
That sounds like something you have heard before?
Warren, I wish you could have heard the way
He jumbled everything. I stopped to look
Two or three times—he made me feel so queer—
To see if he was talking in his sleep.
He ran on Harold Wilson—you remember—
The boy you had in haying four years since.
He's finished school, and teaching in his college.   60
Silas declares you'll have to get him back.
He says they two will make a team for work:
Between them they will lay this farm as smooth!
The way he mixed that in with other things.
He thinks young Wilson a likely lad, though daft
On education—you know how they fought
All through July under the blazing sun,
Silas up on the cart to build the load,
Harold along beside to pitch it on."

"Yes, I took care to keep well out of earshot."   70

"Well, those days trouble Silas like a dream.
You wouldn't think they would. How some things linger!

Harold's young college boy's assurance piqued him.
After so many years he still keeps finding
Good arguments he sees he might have used.
I sympathize. I know just how it feels
To think of the right thing to say too late.
Harold's associated in his mind with Latin.
He asked me what I thought of Harold's saying
He studied Latin like the violin   80
Because he liked it—that an argument!
He said he couldn't make the boy believe
He could find water with a hazel prong—
Which showed how much good school had ever done him.
He wanted to go over that. But most of all
He thinks if he could have another chance
To teach him how to build a load of hay—"

"I know, that's Silas' one accomplishment.
He bundles every forkful in its place,
And tags and numbers it for future reference,   90
So he can find and easily dislodge it
In the unloading. Silas does that well.
He takes it out in bunches like big birds' nests.
You never see him standing on the hay
He's trying to lift, straining to lift himself."

"He thinks if he could teach him that, he'd be
Some good perhaps to someone in the world.
He hates to see a boy the fool of books.
Poor Silas, so concerned for other folk,
And nothing to look backward to with pride,   100
And nothing to look forward to with hope.
So now and never any different."

Part of a moon was falling down the west,
Dragging the whole sky with it to the hills.
Its light poured softly in her lap. She saw
And spread her apron to it. She put out her hand
Among the harp-like morning-glory strings,
Taut with the dew from garden bed eaves,
As if she played unheard the tenderness
That wrought on him beside her in the night.   110
"Warren," she said, "he has come home to die:
You needn't be afraid he'll leave you this time."

"Home," he mocked gently.

"Yes, what else but home?
It all depends on what you mean by home.
Of course he's nothing to us, any more
Than was the hound that came a stranger to us
Out of the woods, worn out upon the trail."

"Home is the place where, when you have to go there,
They have to take you in."

"I should have called it
Something you somehow haven't to deserve."   120

Warren leaned out and took a step or two,
Picked up a little stick, and brought it back
And broke it in his hand and tossed it by.
"Silas has better claim on us you think
Than on his brother? Thirteen little miles
As the road winds would bring him to his door.
Silas has walked that far no doubt to-day.
Why didn't he go there? His brother's rich,
A somebody—director in the bank."

"He never told us that."

"We know it though."   130

"I think his brother ought to help, of course.
I'll see to that if there is need. He ought of right
To take him in, and might be willing to—
He may be better than appearances.
But have some pity on Silas. Do you think
If he'd had any pride in claiming kin
Or anything he looked for from his brother,
He'd keep so still about him all this time?"

"I wonder what's between them."

"I can tell you.
Silas is what he is—we wouldn't mind him—   140
But just the kind that kinsfolk can't abide.
He never did a thing so very bad.
He don't know why he isn't quite as good
As anyone. He won't be made ashamed
To please his brother, worthless though he is."

"*I* can't think Si ever hurt anyone."

"No, but he hurt my heart the way he lay
And rolled his old head on that sharp-edged chair-back.

He wouldn't let me put him on the lounge.   150
You must go in and see what you can do.
I made the bed up for him there to-night.
You'll be surprised at him—how much he's broken.
His working days are done; I'm sure of it."

"I'd not be in a hurry to say that."

"I haven't been. Go, look, see for yourself.
But, Warren, please remember how it is:
He's come to help you ditch the meadow.
He has a plan. You mustn't laugh at him.
He may not speak of it, and then he may.
I'll sit and see if that small sailing cloud
Will hit or miss the moon."   160
                              It hit the moon.
Then there were three there, making a dim row,
The moon, the little silver cloud, and she.
Warren returned—too soon, it seemed to her,
Slipped to her side, caught up her hand and waited.

"Warren," she questioned.

                         "Dead," was all he answered.

Early Draft

                                        Hargrove 1

    Jennifer Hargrove

    Professor Bell

    English 105-13

    14 April 20--

      A Comparison of Mary and Warren in Robert Frost's

               "The Death of the Hired Man"

      Robert Frost in "The Death of the Hired Man"

    presents two different views of how to respond to

    human need. Into the home of Mary and Warren comes

the derelict hired hand, Silas. Mary and Warren
disagree over how to treat him.

Mary tells Warren to "Be kind" (7) to Silas.
Warren, however, is upset with Silas for having run
out on him the year before, when he needed him most.
"There's no depending on [him]," Warren says (17).
Mary shushes Warren so Silas will not hear him, but
Warren does not care if Silas hears or not: "I want
him to: he'll have to soon or late" (32).

In my opinion, Mary understands Silas much
better than Warren. She is also much more sympathetic than Warren. Her sympathy is like that extended to all people by the Virgin Mary. This may
be why Frost chose Mary's name, to underscore this
quality. She reminds Warren, for example, of
Silas's longstanding argument with the college student Harold Wilson. Warren agrees that Silas is
proud of his one accomplishment, building a load
of hay:

> He bundles every forkful in its place,
> And tags and numbers it for future refer-
>   ence,
> So he can find and easily dislodge it
> In the unloading. (89-92)

Mary then tells Warren that Silas has come home to
die: "You needn't be afraid he'll leave you this
time" (112).

One of the things that most upsets Warren is
that Silas comes to them rather than going to
Silas's brother for help:

Hargrove 3

Why didn't he go there? His brother's rich

A somebody--director in the bank. (128-129)

But Mary explains that probably there is some misunderstanding between Silas and his brother. Also,
she says that Silas is "just the kind that kinsfolk
can't abide" (141). He may be "worthless," she argues, but he "won't be made ashamed / To please his
brother" (144-145).

The climax of the poem comes when Warren seems
to agree reluctantly with Mary that Silas should
stay. She tells him to go inside and check on him.
He quietly returns and catches up her hand. When
she asks him what happened, he replies, simply,
"Dead."

In sum, Warren has many qualities that Mary
does not have. He is quick to blame, cynical, and
even a little stingy. But most of all he lacks the
sympathy, the kindness, and the understanding that
Mary has. She seems also to be more imaginative
than he. Finally, though, her kindness wins him
over to her side. Even though Silas dies, Warren
seems ready to do what Mary wants.

Comments on the Early Draft

This draft was one of several the author wrote before she produced
the final draft. You can see in the first few paragraphs that she is moving toward a concept of how Mary and Warren are different. In the
final paragraph she even states some specific ways in which they are
different. You can see, also, how the details and quotations she gives

between the beginning and end of the essay *might* be relevant to her claims about difference. But notice how almost all the paragraphs in the body of the paper lack topic ideas (topic sentences). Notice also how she never connects any of the poem's details to specific claims. As a result, although the paper begins and ends promisingly, it is more like a summary of the poem than an argument in support of a thesis.

To make the paper better, the author needs to do several things. In the introduction, she needs to clarify and emphasize her thesis. If she put the thesis at the end of the introduction rather than at the beginning, she could better show how all the sentences in the introduction relate to the thesis. In the body of the paper, she needs to state her claims about how Mary and Warren are different and support each with evidence from the text. Each claim could be the topic sentence of a paragraph, followed by supporting evidence. In the conclusion, she needs to restate her thesis, summarize her reasoning, and offer some generalizing idea that pulls the entire essay together.

Final Draft

Hargrove 1

Jennifer Hargrove

Professor Bell

English 105-13

14 April 20--

A Comparison of Mary and Warren in Robert Frost's

"The Death of the Hired Man"

When Silas, the unreliable hired hand, returns to the farm owned by Mary and Warren in Robert Frost's "The Death of the Hired Man," Mary and Warren immediately disagree about what to do with him. Warren wants to send him packing. Mary wants to keep him on and care for him. In recounting their disagreement about how to treat Silas, the poem reveals fundamental differences between them.

The most obvious difference is that Mary is compassionate and Warren is not. The poem continually reveals Mary's pity for the sick and troubled Silas. She tells Warren that she discovered him

> Huddled against the barn-door fast asleep,
> A miserable sight, and frightening, too--.
> (35-36)

His physical weakness

> hurt my heart the way he lay
> And rolled his old head on that sharp-
> edged chair-back. (147-48)

She says that his prospects are bleak:

> Poor Silas, so concerned for other folk,
> And nothing to look backward to with pride,
> And nothing to look forward to with hope.
> So now and never any different. (99-102)

Mary's pity leads her to certain moral conclusions. She feels that they should not just take Silas in, but should try to protect his pride as well. "Be kind," she tells Warren (7). Warren, in contrast, resists hints that he has not done right by Silas. Mary's gentle request to be kind elicits an almost angry response: "When was I ever anything but kind to him?" (11). He is impatient with Silas's shortcomings and unforgivingly judgmental:

Hargrove 3

>   "I told him so last haying, didn't I?
>   'If he left then,' I said, 'that ended
>   it.'" (13-14)

Not caring if Silas hears, he loudly expresses his
bitterness (32). He dismisses Silas's plans to
"ditch the meadow" as the foolish promises of an
insincere old man (44-46).

Underlying their disagreement about how
to treat Silas are more fundamental differences.
One is that they value people differently.
Warren values people for their usefulness and
wants to cast them off when they are no longer
useful:

>   What good is he [Silas]? Who else will har-
>   bor him
>   At his age for the little he can do?
>   What help he is there's no depending on.
>   (15-17)

Even one of Warren's few positive comments about
Silas concerns a useful skill, Silas's ability to
load hay: "Silas does that well" (92). Warren believes, then, that one should be kind to people
only if they are useful. Mary's compassion for
Silas reveals a different view of people. She sees
them as good in themselves. She admits that Silas
may be "worthless" (145) as a hired hand:

>   You'll be surprised at him--how much he's
>   broken.

Hargrove 4

His working days are done; I'm sure of it.
(152-53)

But she insists that their farm is his "home," and
it is their responsibility to receive him. Warren's
definition of home is in keeping with his attitude
toward people:

"Home is the place where, when you have to
go there,

They have to take you in." (118-19)

At "home," in other words, people take care of you
out of duty, not love. Mary's counterdefinition is
in keeping with her belief that people are valuable
in themselves:

I should have called it
Something you somehow haven't to deserve.
(119-20)

People at home give you tenderness no matter what
you've done.

Another difference between them is that Mary
is imaginative and Warren is not. Frost suggests
this quality in the opening line of the poem: "Mary
sat musing on the lamp-flame at the table." The word
<u>muse</u> means "to ponder or meditate," "to consider
reflectively." The word is associated with the Muses
of Greek mythology, "each of whom presided over a
different art or science." Because of this association, the noun <u>muse</u> means "the spirit or power regarded as inspiring and watching over poets,
musicians, and artists; a source of inspiration"

(<u>American Heritage Dictionary</u>). Frost's use of the
term presents Mary as something of a poet. Her
imagination allows her to "understand" Silas. She
guesses why he says he wants to ditch the meadow,
even though he probably knows he cannot:

> Surely you wouldn't grudge the poor old man
> Some humble way to save his self-respect.
>
>   (49-50)

She recognizes why Silas remains troubled by his
arguments with the college boy Harold Wilson:

> I sympathize. I know just how it feels
> To think of the right thing to say too
>   late. (75-76)

She realizes that "he has come home to die" (111).
Warren, in contrast, lacks the imagination to see
past his own practical needs. This limited vision
causes him to be unsympathetic to people who hinder
them. When Warren asks why Silas's brother (a
"somebody--director in the bank," [129]) cannot
take care of Silas, Mary has to tell him that the
banker brother may not want to take Silas in. When
Warren wonders why, Mary uses her imagination to
guess what the trouble may be:

> He don't know why he isn't quite as good
> As anyone. He won't be made ashamed
> To please his brother, worthless though he
>   is. (143-45)

Their different imaginative capacities lead them to
different moral conclusions. Warren wants to get as

much as he gives. Mary's ability to put herself in
the place of troubled people leads her to want to
help them.

A final difference between them is that Mary is
allied to nature and Warren is not. Frost connects
Mary to nature twice. Just before Mary and Warren
exchange definitions of <u>home</u>, Frost describes nature
in metaphoric terms:

> Part of a moon was falling down the west,
> Dragging the whole sky with it to the hills.
> Its light poured softly in her lap.
>   (103-05)

Mary's sympathetic response to this fanciful and
beautiful quality in nature fortifies her compassionate impulses:

> She saw
> And spread her apron to it. She put out her
>   hand
> Among the harp-like morning-glory strings,
> Taut with the dew from the garden bed
>   eaves,
> As if she played unheard the tenderness
> That wrought on him beside her in the
>   night. (105-10)

At the end, Mary sends Warren to check on Silas and
again urges him to be kind. While she waits, she
says, she will

> see if that small sailing cloud
> Will hit or miss the moon. (160-61)

Frost blends her in with nature: The cloud

                      hit the moon.

       Then there were three there, making a dim

           row,

       The moon, the little silver cloud, and

           she. (161-63)

Mary's sympathy with nature, like her view of people and her imagination, also leads to moral conclusions:

       Of course he's nothing to us, any more

       Than was the hound that came a stranger

           to us

       Out of the woods, worn out upon the trail.

           (115-17)

They should care for Silas for the same reason
they cared for the stray dog: Both are living
creatures. Frost does not say anything about
Warren's attitude toward nature, but Warren's not
responding suggests that he lacks Mary's poetic
love for nature. He is a farmer who has reduced
nature to its economic value, just as he has done
with people.

     We might wonder why, if Warren and Mary are
so different, they ever got married. But as it
turns out, Warren is not quite so different from
Mary as he at first seems. Who knows, he may have
married Mary just for her imaginative and compassionate qualities. By the end of their conversation he has come around to her view. He is now

Hargrove 8

sympathetic to Silas and takes his side against the status-minded brother: "I can't think Si ever hurt anyone" (146). He even asserts that maybe Silas's working days are not over after all (154). When he brings news of Silas's death, he does so as Mary would have done, with solemnity and tenderness.

Works Cited

The American Heritage Dictionary of the English
      Language. New College Edition. New York:
      Houghton, 1981.

Frost, Robert. "The Death of the Hired Man."
      North of Boston. New York: Henry Holt, 1914.
      14-23.

Note: Normally, the Works Cited list would appear on a separate page, but we print it here, right after the essay, to save space.

Comments on the Final Draft

The final draft is much better than the early draft. The author opens with just enough information to give readers their bearings and get quickly to her thesis. In the body of the paper, each of the paragraphs has an unmistakable topic sentence. Each of the topic ideas is supported with reasoning and facts from the poem. The last paragraph closes the essay with a summary of the differences between Mary and Warren and an explanation of how, at the end of the poem, they reach harmony.

Notice how the final draft is more complex in its interpretation of the poem than the early draft. The rewriting process often brings about this enhancement. Good argumentative essays have a necessary structure: thesis clearly stated, claims supporting the thesis, evidence supporting claims, conclusion tying everything together. If there is a problem with an essay's structure—as there was in the early draft of this essay—it usually reflects problems with reasoning and organization. Most writers struggle just to get ideas on the page. Their early drafts typically have gaps and inconsistencies. But during the rewriting process, writers force themselves to pay attention to the necessary structures of the essay. By doing so, they make their ideas, reasoning, and organization better.

Checklist for Revising and Editing

❖ Regard your final draft as a "publication" that requires the same care and orderliness as real publications.

❖ Write clear and readable prose.

❖ Follow helpful and expected rules of usage for

- Quotations

- Tense

- Names

- Underlinings

- Words used as words

- Titles

- Foreign language terms.

❖ Format your paper neatly and correctly.

Works Cited

Darling, Charles. *Guide to Grammar and Writing.* Capital Community College Foundation. 2004. 10 Dec. 2004. <http://www.ccc. commnet.edu/grammar>.

Gibaldi, Joseph. *MLA Handbook for Writers of Research Papers,* 6th ed. New York: Modern Language Association of America, 2003.

Glenn, Cheryl, et al. *Hodges' Harbrace Handbook,* 15th ed. Boston: Thomson-Wadsworth, 2004.

Strunk, William, Jr. *The Elements of Style.* Ithaca, NY: W. P. Humphrey, 1918. Bartleby.com. May 1999. 10 Dec. 2004. <http//www. bartleby.com/141/index>.

Truss, Lynne. *Eats, Shoots and Leaves: The Zero Tolerance Approach to Punctuation.* New York: Gotham Books, 2004.

11

Documentation and Research

Documentation, or "giving credit," means identifying the sources you consult when you prepare your essays. Two kinds of sources are relevant to writing about literature: primary sources and secondary sources.

PRIMARY SOURCES

Primary sources are the works of literature themselves. If your essay is about *Hamlet,* then *Hamlet* is your primary source. If you are writing about all of Shakespeare's sonnets, then all of these comprise your primary source. Primary sources are crucial for essays about literature. After all, they are what your essays are about, what you want to interpret. Your most important facts, the ones that support your claims, will come from primary sources.

SECONDARY SOURCES

Facts. For many of your essays, primary sources are the only ones you will need. But if you want to include facts from outside the work or commentary from people outside the work, then you need to use secondary sources. Facts from *secondary sources* include such things as information about the author's life, the period in which the author lived, the author's philosophy, literary history, other authors, the original audience, the work's influence, and similarities to other works. Secondary sources are valuable for what they teach us about the work. They give information that helps us form our own opinions. When we study Hawthorne's fiction, our perception of his themes sharpens when we learn that he was ashamed of his Puritan ancestors' dire deeds. When we learn that Jane Austen used an actual calendar to plot the events of *Pride and Prejudice,* we appreciate the care with which she crafted her fiction. When we compare Shakespeare's sources to his plays, we see his genius for deepening characterization and philosophical themes.

Employ secondary sources, then, to learn as much as you can about a work. Use reliable secondary sources—accurate histories, biographies, autobiographies, memoirs, and interviews. When you include facts from secondary sources, cite them and your sources for them. Keep in mind, though, that secondary sources must be backed up by facts from primary sources. When you quote or summarize critics, make it a practice to buttress their claims with your own analysis of the works themselves.

Testimony.　In addition to facts, secondary sources also contain *testimony,* interpretation by critics. You can find testimony in such places as introductions to individual works, head notes in anthologies, opinion columns on websites, articles in professional journals, chapters in books, and book-length studies.

Although testimony is no substitute for your own skillful argumentation, it can add to the persuasive power of your essays. If you show that certain literary critics agree with your interpretation, readers may more readily accept your claims. Furthermore, testimony indicates that your argument is part of an ongoing debate about the work. Testimony signals that you are aware of the debate and, therefore, of the different solutions already proposed to your problem. By explaining other solutions, you can highlight the one that seems most reasonable or offer new solutions of your own.

Use testimony, then, as a complement to your reasoning and facts. If critics make especially good points or give especially good analyses, summarize their ideas and include apt or telling quotations from their writings. Think of critics as witnesses on your behalf or points of departure for your own ideas.

RESEARCH PAPERS AND THE USE
OF SECONDARY SOURCES

Research paper as interpretation. Because most people associate the use of secondary sources with "research" and "research papers," it is appropriate here to address just what research papers are. Although research papers about literature sometimes deliver information for its own sake, they usually are interpretive. They use information to develop interpretations of one or more works of literature. The writer searches through secondary sources to find facts and opinions that lead to an interpretation. Some research papers begin with summaries of different interpretations before settling on one. Others use only a few secondary sources, either to support and illustrate the author's own ideas or as springboards for alternative interpretations. The sample essay on E. A. Robinson's "Richard Cory" in Chapter 13, for example, takes issue with one critic's opinion in order to present another view.

Research paper as an essay. Interpretive research papers are essays. Here, the terms *research paper* and *research essay* are synonymous. Like all essays, research essays present opinions about a subject. They synthesize *your* discoveries about a topic and *your* evaluation of those discoveries. The reader should hear *your* voice speaking throughout the paper and should be constantly aware of *your* intelligence and consciousness. Research essays are not mere anthologies of facts or of other people's ideas. They have the same qualities of all essays: a unifying idea expressed directly and emphatically in a thesis, an introduction and a conclusion, and paragraphs that relate to the essay's thesis and that follow a logical plan. The sample essay at the end of this chapter exemplifies these traits.

HOW TO FIND INFORMATION AND OPINIONS
ABOUT LITERATURE

How do you find information and opinion about literature? Where do you start? In the next four sections, we present a plan for learning about and gaining access to secondary sources. Since most secondary sources are located in libraries, we base this plan on three major places typical of university libraries: the stacks, the reference room, and the periodicals room. We conclude with a fourth "place," one that exists outside libraries, the Internet.

I. LIBRARY CATALOGS AND STACKS

Your research needs will vary from writing project to writing project. Some projects will require minimal research, others more elaborate research. Let's say, however, that you want to write an essay about one work, "Porphyria's Lover," a well-known poem by Robert Browning. Your instructor asks only that you use the primary source (the poem), but you want to read some secondary sources to get yourself thinking about the poem. Go to the *card catalog* or *online catalog* of your college library, find where the author's works are located in the *stacks*—the shelves where books are stored—and browse among the books in that section. Most college libraries have many books about well-known authors. For Browning, choose several books. Look up "Porphyria's Lover" in the indexes, and read what each book has to say about the work. This should not take long, a few minutes per book.

By doing this kind of exploratory reading, you familiarize yourself with critics' ideas about the work. Sometimes, no matter how carefully you read a work, you may be at a loss for what it means. Doing some introductory reading in secondary sources can clue you in to issues critics have been debating about the work. In your own writing, you can join the discussion by seizing upon one of these issues as your topic. If it turns out you want to incorporate some of this material in your essay, then you need to read the sources carefully, take notes, and give credit for the sources you use.

II. LIBRARY REFERENCE ROOM

What if there is little in the stacks on your author, or what if your teacher asks you to do a full-fledged research paper? You can supplement material you find in the stacks with what you turn up in a second place in the library, the *reference room*. The reference room is especially helpful when books are missing from the stacks (lost or checked out) or when your library's collection on an author is small.

Background information. The reference room of a college library typically includes several kinds of materials. First, it contains books with background information, such as encyclopedias, literary histories, brief biographies, books that describe and illustrate critical reactions to authors, handbooks to literary terms, surveys of contemporary authors, and guides to works by ethnic minorities. Consider beginning your writing project with one of these. They can tell you when and what your author wrote, the author's cultural context, and how critics have interpreted and evaluated the author's work. Some examples are as follows:

Benson, Eugene, and William Toye. <u>The Oxford Companion to</u>

   <u>Canadian Literature</u>. 2nd ed. New York: Oxford UP, 1997.

Brownstone, David, and Irene Franck. <u>Timelines of the Arts and</u>

   <u>Literature</u>. New York: HarperCollins, 1994.

<u>Dictionary of Literary Biography</u>. Detroit: Gale, 1978–.

Drabble, Margaret, ed. <u>The Oxford Companion to English</u>

   <u>Literature</u>. 6th ed. New York: Oxford UP, 2000.

Hart, James D., and Phillip W. Leininger. <u>The Oxford Companion</u>

   <u>to American Literature</u>. 6th ed. New York: Oxford UP, 1995.

Howatson, M. C., ed. <u>The Oxford Companion to Classical</u>

   <u>Literature</u>. 2nd ed. New York: Oxford UP, 1989.

Magill, Frank N., ed. <u>Cyclopedia of World Authors</u>. Rev. 3rd

   ed. 5 vols. Pasadena: Salem, 1997.

<u>Merriam-Webster's Encyclopedia of Literature</u>. Springfield, MA:

   Merriam-Webster, 1995.

Murray, Chris, ed. <u>Encyclopedia of Literary Critics and</u>

   <u>Criticism</u>. 2 vols. London: Fitzroy Dearborn, 1999.

<u>The New Encyclopaedia Britannica</u>. Chicago: Encyclopaedia

   Britannica, 2002.

Scott-Kilvert, Ian, ed. <u>British Writers</u>. 8 vols. plus supple-

   ments. New York: Scribner's, 1979–99.

Stade, George, ed. <u>European Writers</u>. 14 vols. New York:

   Scribner's, 1983.

Unger, Leonard, ed. <u>American Writers: A Collection of Literary</u>

   <u>Biographies</u>. 4 vols. plus supplements. New York: Scribner's,

   1974–98.

Information about primary sources. Another kind of resource in the reference room is books that give specific and specialized information about primary sources. These include concordances and indexes to standard authors like Tennyson, Milton, and Shakespeare as well as books dealing with specialized qualities of works, such as author's use of allusions, Greek mythology, or the Bible.

Bibliographies. Finally, reference rooms house bibliographies. With these, you can make your research systematic and thorough. There are many kinds of bibliographies for the study of language and literature, but for the sake of simplicity they are here divided into five categories.

A. General Reference

Baker, Nancy L., and Nancy Huling. <u>A Research Guide for
   Undergraduate Students: English and American Literature</u>.
   5th ed. New York: MLA, 2000.

<u>Book Review Digest</u>. New York: Wilson, 1905- . Also available
   online.

<u>Book Review Index</u>. Detroit: Gale, 1965-69, 1972- . Also avail-
   able online.

<u>The Essay and General Literature Index</u>. New York: Wilson,
   1931- . Also available online.

Harner, James L. <u>Literary Research Guide: An Annotated Listing
   of Sources in English Literary Studies</u>. 4th ed. New York:
   MLA, 2002.

<u>Humanities Index</u>. New York: Wilson, 1975- . Also available on-
   line as <u>Humanities Abstracts</u>.

<u>MLA International Bibliography of Books and Articles on the
   Modern Languages and Literatures</u>. New York: MLA, 1922- .
   Also available online.

<u>Readers' Guide to Periodical Literature: An Author and Subject
   Index</u>. New York: Wilson, 1901- . Also available online.

MLA International Bibliography. The best place to begin your quest for secondary sources on an author or work is the *MLA International Bibliography (MLAIB)*. The *MLAIB* is the most comprehensive bibliography of books and articles on authors and their works. In fact, it is so comprehensive that it may give you *too* much material, so much that you feel overwhelmed. If that is the case, try some of the more selective bibliographies listed in the next few sections. The *MLAIB* is published annually and covers nearly everything published each year on modern languages, literature, folklore, and linguistics. Since 1981 the bibliography has been published in five parts: Part 1 (British Isles, British Commonwealth, English Caribbean, and American Literatures); Part 2 (European, Asian, African, and South American); Part 3 (Linguistics); Part 4 (General Literature and Related Topics); and Part 5 (Folklore). Most libraries will have all five parts bound together in a single volume. A very helpful feature of the bibliography since 1981 is a subject index for each of the five parts. You can use these subject indexes to locate works about topics and authors. Before 1981, you have to look up an author by country and period and look up topics under a limited number of headings. The online version of the *MLAIB,* available by subscription, covers editions from 1963 to the present and is much easier to search than the print version.

Other resources. Harner is a selective but comprehensive guide to reference works for the study of literature in English. He covers just about every area of the study of literature, with chapters on, among other things, research methods, libraries, manuscript collections, databases, biographical sources, genres, national literatures in English (English, Irish, American, and so forth), and foreign language literature. Harner is most valuable for accessing *areas* of study rather than specific authors. If, for example, you are interested in the English Renaissance, find the section on the Renaissance and locate the reference works—encyclopedias and bibliographies—that lead you to the information you need. The book's index is very helpful for locating topics.

    Baker is an excellent brief introduction to research methods in English and American literature. The author, a reference librarian, provides a guide to the basic tools of the library. She discusses, among other things, research strategies and how to use bibliographies, library catalogs, and computer databases.

    The *Humanities Index* (the online version is called *Humanities Abstracts*) lists articles about all the humanities (including literature) in nearly 300 periodicals. It is organized alphabetically by topic and author and is issued four times a year. Its title from 1920 to 1965 was *International Index to Periodicals* and from 1965 to 1974 was *Social Sciences and Humanities Index.* (In 1975 the index was separated into two individual indexes: *Social Sciences Index* and *Humanities Index.*)

The *Essay and General Literature Index* lists essays that appear in books. Library catalogs and many bibliographies do not do this. Someone, for example, might have written an essay on Robert Browning's "Porphyria's Lover" for an anthology of essays titled *Psychotics in Literature.* If you were doing a paper on this poem, you might overlook this essay because it is "hidden" by the title of the book. *The Essay and General Literature Index,* however, would have it. This bibliography comes out twice a year and is easy to use. Authors and topics are listed alphabetically.

The *Readers' Guide to Periodical Literature,* the *Book Review Digest,* and the *Book Review Index* list articles and reviews in newspapers and popular journals.

B. Genres

Drama

Breed, Paul F., and Florence M. Sniderman, comps. <u>Dramatic</u>
   <u>Criticism Index: A Bibliography of Commentaries on</u>
   <u>Playwrights from Ibsen to the Avant-Garde</u>. Detroit: Gale,
   1972.

Eddleman, Floyd Eugene, comp. <u>American Drama Criticism:</u>
   <u>Interpretations 1890–1977</u>. 2nd ed. Hamden, CT: Shoe String,
   1979. <u>Supplement 1</u> (1984). <u>Supplement 2</u> (1989). <u>Supplement 3</u>
   (1992). <u>Supplement 4</u> (1996).

Palmer, Helen H., comp. <u>European Drama Criticism: 1900 to</u>
   <u>1975</u>. Hamden, CT: Shoe String, 1977.

Salem, James, comp. <u>A Guide to Critical Reviews: Part I:</u>
   <u>American Drama, 1909–1982</u>. 3rd ed. Metuchen, NJ: Scarecrow,
   1984. <u>Part II: The Musical, 1909–1989</u>, 3rd ed. (1991). <u>Part</u>
   <u>III: Foreign Drama, 1909–1977</u>, 2nd ed. (1979). <u>Part IV:</u>

Screenplays from The Jazz Singer to Dr. Strangelove (1971).
Part IV, Supplement 1: Screenplays 1963–1980 (1982).

Fiction

Adelman, Irving, comp. The Contemporary Novel: A Checklist of
   Critical Literature on the English Language Novel since
   1945. 2nd ed. Lanham, MD: Scarecrow, 1997.

Beene, Lynndianne. Guide to British Prose Fiction Explication:
   Nineteenth and Twentieth Centuries. New York: G. K. Hall,
   1997.

Kearney, E. I., and L. S. Fitzgerald, comps. The Continental
   Novel: A Checklist of Criticism in English 1900–1966.
   Metuchen, NJ: Scarecrow, 1968.

---. The Continental Novel: A Checklist of Criticism in
   English 1967–1980. Metuchen, NJ: Scarecrow, 1983.

Palmer, Helen H., and Anne Jane Dysen, comps. English Novel
   Explication: Criticism to 1972. Hamden, CT: Shoe String,
   1973. Supplement 1 (1976). Supplement 2 (1981). Supplement 3
   (1986). Supplement 4 (1990). Supplement 5 (1994).

Walker, Warren S., comp. Twentieth-Century Short Story
   Explication: Interpretations 1900–1975, of Short Fiction
   since 1800. 3rd ed. Hamden, CT: Shoe String, 1977.
   Supplement 1 (1980). Supplement 2 (1984). Supplement 3
   (1987). Supplement 4 (1989). Supplement 5 (1991). Index to
   Supplements 1–5 (1992). New Series Vol. 1 (1993). New Series
   Vol. 2 (1995). New Series Vol. 3 (1993–94). New Series Vol.
   4 (1995–96). Vol. 5 (1997–98).

Poetry

Kuntz, Joseph, and Nancy Martinez, comps. Poetry Explication:
   A Checklist of Interpretation since 1925 of British and
   American Poems Past and Present. 3rd ed. Boston, MA:
   G. K. Hall 1980.

Martinez, Nancy C., Joseph G. R. Martinez, and Erland Anderson.

  Guide to British Poetry Explication. 4 vols. New York: G. K.

  Hall, 1991.

Ruppert, James, and John R. Leo. Guide to American Poetry

  Explication. 4 vols. Boston, MA: G. K. Hall, 1989.

If the *MLAIB* seems too daunting, try more selective bibliographies, like those that focus on genres of literature—drama, novel, poetry, short story. These bibliographies provide lists of books and essays about authors and works that the editors deem important. Their disadvantage is that they may leave out works on the very topics you want to research. To use these bibliographies, look up the author and the work in the appropriate bibliography; there you will find a list of critical essays on the work you are studying. These bibliographies undergo constant revision, so check for supplements that bring them up to date. You can bring them up to date yourself with the *MLAIB*. The works listed above are only a few of the ones available. Your library may carry these or others like them.

C. Regions and Countries

World

Contemporary Authors. Detroit: Gale Research, 1962– .

Fister, Barbara. Third World Women's Literature: A Dictionary

  and Guide to Materials in English. Westport, CT: Greenwood,

  1995.

Pendergast, Sara, and Tom Pendergast. Reference Guide to World

  Literature. 3rd ed. 2 vols. Farmington Hills, MI: St. James,

  2003.

Serafin, Steven R, ed. Encyclopedia of World Literature in the

  Twentieth Century. 3rd ed. 4 vols. Farmington Hills, MI: St.

  James, 1999.

Africa and the African Diaspora

Cox, C. Brian, ed. African Writers. 2 vols. New York:

  Scribner's, 1997.

Valade, Roger M., III, ed. <u>The Schomburg Center Guide to Black
   Literature: From the Eighteenth Century to the Present</u>. New
   York: Gale, 1996.

Ancient Greece and Rome

Gwinup, Thomas, and Fidelia Dickinson. <u>Greek and Roman
   Authors: A Checklist of Criticism</u>. Metuchen, NJ: Scarecrow,
   1982.

Luce, T. James, ed. <u>Ancient Writers: Greece and Rome</u>. 2 vols.
   New York: Scribner's, 1982.

Eastern

Lang, David M. <u>A Guide to Eastern Literatures</u>. New York:
   Praeger, 1971.

Nienhauser, William H., et al. <u>The Indiana Companion to
   Traditional Chinese Literature</u>. Bloomington: Indiana UP,
   1986.

English Language

Hawkins-Dady, Mark, ed. <u>Reader's Guide to Literature in
   English</u>. Chicago: Fitzroy-Dearborn, 1996.

Shattock, Joanne, ed. <u>The Cambridge Bibliography of English
   Literature</u>. 3rd ed. Vol. 4 (1800–1900). New York: Cambridge
   UP, 1999. (This is the first available volume of a new edi-
   tion of <u>The New Cambridge Bibliography of English
   Literature</u>, listed below.)

Spiller, Robert E., et al., eds. <u>Literary History of the
   United States</u>. 4th ed. rev. Vol. 2. New York: Macmillan,
   1974. 2 vols. (Vol. 1 is the literary history; Vol. 2 is the
   bibliography.)

Watson, George, ed. <u>The New Cambridge Bibliography of
   English Literature</u>. 5 vols. Cambridge: Cambridge UP,
   1969–77.

Europe

Stade, George, ed. <u>European Writers</u>. 14 vols. New York:
  Scribner's, 1983.

Native America

Marken, Jack W. <u>The American Indian Language and Literature</u>.
  Arlington Heights, IL: AHM, 1978.

Latin America

Fenwick, M. J. <u>Writers of the Caribbean and Central America:</u>
  <u>A Bibliography</u>. 2 vols. New York: Garland, 1992.

Sole, Carlos A., ed. <u>Latin American Writers</u>, 3 vols. New York:
  Scribner's, 1989.

Like the bibliographies on genres, these bibliographies provide *selected* lists of sources on regional literatures and on specific authors within regions. The *Literary History of the United States, The New Cambridge Bibliography of English Literature,* and the emerging *Cambridge Bibliography of English Literature* are especially helpful in pointing to important studies done on American and English literature up to their dates of publication. Many of these bibliographies are more like encyclopedias in that they combine biography with bibliography. They provide information about regional literature and authors as well as a brief list of secondary studies on them.

The above list is itself a short selection. Your library may have these bibliographies as well as others that are equally useful. New bibliographies come out regularly, and many existing ones are updated periodically. You can supplement and update any of these bibliographies with the *MLAIB.*

D. Authors

Weiner, Alan R, and Spencer Means. <u>Literary Criticism Index</u>.
  2nd ed. Metuchen, NJ: Scarecrow, 1994.

Literary Criticism Index is a bibliography of bibliographies. It is organized alphabetically by authors, and keys their works to specific bibliographies. If, for example, you wanted to know where to find critical studies of Browning's "Porphyria's Lover," you would look for the title of the poem under "Browning, Robert." The entry would tell you which bibliographies contain lists of works on the poem.

For the most thorough bibliographies of works by and about authors, seek out bibliographies devoted solely to individual authors. In contrast to the bibliographies listed above, these bibliographies usually contain *complete* listings of works by and about an author. These listings are complete—up to the publication date of the bibliography. For anything after that date, consult the *MLAIB*.

E. Computer Databases Available through Purchase or Subscription

Computer databases can save you enormous amounts of time. Using a bibliography database, for example, is the same as going through hardbound print bibliographies, only the computer does it for you and much faster. Computer databases are available on compact disc (CD-ROM), magnetic tape, diskette, and the Internet. Most college and university libraries subscribe to various databases. Ask your librarian for guidance in choosing and using databases pertinent to your projects.

Of all the bibliography databases, the most useful for discovering secondary sources about literature is the *MLAIB* (1963–present). Its coverage is very comprehensive. Like most bibliography databases, you can search it by author, title, and subject as well as by keywords. Several interdisciplinary databases that cover nonliterary subjects and their connection with literature are *Essay and General Literature Index, Humanities Abstracts,* and *Arts and Humanities Search.* These allow you to research interdisciplinary topics (art and literature, psychology and literature, science and literature, and so forth). Some excellent content databases are *Literature Resource Center, The Encyclopaedia Britannica Online,* and *DiscLit,* all of which provide information about authors and movements as well as historical background. *The Literary Resource Center* includes various reference works published by Gale: *Contemporary Authors, Dictionary of Literary Biography,* and *Contemporary Literary Criticism. DiscLit* reproduces the introductory books published by Twayne Publishers. These books cover major American, British, and world authors.

Several other databases may help as well: *Reader's Guide to Periodical Literature, New York Times, Book Review Digest, America: History and Life, American National Biography, Biography Index,* and the *Oxford English Dictionary.* Databases are constantly being created, expanded, renamed, and incorporated into other databases, so check your library's resources to see which ones it shelves that might pertain to your area of research.

One more database is worthy of mention here: the online catalog of your library. Many online catalogs have the capacity to perform sophisticated and thorough searches of authors and topics. Your library's online catalog may be limited to only the material in that library, but it may be all you need. Many online catalogs link to other databases: to the Internet and to catalogs of nearby libraries, of newspapers, scholarly journals, and popular magazines.

III. LIBRARY PERIODICALS ROOM AND STACKS

Now that you have drawn up a list of resources for your project—by consulting bibliographies and databases—your next step is to locate these resources in the library. Does your library own them or provide access to them? To find out, use your library's online catalog to see which books the library owns. Then locate them in the stacks. For computer databases and Internet resources, use either the computers on campus (in the library or labs) or your own computer. For journal articles, look up the title of the journal in the online catalog or in a "serials holding catalog." Either should tell you whether the library subscribes to it and, if so, where it is located. Recent issues of journals are usually stored in the *periodicals room* of the library, and back issues are kept in the stacks. To save space, some libraries also store past issues of journals on microfilm. If you have difficulty finding the journal articles you need, ask the librarian in the periodicals room for help.

This discussion of how to find information is basic. If you want more thorough guidance on a particular project, see Nancy L. Baker's *A Research Guide for Undergraduate Students: English and American Literature,* listed above under "General Reference." Perhaps the most valuable resource for doing research is the reference librarian. Reference librarians are experts on locating sources of information and opinion. They are usually eager to help and can save you time.

IV. INFORMATION AND OPINION ON THE INTERNET

The Internet is an enormous, constantly changing, continuously growing collection of documents. It is an "ocean" we have to "navigate." This ocean is so vast and changes so fast that almost anything published about it is dated as soon as it is released. What follows, then, are a few observations about how to use the Internet for conducting research about literature. Once you get the hang of using the Internet, you can catch up with new developments on your own.

More than anything, the emergence of the World Wide Web in 1993 has made the Internet easier to search than ever before. Most web documents are hypertexts. *Hypertext* is a document containing *links* (also known as *hyperlinks* or *embedded links*), highlighted phrases that take you to other portions of the document or other hypertexts. Click on a link, and you are whisked to another place within the document or to a completely new website. That site will have links of its own, which take you to other sites, which in turn connect to new sites—many of which may link back to your original site. You can see why the World Wide Web is called a "web."

Because of the web's ease of use, it has just about subsumed everything else on the Internet. You can gain access to the web through *online services* such as America Online, Prodigy, and Earthlink. You can also log onto the Internet by means of a *browser* such as Microsoft Explorer or Netscape Navigator. These are available through companies known as *Internet Service Providers* (or *ISPs*). If your college or university already subscribes to a service, you may be able to log on from your dorm room or computer lab. Once on the Internet, you can use a *search engine* such as Google, Alta Vista, Webcrawler, or Yahoo to scan websites. Most services offer a choice of search engines. Whichever one you choose, it will typically have a box, located near the beginning of the document, that allows you to search by typing in *keywords*. Doing this is an effective way of finding things on the Internet. Type in any terms or combination of terms you want: an author's name ("William Shakespeare"), a literary movement ("English Romanticism"), a geographical or national region ("Canadian literature"). The search engine will find documents related to your keywords, tell you how many documents it has found, and arrange them in descending order of relevance: the most relevant documents first, the least relevant last. If one search engine fails to turn up what you want, try another. Some are more detailed and comprehensive than others. A useful feature of most web browsers is the *Favorites* option, located at the top of the screen. If you find a site you want to keep for future reference, click Favorites to store the web address or Uniform Resource Locator (URL). When you want to get to that site quickly, open your Favorites file and go directly to the addresses stored there. Favorites save you from having to retrace steps to get back to sites you want.

You can also go directly to any site on the web if you know its address. Look for a box at the top of the screen that contains the address of the site where you are. The address for the search engine Yahoo, for example, is http://www.yahoo.com. The "http" part of the address stands for Hypertext Transfer Protocol, the program that establishes a common language between computers and accommodates the transmission of all documents on the web. Click on the address, delete all or part of it, type in a new address, and press Enter. The browser takes you to the site of the new address. Though a bit dated, Evan Morris's *The Book Lover's Guide to the Internet* (2nd ed., New York: Fawcett Columbine, 1998) gives an excellent, nontechnical introduction to the Internet: a brief history, definitions of terms, how to hook up, pathways through the Internet (Gopher, File Transfer Protocol [FTP] sites, Telnet, Internet Relay Chat [IRC]), and different ways of using the Internet (discussion/news groups, mailing lists, self-publication, e-mail, online resources). Especially valuable is his long list of addresses, arranged by category (authors, cultural studies, poetry, mystery literature, science fiction, humor, hypertext literature, magazines, bookstores, and so forth).

General databases
Three databases are especially helpful for starting literary research on the Internet.

Literary Resources on the Net, maintained by Jack Lynch.
   <http://andromeda.rutgers.edu/~jlynch/Lit/>

Voice of the Shuttle: Electronic Resources for the Humanities, maintained
   by Alan Liu
   <http://vos.ucsb.edu/>

The Internet Public Library
   <http://www.ipl.org/>

Literary Resources on the Net, one of the best sites on the Internet, is the obvious place to begin a search for information and opinion about literature. It covers literary periods, literary movements, language study, women's studies, ethnic studies, literary theory, research materials, and much more. You can search the site by category and keyword. *Voice of the Shuttle,* another outstanding site, covers not just literature but all the humanities. *The Internet Public Library* provides access to all areas of knowledge. These three sites are the best places to begin your quest for research materials on the Internet. The following is a very selected list of more narrowly focused sites:

Literary criticism of authors and works
Online Literary Criticism Collection
  <http://www.ipl.org/div/litcrit/>

Author sites
Jane Austen Information Page
  <http://pemberley.com/janeinfo/janeinfo>

Mr. William Shakespeare and the Internet
  <http://daphne.palomar.edu/>

Absolute Shakespeare
  <http://absoluteshakespeare.com>

The William Blake Archive
  <http://www.blakearchive.org>

Virginia Woolf Web
  <http://orlando.jp.org/VWW>

Multiauthor sites
American Studies Crossroads Project
  <http://www.georgetown.edu/crossroads/index/>

Latina/o Literature and Literature of the Americas
  <http://asweb.unco.edu/latina/>

The Literary Encyclopedia
  <http://litercyc.com>

The Literary Gothic
  <http://www.litgothic.com/index_fl>

The ORB: On-line Reference Book for Medieval Studies
  <http://www.the-orb.net>

OzLit [Australian literature]
  <http://www.ozlit.org/>

Postcolonial Studies
  <http://www.emory.edu/ENGLISH/Bahri/>

Romantic Circles [the Romantic movement]
   <http://www.rc.und.edu/>

Storytellers: Native American Authors Online
   <http://hanksville.org/storytellers/>

The Victorian Web
   <http://www.victorianweb.org>

Electronic texts
Bartleby.com
   <http://www.bartleby.com/>

English Online Resources
   <http://etext.lib.virginia.edu/uvaonline>

The On-Line Books Page
   <http://digital.library.upenn.edu/books/>

Project Gutenberg
   <http://www.gutenberg.net/>

Hypertexts and annotated texts
Pride and Prejudice (by Jane Austen), a hypertext
   <http://www.pemberley.com/janeinfo/janeinfo>

A Midsummer Night's Dream (by William Shakespeare), an annotated
text
   <http://cmc.uib.no/dream/>

Robert [Hypermedia] *Browning and Others* (hypertexts, some illustrated with paintings)
   <http://faculty.stonehill.edu/geverett/rb/rb/htm>

Grammar, style, documentary guidelines
The Elements of Style (by William Strunk, Jr.)
   <http://www.bartleby.com/141/index>

Guide to Grammar and Writing
   <http://www.ccc.communet.edu/grammar>

MLA Style (Modern Language Association guidelines for citing
sources)
   <http://www.mla.org/style/>

Poetic techniques
Poetry: Meter, Form, and Rhythm
   <http://www.uncg.edu/~htkirbys/>

Online journals

Domestic Goddesses: AKA "Scribbling Women"
"A moderated E-journal devoted to women writers, beginning in
the 19th century, who wrote 'domestic fiction.'"
<http://www.womenwriters.net/domesticgoddess/>

Other Voices: The (e)Journal of Cultural Criticism
<http://dept.english.upenn.edu/~ov/index2.html/>

Renaissance Forum
<http://www.hull.ac.uk/Hull/EL_Web/renforum/>

Newsletters, discussion groups, and electronic mail

Interpersonal communication by means of newsletters, discussion
groups, and e-mail is a wonderful opportunity for people doing research. You can exchange opinions, share information, and keep up
with trends. Jack Lynch's website, just mentioned, includes a direc-
tory of literary discussion lists. Bear in mind that newsletters and discussion lists are most valuable for researchers who have *long-term*
projects. They are less helpful for people who need to get research
papers done quickly, say within a semester. It is a breach of
"Netiquette" (etiquette for using the Internet) for someone to send
out a message on a discussion list saying something like, "I have a
paper due in three weeks on *Beowulf.* Can anyone out there help me
think of a topic?"

EVALUATING THE QUALITY OF INTERNET SITES

How do you know if a website is good? In contrast to scholarly books
and journals, which are published by reputable publishers with high
standards of acceptance, websites can be created by anyone with an
Internet address. One way to evaluate the quality of websites is to read
reviews of them. The online version of *Forbes* magazine, for example,
maintains a list of the 300 best websites. Among these are *Mr. William
Shakespeare and the Internet* and Jack Lynch's *Literary Resources on the
Net.* See the complete list and reviews at

Forbes.com
<http://www.forbesbest.com/bow>

But as valuable as *Forbes* and other organizations that review websites
are, most of the sites you visit will probably not be reviewed any-

where. You should then evaluate them yourself. Ask questions like the following:

1. **Who is the developer of the site?** How trustworthy is this person? Is the developer a scholar, well-versed in the subject, or an amateur who may be enthusiastic but have limited knowledge? Does the developer give his or her name (something other than "Webmaster")? Can you get in touch with the developer?

2. **How authoritative is the site?** Who publishes the site? Does it originate from a school (university, college, high school) or from a single individual? How commercial is it? Does it seem more interested in selling you things than in presenting information and interpretation?

3. **Is the site well maintained?** Has the site been updated recently? How thorough, thoughtful, and careful is the site? Does the developer seem active in maintaining the site? Are the links current? (How many dead links are there?) Does the information on the site seem dated?

4. **How knowledgeable are the authors who write for the site?** Do the writers document their information and opinions? Do they refer to just a few sources? Do they seem well-read in their subject, familiar with groundbreaking and essential treatments of their subject? How detailed is the treatment of the subject? Is the information accurate?

5. **For e-texts, how reliable are they?** Are e-texts well-edited? Are they accurate? Is the source of the text given? How trustworthy is the source?

In general, websites are best when they meet the following criteria:

❖ The developers are scholars in the field.
❖ The developers are accountable. They tell you who they are and how to get in touch with them.
❖ They constantly and thoughtfully maintain the site, keeping information and links current.
❖ The site is noncommercial and is associated with a school or press. Be wary of the .com sites. More reliable are the nonprofit domains: .edu, .gov, .org, and .net.
❖ Information and interpretation is well-documented and gives evidence of sound knowledge of the subject.
❖ E-texts are edited recently by scholars.

GIVING CREDIT TO SOURCES

Why Should You Give Credit?

First, give credit so readers can find and read the same material you read. They may also want to check the reliability of your sources or your ability to use them fairly and accurately. Giving credit, to put it positively, is one more means of arguing. The more careful and honest you are in giving credit, the stronger your argument will be. Second, give credit to distinguish your ideas from those of others. The purpose of the essay, after all, is to express *your* ideas, to argue *your* position. You may use facts, ideas, and words from other sources to clarify and support your ideas, but readers are interested, finally, in knowing what *you* think. That is why they are reading your paper. By giving credit, you show them exactly where your ideas begin and where other writers' ideas leave off.

Finally, give credit to be ethical. Honor policies stress this reason heavily. Although the ethical principle is obvious, it is not always simple. The usual definition of *plagiarism* is "the presentation of someone else's ideas, work, or facts as your own." The moral judgment that follows is, "Plagiarism is stealing and therefore wrong." These judgments are apt when applied to blatant plagiarism, cases in which someone copies the work of someone else and claims it as his or her own. Most cases of student plagiarism, however, are not so egregiously criminal. The issue of plagiarism is clouded with some uncertainties. Everything you know comes from a "source." When is what you know "yours" and not someone else's? Another uncertainty is that when you summarize someone else's ideas, you will probably use some of that writer's words. How many and what kind of words can you use without plagiarizing? A third uncertainty is the nature of facts. Some facts, even when they appear in a source, do not need documentation. But which ones? Because of uncertainties like these, most students who "plagiarize" do so unintentionally. The following are principles and guidelines that anyone using sources in essays about literature should follow. They can help you use sources meaningfully, clearly, and ethically.

When Should You Give Credit?

For primary sources.   Whenever you make specific reference to an incident or words in a work and whenever you quote from a work, you need to cite the source (give credit) from which you obtained the information. This is as true for primary as for secondary sources. You must do this for several reasons. Works of literature, especially famous ones, often go through many editions. Readers need to know which edition you used so they can find the parts of the work you discuss. You document your primary source, then, for their convenience. Another reason is that the edition you use may affect the validity of your argument. If the edition is unscholarly and contains misprints or omissions, your interpretations will be suspect. A well-known example is Emily Dickinson's poetry. After her death in 1886, Thomas Wentworth Higginson and Mabel Loomis Todd edited Dickinson's poetry for publication. They published it (or some of it) in four volumes throughout the 1890s. Instead of printing it as Dickinson had written it, they "regularized" it for the tastes of nineteenth-century readers. They changed the meter to make it more conventional, changed words to make them rhyme, normalized punctuation, and altered metaphors that seemed illogical. Not until Thomas H. Johnson published a new edition of Dickinson's poems in 1955 did we have versions of her poetry as she had written it. If you write an essay about her poetry, your readers will want to know that you used Johnson's edition (or reprints therefrom). By giving full information about the editions you use, you enhance the reliability of your essay.

Often the nature of college courses allows you to omit complete citations for primary sources. If you write about a work assigned for a course, page numbers may be the only documentation you need. Check with your professor to be sure this practice is acceptable. If so, follow each quotation or reference with appropriate page numbers in parentheses, placing your final mark of punctuation after the closing parenthesis.

Quotation

Lawrence says that when she is with her children she feels "the center of her heart go hard" (125).

A specific reference but not a quotation

When she returns home from the party, she finds Paul riding the rocking horse. Lawrence contrasts her elegant, icy dress to Paul's frenzied and exhausted state (134–35).

More formal usage requires a complete citation for the edition you are using. Complete citations—located on a Works Cited page—are necessary when you use a book that is not a basic text in your course.

For facts that are not common knowledge.   "Common knowledge" facts are those the average well-read person would likely know: very basic facts about history (that Woodrow Wilson was president of the United States during World War I, that the United States entered the war several years after it began), birth and death dates, occupations, publication dates, basic biographical facts about famous people (that Ernest Hemingway began his writing career as a newspaper reporter, that he entered World War I as an ambulance driver, that in 1929 he published a famous novel, *A Farewell to Arms,* based on his wartime experiences, that just before the outbreak of World War II he published a novel, *For Whom the Bell Tolls,* about the Spanish Civil War). Facts that are not common knowledge (what Hemingway's parents thought of his newspaper career, where he saw action during the war, how he was wounded, the identity of the nurse he fell in love with while recuperating, what he actually said to people about the war) come from secondary sources and must be cited. Also, controversial facts need to be documented. If you claim that Theodore Roosevelt was a secret Marxist, or had an affair with Emma Goldman, or conspired to assassinate President McKinley, you must give sources for such outlandish assertions; otherwise readers will write you off as ignorant and irresponsible.

For all direct quotes.   This kind of documentation is crucial, whether you quote from primary or secondary sources.

For summaries or paraphrases of someone else's ideas.   Even when you do not quote directly from the work, you must provide documentation when you repeat someone else's ideas. This includes ideas held by other writers, by your instructor, or even by other students. It also includes ideas you arrive at on your own and then find expressed in print.

For ideas not "assimilated" by you.   Once you have absorbed someone's ideas, thought about them over a time, added ideas of your own or of others, you can assume that these ideas are now "yours." If, however, your memory is so good that these ideas remain in your mind exactly as they were when you read and heard them, then you must give credit to the original author.

A final word.   The dividing line between facts that are common knowledge and those that are not is sometimes frustratingly vague. So too is the line between ideas assimilated by you and those that are not. *When in doubt about where that line is, give credit.* Doing so takes a little extra time and trouble, but the trouble and time are worth it to protect yourself against charges of plagiarism and to provide curious readers with enough information to check your facts.

Where Should You Give Credit?

By introducing your source in your text.   When you use the ideas and specialized or controversial facts of another person, introduce them *in your own text*, not just in parenthetical references. To do this, use introductory phrases like the following:

```
As Jane Tompkins says, "The ground for complaint . . ."

One critic has called attention to "the absurdity of
    Huck's shore experience."

Annette Kolodny suggests . . .

Tuchman's second point is . . .

Judith Butler sees queer theory as . . .
```

All of these introduce paraphrases, summaries, and short quotations. The following example introduces an indented or blocked quotation (that is, a long quotation moved right ten spaces [1 inch] from the established left margin).

```
Friedman's definition of plot focuses on the changes the
protagonist undergoes:

            The end of plot, then, is to represent some
            completed process of change in the protagonist.
```

Acknowledgments for facts are also necessary when the facts are very specialized or controversial. For example, details about F. Scott Fitzgerald's love life in Hollywood during his last years can come from only a few people. You must mention such people *in your text* when you use them:

```
Sheilah Graham claims that . . .

Budd Schulberg saw that Fitzgerald was . . .

Nathanael West said that at the party Fitzgerald concen-
    trated his attention on . . .
```

Note, however, that facts available from many sources do not have to be introduced in your text. Details about English history, for example, are available in many textbooks and are not associated with any one person or group. You do, however, need to provide parenthetical references for such information and to cite your sources in the Works Cited list.

```
Anarchism was such a compelling theory at the turn of the

century that six heads of state--of France, Austria,

Italy, the United States, and two of Spain--were executed

by anarchists (Tuchman 72).
```

In parenthetical citations. See Guidelines for Parenthetical Citations on pages 304–10.

In a Works Cited list. The parenthetical citations and Works Cited list work together to give readers complete information about your sources and how you use them. In parenthetical citations, give enough information so readers can find the sources in the Works Cited list. The Works Cited list enables readers to check out the sources themselves.

CORRECT DOCUMENTARY FORM

Documentary form varies from discipline to discipline. For people writing about literature, the authoritative guide to documentary form is the *MLA Handbook for Writers of Research Papers, Theses, and Dissertations.* (*MLA* stands for Modern Language Association, the preeminent scholarly organization devoted to the study of modern languages and literature.) In 1984 the MLA created a new documentary format, one that resembles the formats of the social and natural sciences. The guidelines in this chapter are from the most recent edition of the *MLA Handbook:*

The MLA Handbook for Writers of Research Papers. Joseph Gibaldi. 6th ed. New York: MLA, 2003.

You can get an abbreviated set of these guidelines from the MLA website:

MLA Style
  <http://www.mla.org/style_faq4>

Although this site is not nearly as thorough as the *MLA Handbook,* it does provide the basic formula for citing sources on the web. For a comparison of various documentary styles (MLA, APA, Chicago), see the following site:

The Columbia Guide to Online Style
  <http://www.columbia.edu/cu/cup/cgos/index>

Guidelines for Parenthetical Citations

Purpose.   Parenthetical citations are markings, placed in parentheses, that point to exact locations in the primary and secondary sources you draw upon for your paper. These markings can be page numbers (for prose), line numbers (for poetry), act, scene, and line numbers (for verse drama), and chapter and verses (for religious texts).

Your goals in making parenthetical citations are twofold. First, you show readers where they can locate, in the sources themselves, any quotations, facts, and ideas that you incorporate in your paper. If, for example, you provide a page number for a quotation, readers should be able to go to that page in the source and find the section you quoted.

Second, you give enough information for readers to locate the source in the Works Cited list at the end of your paper. For guidelines about setting up a Works Cited list, see pages 312–26 in this chapter.

Placement.   For **material that's not indented,** place the parenthetical citation immediately after the material that needs referencing. Usually this is at the end of a sentence or paragraph, but sometimes it can be within a sentence as well. Put the reference before the closing punctuation of the phrase or sentence (comma, period, semicolon, colon, exclamation point).

James Joyce, as Arnold Kettle notes, was consistent about employing his artistic principles (301), but that does not mean his works are all the same.

John H. Arnold points out that although Herodotus seems strikingly modern to us, his histories cannot be fully trusted (17).

The Major's wife cried out, "No, Ekeby shall belong to the cavaliers so that it may be their ruin!" (293).

For **indented material** (quotations), place the citation outside the closing punctuation. Note that indented quotations require no quotation marks and should be set back from the left margin 1 inch (10 spaces).

Near the climax of the story, Wells has Nunez recognize the pleasing qualities of life in the Country of the Blind:

> They led a simple, laborious life, these people, with all the elements of virtue and happiness, as these things can be understood by men. They toiled, but not oppressively; they had food and clothing sufficient for their needs; they had days and seasons of rest; they made much of music and singing, and there was love among them, and little children. (15)

Primary sources.

Prose.   When referring to primary sources, use page numbers for prose works.

In Shirley Jackson's "The Lottery" the people are at first reluctant to participate in the lottery. The men standing around waiting are subdued: "Their jokes were quiet and they smiled rather than laughed" (219). The children, when called, come "reluctantly, having to be called four

> or five times" (220). Once the black box is brought out,
> the villagers keep "their distance" (221).

Verse drama. For plays written in poetry, use act, scene, and line numbers.

> In <u>Hamlet</u> the queen bids farewell to Ophelia by saying, "I
> hoped thou shouldst have been my Hamlet's wife" (V.i.211).

Here the reference is to act five, scene one, line 211. You may also use arabic numbers instead of roman numerals to cite acts and scenes.

> In <u>Hamlet</u> the queen bids farewell to Ophelia by saying,
> "I hoped thou shouldst have been my Hamlet's wife"
> (5.1.211).

Poetry. For poems, especially long ones (more than about twenty lines), cite line numbers.

> In commenting on our growing distance from heaven,
> Wordsworth says in "Intimations of Immortality,"
>   Heaven lies about us in our infancy!
>   Shades of the prison-house begin to close
>   Upon the growing Boy. (66-68)

The Bible. Refer to the Bible by indicating chapter and verse numbers:

> When Solomon became old, his many wives "turned away his
> heart after other gods." He worshiped the goddess
> Ashtoreth and "did evil in the sight of the Lord"
> (1 Kings 11.4-6).

More than one page. Use hyphens between line or page numbers to indicate material that lies within a continuous sequence of lines or pages.

> (231-33).

Use commas between line or page numbers to indicate interruptions in sequence.

```
(200, 219).
```

Multivolume works.   If your reference is to a work with more than one volume, indicate in your parenthetical reference the volume to which you refer. Separate volume and page numbers with a colon. Insert a space between the colon and the page number.

```
Even on the point of death, Clarissa writes to her father

asking his forgiveness. She begs him "on her knees" to

forgive her for "all her faults and follies," especially

"that fatal error which threw her out of [his] protec-

tion" (4:359).
```

Here the reference is to the fourth volume, page 359. If you use only one volume from a multivolume work, you need not give the volume number in the parenthetical reference. Instead, include the volume number in the Works Cited listing.

Secondary sources.

Single author books.   For most parenthetical references, especially for books, it is usually enough to give the author's last name and the page number(s) of the reference. Place the reference at the end of the sentence before the period.

```
Long historical poems, such as The Battle of Maldon, pro-

vide "the soundest evidence we have" for recreating the

Europe of 1000 years ago (Reston 5).
```

An alternative way of giving the this information is to mention the author's name in your text. In this case, only the page number need appear in the parenthetical reference.

```
James Reston, Jr. says that poetic depictions of histori-

cal events, such as The Battle of Maldon, provide "the
```

```
soundest evidence we have" for recreating the Europe of
1000 years ago (5).
```

In both instances, the author's name points to the work in the Works Cited list, and the page number points to the citation in the work itself. The above citation is to the following work in the Works Cited list:

```
Reston, James, Jr. The Last Apocalypse: Europe at the Year
   1000 A.D. New York: Anchor Books, 1998.
```

Two or three authors.   When referring to a work by two or three authors, give all their names in the text or in the reference.

```
One work makes the useful distinction between "represen-
tational" and "illustrative" narrative (Scholes and
Kellogg 84).

Scholes and Kellogg make the useful distinction between
"representational" and "illustrative" narrative (84).
```

More than three authors.   When referring to a work by more than three authors, give all their names or, more simply, give the first name and "et al." (abbreviation for Latin *et alii,* "and others").

```
The trickster has been a traditional folk hero not just
of American "Yankee" narrative but of American Indian and
African-American narrative as well (Spiller et al. 729).
```

Several works by the same author.   If you use several works by the same author, give the author's last name, a portion of the title, and the page number.

```
Reston claims that Olaf Trygvesson's conversion to
Christianity in 994 AD diminished Viking hostility in
southern England (Last Apocalypse 18).
```

When you use more than one work by the same author, you can refer to the work in the text or in a parenthetical reference.

Lawrence describes the two mothers differently. Elizabeth
Bates is "a tall woman of imperious mien, handsome, with
definite black eyebrows" ("Odour of Chrysanthemums" 248),
whereas Paul's mother is simply "a woman who was beautiful" ("The Rocking-Horse Winner" 271).

Lawrence describes the two mothers differently. Elizabeth
Bates in "Odour of Chrysanthemums" is "a tall woman of
imperious mien, handsome, with definite black eyebrows"
(248), whereas Paul's mother in "The Rocking-Horse
Winner" is simply "a woman who was beautiful" (271).

Authors with the same last name.   If you have several authors
with the same last name, give initials or the whole name to distinguish
among them:

(J. Reston 58-60)

Titles without authors.   If the author of a work is anonymous,
give the complete title or the first few words of the title, plus the page
number. (Anonymous works are alphabetized by title in the Works
Cited list.)

Unlike the pilgrims, the Puritans remained members of the
Anglican church. But like the Pilgrims, they adhered to a
Calvinistic theology ("Early American Literature" 2).

Whole works.   When you refer to an entire work (not some
part of it), you may omit a parenthetical reference to it if you identify
the author and the title of the work in your text:

E. M. W. Tillyard devotes a short book to explaining how
the Elizabethans saw the structure of the cosmos.

If readers are interested in Tillyard's book, they can find it in the
Works Cited list.

More than one work.   Refer to more than one work in a single
parenthetical reference by separating the works with semicolons.

> At least two critics have seen the similarity between
> Voltaire's character Candide and the young Benjamin
> Franklin in the <u>Autobiography</u> (Orkney 13; Scott 151-52).

If, however, you want to refer to more than two or three works, use a footnote or endnote instead of a parenthetical reference. (See the discussion of footnotes and endnotes below.)

Works quoted in other works. If you find a quotation in a book or article but cannot find the original source for the quotation, rather than abandon the quotation, cite the place where you found it. Use "qtd. in" ("quoted in").

> When Dreiser was a magazine editor, he would write on re-
> jection slips, "We like realism, but it must be tinged
> with sufficient idealism to make it all a truly uplifting
> character" (qtd. in Fiedler 46).

Internet sources. Some works, like many on the Internet, may not have page numbers. If so, give other information to mark the location of references.

> Diane Elam worries that because a university education is
> becoming more of "a vocational exercise," the value of
> reading literature "is no longer a self-evident proposi-
> tion in market-driven universities" (par. 4).

If you refer to more than one paragraph, use the abbreviation "pars.": (pars. 15–18). You could refer also to screens, if they are numbered: (screens 8–9).

Magazines and newspapers. Like Internet sources, magazine and newspaper articles may have unusual page indicators. As always, give enough information so readers can find your references. The following example is from a newspaper article:

> Kunitz said that one of the advantages of being so old is
> that "I encountered a good portion of the best poets of
> the twentieth century" (C5).

Guidelines for Using Footnotes and Endnotes

You can place explanatory notes either at the foot of pages (footnotes) or on separate sheets at the end of the paper (endnotes). Unless your instructor tells you otherwise, place all notes at the end.

Citing several sources (more than two or three) all at once.
Text

> A host of critics agree that Swift does not share
>
> Gulliver's condemnation of human beings at the end of
>
> <u>Gulliver's Travels</u>.[1]

Note

> [1] Abrams 23-28; Converse 55-70; Portnoy 150-65; Clore
>
> and Barchester 300-05; Kellerman 83; Soles 15-20.

Comments or information relating to something in your text.
These comments or facts are not necessary to your line of thought, but you may want to include them because you think your readers would find them useful and interesting.

Text

> Irving adopts the stance of the ironic narrator in his
>
> comic masterpiece "The Legend of Sleepy Hollow."[2]

Note

> [2] The ironic narrator was a common fictional device in
>
> eighteenth-century English fiction and was most notably pres-
>
> ent in one of Irving's favorite authors, Henry Fielding.

Setting up a footnote or endnote
❖ In the text of your essay where you want the reference to appear, place a number raised slightly above the line (*superscript;* note the examples above).
❖ Place a corresponding superscript number, slightly raised, just before the note itself (see the examples above) and add a space between the number and the note.

❖ Indent the note five spaces (one-half inch).
❖ Number the notes sequentially throughout the paper. In other words, do not restart your numbering (with "1") when you come to a new page. Rather, go from "1" to the final number all the way through the paper.
❖ Place your notes at the end of the paper (endnotes). You can also place them at the bottom of the page (footnotes), but it's much easier to format endnotes than footnotes.
❖ Place endnotes on a separate page or pages and position them between the text of your essay and the Works Cited page. Center the title "Notes" one inch from the top of the page. Double space.
❖ Indent the first line of each note. Put the number slightly raised before the first word of the note. Put a single space between the number and the first letter. The rest of the note goes all the way to the left margin. Double-space within and between endnotes. For a "real life" example of the use of endnotes, see the sample paper at the end of this chapter.
❖ Place footnotes at the bottom of the page, four lines below the text (two double spaces). Use the same format as for endnotes, only single space them. If you have more than one footnote on a page, put a double space between them.

Guidelines and Form for the Works Cited List: General Rules

The Works Cited list, placed at the end of the paper, contains citations for all the resources—primary and secondary—to which you refer in the body of your paper. Be sure that every source you referred to is included in your Works Cited list. Your goal here is to give enough information so readers can find these same sources and verify their content and reliability. Follow the guidelines below. Use the sample entries as models for each guideline or category.

1. **Arrange entries alphabetically by author.** If the author is anonymous, list the entry alphabetically by its title. For the purpose of alphabetizing, ignore *A, An,* and *The* at the beginning of titles.

2. **Do not number entries.** Since the entries are listed alphabetically, numbers are unnecessary.

3. **In each entry, put the author's last name first.** The author's last name appears first because the list is in alphabetical order. If more than one author appears in an entry, put the last name first for the first author: Rochester, Henry. Put the names of the other authors in regular order: Rochester, Henry, Roch Small, and Leonard Handy.

4. **Put the first line flush with the left margin.** Indent any subsequent (turnover) lines of the entry five spaces (one-half inch) from the left-hand margin.

5. **Include without exception every source—primary or secondary—cited in your paper.**

6. **Divide your entries into three main sections:**

   ❖ author's name (last name first)
   ❖ the name of the article or book
   ❖ information about publication

   Sometimes more sections are necessary—information about editors, about volume numbers, or about reprinted editions. But these three divisions are essential for all entries. Punctuate citations as indicated in the sample entries below.

7. **If information seems missing from a source, don't panic.** Provide as much information as you can.

8. **Put the Works Cited list at the end of your paper, on sheets separate from your text.** Center the title, "Works Cited." Double space. Begin the list of entries, double spacing between and within them.

Sample Entries for Books

One author

```
Lewis, C. S. The Allegory of Love: A Study in Medieval
     Tradition. New York: Oxford UP, 1936.
```

You can usually find the date of publication of books on the copyright page (the reverse of the title page) or, for some books published outside the United States, at the back of the book. If there is more than one date, choose the most recent one. If several cities are listed as places of publication, use the first one. The "UP" after "Oxford" in the above entry represents "University Press."

No known author

<u>Sir Gawain and the Green Knight</u>. Trans. Keith Harrison. New
   York: Oxford UP, 1998.

If the work is anonymous, begin the entry with the title.

More than one work by an author

Jewett, Sarah Orne. <u>A Country Doctor</u>. New York: Garret, 1970.

---. <u>A White Heron and Other Stories</u>. Boston: Houghton, 1886.

When you include more than one work by an author, substitute three hyphens for the author's name after the first citation. Arrange the works in alphabetical order by title.

Two or three authors

Berry, Lester V., and Melvin Van den Bark. <u>The American
   Thesaurus of Slang: With Supplement</u>. New York: Crowell,
   1947.

Reverse the name of the first author only.

Translation

Salih, Tayeb. <u>Season of Migration to the North</u>. Trans. Denys
   Johnson-Davies. London: Heinemann, 1969.

Multivolume work

Richardson, Samuel. <u>Clarissa; or, the History of a Young Lady</u>.
   Vol. 4. London: Everyman, 1932.
Richardson, Samuel. <u>Clarissa; or, the History of a Young Lady</u>.
   4 vols. London: Everyman, 1932.

If you refer to just one volume of a multivolume set, indicate the volume you use, as in the first example. If you use all the volumes, indicate how many volumes the set contains, as in the second example.

More than three authors, several editions, and one of several volumes

Spiller, Robert E., et al. <u>Literary History of the United</u>
    <u>States</u>. 4th ed. rev. Vol. 1. New York: Macmillan, 1974.

Using "et al." saves you from listing all the other authors of the work.

Introduction or an afterword to a primary source

Charvat, William. Introduction. <u>The Last of the Mohicans</u>. By
    James Fenimore Cooper. Boston: Riverside, 1958. iii-xiv.

Magarshack, David. Afterword. <u>The Death of Ivan Ilych and</u>
    <u>Other Stories</u>. By Leo Tolstoy. New York: Signet, 1960.
    295-304.

Edition of an author's work

Trollope, Anthony. <u>The Last Chronicle of Barset</u>. Ed. Arthur
    Mizener. Boston: Riverside, 1964.

In this example, Arthur Mizener is the editor of this edition of Trollope's *The Last Chronicle of Barset.*

Article in a reference book

"La Fontaine, Jean de." <u>The New Encyclopaedia Britannica:</u>
    <u>Macropaedia</u>. 15th ed. 1987.

For familiar reference works, especially ones that undergo frequent revision, you need not give complete publishing information. Give the author's name (if known), the title of the article, the title of the reference work (underlined or italicized), the edition number, and the date of publication. If the entries are listed alphabetically, there is no need to give volume or page numbers. For less familiar references books, give full publication information.

"Blank Verse." <u>The New Princeton Encyclopedia of Poetry and</u>
    <u>Poetics</u>. Ed. Alex Preminger and T. V. F. Brogan. Princeton:
    Princeton UP, 1993.

Anonymous introduction or article in an anthology of literature

"The Middle Ages to ca. 1485." <u>Norton Anthology of English</u>

<u>Literature</u>. Ed. M. H. Abrams et al. 7th ed. Vol. 1. New

York: Norton, 2000. 1-22.

Here the reference is to the first volume, pages 1–22. Note that when you cite sections of books, you usually give page numbers for the whole section. The abbreviation "Ed." after the titles in the examples above means "edited by"; no need to add an "s" to the abbreviation if the book is edited by more than one person.

Work from an anthology

Christie, Agatha. "The Dream." <u>Detective Stories from the</u>

<u>Strand Magazine</u>. Ed. Jack Adrian. New York: Oxford UP, 1992.

21-43.

Jackson, Shirley. "The Lottery." <u>Literature: Reading,</u>

<u>Reacting, Writing</u>. Ed. Laurie G. Kirszner and Stephen R.

Mandell. Compact 3rd ed. Fort Worth: Harcourt, 1997. 261-69.

Lyon, Thomas J. "The Literary West." <u>The Oxford History of the</u>

<u>American West</u>. Ed. Clyde A. Milner, II, Carol A. O'Connor,

and Martha A. Sandweiss. New York: Oxford UP, 1994. 707-41.

Montaigne, Michel de. "Of Cannibals." Trans. Donald Frame. <u>The</u>

<u>Norton Anthology of World Masterpieces: The Western</u>

<u>Tradition</u>. Ed. Sarah Lawall and Maynard Mack. 7th ed. Vol.

1. New York: Norton, 1999. 1933-42.

One or more editors

Drabble, Margaret, ed. <u>The Oxford Companion to English</u>

<u>Literature</u>. Rev. ed. New York: Oxford UP, 1995.

Suleiman, Susan R., and Inge Crosman, eds. <u>The Reader in the</u>

<u>Text: Essays on Audience and Interpretation</u>. Princeton:

Princeton UP, 1980.

The abbreviation "ed." above means "editor." Add an "s" to the abbreviation if the book is edited by more than one person.

Published before 1900

Scott, Sir Walter. <u>Kenilworth</u>. Chicago, 1890.

You may, when citing a book published before 1900, omit the name of the publisher and use a comma (rather than a colon) after the place of publication.

Sample Entry for Articles in Scholarly Journals

Leverenz, David. "The Last Real Man in America: From Natty
   Bumppo to Batman." <u>American Literary History</u> 3 (1991):
   753-81.

In this entry, *American Literary History* is the journal, 3 is the volume number, 1991 is the year of publication, and 753–81 are the page numbers. Note that you give page numbers not just for the pages you cite but for the entire article.

Sample Entries for Articles in Popular Publications

Weekly or biweekly magazine

Dubos, Andre. "Witness." <u>New Yorker</u> 21 July 1997: 33-36.

Monthly magazine

Malone, Michael. "Books in Brief." <u>Harper's</u> June 1977: 82-84.

Book review in a weekly magazine

Blake, Patricia. "Gingerly Removing the Veil." Rev. of
   <u>Josephine Herbst</u>, by Elinor Langer. <u>Newsweek</u> 3 Sept.
   1984: 80.

Article in a newspaper

Coneroy, Herman. "<u>David Copperfield</u> Revisited." <u>New York Times</u>
   19 Aug. 1962, late ed.: F23.
Weeks, Linton. "Stanley Kunitz, 95, Becomes Poet Laureate for
   a New Century." <u>Washington Post</u> 29 July 2000: C1+.

When citing newspaper articles, indicate if possible the edition of the paper ("late edition," "national edition," "city edition"). The reason is that the content of articles may vary from edition to edition. The edition is usually indicated in the newspaper's masthead. The plus sign at the end of the second citation indicates that the article continues on another page.

Sample Entries for Computer Databases

The documentary format for computer resources continues to evolve along with the resources themselves. The sixth edition of the *MLA Handbook for Writers of Research Papers* is the source for the guidelines below, but even these will change as technology evolves. For the most up-to-date MLA guidelines for documenting online resources, check the *MLA Style* website at <http://www.mla.org/style_faq4>.

When you are faced with the sometimes puzzling problem of documenting electronic resources, keep in mind the reasons to document *anything:* You want to verify the existence and reliability of your resources. You want to help readers find these resources. You want to show that you have conscientiously sifted through the relevant evidence and opinion. So, if you are confused about how to document a resource, use common sense. Give the information necessary to accomplish the above goals. Since databases often cease publication, especially on the Internet, you might want to print out the relevant sections of documents you cite, in case you have to show readers (including your instructor) they really existed.

Portable databases published periodically. For CD-ROMs, diskettes, and magnetic tapes that are continually updated, use the following format:

Dolan, Marc. "The (Hi)story of Their Lives: Mythic

Autobiography and 'The Lost Generation.'" <u>Journal of</u>

<u>American Studies</u>. 27 (1993): 35-56. <u>America: History and</u>

<u>Life on Disc</u>. CD-ROM. ABC-Clio. 1996.

Earthman, Elise Ann. "Creating the Virtual Work: Readers'

Processes in Understanding Literary Texts." Conference on

College Composition and Communication. Seattle,

```
Washington, 17 March 1989. ERIC. CD-ROM. SilverPlatter.

   June 1996.
```

Your citations should include as much of the following information as you can find:

- ❖ Author's name—if the work is anonymous, omit the name.
- ❖ Publication information—if the work appears in print (for example, in a scholarly journal), use the same format for giving publication information as you would for the printed version. (See the above sample entries for books, scholarly journals, and popular publications.)
- ❖ Title of the database (underlined)
- ❖ Publication medium (CD-ROM, diskette, magnetic tape)
- ❖ Name of the vendor—you can usually spot the name of the vendor somewhere on the first screen. If it is not there, check to see if you can click on "information about this database." If that does not work, leave out the information and move on.
- ❖ Electronic publication date (when the database was released)—the sources of information just mentioned should give you this date.

The first example above is an abstract of an article in a scholarly journal. If you wanted to summarize or quote from this abstract, you would cite the computer database *(America: History and Life on Disc)* that provides it. The second entry is a lecture available only from the computer database *ERIC*. If you wanted to use it, you would cite the database.

Portable databases not published periodically. These are CD-ROMs, diskettes, and magnetic tapes published only once, like a book.

```
Hallam, Walker. Molière. Boston: Twayne, 1990. CD-ROM. Boston:

   DiscLit, 1992.

"Mingle." The Oxford English Dictionary. 2nd ed. CD-ROM.

   Oxford: Oxford UP, 1992.
```

For these databases, include the following information:

- ❖ Author's name—If the work is anonymous, omit the name. If the name is for an editor, translator, or compiler, indicate that with the appropriate abbreviation (ed., comp., trans.).

❖ Title of the publication (underlined)
❖ Name of the editor, translator, or compiler. This is relevant if the work is not in its original published form.
❖ Publishing information for print version, if relevant
❖ Publication medium (CD-ROM, diskette, magnetic tape)
❖ Edition, release, or version, if relevant
❖ Place of publication
❖ Name of the publisher
❖ Date of publication

The first example on page 319 is a book from the Twayne Publishers series of books about authors. For this entry, publication information about the printed book is followed by information about the CD-ROM. The second example is the definition of a word from *The Oxford English Dictionary.*

Online databases accessed through a computer service and featuring material published in print.   Such databases are available over the Internet, usually through subscription. You typically gain access to them through your college or library computer network.

Halberstam, Judith. "Technologies of Monstrosity: Bram

   Stoker's Dracula." Victorian Studies 36 (1993): 20. Expanded

   Academic ASAP. Infotrac Online. Jackson Library, UNC at

   Greensboro. 21 Sept. 2004.

Hutchinson, Mark. "In Defense of Fiction." New York Times 22

   October 1995, late ed., sec. 7:30. New York Times. Proquest.

   Jackson Library, UNC at Greensboro. 21 Sept. 2004.

For these databases, supply the following information:

❖ Name of the author (if given)
❖ Publication information for the printed source. Use the same format as described above for printed material. See the sample entries for books, scholarly journals, and popular publications.
❖ Title of the database (underlined or italicized)
❖ Name of the computer service
❖ Name of the library that gave you access to the database
❖ Date of access (the date you used the service to read or print this material)

In the first example on page 320, the computer service, Infotrac Online, provides an abstract and the full text of an article that appeared in a printed scholarly journal. There are no page numbers in this document, but the information about it includes the number of pages (twenty) of the printed essay. In the second example, the service gives an abstract of a newspaper article.

Online databases accessed via a computer service and featuring material with no printed source

```
"Courtly Love." 2004. Encyclopaedia Britannica Online. Jackson

    Library, UNC at Greensboro. 24 Sept. 2004.
```

For these databases, supply the following information:

- ❖ Author's name (if available)
- ❖ Title of the article or chapter (in quotation marks)
- ❖ Date of the material (if given)
- ❖ Title of the database (underlined)
- ❖ Name of the computer service
- ❖ Name of the library through which you accessed to the database
- ❖ Date of access (the date you used the service)

In the example above, the author is unknown (so not included) and the article was accessed from the Internet via subscription to *Encyclopaedia Britannica Online.* Were you to look up "courtly love" in the printed version of the *Encyclopaedia Britannica,* you might find the same article as the one cited above, but the editors of *Encyclopaedia Britannica Online* claim that they update their entries regularly, so their version of the article might be different from the printed version.

Articles in online periodicals and websites

```
Cohen, Rachel. "A Private History: Moments in the Friendship

    of Mark Twain and Ulysses S. Grant." Doubletake 21 (Summer

    2000): 31 pars. 21 Sept. 2004 <http://www.double

    takemagazine.org/mag/html/backissues/21/cohen/index>.

Elam, Diane. "Why Read?" Culture Machine. 2 (2000):

    18 pars. 28 Aug. 2004 <http://culturemachine.tees.ac.

    uk/frm_f1/htm>.
```

Many essays and commentaries are published only on the Internet in such places as websites, journals, magazines (e-zines), and newsletters. For these resources, give as much of the following information as you can:

❖ Author's name (if available)
❖ Title of the article (in quotation marks)
❖ Title of the website or publication (underlined)
❖ Volume number, issue number, or other identifying number (if available)
❖ Date of publication (if available)
❖ The number of pages, screens, paragraphs, or sections, if they are numbered
❖ Date of access
❖ Electronic address of the site (URL), contained within angle brackets ($<$ $>$)

Professional and personal websites

Churchyard, Henry. <u>Jane Austen Information Page</u>. 29 July 2004

<http://pemberley.com/janeinfo/janeinfo.html>.

When you cite the website itself, not an article within the website, give as much of the following information as you can:

❖ Name of the person who created or maintains the site
❖ Title of the site (underlined)
❖ If there is no title, a description such as "Home Page" (not underlined or in quotation marks)
❖ Name of any institution or organization connected with the site
❖ Date of the last update (if known)
❖ Date of access
❖ Electronic address (URL), contained within angle brackets

Electronic texts

Keats, John. "La Belle Dame sans Merci." <u>The Poetical Works of</u>

<u>John Keats</u>. London: Macmillan, 1884. bartleby.com. Feb.

1999. 28 Aug. 2000 <http://bartleby.com/126/55.html>.

Milton, John. <u>Paradise Lost</u>. Ed. Joseph Raben. 1965. Project

Gutenberg. Feb. 1992. 27 Mar. 2004 <ftp://metalab.

unc.edu/pub/docs/books/gutenberg/etext92/plrabn12.txt>.

For e-texts, give the following information:

❖ Author's name (if given)
❖ Title of the text—if the title is a work within a larger work, such as a poem or short story, put it within quotation marks; if the title is a self-contained work, such as a novel, play, or collection, underline it.
❖ Name of editor, translator, or compiler (if available)
❖ Publication information about the printed source (to the extent available)
❖ Information about electronic publication, such as the site title (underlined), editor, version number, date of e-publication, name of sponsoring institution or organization.
❖ Date of access
❖ Electronic address (URL), contained within angle brackets

The first example above is a poem by John Keats located in a collection of his poems published in 1884. Information about the printed source for the poem is made clear at the beginning of the site. The second example is the complete version of John Milton's *Paradise Lost*. The publisher of the text, Project Gutenberg, provides an introduction to this edition that indicates who created it and what the edition is like.

Online discussion groups and newsgroups

```
Foner, Heather. "Time Travel Fiction." Online posting. 10
    June 1999. Weird Science Discussion Group. 12 June 1999
    <darwin-1@_uconnaix.cc.uconn.edu>.
Grayfield, John. "Two Years Before the Mast." Online posting.
    3 June 1999. Naval Science News Group. 12 Aug. 1999
    <sci.military.naval.rec.ships>.
```

Discussion groups abound on the Internet. For these resources, supply the following information:

❖ Author's name (if known)
❖ The title of the posting (in quotation marks)
❖ The kind of communication (online posting)
❖ The date of publication
❖ The name of the forum (discussion group, newsgroup)
❖ The access date
❖ Electronic address (URL), enclosed in angle brackets

Electronic mail (e-mail)

```
Finney, Jack. "Re: Time travel fiction." E-mail to Kelley
    Griffith. 11 Oct. 1993.
```

For e-mail messages, give the following information:

- ❖ Author's name
- ❖ The subject line from the posting (in quotation marks)
- ❖ The recipient of the posting
- ❖ The date of publication (the day the message was sent)

For *all* electronic resources, you may find some of the information missing or difficult to come by. Don't be frustrated. Give as much of the information as you can. Omit what you cannot find.

Sample Entries for Other Nonprint Sources

Interview

```
Rogers, Fred. Interview with Noah Adams. All Things
    Considered. National Public Radio. WFDD, Winston-Salem. 19
    Feb. 1993.
Trillin, Calvin. Personal interview. 16 Mar. 1993.
```

The basic information for interviews is (1) the interviewee's name, (2) the title or nature of the interview and the interviewer (if known), and (3) the place and date of the interview. The first entry above indicates that Fred Rogers was interviewed on the radio program *All Things Considered* by Noah Adams. If you personally interviewed someone, your citation would look like the second entry.

Lecture

```
Gay, Geneva. "Ethnic Identity in a Diverse Society: The
    Challenge for Education." Temple University. Philadelphia.
    30 Mar. 1993.
May, Marilyn. Class lecture. English 368: English Romantic
    Poetry. University of North Carolina at Greensboro. 10
    Apr. 1991.
```

For lectures, give the lecturer's name, then the title or nature of the lecture, and finally the place and date.

Television or radio program

<u>Soundings</u>. NPR. WFDD, Winston-Salem. 7 Mar. 1993.

<u>Sixty Minutes</u>. CBS. WFMY, Greensboro. 24 Jan. 1993.

"Mistaken Identity." Millennium: Tribal Wisdom and the Modern

   World. Narr. Adrian Malone. WUNC, Chapel Hill. 12 Feb. 1992.

Radio and television programs should contain the following basic information: the title of the episode (in quotation marks), the title of the program (underlined), the network (CBS, NPR), the title of the series (no underscore), the call letters of the local station where you heard or saw the program, and the date of broadcast. The first entry above is a radio program, the second a television program. The third entry illustrates an episode in a series narrated by an individual.

Sound recording

Holbrook, Hal. "Journalism on Horseback." <u>Mark Twain Tonight</u>.

   LP. Columbia, n.d.

McKennitt, Loreena. "The Lady of Shalott." <u>The Visit</u>. Music by

   Loreena McKennitt. Lyrics by Alfred, Lord Tennyson. Warner

   Brothers, 1991.

Thomas, Dylan. "Fern Hill." <u>Dylan Thomas Reading A Child's</u>

   <u>Christmas in Wales and Five Poems</u>. LP. Caedmon, 1952.

For commercially available recordings, put the person cited first. Depending on your emphasis, this person may be the author, composer, performer, or director. Then list the title or titles, the artist or artists, the medium, the manufacturer, and the year of issue. If you do not know the year of issue, put *n.d.* ("no date"). If the medium is not compact disc, indicate the medium: audiocassette, audiotape, or LP (long-playing record).

Film or videotape recording

<u>Crete and Mycenae</u>. Prod. and dir. Hans-Joachim Horsfeld.

   Videocassette. Kartes Video Communications, 1986.

<u>Star Wars</u>. Dir. George Lucas. Prod. Gary Kurtz. Screenplay by
    George Lucas. Music by John Williams. Perf. Mark Hamill,
    Harrison Ford, Carrie Fisher, Peter Cushing, and Alec
    Guiness. Twentieth Century-Fox, 1977.

When citing films, begin with the title (underlined), then give information such as director, writer, performers, and conclude with distributor and date. For videotapes and DVDs (and filmstrips and slide programs, as well), include the medium right before the name of the distributor, as in the first entry.

FREQUENTLY USED ABBREVIATIONS

Abbreviations save space. You will run into them when you read essays and books about literature, and you may want to use them yourself. Here is a brief list. For a much longer list, see *The MLA Handbook*.

adapt.	adapter, adaptation, adapted by
app.	appendix
c., ca.	*circa,* "about" (usually used with dates when the exact date is not certain—for example, ca. 1594)
cf.	*confer,* "compare" (not the equivalent of "see")
ch., chs.	chapter, chapters
comp.	compiler
d.	died
ed., eds.	edited by, editor, editors
esp.	especially
e.g.	*exempli gratia,* "for example"
et al.	*et alii,* "and others"
etc.	*et cetera,* "and so forth"
i.e.	*id est,* "that is"
l., ll.	line, lines
ms., mss.	manuscript, manuscripts
NB	*nota bene,* "note well"
p., pp.	page, pages
par.	paragraph
pt.	part
rev.	revised by, revision; review or reviewed by (for reviews, use *review* where *rev.* might be confused with *revision* or *revised by*)
trans.	translated by

U, UP	university, university press (in documentation)
vol., vols.	volume, volumes

SAMPLE RESEARCH PAPER

The following sample student research paper illustrates the use of the MLA documentary style as well as the principles of the argumentative research essay. As in this paper, the first page of your paper should have your name and course information in the upper-left corner, the title centered just below this information, and the text just below the title. The *MLA Handbook* says that you do not need a title page, but ask your instructor for his or her preference. Usually, you do not need a title page. If you have endnotes, place them on a new page immediately following your text. Put your Works Cited list after the endnotes, beginning on a new page. For more detailed instructions on the format of your paper, see Chapter 10.

Wright 1

Harold Wright

Professor Helen May

English 105-06

12 April 20--

The Monster's Education in Mary Shelley's

Frankenstein

Education is a prominent endeavor in Mary

Shelley's Frankenstein. Nearly all the major charac-

ters--Walton, Victor, Elizabeth, Henry, Safie, and the

monster--are at school or searching for knowledge.

Victor's education leads to the best known event of

the novel, his creation of a human being. But the

similarity of the monster to Mary Shelley herself

suggests that she uses the monster, and especially

his education, to express ideas that were close to
her heart.

The monster's education begins immediately
after his creation. His creator, Victor
Frankenstein, while at school in Germany, learns
how to bring dead tissue back to life. He assembles
a creature from body parts, but when he awakens it,
he shrinks from it in horror and runs away. Two
years later, the monster, now "grown up," meets
Victor in the Alps and tells him his story.

Although the monster's education is improbably
rapid, Shelley makes clear that it follows the pattern of any person's growth from infancy to adoles-
cence. To establish the normality of the monster's
growth and education, she drew upon two works she
read while writing <u>Frankenstein</u>: John Locke's <u>Essay
Concerning Human Understanding</u> (1690) and
Rousseau's <u>Discourse on the Origins of Human
Inequality</u> (1755). The monster's childhood fits the
pattern of Rousseau's noble savage, who must learn
how to survive in the wilderness by trial and
error. And he acquires knowledge according to
Locke's theory that everything people learn origi-
nates from sensations (Woodbridge pars. 15-17).

At the beginning of the monster's life, he is
like any newborn baby, completely innocent, empty
of knowledge, registering only sensations.
Gradually he moves into a kind of early childhood
by learning to feel hot and cold, to experience

fear and pleasure, to walk, eat, sleep, and clothe
himself. His initial encounters with human beings
are not happy. The first person who sees him runs
shrieking away. When he ventures into a village,
the townspeople pelt him with rocks and chase him
out. After wandering cold and hungry around the
countryside, the monster comes upon a cottage with
a lean-to shed attached to it. He crawls into the
shed and makes it his home for the next year
(Shelley 98-101).

The cottage is occupied by the De Laceys, a
family of political exiles from France. The family
consists of an old, blind father, a son, a daughter, and, somewhat later, the son's fiancée, the
daughter of a Turkish businessman. Through a chink
in a window, the monster observes and listens to
them. He is deeply impressed by this family, because, although they are poor, they love and care
for one another. Fearing that his appearance might
frighten them, he keeps out of sight. But in imitation of them, he acts with kindness. At night, he
piles firewood outside their door and shovels snow
from their pathways. The more he observes them, the
more he yearns to join their warm family circle
(101-09).

His opportunity comes, he thinks, when the fiancée arrives. Since the fiancée cannot speak their
language and knows nothing about Europe, the family
begins to teach her. As they do, the monster becomes

her co-student. The monster is astonishingly adept. He learns French more quickly than Safie, the fiancée. He studies European history, economics, and politics. He reads Goethe's <u>The Sorrows of Young Werther</u>, Plutarch's <u>Lives</u>, and Milton's <u>Paradise Lost</u> (109–123). As a result, he begins to think about who he is: "My person was hideous and my stature gigantic. What did this mean? Who was I? What was I? Whence did I come? What was my destination?" (123).

He decides, finally, to reveal himself to the family and beg them to accept him as one of their own. One day, with fear and trepidation, while the rest of the family is away, he visits the blind father. At first all goes well. The monster explains, "I have good dispositions; my life has been hitherto harmless and in some degree beneficial; but a fatal prejudice clouds their [people's] eyes, and where they ought to see a feeling and kind friend, they behold only a detestable monster" (128). The father responds eagerly and recognizes in the monster a kindred spirit: "I also am unfortunate; I and my family have been condemned, although innocent; judge, therefore, if I do not feel for your misfortunes" (128). The monster weeps in gratitude.

But when the others return, they view the monster with horror. The daughter faints, Safie runs out of the cottage, and the son beats the monster with a stick. Two days later, the monster returns,

finds the De Laceys gone, and burns the cottage to
the ground. Shortly thereafter, when the monster
rescues a little girl, he completes his education.
Instead of expressing gratitude, the girl's companion shoots and wounds him. The monster then vows
revenge on all humankind. From this point onward,
he becomes what he is most famous for being--a
killer (123-135).

Mary Shelley's childhood and education parallel the monster's in striking ways. She was born 30
August 1797 to two of the most notorious political
radicals of their day. Her father, William Godwin,
was a social critic, philosopher, political re-
former, and novelist. Her mother, Mary
Wollstonecraft, was the first feminist author.
Together, they condemned tyrannical governments and
enthusiastically supported the French Revolution.
They shared a passionate and deeply satisfying relationship. Neither believed in marriage, but when
Wollstonecraft became pregnant, they married to
protect the child. Ten days after Mary's birth,
Wollstonecraft died from natal complications
(Spark 3-11).

Mary grew up in a large and busy family, consisting of Godwin's new wife, Jane Clairmont, a
stepsister, stepbrother, half-sister, and half-
brother. Although her brothers went to the best
schools, she had no formal education. Instead, she
was taught at home by her father, her stepmother,

and tutors. She read from her father's large library. She listened to the conversation of famous visitors, like William Wordsworth, Charles Lamb, and William Hazlitt. Once she hid behind the sofa to hear Samuel Taylor Coleridge recite "The Rime of the Ancient Mariner" (Spark 13).

By the time Mary was a teenager, relations with her family had become strained. She didn't get along with her stepmother, and her father distanced himself from her. To escape tensions at home, she made several extended visits to friends in Scotland. It was after one of these that she met the poet Percy Shelley, who had become a frequent visitor in her father's house. He was five years older than Mary, already married, and father of one child with a second on the way. He and Mary fell in love and began a passionate affair. After stormy opposition from her family, they ran away together to Europe in July 1814. Percy was twenty-one years old. She was sixteen and had just discovered that she was pregnant (Spark 28–29).

Until Percy's death in 1822 from a boating accident, the couple lived a difficult, often tumultuous life together. After they "eloped," her father condemned her and refused to see or write to her for three and a half years. She and Percy were almost always in financial difficulty, often, at first, having no place to stay so that they slept outdoors or in barns (Spark 28–29). Giving birth

and caring for babies dominated her relationship
with Percy. She was pregnant five times until
Percy's death. She had two miscarriages, the second
of which almost killed her. Two of her children
died as infants, and only one survived to adulthood.

Amidst these difficulties, Mary wrote
Frankenstein. To create the novel, she drew upon
the huge amount of reading she had done during this
period, the conversations she had with Percy and
their friends, her mother and father's writings,
and her own experiences. She began the novel in
July 1816 and finished it by May 1817. It was published in January 1818 (Spark 56–60).

The difficulties of Mary's own education and
coming of age gave rise to the ideas she embedded
in the story of the monster's education. The first
of these ideas is that children who are abandoned
or neglected by their parents can become "monsters." Ellen Moers argues that Mary's experience
of continual pregnancy, childbirth, childcare, and
child death led her to write about a careless and
inept scientist who gives birth, so to speak, to a
mis-formed child. Moers calls Frankenstein a "birth
myth" (140). The novel is "interesting, most powerful, and most feminine" in its "motif of revulsion
against newborn life, and the drama of guilt,
dread, and flight surrounding birth and its consequences," especially in its dealing "with the ret-

ribution visited upon monster and creator for defi-
cient infant care" (142). Mary thus writes a "fantasy of the newborn as at once monstrous agent of
destruction and piteous victim of parental abandon-
ment" (148).

As a daring and anxious creator of life, Mary
is similar to Victor. But her childhood experiences, gifts, and education link her also to the
monster. Like the monster she felt "abandoned" by
her parents, first, at childbirth by her mother,
then by her father when he remarried and when she
ran away with Shelley (Sunstein 34, 114).
"Obviously," Emily Sunstein says, "the monster created from corpses reflects the primitive Mary
Shelley: her guilt at being her mother's killer-
reincarnation, her rage that her father abandoned
her, and her resentment of her half brother,
William" (131). Like the monster Mary grew up rapidly and was extremely young when she took on the
responsibilities of adulthood. Like the monster she
had to pick up an education by "looking on." Like
the monster she was precocious, a rapid learner.
Like the monster she was something of an outlaw,
stepping across the border of conventional female
morality. Like the monster, she was scorned and exiled.

Mary transfers her feelings of parental vic-
timization to the monster. Upon his first meeting
with Victor, he holds Victor accountable for mis-

treating him: "Remember that I am thy creature; I ought to be thy Adam, but I am rather the fallen angel, whom thou drivest from joy for no misdeed" (95). Victor reluctantly agrees: "For the first time, also, I felt what the duties of a creator towards his creature were, and that I ought to render him happy before I complained of his wickedness" (97). The monster compares the happy De Lacey family to his own lack of family: "But where were my friends and relations? No father had watched my infant days, no mother had blessed me with smiles and caresses" (115). At the end of his story, the monster once again accuses Victor of failing as a parent: "You endowed me with perceptions and passions and cast me abroad an object for the scorn and horror of mankind" (133).

The second idea in <u>Frankenstein</u> suggested by Mary's life is that, like bad parents, an unjust society can create monsters. Her main source for this idea probably originated with her parents' beliefs about the French Revolution. In her <u>An Historical and Moral View of the Origin and Progress of the French Revolution</u> (1794), Wollstonecraft responds to conservative critics of the French Revolution, like Edmund Burke, who labeled the revolutionaries "monsters" (Sterrenburg 153). Wollstonecraft, Lee Sterrenburg says, "admits that rebels are monsters. But she resolutely insists that these monsters are social products. They are not the living dead, nor are they specters arisen from the tomb of the murdered monarchy. Rather, they are the products of oppression, misrule, and despotism under the ancien régime. The lower orders are driven to rebellion" (162).

The monster embodies Wollstonecraft's belief that social rebels are formed by society. At birth the monster is innocent. As he begins his education, he wants to do good deeds and to have loving relationships. But the failure of society (Victor, the De Laceys, other people) to accept him, love him, and treat him fairly causes him to become a monster. He tells Victor, "I was benevolent and good; misery made me a fiend" (95-96). After the De Laceys drive him out of the cottage and the little girl's companion shoots him, he feels "the oppressive sense of injustice and ingratitude" of the people who have hurt him and vows "eternal hatred and vengeance to all mankind" (135). "I am malicious," he says, "because I am miserable" (138). As Sterrenburg states, "The Monster proves a very philosophical rebel. He explains his actions in traditional republican terms. He claims he has been driven to rebellion by the failures of the ruling orders. His superiors and protectors have shirked their responsibilities toward him, impelling him to insurrection" (161).

Although the monster is just one person, and an unusual one, at that, Mary extends her social

criticism to include others. She does so by means
of his education. Through his and Safie's reading of
Volney's <u>Ruins of Empires</u>,[1] he hears about the
tragic history of human societies: "For a long time
I could not conceive how one man could go forth to
murder his fellow, or even why there were laws and
governments; but when I heard details of vice and
bloodshed, my wonder ceased and I turned away with
disgust and loathing" (114). The De Laceys reveal
that society is unfair to all but a few citizens:
"I heard of the division of property, of immense
wealth and squalid poverty, of rank, descent, and
noble blood. . . . I learned that the possessions
most esteemed by your fellow creatures were high
and unsullied descent united with riches" (115).

    The De Laceys, Safie, Justine Moritz, the mon-
ster are all victims of an unjust society. So, too,
Mary no doubt believed, were the oppressed workers
of her own day. While she was writing <u>Frankenstein</u>,
England suffered from an economic depression that
caused widespread unemployment and hunger among
workers. These conditions led workers to hold
protest rallies that sometimes ended in violence.
The worst of these occasions was the "Peterloo"
riot of 1819, when 80,000 people demonstrated in
St. Peter's Fields in Manchester for political reform and were fired upon by soldiers. Eleven people
were killed and 400 injured. The government's response to such protests was unsympathetic, harsh,

and repressive (Lerner 786). In Mary's mind, the monster could have been any of these workers, driven to rebellion by poverty, hunger, and the meanness of powerful people.[2]

The third idea suggested by Mary's life is that women, too, are made monstrous by society. Sandra Gilbert and Susan Gubar hold that Mary saw herself as a monster because women are taught to feel like monsters: "As we argued earlier, women have seen themselves (because they have been seen) as monstrous, vile, degraded creatures, second-comers, and emblems of filthy materiality, even though they have also been traditionally defined as superior beings, angels, better halves" (240).

Mary got a taste of this attitude when she learned about her mother's life and ideas. A year after Wollstonecraft's death, Godwin published his <u>Memoirs of the Author of A Vindication of the Rights of Woman</u> (1798), in which, Emily Sunstein says, "he revealed the details of her intimate life, which comparatively few had known about: her love for Fuseli, her liaison with Imlay, her premarital affair with him--'stripping his dead wife naked,' said Robert Southey" (19). As a re-sult, the conservative press ruthlessly attacked Godwin and her, calling her a "lascivious whore" (Sunstein 20).

Mary read Godwin's <u>Memoirs</u> when she was four-teen, along with <u>A Vindication of the Rights of</u>

Woman (1794), Wollstonecraft's best-known book, and
her other works. Fully aware of the press's charges
against her mother, Mary became a fierce partisan of
Wollstonecraft's feminist beliefs. She "worshiped"
her mother, according to Sunstein, "both as rational intellectual and romantic heroine" (53).
Through her mother's writings and actions, Mary saw
that women who advocate and practice liberation are
labeled "monsters."

The monster's embodiment of women is most visible in his education. In A Vindication of the
Rights of Woman, Wollstonecraft declared the equal-
ity of the sexes and demanded equal rights for
women. She argued that the key to women's sharing
of power with men is education. Yet Mary, although
extremely able as a student, did not go to school.
Her brothers and husband went, but not she. And
there was probably no college or university at the
time that would have accepted females as students.
Instead, like the monster, Mary did much of her
learning on her own. As if to call attention to her
identity with the monster, she had him read the
same things that she had been reading under Percy's
tutelage. The similarity of their reading program
leads Gilbert and Gubar to claim that Mary and the
monster are "parented, if at all, by books" (239).

The similarity of Mary's life to the monster's, then, suggests that, through neglect and
mistreatment, three groups can be turned into "mon-

ters": children, citizens, and women. If the monster's experience is anything to go by, education,
though exciting, only adds to their monstrousness.
It makes them more aware of their alienation and
unjust treatment. "Increase of knowledge," the monster tells Victor, "only discovered to me more
clearly what a wretched outcast I was" (125).
Furthermore, education drives them toward vengeance
rather than acceptance: "My sufferings were augmented also by the oppressive sense of the injustice and ingratitude of their infliction. My daily
vows rose for revenge--a deep and deadly revenge,
such as would alone compensate for the outrages and
anguish I endured" (135). But the monster's education is also our education. Just as he learned by
looking over Safie's shoulder, we learn by looking
over his. Mary Shelley perhaps hoped that if we
shared the monster's education, we might help prevent the creation of monsters--by caring for our
children, by treating people fairly, and by establishing just societies.

Notes

[1] One of Shelley's sources for the scene
wherein the monster learns about the history of
human vice is <u>Pygmalion et Galatée</u> (1803), a play
by Stéphanie-Felicité Ducrest de Saint-Aubin,
Comtesse de Genlis. In this play, a pure and
innocent character, Galatea, is, like the monster,
"awakened" to life fully grown. When an old servant fills her in on human history, she is shocked
by revelations of human meanness and misery
(slavery, tyranny, extreme distance between rich
and poor, treachery). This play, Burton Pollin
maintains, "helped to suggest the device of
awakening and the actual injustices of society
with which both naive intellects become acquainted" (101).

[2] Elizabeth Bohls claims that Mary extends her
social criticism to "colonized" peoples: "Shelley
weaves into her creature's indeterminate identity
middle-class Britons' collective anxieties about
otherness of more than one kind" (25). Safie, as a
Turk and Christian, and the monster, as the alien-
ated outlaw, represent colonized peoples (32).
After reading Volney's book, they both lament the
"genocide of the American Indians" (29). The monster's exclusion from happy middle class families
like the Frankensteins and the De Laceys, "is in-
separable from, in fact depends on, the violence
their civilization does to those whom its struc-

ture of value needs to exclude and condemn" (29).
In the monster's expressions of alienation, we
"hear the anguish of a colonized self who has in-
ternalized the values that judge him forever defi-
cient" (32).

Works Cited

Bohls, Elizabeth A. "Standards of Taste, Discourses
of 'Race,' and the Aesthetic Education of a
Monster: Critique of Empire in <u>Frankenstein</u>."
<u>Eighteenth-Century Life</u> (Nov. 1994): 23-36.

Gilbert, Sandra M., and Susan Gubar. <u>The Madwoman in
the Attic: The Woman Writer and the Nineteenth-
Century Literary Imagination</u>. New Haven, CT:
Yale UP, 1979.

Lerner, Robert E., Standish Meacham, and Edward
McNall Burns. <u>Western Civilizations: Their
History and Their Culture</u>. 11th ed. New York:
Norton, 1988.

Moers, Ellen. <u>Literary Women: The Great Writers</u>.
Garden City, NY: Anchor Books, 1977.

Pollin, Burton R. "Philosophical and Literary
Sources of <u>Frankenstein</u>." <u>Comparative
Literature</u> 17 (Spring 1965): 97-108.

Shelley, Mary. <u>Frankenstein: Or, The Modern
Prometheus</u>. New York: Signet Classic (New
American Library), 1965.

Spark, Muriel. <u>Mary Shelley</u>. New York: Dutton, 1987.

Sunstein, Emily W. <u>Mary Shelley: Romance and
Reality</u>. Boston: Little, Brown, 1989.

Woodbridge, Kim. "Mary Shelley and the Desire to
Acquire Knowledge: Demonstrated in the Novel
Frankenstein." <u>Mary Shelley and Frankenstein</u>.
28 Aug. 2000 <http://desert-fairy.com/
knowledge.shtml>.

Comments on the Research Paper

In the first paragraph—the introduction—the author states his purpose: to use Mary Shelley's life as a means of identifying important ideas in *Frankenstein*. He indicates that he will focus on one part of the novel, the section about the monster's education. Although he does not state his purpose in the form of a question, we can infer the question that lies behind his purpose: How might the monster's education apply to the real world? Put another way, what ideas might Shelley have wanted to convey in her story of the monster's education?

The body of the paper is structured by three answers to this question. First, neglectful parents can turn children into monsters. Second, unjust societies can turn citizens into monsters. Third, prejudiced societies can turn women into monsters. Each of these claims constitutes a major unit of the paper. Within each unit the author draws upon details from the novel, information about Mary Shelley's life, and opinions of critics to explain and support his claims.

In the final paragraph, the author's conclusion, he restates his three major claims. This summary, the first sentence of the paragraph, is his thesis. He then uses the thesis to make a conjecture about what his line of thought adds up to, how the monster's education might apply to people today. Throughout the paper, he follows MLA procedure for introducing facts and testimony in his text. He includes two explanatory notes, which he places at the end of the paper. His parenthetical references refer clearly to the sources in the Works Cited list.

Notice that for all the author's inclusion of secondary sources, the paper is nonetheless his argument, his creative investigation of the meaning of the novel. He never presents facts and other people's opinions as ends in themselves, but rather as support for his own ideas. As such, his paper is a fine model of a research essay about literature.

Checklist for Documentation and Research

❖ Plan a research paper that uses secondary sources to develop and help support your interpretation of a work or works of literature.

❖ Use the library and computers to locate resources in books, journals, newspapers, databases, and Internet sites.

❖ Evaluate the quality of any Internet sites you consult.

❖ In your paper, give proper credit to all primary and secondary sources you include.

❖ Give credit in your text (parenthetical references) and in a Works Cited section, located at the end. Follow correct documentary style.

12

Taking Essay Tests

So far, this book has dealt with essays written outside the classroom. Tests and examinations, however, are work you do in class, usually within a given time frame. When your instructor tests you, he or she wants to know two things: how familiar you are with the course material (the literature, the instructor's lectures, the secondary material you may be required to read) and how creatively you can think about this material. Tests fall into two categories—objective and essay. Sometimes, the instructor may include questions or assignments from both categories on the same test.

Objective vs. essay tests. Objective tests ask you to account for, explain, and identify details about the course material. Essay tests ask you to state your ideas about literary works and to support those ideas with facts and reasoning. Some essay tests call for short, one-paragraph essays; some call for long essays. The same methods for writing out-of-class essays apply to test essays, short or long. Your test essays are arguments: They should have a thesis and should try to convince an audience of the validity of that thesis. They should use sound logic and apt illustrations. Most of all, because of time limits, they need good organization.

Performance on tests. Perhaps the most important general consideration to keep in mind is that your grade will depend on how well you *perform* on a particular assignment, not simply on how much you know. You may know the material very well, but if you do not perform well, your grade will not reflect the abundance or quality of your knowledge. The following guidelines should help you perform well on essay tests.

GUIDELINES FOR TAKING ESSAY TESTS

1. **Prepare thoroughly.**
   a. First, learn the facts of the work or works on which you are being tested. Know who the characters are, what they do, and what happens to them, as well as the specifics of setting, and so forth. When you are taking the test, you should know the details so well that they emerge from your memory almost automatically. This subliminal knowledge saves your creative energy for dealing with interpretive problems the instructor gives you. If you have to slowly dredge up facts from your memory, you lose time for interpretation.
   b. Systematically review the key issues relevant to the works, literary periods, or genres covered by the test. A wise first step is to review the aspects of the works the instructor has emphasized in class. Then ask questions about the works, as you would for finding essay topics. Here, however, cover a range of important questions. Focus on the elements of literature. How does the author handle setting, characterization, theme, point of view, and so forth. If the test covers a number of works, consider ways in which the works are linked. Assume that your instructor will ask you to compare works, noting similarities and differences among them.
   c. When you review class notes, do so *along with* a review of the literary works. Reviewing your notes on the instructor's class comments will help you pinpoint important aspects of the works and help you anticipate test questions. Remember, however, that memorizing class notes is no substitute for reviewing the works themselves. The two go together.

2. **Understand the assignment.** When you get the test, carefully read all of the assignments before you begin writing. If you do not understand any of them, ask the instructor to explain more fully. Sometimes instructors unintentionally write ambiguous

assignments. You have a right to know exactly what you are supposed to do.

3. Plan your answer.

    a. *Think through* your answer by making a short, topical outline. Making an outline frees you from worrying about relevance and completeness while you write. Instead, once you have planned your answer and jotted down an outline of your plan, you can devote your writing time to a creative development of each main point. If you have fifty minutes to write an essay, ten minutes making an outline is time well spent. Your outline might look something like this:

> Thesis (state it in a phrase)
>
> Claim # 1 (state it in a phrase)
>   Supporting facts (list several)
>
> Claim # 2
>   Supporting facts
>
> Claim # 3
>   Supporting facts

    b. Cross through items on your outline that do not fit the topic.

    c. Arrange the remaining items in a logical order. Descending order of importance is probably best. That way, if you run out of time, you will have covered the most important items.

    d. Once you have edited your outline, you are ready to write. If you think of additional items to cover, add them in the appropriate place to your outline.

4. Respond directly to the assignment. One or two sentences at the beginning of the essay and at strategic places throughout should do the job. This way the instructor will know that you have kept the assignment in mind and that you have tried to deal with it. Your direct response to the assignment is the thesis of your essay and therefore should usually come near the beginning or end of your essay. Note the following example:

```
Assignment: Huck tricks Jim into believing that he
dreamed they were separated in the fog. But Jim finally
sees the trick for what it is. What does Huck learn from
Jim's reaction?
```

```
Direct Response: Huck learns that Jim has feelings and
dignity just as white people do.
```

The complete answer, of course, would explain and illustrate this point, but the direct response connects the whole answer to the assignment. Without a direct response, your answer may seem irrelevant.

5. **Write on one side of the page.** Writing on both sides of the page is messy and hard to read (ink bleeds through). Also, the instructor might overlook what's on the back side, especially if it is just a few sentences. To avoid these problems, write on one side of the page. Do this even if you use blue books.

6. **Add inserts when necessary.** It is acceptable, after you have read your answer through, to add new material. This is another reason to write on only one side of the page. If the new material is short, write it in the margin, with an arrow to indicate where it fits. If the new material is long, write the words "insert (see the back of this page)" in the margin, accompanied with the arrow, and write the new material on the back of the page.

7. **Write clear, simple, and correct prose.** The limited time and the pressure of the occasion make some mechanical slips likely, but strive to avoid them. Be wary of serious errors such as sentence fragments, ambiguous pronoun references, and subject-verb disagreements. If your handwriting is normally difficult to read, take care to make it legible.

8. **Develop your answer thoroughly.**
   a. State claims that respond directly to the assignment. Often, these claims will serve as topic sentences for paragraphs.
   b. Offer specific details from the works that support and illustrate your claims.
   c. Represent the work or works adequately. The more thoroughly and appropriately you relate the work to your claims (and thus to the assignment), the better your answer will be.
   d. Your answer is an argument. Back up claims with evidence. Show your readers, do not just tell them.

9. **Be creative.** Some instructors want you to reproduce what they have said in class. Studying for their tests is straightforward. Just memorize what the instructor has said and paraphrase it on

the test. The more perfect your reproduction, the better your grade. Other instructors, however, want more—and they design their tests to get more. They want *your* thinking, not just their own. They want your creativity. But how can you be creative on tests? The answer is—think for yourself! Here are some ways to do so.

a. Use the instructor's points, but provide your own facts from the works. This shows that you are doing more than just memorizing lectures. It shows that you have thought through and applied the instructor's ideas on your own.

b. Make your own claims. Although instructors try to cover the most important aspects of a work, limited class time makes it impossible for them to cover every aspect, even all the important ones. There are usually plenty of other claims to be made. Study the work yourself, and come up with your own claims. Read what others have said about the work and discover claims that way. Do not neglect claims made by the instructor, but make other claims as well.

c. Describe and take a stand on controversies—disagreements about meaning—in works of literature. Instructors often enjoy presenting controversies for class discussion. You can dip into them yourself by reading criticism of the works you are studying. Understanding literary controversies can sharpen your perception of the work. Showing your awareness of them and taking a stand on them will demonstrate your creative involvement with the work.

d. Be detailed in your support and illustration of points. The more details you provide, the clearer your creative involvement becomes, especially if you include details you have noticed on your own.

SAMPLE TEST ESSAYS

All of the following essays respond to the assignment below. The writers had about twenty minutes to write their essays.

ASSIGNMENT: *Explain the possible symbolic meanings of the rocking horse in D. H. Lawrence's "The Rocking-Horse Winner."*

Essay 1

Paul seems desperately to want his mother to love him. He senses that somehow she disapproves of him, that he stands in her way of achieving happiness. He seeks solace in the rocking horse. She has told him that "luck" means having money, so he rides the horse to get money. He hopes that by giving his mother money, he can buy his way into her heart. But, unfortunately, when he gives her an enormous sum of money, she is even more unhappy than before. Paul returns to the rocking horse to get more money for her. He frantically rides the horse one last time. But although he wins the jackpot, he dies from overexcitement and exhaustion.

Comments on Essay 1

Although this essay has good qualities, it is nonetheless mediocre because it does not directly address the assignment. It describes the action of the story accurately. It is clearly written. Its organization is easy to follow. It seems to have the assignment vaguely in mind, but nowhere does it say what the rocking horse symbolizes. The instructor may guess what the writer has in mind, but he or she cannot know for sure. The essay also omits important details. The writer does not say, for example, how Paul uses the horse to win money. The instructor may wonder whether the writer has read the story carefully.

Essay 2

Paul's mother claims that she is "unlucky," and she explains to Paul that being unlucky means having no money. But the details of the story suggest that Paul's family does have money, because they live very well. The family has the trappings of wealth--a nurse, a large house, comfortable furnishings, and a gardener. The mother, then, isn't really poor but is obsessed with money. Her children sense this obsession. Most sensitive of all is Paul, who hears voices saying, "There must be more money." As a result, Paul sets out to win his mother's love by being "lucky." His means of achieving luck and thus his mother's love is the rocking horse. He finds that by riding the horse hard enough, he can predict winners of horse races. The rocking horse, then, symbolizes the love his mother has withheld from him. He even experiences something like the ecstasy of love when riding the horse to a winner. But his plan fails when his gift of 5,000 pounds only makes his mother's greed greater. He then becomes so desperate for love that he rides the rocking horse to his death.

Comments on Essay 2

This is a good essay. It not only recounts details from the story accurately, it also directly responds to the assignment, and it relates all the details cited from the story to that response. In other words, the details become "evidence." Because it deals directly with the assignment, it treats the story more specifically and thoroughly than does essay 1.

Essay 3

The rocking horse symbolizes many things in "The Rocking-Horse Winner." Paul's mother complains that she has no money, and she tells Paul that to be "lucky" is to have money. Paul is very impressed by what she says and decides to prove to her that he is lucky. He wants also to stop the voices in the house that incessantly demand more money. He feels that the rocking horse can take him where luck is. Sure enough, when he rides the rocking horse and it takes him "there," he can predict the winners of horse races and make a great deal of money. So one thing the rocking horse symbolizes is luck, which, in turn, means money.

But the rocking horse also seems to represent a second idea. Paul's uncle says after Paul dies that Paul is better off being dead than living in a world where he had to ride a rocking horse to find a winner. The implication is that Paul was using the rocking horse to get what his mother never gave him: her love. So the rocking horse also symbolizes Paul's need for love and his parents' failure to give him love.

Finally, the rocking horse symbolizes success. When Paul rides the rocking horse far enough, it brings him financial success. But this success is only ironic, for it never brings him the "success" he desperately wants--his mother's love--and in the end it brings him death. Lawrence seems to suggest that some kinds of success are better than others; it is better to be loved than to be rich.

Comments on Essay 3

This is an excellent answer. Like essay 2, the essay responds to the assignment directly, and it plausibly and logically connects details of the story to its points. But it is more detailed and creative than essay 2. The writer makes a strong case for the complexity of the rocking horse as symbol and, by so doing, points to the multiple meanings and richness of the story.

Checklist for Taking Essay Tests

Preparation

❖ Know exceedingly well the details in works covered by the test.

❖ Review key issues of interpretation raised by the instructor or critics.

❖ Ask your own interpretive questions about the work. Anticipate questions that might appear on the test.

❖ Study class notes while reviewing the works.

Before You Begin Writing

❖ Understand the assignment.

❖ Make a rough outline of your essay.

While You Write

❖ Respond directly to the assignment.

❖ Write on one side of the page.

❖ Insert afterthoughts and corrections where necessary.

❖ Write clearly.

❖ Cover the assignment thoroughly.

❖ Support claims with evidence from the works.

❖ Be creative.

13

Sample Essays

This chapter contains four sample essays: one on a poem, one on a short story, one on a play, and one on a novel. All essays about literature are different. Interpretive questions vary enormously from essay to essay; authors employ different methods of answering them. These essays, then, are not models to be slavishly imitated. They do, however, embody the main points of this book: that essays about literature are interpretations, that they address explicit or implicit questions, that their theses answer those questions, and that, as arguments, they employ sound logic and well-supported claims.

ESSAY ON A POEM

RICHARD CORY

by Edwin Arlington Robinson

[First published in 1897]

Whenever Richard Cory went down town,
We people on the pavement looked at him:
He was a gentleman from sole to crown,
Clean favored, and imperially slim.

And he was always quietly arrayed,
And he was always human when he talked;
But still he fluttered pulses when he said,
"Good-morning," and he glittered when he walked.

And he was rich—yes, richer than a king—
And admirably schooled in every grace:
In fine, we thought that he was everything
To make us wish that we were in his place.

So on we worked, and waited for the light,
And went without the meat, and cursed the bread;
And Richard Cory, one calm summer night,
Went home and put a bullet through his head.

Cannon 1

George Cannon

Professor Landsdown

English 251-10

12 February 20--

Point of View in Edwin Arlington Robinson's
"Richard Cory"

Yvor Winters, an American critic, condemns
Edwin Arlington Robinson's poem "Richard Cory" for
containing "a superficially neat portrait of the elegant man of mystery" and for having a "very cheap
surprise ending" (52). It is true that because
Richard Cory fits the stereotype of "the man who has
everything," his suicide at the end is surprising,
even shocking. But the poet's handling of point of
view makes the portrait of Richard Cory only apparently superficial and the ending only apparently
"cheap."

In the second line of the poem, we learn that the speaker is not an omniscient narrator, but someone with a limited view of things. He is one of the "people" of the town (38). It is as if he has cornered a visitor on a sidewalk somewhere and is telling him about a fellow townsman whose suicide has puzzled and troubled him. He cannot understand it, so he talks about it. Throughout this speaker's narration, we learn a lot about him and his peers and how they regarded Richard Cory.

Clearly they saw him as something special. The imagery of kings and nobility ("crown," "imperially slim" and "richer than a king") permeates their conception of Richard Cory. To them he had the bearing and trappings of royalty. He was a "gentleman," a word that suggests courtliness as well as nobility. He had good taste ("he was always quietly arrayed"). He was wealthy. He had good breeding (he was "admirably schooled in every grace"). He "glittered when he walked," suggesting, perhaps, that he wore jewelry and walked with confidence.

Because of this attitude, the speaker and his peers placed themselves in an almost feudal relationship to Cory. They saw themselves as "people on the pavement," as if they walked on the ground and Richard Cory somehow walked above them. Even if he did not literally walk above them, they saw him as "above" them socially. They seemed to think it unusual that he was "human when he talked." The word

human suggests several things. One is that the people saw Cory as somehow exempt from the problems
and restrictions of being a human being (thus
"human") but that when he talked, he stepped out of
character. Another is that he, who was so much
above them, could be kind, warm, and thoughtful
(another meaning of "human"). They were so aston-
ished by this latter quality that when he did such
a simple and obvious thing as say "Good-morning,"
he "fluttered pulses."

In the final stanza, the speaker brings out the
most important differences between the people and
Richard Cory. Most obvious is that he was rich and
they were poor; they "went without the meat, and
cursed the bread." But another difference is suggested by the word light: "So on we worked, and
waited for the light." Light in this context most
apparently means a time when things will be better,
as in the expression "the light at the end of the
tunnel." But another meaning of "light" is revelation. Light has traditionally symbolized knowledge
and truth, and it may be that this is the meaning
the speaker--or at least Robinson--has in mind. If
so, another difference that the people saw between
Richard Cory and themselves was that Cory had
knowledge and understanding and they did not. After
all, they had no time to pursue knowledge; they
needed all their time just to survive. But Richard
Cory did have the time. He was a man of leisure who

had been "schooled." If anyone would have had the
"light"--a right understanding of things--then
Richard Cory would have been that person.

   Although Robinson does not tell us why
Richard Cory killed himself, he leaves several
hints. One of these is the assumptions about
Richard Cory held by the narrator and the "people."
Cory may have been a victim of their attitude. The
poem gives no evidence that he sought to be treated
like a king or that he had pretensions to nobility.
He seems, in fact, to have been democratic enough.
Although rich, well-mannered, and tastefully
dressed, he nonetheless came to town, spoke with
kindness to the people, and greeted them as if they
deserved his respect. Could he have wanted their
friendship?

      But the people's attitude may have isolated
         Richard Cory. Every time he came to town, they
      stared at him as if he were a freak in a sideshow
         (lines 1-2). In their imagination, furthermore,
         they created an ideal of him that was probably
         false and, if taken seriously by Richard Cory,
      would have been very difficult to live up to. Cory
      did not, at least, have the "light" that the people
         thought he had. His suicide attests to that. He
         was, in short, as "human" as they; but, unlike
         them, he lacked the consolation of fellowship.
      Ironically, then, the people's very admiration of
         Richard Cory, which set him apart as more than

Cannon 5

human and isolated him from human companionship,
may have been the cause of his death.

Had Robinson told Cory's story as an omniscient
narrator, Winters's complaint about the poem would
be justified. The poem would seem to be an attempt to
shock us with a melodramatic and too-obvious irony.
But Robinson has deepened the poem's meaning by having one of Cory's fellow townspeople tell his story.
This presentation of Cory's character, his relationship to the townspeople, and his motives for suicide
open up the poem to interpretation in a way that
Winters does not acknowledge or explore.

Works Cited

Robinson, Edwin Arlington. <u>Tilbury Town: Selected
     Poems of Edwin Arlington Robinson</u>. New York:
     Macmillan, 1951.

Winters, Yvor. <u>Edwin Arlington Robinson</u>. Norfolk:
     New Directions, 1946.

Note: Normally, the Works Cited list would appear on a separate page, but we print it here, right after the essay, to save space.

ESSAY ON A SHORT STORY

THE CASK OF AMONTILLADO

By Edgar Allan Poe

[First published in 1846]

The thousand injuries of Fortunato I had borne as I best could, but when he ventured upon insult I vowed revenge. You, who so well know the nature of my soul, will not suppose, however, that I gave utterance to a threat. *At length* I would be avenged; this was a point definitely settled—but the very definitiveness with which it was resolved precluded the idea of risk. I must not only punish but punish with impunity. A wrong is unredressed when retribution overtakes its redresser. It is equally unredressed when the avenger fails to make himself felt as such to him who has done the wrong.

It must be understood that neither by word nor deed had I given Fortunato cause to doubt my good will. I continued, as was my wont, to smile in his face, and he did not perceive that my smile *now* was at the thought of his immolation.

He had a weak point—this Fortunato—although in other regards he was a man to be respected and even feared. He prided himself on his connoisseurship in wine. Few Italians have the true virtuoso spirit. For the most part their enthusiasm is adopted to suit the time and opportunity, to practice imposture upon the British and Austrian *millionaires.* In painting and gemmary, Fortunato, like his countrymen, was a quack, but in the matter of old wines he was sincere. In this respect I did not differ from him materially;—I was skilful in the Italian vintages myself, and bought largely whenever I could.

It was about dusk, one evening during the supreme madness of the carnival season, that I encountered my friend. He accosted me with excessive warmth, for he had been drinking much. The man wore motley. He had on a tight-fitting parti-striped dress, and his head was surmounted by the conical cap and bells. I was so pleased to see him that I thought I should never have done wringing his hand.

I said to him—"My dear Fortunato, you are luckily met. How remarkably well you are looking to-day. But I have received a pipe of what passes for Amontillado, and I have my doubts."

"How?" said he. "Amontillado? A pipe? Impossible! And in the middle of the carnival!"

"I have my doubts," I replied; "and I was silly enough to pay the full Amontillado price without consulting you in the matter. You were not to be found, and I was fearful of losing a bargain."

"Amontillado!"

"I have my doubts."

"Amontillado!"

"And I must satisfy them."

"Amontillado!"

"As you are engaged, I am on my way to Luchresi. If any one has a critical turn it is he. He will tell me—"

"Luchresi cannot tell Amontillado from Sherry."

"And yet some fools will have it that his taste is a match for your own."

"Come, let us go."

"Whither?"

"To your vaults."

"My friend, no; I will not impose upon your good nature. I perceive you have an engagement. Luchresi—"

"I have no engagement;—come."

"My friend, no. It is not the engagement, but the severe cold with which I perceive you are afflicted. The vaults are insufferably damp. They are encrusted with nitre."

"Let us go, nevertheless. The cold is merely nothing. Amontillado! You have been imposed upon. And as for Luchresi, he cannot distinguish Sherry from Amontillado."

Thus speaking, Fortunato possessed himself of my arm; and putting on a mask of black silk and drawing a *roquelaire** closely about my person, I suffered him to hurry me to my palazzo.

There were no attendants at home; they had absconded to make merry in honor of the time. I had told them that I should not return until the morning, and had given them explicit orders not to stir from the house. These orders were sufficient, I well knew, to insure their immediate disappearance, one and all, as soon as my back was turned.

I took from their sconces two flambeaux, and giving one to Fortunato, bowed him through several suites of rooms to the archway that led into the vaults. I passed down a long and winding staircase, requesting him to be cautious as he followed. We came at length to the foot of the descent, and stood together upon the damp ground of the catacombs of the Montresors.

The gait of my friend was unsteady, and the bells upon his cap jingled as he strode.

"The pipe," he said.

"It is farther on," said I; "but observe the white web-work which gleams from these cavern walls."

He turned towards me, and looked into my eyes with two filmy orbs that distilled the rheum of intoxication.

"Nitre?" he asked, at length.

"Nitre," I replied. "How long have you had that cough?"

"Ugh! ugh! ugh!—ugh! ugh! ugh!—ugh! ugh! ugh!—ugh! ugh! ugh!—ugh! ugh! ugh!"

My poor friend found it impossible to reply for many minutes.

"It is nothing," he said, at last.

"Come," I said, with decision, "we will go back; your health is precious. You are rich, respected, admired, beloved; you are happy, as I once was. You are a man to be missed. For me it is no matter. We will go back; you will be ill, and I cannot be responsible. Besides, there is Luchresi—"

"Enough," he said; "the cough is a mere nothing; it will not kill me. I shall not die of a cough."

"True—true," I replied; "and, indeed, I had no intention of alarming you unnecessarily—but you should use all proper caution. A draught of this Medoc will defend us from the damps."

*A long cloak

Here I knocked off the neck of a bottle which I drew from a long row of its fellows that lay upon the mould.

"Drink," I said, presenting him the wine.

He raised it to his lips with a leer. He paused and nodded to me familiarly, while his bells jingled.

"I drink," he said, "to the buried that repose around us."

"And I to your long life."

He again took my arm, and we proceeded.

"These vaults," he said, "are extensive."

"The Montresors," I replied, "were a great and numerous family."

"I forget your arms."

"A huge human foot d'or, in a field azure; the foot crushes a serpent rampant whose fangs are imbedded in the heel."

"And the motto?"

"*Nemo me impune lacessit.*"*

"Good!" he said.

The wine sparkled in his eyes and the bells jingled. My own fancy grew warm with the Medoc. We had passed through long walls of piled skeletons, with casks and puncheons intermingling, into the inmost recesses of the catacombs. I paused again, and this time I made bold to seize Fortunato by an arm above the elbow.

"The nitre!" I said; "see, it increases. It hangs like moss upon the vaults. We are below the river's bed. The drops of moisture trickle among the bones. Come, we will go back ere it is too late. Your cough—"

"It is nothing," he said; "let us go on. But first, another draught of the Medoc."

I broke and reached him a flagon of De Grâve. He emptied it at a breath. His eyes flashed with a fierce light. He laughed and threw the bottle upwards with a gesticulation I did not understand.

I looked at him in surprise. He repeated the movement—a grotesque one.

"You do not comprehend?" he said.

"Not I," I replied.

"Then you are not of the brotherhood."

"How?"

"You are not of the masons."

"Yes, yes," I said; "yes, yes."

"You? Impossible! A mason?"

"A mason," I replied.

"A sign," he said, "a sign."

"It is this," I answered, producing from beneath the folds of my *roquelaire* a trowel.

---

*No one attacks me with impunity.

"You jest," he exclaimed, recoiling a few paces. "But let us proceed to the Amontillado."

"Be it so," I said, replacing the tool beneath the cloak and again offering him my arm. He leaned upon it heavily. We continued our route in search of the Amontillado. We passed through a range of low arches, descended, passed on, and descending again, arrived at a deep crypt, in which the foulness of the air caused our flambeaux rather to glow than flame.

At the most remote end of the crypt there appeared another less spacious. Its walls had been lined with human remains, piled to the vault overhead, in the fashion of the great catacombs of Paris. Three sides of this interior crypt were still ornamented in this manner. From the fourth side the bones had been thrown down, and lay promiscuously upon the earth, forming at one point a mound of some size. Within the wall thus exposed by the displacing of the bones, we perceived a still interior crypt or recess, in depth about four feet, in width three, in height six or seven. It seemed to have been constructed for no especial use within itself, but formed merely the interval between two of the colossal supports of the roof of the catacombs, and was backed by one of their circumscribing walls of solid granite.

It was in vain that Fortunato, uplifting his dull torch, endeavored to pry into the depth of the recess. Its termination the feeble light did not enable us to see.

"Proceed," I said; "herein is the Amontillado. As for Luchresi—"

"He is an ignoramus," interrupted my friend, as he stepped unsteadily forward, while I followed immediately at his heels. In an instant he had reached the extremity of the niche, and finding his progress arrested by the rock, stood stupidly bewildered. A moment more and I had fettered him to the granite. In its surface were two iron staples, distant from each other about two feet, horizontally. From one of these depended a short chain, from the other a padlock. Throwing the links about his waist, it was but the work of a few seconds to secure it. He was too much astounded to resist. Withdrawing the key I stepped back from the recess.

"Pass your hand," I said, "over the wall; you cannot help feeling the nitre. Indeed, it is *very* damp. Once more let me *implore* you to return. No? Then I must positively leave you. But I must first render you all the little attentions in my power."

"The Amontillado!" ejaculated my friend, not yet recovered from his astonishment.

"True," I replied; "the Amontillado."

As I said these words I busied myself among the pile of bones of which I have before spoken. Throwing them aside, I soon uncovered a quantity of building stone and mortar. With these materials and with the aid of my trowel, I began vigorously to wall up the entrance of the niche.

I had scarcely laid the first tier of the masonry when I discovered that the intoxication of Fortunato had in a great measure worn off. The earliest indication I had of this was a low moaning cry from the depth of the recess. It was *not* the cry of a drunken man. There was then a long and obstinate silence. I laid the second tier, and the third, and the fourth; and then I heard the furious vibrations of the chain. The noise lasted for several minutes, during which, that I might hearken to it with the more satisfaction, I ceased my labours and sat down upon the bones. When at last the clanking subsided, I resumed the trowel, and finished without interruption the fifth, the sixth, and the seventh tier. The wall was now nearly upon a level with my breast. I again paused, and holding the flambeaux over the mason-work, threw a few feeble rays upon the figure within.

A succession of loud and shrill screams, bursting suddenly from the throat of the chained form, seemed to thrust me violently back. For a brief moment I hesitated, I trembled. Unsheathing my rapier, I began to grope with it about the recess; but the thought of an instant reassured me. I placed my hand upon the solid fabric of the catacombs, and felt satisfied. I reapproached the wall; I replied to the yells of him who clamoured. I re-echoed, I aided, I surpassed them in volume and in strength. I did this, and the clamorer grew still.

It was now midnight, and my task was drawing to a close. I had completed the eighth, the ninth and the tenth tier. I had finished a portion of the last and the eleventh; there remained but a single stone to be fitted and plastered in. I struggled with its weight; I placed it partially in its destined position. But now there came from out the niche a low laugh that erected the hairs upon my head. It was succeeded by a sad voice, which I had difficulty in recognizing as that of the noble Fortunato. The voice said—

"Ha! ha! ha!—he! he! he!—a very good joke, indeed—an excellent jest. We will have many a rich laugh about it at the palazzo—he! he! he!—over our wine—he! he! he!"

"The Amontillado!" I said.

"He! he! he!—he! he! he!—yes, the Amontillado. But is it not getting late? Will not they be awaiting us at the palazzo, the Lady Fortunato and the rest? Let us be gone."

"Yes," I said, "let us be gone."

"For the love of God, Montresor!"

"Yes," I said, "for the love of God!"

But to these words I hearkened in vain for a reply. I grew impatient. I called aloud—

"Fortunato!"

No answer. I called again—

"Fortunato!"

No answer still. I thrust a torch through the remaining aperture and let it fall within. There came forth in return only a jingling of the bells. My heart grew sick; it was the dampness of the catacombs that made it so. I hastened to make an end of my labour. I forced the last stone into its position; I plastered it up. Against the new masonry I re-erected the old rampart of bones. For the half of a century no mortal has disturbed them. *In pace requiescat!**

---

*May he rest in peace.

Blake Long

Prof. Johnson

English 212-04

3 April 20--

Montresor's Fate in Edgar Allan Poe's
"The Cask of Amontillado"

Montresor, the narrator of Edgar Allan Poe's story "The Cask of Amontillado," tells the story not to us but to someone else. We see this in the first two sentences: "The thousand injuries of Fortunato I had borne as I best could, but when he ventured upon insult I vowed revenge. You, who so well know the nature of my soul, will not suppose, however, that I gave utterance to a threat" (167). In the story, Montresor reveals that fifty years ago he murdered Fortunato and no one found out. He committed the perfect crime. Why would he be telling anyone about it now?

Details in the story suggest that Montresor's listener is a priest and that the story is a confession. If this is correct, Montresor's motive for telling the story would be to gain absolution for his sin. Montresor is the right age to worry about the fate of his soul. At the time of the crime, he had to be old enough to live through Fortunato's "thousand injuries" and worldly wise enough to plan his complicated revenge. Let's say he was about thirty. Fifty years have passed, so Montresor is

now around eighty. Death is staring him in the
face. His categorization of the listener as someone
who "so well" knows "the nature of my soul" points
to someone whose calling is to care for souls--a
priest. The final line of the story--<u>In pace requiescat!</u>--echoes the words a priest would say at the
end of a service for the dead: "May he rest in
peace." A priest would know these words as a pious
expression. Montresor perhaps thinks that the
priest will take them as an expression of remorse,
as if, after much reflection, Montresor is sorry for
what he did and now wishes "peace" for Fortunato in
the afterlife. In his own mind, Montresor might
also be applying the phrase to himself: "Since I am
about to die, may <u>I</u> rest in peace. And I will if
this priest will only absolve me."

If the listener is indeed a priest, will he do
this, grant Montresor absolution? Since the story
ends before the listener speaks, Poe leaves it to
us to imagine the ensuing scene. What will the
priest decide? In order to answer this question, we
need to judge two things: the magnitude of
Montresor's crime and his attitude toward it.

First, did Fortunato deserve to die? A priest
might be willing to grant absolution if Montresor
had been an instrument of justice. Maybe Fortunato
had done terrible deeds but escaped the law. In
that case, Montresor's crime would have visited
just retribution upon Fortunato. From what we see

of Fortunato, he is not especially likable. He is so egotistical that he goes on a wild goose chase just to prove his superiority to Luchresi, his rival in wine connoisseurship. He pooh poohs his ill-health with macho bravado, as if he is above mortal limitations. His pretense of not knowing Montresor's family crest (171) reveals his disdain for people. His drunkenness and costume--that of a fool--underscore his boorishness and stupidity. All of these qualities support Montresor's claim that Fortunato is guilty of committing "injuries" and "insults." But does someone deserve to die for being boorish and stupid? Montresor doesn't say what the injuries are, but they don't seem to have harmed him greatly. He is still alive, still the owner of a palazzo, still a person of high station. His unwillingness to specify what Fortunato did makes us suspicious that Fortunato wounded Montresor's pride rather than caused him serious harm. The punishment Montresor dishes out seems to far outweigh the "injuries" and "insults" of which Fortunato stands accused.

Well, OK, Montresor went too far. Perhaps he realizes that now. Does he show contrition for killing Fortunato? If so, the priest might grant him absolution. No, Montresor does not. The tone of his narrative reflects pride in his cleverness, not sorrow for his deed. Presenting his plan for re-venge as a kind of game, he states the "rules" at

the beginning: "A wrong is unredressed when retribution overtakes its redresser. It is equally unredressed when the avenger fails to make himself felt
as such to him who has done the wrong" (167). He
proceeds to gloat about how clever he was in getting Fortunato to go down into the catacombs.
Montresor is an astute psychologist. He knows that
if he plucks the strings of Fortunato's vanity,
Fortunato will keep on walking. All he has to do is
mention Luchresi and Fortunato's cold, and Fortunato will keep going. Montresor revels in telling
how he sadistically needled Fortunato about his
cold by calling attention to the nitre and dampness. Montresor also enjoys his little jokes. When
Fortunato says he "shall not die of a cough,"
Montresor replies "True--true" (170). When Fortunato asks him if he is a Mason, Montresor assures
him he is and pulls out a trowel (172). After
Montresor enchains Fortunato, he says, "Once more
let me implore you to return" (173).

Montresor does exhibit some behavior that
might suggest feelings other than self-
congratulation. Fortunato's screams give Montresor
pause: "For a brief moment I hesitated, I trembled" (174). But he trembles from fear of discovery, not contrition. When Fortunato appeals to
Montresor's sense of divine mercy ("For the love
of God, Montresor!"), Montresor blows him off:
"'Yes,' I said, 'for the love of God!'" (175). The

only hint of remorse comes when, after hearing the bells on Fortunato's costume, Montresor says, "My heart grew sick" (175). In his heart of hearts, Montresor may be revolted by his crime. But this recognition never reaches the surface of his consciousness. Instead, he attributes his feeling to "the dampness of the catacombs" (175). His concluding statement--"For the half of a century no mortal has disturbed [Fortunato's bones]"--seems like pride of accomplishment rather than anything close to remorse.

On two counts, then, Montresor fails the test for absolution: His crime was not justified and he expresses no remorse for committing it. We might join the priest here in saying, "May you fry in hell!" But a final twist in the story is that Montresor has already, for fifty years, been in hell, a mental hell. He knows the details of this story so well that we surmise he has replayed it in his mind, like a movie, over and over for years and years. Now he wants a different story, one of ascent: ascent to heaven. The story he will get, however, is one of descent: deeper and deeper into the earth, past the remains of the dead, through cold and damp, ending at his own crypt. He may not have realized it at first, but surely he now knows that his story was not just about Fortunato's descent to death, but about his own as well. His final descent will be to the eternal punishments of hell.

```
                                              Long   6


                          Work Cited

    Poe, Edgar Allan. "The Cask of Amontillado."

         Complete Works of Edgar Allan Poe. Ed. James

         A. Harrison. Vol. 5. New York: Fred De Fau,

         1902.
```

Note: Normally the Works Cited list would appear on a separate page, but we print it here, right after the essay, to save space.

ESSAY ON A PLAY

TRIFLES

By Susan Glaspell

The first performance of the one-act play *Trifles* took place at the Wharf Theater, Provincetown, Massachusetts, on 8 August 1916. Susan Glaspell played the part of Mrs. Hale.

❖ Characters

George Henderson (County Attorney)	Mrs. Peters
Henry Peters (Sheriff)	Mrs. Hale
Lewis Hale (a neighboring farmer)	

SCENE: *The kitchen is the now abandoned farmhouse of* JOHN WRIGHT, *a gloomy kitchen, and left without having been put in order—unwashed pans under the sink, a loaf of bread outside the bread-box, a dish-towel on the table—other signs of incompleted work. At the rear the outer door opens and the* SHERIFF *comes in followed by the* COUNTY ATTORNEY *and* HALE. *The* SHERIFF *and* HALE *are men in middle life, the* COUNTY ATTORNEY *is a young man; all are much bundled up and go at once to the stove. They are followed by the two women—the* SHERIFF's *wife first; she is a slight wiry woman, a thin nervous face.* MRS. HALE *is larger and would ordinarily be called more comfortable looking, but she is disturbed now and looks fearfully about as she enters. The women have come in slowly, and stand close together near the door.*

COUNTY ATTORNEY: *(rubbing his hands)* This feels good. Come up to the fire, ladies.

MRS. PETERS: *(after taking a step forward)* I'm not—cold.

SHERIFF: *(unbuttoning his overcoat and stepping away from the stove as if to mark the beginning of official business)* Now, Mr. Hale, before we move things about, you explain to Mr. Henderson just what you saw when you came here yesterday morning.

COUNTY ATTORNEY: By the way, has anything been moved? Are things just as you left them yesterday?

SHERIFF: *(looking about)* It's just the same. When it dropped below zero last night I thought I'd better send Frank out this morning to make a fire for us—no use getting pneumonia with a big case on, but I told him not to touch anything except the stove—and you know Frank.

COUNTY ATTORNEY: Somebody should have been left here yesterday.

SHERIFF: Oh—yesterday. When I had to send Frank to Morris Center for that man who went crazy—I want you to know I had my hands full yesterday. I knew you could get back from Omaha by today as long as I went over everything here myself—

COUNTY ATTORNEY: Well, Mr. Hale, tell just what happened when you came here yesterday morning.

HALE: Harry and I had started to town with a load of potatoes. We came along the road from my place and as I got here I said, "I'm going to see if I can't get John Wright to go in with me on a party telephone." I spoke to Wright about it once before and he put me off, saying folks talked too much anyway, and all he asked was peace and quiet—I guess you know about how much he talked himself; but I thought maybe if I went to the house and talked about it before his wife, though I said to Harry that I didn't know as what his wife wanted made much difference to John—

COUNTY ATTORNEY: Let's talk about that later, Mr. Hale. I do want to talk about that, but tell now just what happened when you got to the house.

HALE: I didn't hear or see anything; I knocked at the door, and still it was quiet inside. I knew they must be up, it was past eight o'clock. So I knocked again, and I thought I heard somebody say, "Come in." I wasn't sure. I'm not sure yet, but I opened the door—this door *(indicating the door by which the two women are still standing)* and there in that rocker—*(pointing to it)* sat Mrs. Wright.

   (They all look at the rocker.)

COUNTY ATTORNEY: What—was she doing?

HALE: She was rockin' back and forth. She had her apron in her hand and was kind of—pleating it.

COUNTY ATTORNEY: And how did she—look?

HALE: Well, she looked queer.

COUNTY ATTORNEY: How do you mean—queer?

HALE: Well, as if she didn't know what she was going to do next. And kind of done up.

COUNTY ATTORNEY: How did she seem to feel about your coming?

HALE: Why, I don't think she minded—one way or other. She didn't pay much attention. I said "How do, Mrs. Wright it's cold, ain't it?" And she said, "Is it?"—and went on kind of pleating at her apron. Well, I was surprised; she didn't ask me to come up to the stove, or to set down, but just sat there, not even looking at me, so I said, "I want to see John." And then she—laughed. I guess you would call it a laugh. I thought of Harry and the team outside, so I said a little sharp: "Can't I see John?" "No," she says, kind o' dull like. "Ain't he home?" says I. "Yes," says she, "he's home." "Then why can't I see him?" I asked her, out of patience. "Cause he's dead," says she. *"Dead?"* says I. She just nodded her head, not getting a bit excited, but rockin' back and forth. "Why—where is he?" says I, not knowing what to say. She just pointed upstairs—like that *(himself pointing to the room above)* I got up, with the idea of going up there. I walked from there to here—then I says, "Why, what did he die of?" "He died of a rope round his neck," says she, and just went on pleatin' at her apron. Well, I went out and called Harry. I thought I might—need help. We went upstairs and there he was lyin'—

COUNTY ATTORNEY: I think I'd rather have you go into that upstairs, where you can point it all out. Just go on now with the rest of the story.

HALE: Well, my first thought was to get that rope off. It looked . . . *(stops, his face twitches)* . . . but Harry, he went up to him, and he said, "No, he's dead all right, and we'd better not touch anything." So we went back down stairs. She was still sitting that same way. "Has anybody been notified?" I asked. "No," says she unconcerned. "Who did this, Mrs. Wright?" said Harry. He said it business-like—and she stopped pleatin' of her apron. "I don't know," she says. "You don't *know?*" says Harry. "No," says she. "Weren't you sleepin' in the bed with him?" says Harry. "Yes," says she, "but I was on the inside." "Somebody slipped a rope round his neck and strangled him and you didn't wake up?" says Harry. "I didn't wake up," she said after him. We must 'a looked as if we didn't see how that could be, for after a minute she said, "I sleep sound." Harry was going to ask her more questions but I said maybe we ought to let her tell her story first to the coroner, or the sheriff, so Harry went fast as he could to Rivers' place, where there's a telephone.

COUNTY ATTORNEY: And what did Mrs. Wright do when she knew that you had gone for the coroner?

HALE: She moved from that chair to this one over here *(pointing to a small chair in the corner)* and just sat there with her hands held together and looking down. I got a feeling that I ought to make some conversation, so I said I had come in to see if John wanted to put in a telephone, and at that she started to laugh, and then she stopped and looked at me—scared. *(the* COUNTY ATTORNEY, *who has had his notebook out, makes a note)* I dunno, maybe it wasn't scared. I wouldn't like to say it was. Soon Harry got back, and then Dr. Lloyd came, and you, Mr. Peters, and so I guess that's all I know that you don't.

COUNTY ATTORNEY: *(looking around)* I guess we'll go upstairs first—and then out to the barn and around there. *(to the* SHERIFF*)* You're convinced that there was nothing important here—nothing that would point to any motive.

SHERIFF: Nothing here but kitchen things.

(*The* COUNTY ATTORNEY, *after again looking around the kitchen, opens the door of a cupboard closet. He gets up on a chair and looks on a shelf. Pulls his hand away, sticky.*)

COUNTY ATTORNEY: Here's a nice mess.

(The women draw nearer.)

MRS. PETERS: *(to the other woman)* Oh, her fruit; it did freeze. (*to the* LAWYER*)* She worried about that when it turned so cold. She said the fire'd go out and her jars would break.

SHERIFF: Well, can you beat the women! Held for murder and worryin' about her preserves.

COUNTY ATTORNEY: I guess before we're through she may have something more serious than preserves to worry about.

HALE: Well, women are used to worrying over trifles.

(The two women move a little closer together.)

COUNTY ATTORNEY: *(with the gallantry of a young politician)* And yet, for all their worries, what would we do without the ladies? *(the women do not unbend. He goes to the sink, takes a dipperful of water from the pail and pouring it into a basin, washes his hands. Starts to wipe them on the roller-towel, turns it for a cleaner place)* Dirty towels! *(kicks his foot against the pans under the sink)* Not much of a housekeeper, would you say ladies?

MRS. HALE: *(stiffly)*There's a great deal of work to be done on a farm.

COUNTY ATTORNEY: To be sure. And yet *(with a little bow to her)* I know there are some Dickson county farmhouses which do not have such roller towels.

(He gives it a pull to expose its length again.)

MRS. HALE: Those towels get dirty awful quick. Men's hands aren't always as clean as they might be.

COUNTY ATTORNEY: Ah, loyal to your sex, I see. But you and Mrs. Wright were neighbors. I suppose you were friends, too.

MRS. HALE: *(shaking her head)* I've not seen much of her of late years. I've not been in this house—it's more than a year.

COUNTY ATTORNEY: And why was that? You didn't like her?

MRS. HALE: I liked her all well enough. Farmers' wives have their hands full, Mr. Henderson. And then—

COUNTY ATTORNEY: Yes—?

MRS. HALE: *(looking about)* It never seemed a very cheerful place.

COUNTY ATTORNEY: No—it's not cheerful. I shouldn't say she had the homemaking instinct.

MRS. HALE: Well, I don't know as Wright had, either.

COUNTY ATTORNEY: You mean that they didn't get on very well?

MRS. HALE: No, I don't mean anything. But I don't think a place'd be any cheerfuller for John Wright's being in it.

COUNTY ATTORNEY: I'd like to talk more of that a little later. I want to get the lay of things upstairs now.

(He goes to the left, where three steps lead to a stair door.)

SHERIFF: I suppose anything Mrs. Peters does'll be all right. She was to take in some clothes for her, you know, and a few little things. We left in such a hurry yesterday.

COUNTY ATTORNEY: Yes, but I would like to see what you take, Mrs. Peters, and keep an eye out for anything that might be of use to us.

MRS. PETERS: Yes, Mr. Henderson.

(The women listen to the men's steps on the stairs, then look about the kitchen.)

MRS. HALE: I'd hate to have men coming into my kitchen, snooping around and criticising.

(She arranges the pans under sink which the LAWYER *had shoved out of place.)*

MRS. PETERS: Of course it's no more than their duty.

MRS. HALE: Duty's all right, but I guess that deputy sheriff that came out to make the fire might have got a little of this on. *(gives the roller towel a pull)* Wish I'd thought of that sooner. Seems mean to talk about her for not having things slicked up when she had to come away in such a hurry.

MRS. PETERS: *(who has gone to a small table in the left rear corner of the room, and lifted one end of a towel that covers a pan)* She had bread set.

> *(Stands still.)*

MRS. HALE: *(eyes fixed on a loaf of bread beside the bread-box, which is on a low shelf at the other side of the room. Moves slowly toward it)* She was going to put this in there. *(picks up loaf, then abruptly drops it. In a manner of returning to familiar things)* It's a shame about her fruit. I wonder if it's all gone. *(gets up on the chair and looks)* I think there's some here that's all right, Mrs. Peters. Yes—here; *(holding it toward the window)* this is cherries, too. *(looking again)* I declare I believe that's the only one. *(gets down, bottle in her hand. Goes to the sink and wipes it off on the outside)* She'll feel awful bad after all her hard work in the hot weather. I remember the afternoon I put up my cherries last summer.

> *(She puts the bottle on the big kitchen table, center of the room. With a sigh, is about to sit down in the rocking-chair. Before she is seated realizes what chair it is; with a slow look at it, steps back. The chair which she has touched rocks back and forth.)*

MRS. PETERS: Well, I must get those things from the front room closet. *(she goes to the door at the right, but after looking into the other room, steps back)* You coming with me, Mrs. Hale? You could help me carry them.

> *(They go in the other room; reappear, MRS. PETERS carrying a dress and skirt, MRS. HALE following with a pair of shoes.)*

MRS. PETERS: My, it's cold in there.

> *(She puts the clothes on the big table, and hurries to the stove.)*

MRS. HALE: *(examining the skirt)* Wright was close. I think maybe that's why she kept so much to herself. She didn't even belong to the Ladies Aid. I suppose she felt she couldn't do her part, and then you don't enjoy things when you feel shabby. She used to wear pretty clothes and be lively, when she was Minnie Foster, one of the town girls singing in the choir. But that—oh, that was thirty years ago. This is all you was to take in?

MRS. PETERS: She said she wanted an apron. Funny thing to want, for there isn't much to get you dirty in jail, goodness knows. But I suppose just to make her feel more natural. She said they was in the top drawer in this cupboard. Yes, here. And then her little shawl that always hung behind the door. *(opens stair door and looks)* Yes, here it is.

> *(Quickly shuts door leading upstairs.)*

MRS. HALE: *(abruptly moving toward her)* Mrs. Peters?

MRS. PETERS: Yes, Mrs. Hale?

MRS. HALE: Do you think she did it?

MRS. PETERS: *(in a frightened voice)* Oh, I don't know.

MRS. HALE: Well, I don't think she did. Asking for an apron and her little shawl. Worrying about her fruit.

MRS. PETERS: *(starts to speak, glances up, where footsteps are heard in the room above. In a low voice)* Mr. Peters says it looks bad for her. Mr. Henderson is awful sarcastic in a speech and he'll make fun of her sayin' she didn't wake up.

MRS. HALE: Well, I guess John Wright didn't wake when they was slipping that rope under his neck.

MRS. PETERS: No, it's strange. It must have been done awful crafty and still. They say it was such a—funny way to kill a man, rigging it all up like that.

MRS. HALE: That's just what Mr. Hale said. There was a gun in the house. He says that's what he can't understand.

MRS. PETERS: Mr. Henderson said coming out that what was needed for the case was a motive; something to show anger, or—sudden feeling.

MRS. HALE: *(who is standing by the table)* Well, I don't see any signs of anger around here. *(she puts her hand on the dish towel which lies on the table, stands looking down at table, one half of which is clean, the other half messy)* It's wiped to here. *(makes a move as if to finish work, then turns and looks at loaf of bread outside the breadbox. Drops towel. In that voice of coming back to familiar things.)* Wonder how they are finding things upstairs. I hope she had it a little more red-up up there. You know, it seems kind of *sneaking.* Locking her up in town and then coming out here and trying to get her own house to turn against her!

MRS. PETERS: But Mrs. Hale, the law is the law.

MRS. HALE: I s'pose 'tis. *(unbuttoning her coat)* Better loosen up your things, Mrs. Peters. You won't feel them when you go out.

(MRS. PETERS *takes off her fur tippet, goes to hang it on hook at back of room, stands looking at the under part of the small corner table.*)

MRS. PETERS: She was piecing a quilt.

(*She brings the large sewing basket and they look at the bright pieces.*)

MRS. HALE: It's log cabin pattern. Pretty, isn't it? I wonder if she was goin' to quilt it or just knot it?

(*Footsteps have been heard coming down the stairs. The* SHERIFF *enters followed by* HALE *and the* COUNTY ATTORNEY.)

SHERIFF: They wonder if she was going to quilt it or just knot it!

(*The men laugh, the women look abashed.*)

COUNTY ATTORNEY: *(rubbing his hands over the stove)* Frank's fire didn't do much up there did it? Well, let's go out to the barn and get that cleared up.

    (The men go outside)

MRS. HALE: *(resentfully)* I don't know as there's anything so strange, our takin' up our time with little things while we're waiting for them to get the evidence. *(she sits down at the big table smoothing out a block with decision)* I don't see as it's anything to laugh about.

MRS. PETERS: *(apologetically)* Of course they've got awful important things on their minds.

    (Pulls up a chair and joins MRS. HALE *at the table.)*

MRS. HALE: *(examining another block)* Mrs. Peters, look at this one. Here, this is the one she was working on, and look at the sewing! All the rest of it has been so nice and even. And look at this! It's all over the place! Why, it looks as if she didn't know what she was about!

    (After she has said this they look at each other, then start to glance back at the door. After an instant MRS. HALE *has pulled at a knot and ripped the sewing.)*

MRS. PETERS: Oh, what are you doing, Mrs. Hale?

MRS. HALE: *(mildly)* Just pulling out a stitch or two that's not sewed very good. *(threading a needle)* Bad sewing always made me fidgety.

MRS. PETERS: *(nervously)* I don't think we ought to touch things.

MRS. HALE: I'll just finish up this end. *(suddenly stopping and leaning forward)* Mrs. Peters?

MRS. PETERS: Yes, Mrs. Hale?

MRS. HALE: What do you suppose she was so nervous about?

MRS. PETERS: Oh—I don't know. I don't know as she was nervous. I sometimes sew awful queer when I'm just tired. *(*MRS. HALE *starts to say something, looks at* MRS. PETERS, *then goes on sewing)* Well I must get these things wrapped up. They may be through sooner than we think. *(putting apron and other things together)* I wonder where I can find a piece of paper, and string.

MRS. HALE: In that cupboard, maybe.

MRS. PETERS: *(looking in cupboard)* Why, here's a bird-cage. *(holds it up)* Did she have a bird, Mrs. Hale?

MRS. HALE: Why, I don't know whether she did or not—I've not been here for so long. There was a man around last year selling canaries cheap, but I don't know as she took one; maybe she did. She used to sing real pretty herself.

MRS. PETERS: *(glancing around)* Seems funny to think of a bird here. But she must have had one, or why would she have a cage? I wonder what happened to it.

MRS. HALE: I s'pose maybe the cat got it.

MRS. PETERS: No, she didn't have a cat. She's got that feeling some people have about cats—being afraid of them. My cat got in her room and she was real upset and asked me to take it out.

MRS. HALE: My sister Bessie was like that. Queer, ain't it?

MRS. PETERS: *(examining the cage)* Why, look at this door. It's broke. One hinge is pulled apart.

MRS. HALE: *(looking too)* Looks as if someone must have been rough with it.

MRS. PETERS: Why, yes.

(She brings the cage forward and puts it on the table.)

MRS. HALE: I wish if they're going to find any evidence they'd be about it. I don't like this place.

MRS. PETERS: But I'm awful glad you came with me, Mrs. Hale. It would be lonesome for me sitting here alone.

MRS. HALE: It would, wouldn't it? *(dropping her sewing)* But I tell you what I do wish, Mrs. Peters. I wish I had come over sometimes when *she* was here. I—*(looking around the room)*—wish I had.

MRS. PETERS: But of course you were awful busy, Mrs. Hale—your house and your children.

MRS. HALE: I could've come. I stayed away because it weren't cheerful—and that's why I ought to have come. I—I've never liked this place. Maybe because it's down in a hollow and you don't see the road. I dunno what it is, but it's a lonesome place and always was. I wish I had come over to see Minnie Foster sometimes. I can see now—*(shakes her head)*

MRS. PETERS: Well, you mustn't reproach yourself, Mrs. Hale. Somehow we just don't see how it is with other folks until—something comes up.

MRS. HALE: Not having children makes less work—but it makes a quiet house, and Wright out to work all day, and no company when he did come in. Did you know John Wright, Mrs. Peters?

MRS. PETERS: Not to know him; I've seen him in town. They say he was a good man.

MRS. HALE: Yes—good; he didn't drink, and kept his word as well as most, I guess, and paid his debts. But he was a hard man, Mrs. Peters. Just to pass the time of day with him—*(shivers)* Like a raw wind that gets to the bone *(pauses, her eye falling on the cage)* I should think she would 'a wanted a bird. But what do you suppose went with it?

MRS. PETERS: I don't know, unless it got sick and died.

(She reaches over and swings the broken door, swings it again, both women watch it.)

MRS. HALE: You weren't raised round here, were you? (MRS. PETERS *shakes her head)* You didn't know—her?

MRS. PETERS: Not till they brought her yesterday.

MRS. HALE: She—come to think of it, she was kind of like a bird herself— real sweet and pretty, but kind of timid and—fluttery. How—she— did—change. *(silence; then as if struck by a happy thought and relieved to get back to everyday things)* Tell you what, Mrs. Peters, why don't you take the quilt in with you? It might take up her mind.

MRS. PETERS: Why, I think that's a real nice idea, Mrs. Hale. There couldn't possibly be any objection to it, could there? Now, just what would I take? I wonder if her patches are in here—and her things.

(They look in the sewing basket.)

MRS. HALE: Here's some red. I expect this has got sewing things in it. *(brings out a fancy box)* What a pretty box. Looks like something somebody would give you. Maybe her scissors are in here. *(Opens box. Suddenly puts her hand to her nose)* Why—(MRS. PETERS *bends nearer, then turns her face away)* There's something wrapped up in this piece of silk.

MRS. PETERS: Why, this isn't her scissors.

MRS. HALE: *(lifting the silk)* Oh, Mrs. Peters—it's—

(MRS. PETERS *bends closer.)*

MRS. PETERS: It's the bird.

MRS. HALE: *(jumping up)* But, Mrs. Peters—look at it! It's neck! Look at it's neck! It's all—other side *to.*

MRS. PETERS: Somebody—wrung—its—neck.

(Their eyes meet. A look of growing comprehension, of horror. Steps are heard outside. MRS. HALE slips box under quilt pieces, and sinks into her chair. Enter SHERIFF and COUNTY ATTORNEY. MRS. PETERS rises.)

COUNTY ATTORNEY: *(as one turning from serious things to little pleasantries)* Well ladies, have you decided whether she was going to quilt it or knot it?

MRS. PETERS: We think she was going to—knot it.

COUNTY ATTORNEY: Well, that's interesting. I'm sure. *(seeing the birdcage)* Has the bird flown?

MRS. HALE: *(putting more quilt pieces over the box)* We think the—cat got it.

COUNTY ATTORNEY: *(preoccupied)* Is there a cat?

(MRS. HALE *glances in a quick covert way at* MRS. PETERS.)

MRS. PETERS: Well, not *now.* They're superstitious, you know. They leave.

COUNTY ATTORNEY: (*to* SHERIFF PETERS, *continuing an interrupted conversation*) No sign at all of anyone having come from the outside. Their own rope. Now let's go up again and go over it piece by piece *(they start upstairs)* It would have to have been someone who knew just the—

> (MRS. PETERS *sits down. The two women sit there not looking at one another, but as if peering into something and at the same time holding back. When they talk now it is in the manner of feeling their way over strange ground, as if afraid of what they are saying, but as if they can not help saying it.)*

MRS. HALE: She liked the bird. She was going to bury it in that pretty box.

MRS. PETERS: *(in a whisper)* When I was a girl—my kitten—there was a boy took a hatchet, and before my eyes—and before I could get there—*(covers her face an instant)* If they hadn't held me back I would have *(catches herself, looks upstairs where steps are heard, falters weakly)*—hurt him.

MRS. HALE: *(with a slow look around her)* I wonder how it would seem never to have had any children around. *(pause)* No, Wright wouldn't like the bird—a thing that sang. She used to sing. He killed that, too.

MRS. PETERS: *(moving uneasily)* We don't know who killed the bird.

MRS. HALE: I knew John Wright.

MRS. PETERS: It was an awful thing was done in this house that night, Mrs. Hale. Killing a man while he slept, slipping a rope around his neck that choked the life out of him.

MRS. HALE: His neck. Choked the life out of him.

> *(Her hand goes out and rests on the bird-cage.)*

MRS. PETERS: *(with rising voice)* We don't know who killed him. We don't *know.*

MRS. HALE: *(her own feeling not interrupted)* If there'd been years and years of nothing, then a bird to sing to you, it would be awful—still, after the bird was still.

MRS. PETERS: *(something within her speaking)* I know what stillness is. When we homesteaded in Dakota, and my first baby died—after he was two years old, and me with no other then—

MRS. HALE: *(moving)* How soon do you suppose they'll be through, looking for the evidence?

MRS. PETERS: I know what stillness is. *(pulling herself back).* The law has got to punish crime, Mrs. Hale.

MRS. HALE: *(not as if answering that)* I wish you'd seen Minnie Foster when she wore a white dress with blue ribbons and stood up there in the choir and sang. *(a look around the room)* Oh, I *wish* I'd come over here once in a while! That was a crime! That was a crime! Who's going to punish that?

MRS. PETERS: *(looking upstairs)* We mustn't—take on.

MRS. HALE: I might have known she needed help! I know how things can be—for women. I tell you, it's queer, Mrs. Peters. We live close to-gether and we live far apart. We all go through the same things—it's all just a different kind of the same thing. *(brushes her eyes, noticing the bottle of fruit, reaches out for it)* If I was you, I wouldn't tell her her fruit was gone. Tell her it *ain't.* Tell her it's all right. Take this in to prove it to her. She—may never know whether it was broke or not.

MRS. PETERS: *(takes the bottle, looks about for something to wrap it in; takes petticoat from the clothes brought from the other room, very nervously begins winding this around the bottle. In a false voice)* My, it's a good thing the men couldn't hear us. Wouldn't they just laugh! Getting all stirred up over a little thing like a—dead canary. As if that could have anything to do with—with—wouldn't they *laugh!*

(The men are heard coming down stairs.)

MRS. HALE: *(under her breath)* Maybe they would—maybe they wouldn't.

COUNTY ATTORNEY: No, Peters, it's all perfectly clear except a reason for doing it. But you know juries when it comes to women. If there was some definite thing. Something to show—something to make a story about—a thing that would connect up with this strange way of doing it—

(The women's eyes meet for an instant. Enter HALE from outer door.)

HALE: Well, I've got the team around. Pretty cold out there.

COUNTY ATTORNEY: I'm going to stay here a while by myself. *(to the SHERIFF)* You can send Frank out for me, can't you? I want to go over everything. I'm not satisfied that we can't do better.

SHERIFF: Do you want to see what Mrs. Peters is going to take in?

(The LAWYER goes to the table, picks up the apron, laughs.)

COUNTY ATTORNEY: Oh, I guess they're not very dangerous things the ladies have picked out. *(Moves a few things about, disturbing the quilt pieces which cover the box. Steps back)* No, Mrs. Peters doesn't need supervising. For that matter, a sheriff's wife is married to the law. Ever think of it that way, Mrs. Peters?

MRS. PETERS: Not—just that way.

SHERIFF: *(chuckling)* Married to the law. *(moves toward the other room)* I just want you to come in here a minute, George. We ought to take a look at these windows.

COUNTY ATTORNEY: *(scoffingly)* Oh, windows!

SHERIFF: We'll be right out, Mr. Hale.

(HALE goes outside. The SHERIFF follows the COUNTY ATTORNEY into the other room. Then MRS. HALE rises, hands tight together, look-ing intensely at MRS. PETERS, whose eyes make a slow turn, finally

meeting MRS. HALE*'s. A moment* MRS. HALE *holds her, then her own eyes point the way to where the box is concealed. Suddenly* MRS. PETERS *throws back quilt pieces and tries to put the box in the bag she is wearing. It is too big. She opens box, starts to take bird out, cannot touch it, goes to pieces, stands there helpless. Sound of a knob turning in the other room.* MRS. HALE *snatches the box and puts it in the pocket of her big coat. Enter* COUNTY ATTORNEY *and* SHERIFF.)

COUNTY ATTORNEY: *(facetiously)* Well, Henry, at least we found out that she was not going to quilt it. She was going to—what is it you call it, ladies?

MRS. HALE: *(her hand against her pocket)* We call it—knot it, Mr. Henderson.

(CURTAIN)

Briner 1

Carolyn Briner

Prof. Hesterman

English 104-12

12 September 20--

The Meaning of Physical Objects

in Susan Glaspell's <u>Trifles</u>

In most performances of plays, the audience sees physical objects on stage--the sets and props that locate the action in time and space. The title of Susan Glaspell's play <u>Trifles</u> calls attention to the importance of such objects. Most of them are the "trifles" that mark the extreme difference between the way the male and female characters value women's work. They are also the evidence in the impromptu trial enclosed by the play: Mrs. Wright is

charged with murdering her husband; the county attorney is the prosecutor; Mr. Hale and the sheriff
(Mr. Peters) are the witnesses; and the women, Mrs.
Hale and Mrs. Peters, are the jury. We, the audience, join the women as jurors. Like them, we piece
together Mrs. Wright's character and her past by
discovering what the physical objects mean.

The action of the play takes place in Mrs.
Wright's kitchen. The characters have arrived the
day after Mr. Hale discovered Mr. Wright's body.
The men have come to find evidence to prove that
Mrs. Wright strangled her husband with a rope. They
have brought the women along, not to help them find
evidence but to gather items to take to Mrs. Wright
in jail. The key exchange, which names the play and
sets the trial in motion, occurs near the beginning:

> COUNTY ATTORNEY: [to the SHERIFF] You're con-
> vinced that there was nothing important here--
> nothing that would point to any motive.
> SHERIFF: Nothing here but kitchen things.
> COUNTY ATTORNEY: [after noticing spilled pre-
> serves in the cupboard.] Here's a nice mess.
> MRS. PETERS: [to Mrs. Hale] Oh, her fruit; it did
> freeze. [to the County Attorney] She worried
> about that when it turned so cold. She said
> the fire'd go out and her jars would break.
> SHERIFF: Well, can you beat the women! Held for
> murder and worryin' about her preserves.

COUNTY ATTORNEY: I guess before we're through
she may have something more serious than preserves to worry about.

HALE: Well, women are used to worrying over
trifles.

COUNTY ATTORNEY: And yet, for all their worries, what would we do without the ladies?
[notices the dirty hand towel.] Dirty towels!
[kicks the pans under the sink.] Not much of
a housekeeper, would you say, ladies?

MRS. HALE: [stiffly] There's a great deal of
work to be done on a farm. (38)

In this exchange, the men dismiss the very evidence that is crucial to the case, evidence that
establishes Mrs. Wright's guilt and her motive.
This evidence--objects the men label as "trifles"--
shows three things about Mrs. Wright. First, it
shows that Mrs. Wright was a hard worker and fine
craftsperson. The men don't understand this, since,
as the passage above indicates, they undervalue
women's work and conclude that Mrs. Wright was "a
bad housekeeper." But the objects in the kitchen,
as the women know, tell a different story. The broken jars of preserves represent Mrs. Wright's hard
work and skill. "She'll feel awful bad," Mrs. Hale
says, "after all her hard work in the hot weather.
I remember the afternoon I put up my cherries last
summer" (39). An expert herself, Mrs. Hale holds
the one good jar to the window and sees that it's

all right. Equally telling are the loaf of bread, covered with a cloth, waiting to be placed in the breadbox, and the quilting pieces the women find in her sewing basket. "It's log cabin pattern," Mrs. Hale says. "Pretty, isn't it?" The sewing is "nice and even" (41). The kitchen has been Mrs. Wright's domain. As playgoers, we view its objects—stove, table, breadbox, loaf of bread, jar of cherries, cupboard, sewing basket, quilting pieces--and see them as the tools of her craft and the products of her hard work.

The second thing that physical objects show about Mrs. Wright is that she led a difficult life with her husband. Even Mr. Hale knows that Mr. Wright was indifferent to his wife: "I didn't know as what his wife wanted made much difference to John" (36). Mrs. Hale admits that Mr. Wright was "good" in that he abstained from drinking, kept his word, and paid his debts. But "he was a hard man, Mrs. Peters. Just to pass the time of day with him-- [shivers] Like a raw wind that gets to the bone" (42). Coldness is the dominant atmosphere of the play and represents the Wrights' life together. At the beginning, we are told that the night before the temperature was below zero (36). Ironically, the object that signifies coldness is the stove. Although the stove is constantly referred to, it never seems adequate to heat the house, to make it warm and cosy. When Mrs. Peters returns from the

front room, she says, "My, it's cold in there"
(40). When the men come from upstairs, the County
Attorney says, "Frank's fire didn't do much up
there, did it?" (41). Mr. Wright was stingy and did
not talk much. The house is "down in a hollow"
where "you don't see the road" (42). There was no
telephone in the house. The severity of Nebraska
winters, the isolation of the house, its location
in a low place, the stingy and obdurate nature of
Mr. Wright all make the house emotionally as well
as physically "cold."

The third thing that physical objects show
about Mrs. Wright is her motivation for killing her
husband. The most important objects here are the
canary and the birdcage. Glaspell openly associates
Mrs. Wright with the canary. Mrs. Hale says, "She--
come to think of it, she was kind of like a bird
herself--real sweet and pretty, but kind of timid
and--fluttery" (43). Before she married Mr. Wright,
she was Minnie Foster, who used to sing (42) and
wear pretty clothes (40). But after marrying him,
she didn't socialize: "I suppose she felt she
couldn't do her part, and then you don't enjoy
things when you feel shabby" (40). The canary also
represents the children she never had, which Mr.
Wright may have denied her. "I wonder," Mrs. Hale
says, "how it would seem never to have had any
children around. . . . No, Wright wouldn't like the
bird--a thing that sang. She used to sing. He

killed that, too" (44). The canary's death, Mrs. Peter's speculates, must have caused an alienating "stillness": "When we homesteaded in Dakota, and my first baby died--after he was two years old, and me with no other then--. . . . I know what stillness is" (44).

We can guess that to Mrs. Wright the canary represented the sum total of what she was as Minnie Foster: young, pretty, sweet, lively, a person who took pleasure in singing, in wearing attractive clothes, in other people's company, in hopes for the future. She must have equated Mr. Wright's strangling of the canary to his destroying the Minnie Foster that was her former self. The bird-cage, too, represents this violation. Mrs. Hale, upon seeing it, says, "Looks as if someone must have been rough with it." She then immediately con-nects it to the house: "I don't like this place" (42). The broken birdcage is equivalent to Minnie Foster's violated self. It is the shell of her pri-vacy, the container of her true self. Mr. Wright breaks into it to find and destroy her. The bird and birdcage, in other words, make clear to the women and to us that Mrs. Wright did in fact kill her husband and that she had a strong motive.

The men, dense as ever, never see any of this. From what they say, Mrs. Wright is likely to be ac-quitted or to get off with a light sentence. They can't find a motive for the crime, and juries, the

Briner 7

county attorney says, are easy on women (44). But
the women know the truth. They "vote" for acquittal
by suppressing the evidence--the dead canary--and
by withholding an interpretation of the "trifles"
that would make the case against Mrs. Wright.

Their last act is to gather objects to take to
Mrs. Wright. In choosing them, they seem almost to
communicate with Mrs. Wright, to express their solidarity with her, as if the objects belong to a
language that only women know: her apron (for hard
work), her jar of cherries (for achievement), her
quilting pieces (for work still to do), and her
shawl (for warmth).

Work Cited

Glaspell, Susan. <u>Trifles. Plays by Susan Glaspell</u>. Ed.

C. W. E. Bigsby. Cambridge: Cambridge UP, 1987.

Note: Normally, the Works Cited list would appear on a separate page, but we print it here, right after the essay, to save space.

ESSAY ON A NOVEL

Mary Ann Evans, the author of *Adam Bede,* wrote under the pen name George Eliot. The novel was first published in 1859. The action takes place in 1799 in an English farm village. The events of the novel featured in the essay below are as follows: Hetty Sorrel, a working-class teenager, and Arthur Donnithorne, an aristocrat, fall in love. Not knowing that she is pregnant, he breaks off the relationship. When she can no longer hide her pregnancy, she undertakes an arduous journey in search of him. She fails to find him, gives birth, and, in a confused state of mind, abandons the baby in the woods. After being tried for infanticide and condemned to hang, she gains a reprieve and is transported to Australia. Dinah Morris, a devout Methodist preacher, ministers to her in prison.

                                                    Forrest 1

Shalita Forrest

Professor Griffith

English 110-02

2 November 20--

    First Love, Lost Love in George Eliot's <u>Adam Bede</u>

        In George Eliot's <u>Adam Bede</u>, I was drawn to
Hetty Sorrel. Hetty's first experience of love somewhat resembles my own. Hetty is misunderstood by
many of the other characters, but I understood her
from the beginning of the book. Hetty is young, in
love for the first time, and blinded by love. I know
this feeling, because I have been there and experienced a love similar to Hetty's. There are similarities between Hetty's first love and my first love, but
we handled our situations in totally different ways.

        The first similarity between Hetty and me is
the type of men we fell in love with. Hetty and I
both loved men who could never be completely ours.
Hetty is in love with Arthur Donnithorne, who is on
a different social level from her. Arthur belongs
to the aristocracy, and Hetty comes from the working class. This class difference creates a tremen-

dous barrier between them. Hetty can never have
Arthur. She knows, however, that Arthur is interested in her: "Hetty had become aware that Mr.
Arthur Donnithorne would take a good deal of trouble
for the chance of seeing her" (99). Despite their
class difference, she welcomes his attentions anyway. I was also in love with a man who I knew could
never be true to one woman. The man I loved wanted
his cake plus his ice cream, too. He had many other
women and was not willing to give them up to be with
me. Yet I pursued him anyway, knowing that it was
nothing but trouble, just as Hetty does.

When you pursue something you know can never
be, you subject yourself to a lot of heartache.
Hetty receives a letter from Arthur, the man of her
dreams, telling her that their relationship has to
end, and this crushes her heart. The same thing
happened to me. I was in love and I got a letter
saying that we could not be together because he was
not ready for a serious relationship. Since this
was my first love and I had never been rejected like
this before, I hurt more than anything in the
world. It was as if the person I loved took a knife
and stabbed me in the heart.

Another way in which Hetty and I are alike is
that we both lost the will to live. In Hetty's
case, she travels to find the man who broke her
heart. The journey is not easy for her. Times get
harder, the nights get colder, and her money begins

to disappear. Hetty is so unhappy she wants to kill
herself: "It was because I was so very miserable,"
she tells Dinah, the Methodist minister. "I didn't
know where to go . . . and I tried to kill myself
before, and I couldn't. O, I tried so to drown myself in the pool, and I couldn't. . . . I went to
find him, as he might take care of me; and he was
gone, and then I didn't know what to do" (451-52).
Hetty has given up on life: "I wished I'd never
been born into this world" (452). In my case I was
young and didn't know any better. My first love
broke my heart, and I did not think that my life
could go on without him. I did not believe there
was anything to move on to. There were times when I
hoped that I would not wake up the next day.

    The last similarity between Hetty and me is
that we both got pregnant at a very young age.
Hetty and I were very young and very naive. We were
just in love; at least, that is what we thought.
Not at one time did we ever stop to think about the
consequences of sharing ourselves and our hearts
with the men we believed we loved. When Hetty gets
pregnant she hides it from everybody for months,
because she knows it would not be accepted. In her
society, getting pregnant out of wedlock is totally
unacceptable. Not only can Hetty not tell anyone,
she also worries what people will think about her
relationship with Arthur: "I daredn't go back home
again--I couldn't bear it. I couldn't have bore to

look at anybody, for they'd have scorned me" (452).
When I got pregnant, I hid it also, because I knew
that I would let my family down. I knew that they
would be disappointed. I was a very good student
with a lot of potential, and I thought that they
would only look down on me.

Even though Hetty and I experienced the same
first love but lost love, we handled our situations differently. Hetty runs after Arthur when
she gets pregnant. She leaves her family behind,
the family she believes will not help her. Hetty
leaves home to find Arthur, thinking that they can
be together: "But it must be done--she must get to
Arthur: oh, how she yearned to be again with somebody who would care for her!" (371). Hetty never
gives up trying to find Arthur; she never stops to
think about what she is doing. She continues to
let herself hurt.

At one point I did leave home, and I did turn
my back on my family, but I had to stop and think
about what I was doing. I was tired of being unhappy. The relationship was too intense. It caused
me to be miserable and never content. I made a very
big decision, and that was to give up and go back
home. I realized that love was not supposed to
hurt. Every day with him I felt the agonizing pain
that he was putting me through and that I allowed
myself to go through. I realized that I deserved
better. I knew when to get out, when enough was

Forrest 5

enough. Hetty did not have the sense to know when enough was enough.

I turned to my family and friends for support. They helped me make it through a very rough time in my life. I was only sixteen years old when I gave birth. Daily, I asked myself, "How am I supposed to raise a child, when I am just a child myself?" I realized then that I could no longer consider my-self a child. At that point in my life, I felt I had to take on the responsibilities of a woman, so that I could be a good mother to my child, and care for her, support her, and love her as a mother should. My family and friends made me realize that life goes on and that I had too much going for my-self to give up on life. My family and friends gave me strength to live and to go on with my life.

Hetty, on the other hand, leaves her child in the woods, thinking that someone will find it so that she can return home and continue as if nothing has happened. Things turn out badly for Hetty. After Hetty leaves the child, it dies: "I did do it, Dinah . . . I buried it in the wood . . . the little baby . . . and it cried . . . I heard it cry . . . ever such a way off . . . all night . . . and I went back because it cried. . . . I didn't kill it--I didn't kill it myself. I put it down there and covered it up, and when I came back it was gone" (451). Hetty does not think that this act will cause her to spend the rest of her days in prison or to be hanged: "I thought I should get rid of all my misery, and go back home, and never let 'em know why I ran away" (452).

 I understand the confusion and the sorrow Hetty feels from lost love. It is a love so deep and consuming that Hetty cannot make a rational decision about the child she is carrying. Hetty should realize that the conception of this child will have to be a symbol of her lost love and to do her best to raise and love this child as every child deserves. Hetty is overcome with grief for a man who does not love her. She does not know how to handle this heartbreak. I, on the other hand, am raising and loving my child, because she is a part of the man I loved and a part of me, and just simply because she is my first love!

Work Cited

Eliot, George. <u>Adam Bede</u>. Oxford World's Classics. New York: Oxford UP, 1998.

Note: Normally, the Works Cited list would appear on a separate page, but we print it here, right after the essay, to save space.

Glossary

Accentual meter   Meter based on the number of stressed syllables per line. See **meter.**

Accentual-syllabic meter   A metrical pattern based on the number of stresses and the number of syllables per line. Accentual-syllabic is the most typical metrical pattern in English poetry. It is marked by repeated units (feet) such as iambs, trochees, anapests, dactyls, and spondees. See **meter.**

Aesthetic quality of literature   The "beauty" of a work; aspects that give pleasure, brought about by its form.

Allegory   A kind of literature in which concrete things—characters, events, and objects—represent ideas.

Alliteration   The repetition of consonant sounds at the beginning of words or at the beginning of accented syllables: "the <u>w</u>oeful <u>w</u>oman <u>w</u>ent <u>w</u>ading <u>W</u>ednesday."

Allusion   A reference within a work to something outside the work, such as historical people and events, mythological and biblical figures, places, and other works of literature.

Analogy   A statement that claims the similarity of things that are basically different. See **figurative language.**

Analysis   The examination of the parts of something in order to discover the relationships among them and the meanings suggested by those relationships.

Anapest   A metrical foot consisting of two unaccented syllables followed by an accented syllable: overwhélm. See **foot** and **meter.**

Anaphora   Repetitions of phrases at the beginning of lines of poetry. A device characteristic of biblical free verse. See **free verse** and **biblical free verse.**

Antagonist   The opponent, whether human or otherwise, of the protagonist. See **protagonist.**

Approximate rhyme   Words that are close to rhymed: "book-buck," "watch-match," "man-in." See **rhyme.**

Archetypal criticism   Literary criticism that brings to light and explores the implications of repeated patterns (archetypes) in works of literature, such as the hero, the scapegoat, the journey, death and rebirth, and the Promethean rebel.

Argument   A line of thought that uses inductive and deductive reasoning to support claims and develop a thesis. See **essay.**

Argumentative structure of essays   The inductive and deductive reasoning that underlies an essay's line of thought. See **inductive reasoning, deductive reasoning,** and **argument.**

Assonance   The repetition of vowel sounds followed by different consonant sounds: "O the groans that opened to his own ears".

Atmosphere   The emotional reaction—such as fear, happiness, foreboding, and tension—that the audience and sometimes characters have to the setting and events of a work.

Attitudinal irony   A person's belief that reality is one way when, in fact, it is very different. See **irony.**

Ballad   A poem that is meant to be sung, that tells a story, and that is arranged in ballad stanzas. *Folk ballads* are anonymous and meant to be sung aloud. *Literary ballads* are written for publication by known authors. See **ballad stanza.**

Ballad stanza   A four-line stanza of poetry, traditional to ballads, that typically has four stresses in lines one and three and three stresses in lines two and four. The rhyme scheme is usually abcb. See **rhyme scheme, ballad,** and **common meter.**

Biblical free verse   Free verse influenced by translations of the Hebrew Bible (Old Testament), featuring long lines, anaphora (repeated phrases at the beginnings of lines), end-stopped lines, musical language, and an elevated tone. See **anaphora** and **free verse.**

Biographical criticism   Literary criticism that shows the relationship between authors' lives and their works of literature.

Blank verse Iambic pentameter with no end rhyme. See **meter, iamb, foot,** and **pentameter.**

Brainstorming A strategy for generating ideas by allowing the mind to flow where it will while it focuses on a problem, topic, or work of literature.

Caesura A strong pause in a sentence, used as a rhythmic and thematic device in lines of poetry. See **meter** and **rhythm.**

Canon The unofficial collection of works of literature that critics deem worthy of admiration and study.

Center of consciousness See **central consciousness.**

Central consciousness The sole character through whose mind we experience a narrative as rendered in the third person limited point of view. See **point of view.**

Character The people in narratives and dramas.

Characterization The presentation and development of the traits of characters in drama and narrative fiction.

Chronological organization of facts In an essay, the presentation of facts in a work of literature in the order in which they occur in time. See **spatial organization of facts.**

Climax The point in a narrative where the conflicts reach a peak of intensity and are resolved or will soon be resolved. See **Freytag pyramid.**

Comedy A subgenre of drama that, among other things, provokes laughter and, through exaggeration and incongruity, depicts the ludicrous. See **tragedy.**

Common meter Ballad meter adapted for hymns, consisting of four lines rhyming abcb or abab. Lines one and three have four stresses; lines two and four have three. Also called *hymn meter.* See **ballad stanza.**

Complex characters See **round characters.**

Complex sentence A sentence containing independent and subordinate (dependent) clauses. See **simple sentence.**

Connotation The subjective, emotional associations that a word has for one person or a group of people. See **denotation.**

Consonance The repetition of final consonant sounds that are preceded by different vowel sounds: "The bea_st_ climbed fa_st_ to the cre_st_." Consonance is also called *half-rhyme.*

Conventions Devices of literature, such as stock characters, omniscient point of view, end-rhyme, and symbolism that an audience easily recognizes and accepts.

Couplet A two-line stanza of poetry whose lines are the same length and have the same end rhymes. See **rhyme scheme.**

Dactyl A metrical foot consisting of one accented syllable followed by two unaccented syllables: róyalty. See **meter** and **foot.**

Database An electronic resource—on a compact disc or on the Internet—that provides, among other things, works of literature and information about them.

Deconstruction A theory of language, developed by Jacques Derrida and based on the linguistics of Ferdinand de Saussure, that rejects certainty of meaning in linguistic communications, including especially literature. To "deconstruct" a work of literature is to expose its contradictory ideas and thus its lack of meaning.

Deductive reasoning A form of logic based on claims. The major premise (a general claim) and minor premise (a claim about a specific instance of the general claim) lead to a conclusion. The three together make up a syllogism. See **syllogism, inductive reasoning,** and **argumentative structure of essays.**

Defamiliarization The concept, developed by Russian Formalists, that authors change familiar aspects of communication so that they are "unfamiliar." Literature is different from other communications because it contains such unfamiliar, "strange" qualities. See **foreground.**

Denotation The object or idea—the referent—that a word represents. See **connotation.**

Dénouement See **falling action.**

Dependent clause See **subordinate clause.**

Descriptive language (imagery) Representations of physical details that appeal to the senses.

Dialogue The words characters speak to one another.

Diction An author's choice of words.

Dimeter A line of poetry consisting of two metrical feet. See **meter** and **foot.**

Drama A genre of literature that is meant to be performed. It features characters, setting, and plot and is acted out on a stage.

Dramatic irony Statements and beliefs by characters that the audience knows to be false or that signal meanings the audience knows but the characters do not. See **irony.**

Dynamic characters Characters who change during the course of drama and narrative fiction. See **static characters.**

Elements of literature Conventions that make up works of literature, such as characterization, plot, regularized rhythm, sound devices, metaphor, and setting. See **conventions.**

Embedded stories   Narratives that appear within a narrative or drama and that seem to digress from the main plot.

End rhyme   Rhymed words that appear at the ends of lines of poetry. See **rhyme.**

End-stopped lines   A line of poetry that has a definite pause at the end. See **line** and **enjambment.**

Enjambment   The continuance of a phrase from one line of poetry to the next so that there is no pause at the end of the line. See **line.**

Enthymeme   A syllogism with one of the premises—usually the major premise—missing: "Anna Karenina is fascinating because she is so complex." The missing premise here—the main premise—is that all people who are complex are fascinating. See **syllogism.**

Epigraph   A pertinent quotation placed at the beginning of a work or unit (for example, a chapter) within the work. Usually an epigraph comments on or reflects the contents of the work or unit.

Epiphany   A term invented by James Joyce to mean a sudden feeling of revelation experienced by a character in a work of literature.

Essay   A piece of writing that is relatively brief, that adheres to rules of usage typical of mainstream publications, that develops an argument—line of thought—that attempts to persuade a general audience of the validity of the author's claims, and that is unified by a thesis. See **usage, argument, general audience for essays,** and **thesis of an essay.**

Ethos   The image that speakers and writers project of themselves in their speaking or writing.

Events   Things that happen in a narrative or drama–actions, statements, thoughts, and feelings.

Experiential quality of literature   A kind of "truth" in works of literature that causes an audience to feel, emotionally and intellectually, a concept, such as racism, triumph, wrongful imprisonment, true love, and transformation.

Exposition   Throughout a narrative, the narrator's explanation of the conflict. See **Freytag pyramid.**

Expressiveness in literature   The presentation in works of literature of authors' personalities, emotions, styles, tastes, and beliefs.

Extended metaphor   An analogy extended throughout an entire poem or a major section of a poem. See **analogy, metaphor,** and **simile.**

External conflicts   Conflicts that take place outside characters—between characters or between characters and physical realities, such as storms, earthquakes, extreme heat, hostile terrain, and machines. See **internal conflicts.**

Facts in works of literature "Facts" consist of anything in the work: details about places and characters, word sounds, rhythm, characterization, physical description, the passage of time—anything.

Falling action The events in a narrative that occur after the climax and lead to the end. Another word for "falling action" is *dénouement.* See **Freytag pyramid.**

Feminine rhyme Rhymed sounds that have two or more syllables: "subtle-rebuttal," "deceptively-perceptively." See **rhyme.**

Feminist criticism Literary criticism that studies the representation of women and issues that concern women in works of literature. See **gender criticism.**

Fiction Generally thought of as a prose narrative that includes made up (invented) materials. More specifically, "fiction" refers to the invented material itself and the stylization of materials so that the audience knows they are different from reality.

Figurative language Generally, the conscious departure from normal or conventional ways of speaking. More specifically, tropes such as metaphor and simile. See **trope, metaphor, simile,** and **analogy.**

First person point of view In narrative fiction, the telling of a story by a character in the story who refers to himself or herself in the first person, as "I."

Fixed forms Stanzas and whole poems that conform to traditional patterns and rules. See **rhyme scheme** and **nonce forms.**

Flat characters Characters with one or two traits who can be described in a short phrase. Another term for flat characters is "simple" characters. See **round characters** and **stock characters.**

Folk ballad See **ballad.**

Foot A unit of rhythm in a line of poetry. See **meter.**

Foreground The method of giving prominence to something in the work of literature that makes it different from everyday use. See **defamiliarization.**

Form The ordering of a work of literature so that it has structure, induces pleasure, and is recognizable as a genre or subgenre. See **aesthetic qualities of literature.**

Formal structural divisions in plays Units, such as acts and scenes, that playwrights or editors indicate. See **structural divisions in plays.**

Frame stories Narratives that "surround"—provide a frame for—other narratives in the work. An example is the account of the pilgrims in Chaucer's *Canterbury Tales,* who agree to tell one another tales as they walk to Canterbury.

Free verse   Poetry without meter. See **meter, biblical free verse,** and **imagist free verse.**

Freewriting   A strategy for generating ideas by writing without stop for a brief period on a topic, problem, or work of literature.

Freytag pyramid   A diagram, developed by Gustav Freytag, that illustrates the typical plot pattern of a five-act tragedy and of most works of fiction.

Gaps in a work   Information left out of a work that the audience usually completes with its imagination.

Gender criticism   An outgrowth of feminist criticism, literary criticism that deals with all matters related to gender in works of literature: heterosexuality, homosexuality, male–female roles, role playing, politics. See **feminist criticism.**

General audience for essays   Anyone who might be interested in the author's topic and who genuinely wants to learn from the essay.

Genre   A type or kind of literature, identifiable by the presence of easily recognizable conventions. Very broad genres include fiction, drama, poetry, and the essay. Subgenres of drama include tragedy, comedy, tragicomedy, farce, and theater of the absurd. Subgenres of fiction include science fiction, detective, gothic, western, and spy. Subgenres of poetry include sonnet, ode, villanelle, and haiku.

Haiku   A poem, originating in Japan, that typically has three lines, with five syllables in the first, seven in the second, and five in the third—a total of seventeen syllables. The haiku also refers to nature, to a specific event, and to actions in the present. See **fixed forms.**

Half-rhyme   See **consonance.**

Heptameter   A line of poetry consisting of seven metrical feet. See **meter** and **foot.**

Hexameter   A line of poetry consisting of six metrical feet. See **meter** and **foot.**

Historical criticism   Literary criticism that studies how historical events, intellectual beliefs, and cultural patterns relate to works of literature.

Hymn meter   See **common meter.**

Hypertext   A World Wide Web database that contains *links*—highlighted phrases that connect (link) to other databases.

Iamb   A metrical foot, consisting of an unaccented syllable followed by an accented syllable: abóve. The iamb is the most used and "natural" foot in English poetry. See **foot** and **meter.**

Iambic pentameter   A line of poetry consisting of five iambic feet. See **foot, iamb, meter,** and **blank verse.**

Imagery   **a.** Descriptions of physical phenomena that appeal to one or more of the senses. **b.** Figurative language, such as metaphor and simile. See **trope, descriptive language,** and **figurative language.**

Imagist free verse   Free verse that abandons the grandiose style of biblical free verse for shorter lines, enjambment, subtle rhythms, colloquial language, understatement, and a realistic depiction of human experience. Also called "meditative," "private," and "conversational" free verse. See **free verse** and **biblical free verse.**

Implied author   Wayne C. Booth's concept of an idealized "author" who manifests himself or herself in a work of literature. The implied author may be similar to but is distinct from the real author.

Incremental repetition   The repetition of phrases, lines, and even whole stanzas. Most of the repetitions include subtle variations that advance the story. Incremental repetition is a traditional device of ballads, especially ones featuring dialogue between two characters. See **ballad.**

Independent clause   See **simple sentence.**

Inductive reasoning   A form of logic based on observing specific instances of something and drawing conclusions about them. See **argumentative structure of essays** and **deductive reasoning.**

Informal structural divisions in plays   Units not identified by the playwright but that nonetheless have a self-contained quality. See **structural divisions in plays** and **formal structural divisions in plays.**

In medias res   Latin for "in the middle of things." A plot that begins in the middle of a story and that uses flashbacks to reveal events that occur prior to the beginning. See **plot** and **story.**

Internal conflicts   Conflicts that take place within the minds of characters.

Internal rhyme   Rhymed words that occur within a line of poetry or that appear close together in prose. See **rhyme.**

Interpretation   The process of examining the details of something in order to make sense of it. Interpretation of literature involves analyzing individual works in order to discover "meaning" in them—how elements cohere inside the works, how the works connect to realities outside the works.

Intertextuality   The formal, thematic, and historical relationship of works of literature to other works of literature. See **conventions** and **genre.**

Irony   The obvious contrast between appearance and reality. See **verbal irony, situational irony, attitudinal irony, dramatic irony.**

Line   One or more words arranged in a line (on a horizontal plane). Line is the most immediately visible structural unit of poetry. See **enjambment** and **end-stopped lines.**

Literary ballad   See **ballad.**

Literary criticism   The analysis and interpretation of works of literature.

Literary theory   The study of the nature of literature and strategies for analyzing it.

Literature   A form of communication, oral and written, that includes some or all of the following elements: language, fiction, truth, aesthetic appeal, and intertextuality.

Marxist criticism   Literary criticism that explores how works of literature reflect the theories of Karl Marx or that examines literature from the perspective of Marx's ideas.

Masculine rhyme   Rhymed sounds that consist of one stressed syllable: "mán-rán," "detéct-corréct." See **rhyme.**

Mask wearing   A character's pretense to be something he or she is not.

Metaphor   In general, any analogy. More specifically, metaphor is a statement that claims a similarity between things that are essentially unlike and that omits the comparative words *like* and *as:* "My love is a red, red rose" rather than "My love is like a red, red rose." See **analogy, simile,** and **figurative language.**

Meter   A regular and repeated pattern of rhythm in a line of poetry. Meter (from the Greek word for "measure") can be based on (measured by) the duration of syllables (quantitative meter), the number of syllables per line (syllabic meter), and the number of stresses per line (accentual meter). The most typical meter in English poetry is accentual-syllabic: stresses and syllables per line. Accentual-syllabic meter is arranged by units (feet) such as iambs, trochees, anapests, dactyls, and spondees. See **foot.**

Monometer   A line of poetry consisting of one metrical foot. See **meter** and **foot.**

Moral center   A character in a work of literature who seems to embody the author's (or implied author's) concepts of right belief and conduct.

Narrated monologue   Characters' thoughts in their own words but presented by narrators in the past tense and third person. See **reported thought, quoted monologue,** and **stream of consciousness.**

Narratee   The person or persons who read or listen to a narrative.

Narrative   A story, told by a narrator, featuring characters who act, think, and talk.

Narrative fiction   A narrative that includes made-up events. See **narrative.**

Narrator   The teller of a story. The narrator can be a person or a medium (images, bodily movements, music) that conveys the story.

New Criticism   Literary criticism that de-emphasizes the value of biography and history for interpreting literature and that instead focuses on the form and unity of works of literature.

New historicist criticism   Literary criticism that endeavors to show how authors and their works of literature are products of their culture. Influenced by Ferdinand de Saussure's linguistics, new historicist critics see culture and all of its products, including literature, as similar to language.

Non sequitur   A conclusion that is unwarranted by—does not follow from—facts or verifiable claims. The literal meaning is "it does not follow."

Nonce forms   Stanzas and whole poems that conform to no traditional patterns or rules. See **fixed forms.**

Octameter   A line of poetry consisting of eight metrical feet. See **meter** and **foot.**

Octave   A stanza consisting of eight lines. See **stanza.**

Onomatopoeia   The use of words that sound like what they mean ("buzz," "boom," "hiss," "fizz," "pop," "glug").

Ottava rima   A stanza of poetry that has eight lines and rhymes abababcc. See **stanza** and **rhyme scheme.**

Overstatement   A type of verbal irony that exaggerates the nature of something while meaning the opposite. See **verbal irony.**

Pastoral poetry   Poetry that includes such conventions as a peaceful rural setting, carefree shepherds, beautiful maidens, eternal spring, pleasant weather, an absence of harsh difficulties, talk of love, and a witty use of language.

Pattern poetry   See **visual poetry.**

Pentameter   A line of poetry consisting of five metrical feet. See **meter** and **foot.**

Personofication   An analogy that attributes human qualities to something not human: Old Man Winter, Father Time, Mother Nature. See **metaphor.**

Petrarchan sonnet   A form of sonnet, named for its inventor Francesco Petrarch, whose typical rhyme scheme (abbaabba/cdecde) divides it into an octave (the first eight lines) and a sestet (the final six lines). See **sonnet.**

Plagiarism   The presentation of other people's ideas, work, and facts as one's own.

Plot An aspect of narrative and drama consisting of three things: first, the author's arrangement of events, which we experience as we read, hear, or witness the work. Second, the connection of events by cause and effect, which gives rise to conflict. Third, devices the author uses to engage us emotionally and intellectually (such as pacing, rising action, climax, surprise, intense conflict, suspense, and foreshadowing). See **events** and **story.**

Plotline In a narrative or drama, a single chain of events linked together by cause and effect. There may be more than one plotline within a narrative or drama. See **events** and **plot.**

Poetry A genre of literature that combines conventions that convey ideas (diction, speakers, imagery, symbolism), musical devices (rhythm, word sounds), structural arrangements (lines, stanzas), and sometimes visual qualities.

Point of view In narrative fiction, the narrator's relationship to the world of the work. The location (point) from which the narrator sees (views) everything in the narrative and from which the narrator tells the story. See **third person omniscient point of view, third person limited point of view, third person objective point of view,** and **first person point of view.**

Primary sources Works of literature: short stories, novels, poems, epics, romances, plays, etc. See **secondary sources.**

Private symbols Objects whose symbolic meaning is unique to one writer. See **symbol** and **public symbol.**

Probable actions In narrative and drama, events and their consequences that seem plausible.

Prose The ordinary speech of people. See **poetry** and **prose poetry.**

Prose poetry Prose that has some of the qualities of poetry, such as nuanced diction, rhythmical devices, imagery, and internal rhyme.

Protagonist The main character of a narrative.

Psychological criticism Literary criticism that attempts to explore the psychological implications of works of literature. In the twentieth century, the theories of Sigmund Freud have heavily influenced this movement.

Public symbols Objects whose meanings the general public would recognize. See **symbol** and **private symbol.**

Quantitative meter See **meter.**

Quatrain A unit of poetry consisting of four lines.

Quoted monologue The thoughts of characters rendered in the characters' own words. See **reported thought, narrated monologue,** and **stream of consciousness.**

Reader-response criticism   Literary criticism that focuses on how readers respond to literature and especially how readers, in the act of reading, help create works of literature.

Referent   The thing to which a word refers.

Reflector   See **central consciousness.**

Repetitions   Repeated actions, patterns of behavior, and thoughts that call attention to characters' traits and beliefs.

Reported thought   The thoughts of characters as rendered by narrators in the narrators' own words. See **quoted monologue, narrated monologue,** and **stream of consciousness.**

Research paper   An essay (research essay) that incorporates research in order to support the author's line of thought about a work or works of literature.

Rhetoric   The art of persuasion.

Rhetorical structure of an essay   All the aspects of an essay that makes it persuasive. These include its prose style, its tone, its beginning, its reasoning, its location of thesis, its organization of key claims, its support of claims, and its ending.

Rhythm   One of the characteristic features of poetic language. See **meter.**

Rhyme   The repetition of the last accented vowel of words and the sounds that follow: slów-grów, Máy-dáy. See **masculine rhyme, feminine rhyme, internal rhyme, end rhyme,** and **approximate rhyme.**

Rhyme scheme   Any pattern of end rhyme. End rhyme is a traditional method of organizing stanzas and poems. Rhyme scheme is indicated by letters. Ballad stanzas, for example, typically rhyme abcb (the second and fourth lines rhyme). See **rhyme** and **end rhyme.**

Rising action   The intensification of conflict in a narrative, leading to ("rising" toward) a climax. See **Freytag pyramid.**

Round characters   Characters who have multiple personality traits, who resemble the complexity of real people. "Complex" characters.

Scanning   The marking of accented and unaccented syllables in lines of poetry. See **meter.**

Scenic narration   Telling an event in real time, so that reading or hearing the event takes about as long as the event to take place. Scenic narration usually features dialogue. See **summary narration.**

Secondary sources   Resources—books, articles, speeches, Internet sites—that provide information about authors and works of literature. See **primary sources.**

Sestet   A unit of poetry consisting of six lines.

Sets   Objects that represent the physical setting of a play.

Setting   The physical, sensuous location of the action, the time in which the action occurs, and the social environment of the characters.

Shakespearean sonnet   A form of sonnet, named after its most famous practitioner. The typical rhyme scheme (abab/cdcd/efef/gg) divides the poem into three quatrains (four lines each) and a couplet. See **sonnet.**

Simile   A statement that claims the similarity of things that are essentially unlike and that uses the comparative words *like* or *as:* "My love is as fair as a dove." See **analogy, trope, metaphor,** and **figurative language.**

Simple characters   See **flat** characters.

Simple sentence   The basic independent clause that constitutes a sentence, usually following the order of subject-verb (Jane loves) or subject-verb-object (Jane loves Joe). See **complex sentence.**

Situational irony   A situation that differs from what common sense indicates it is, will be, or ought to be. See **irony.**

Sonnet   A form of poetry that consists of fourteen lines of iambic pentameter and conforms to one of two patterns of end rhyme: Shakespearean sonnet (abab/cdcd/efef/gg) and Petrarchan sonnet (abbaabba/cdecde). See **Shakespearean sonnet, Petrarchan sonnet,** and **fixed forms.**

Spatial organization of facts   In an essay, the presentation of facts from a work of literature as they appear in the work. See **chronological organization of facts.**

Spenserian stanza   A nine-line stanza of poetry, invented by Edmond Spenser, that rhymes ababbcbcc. See **stanza.**

Spondee   A metrical foot consisting of two accented syllables: bréak, bréak. See **meter** and **foot.**

Stable situation   The end of a narrative, where all or most of the major conflicts have been resolved. See **Freytag pyramid.**

Stanza   In a poem, a unit of lines set apart from other units by spaces. A stanza can encompass the whole poem (for example, a sonnet) or part of the poem (for example, a ballad). Stanzas are often organized by patterns of end rhyme, such as ballad stanza, ottava rima, couplet, and Spenserian stanza. Poems with stanzas are "strophic." Poems without stanzas are "stichic." See **rhyme scheme.**

Static characters   Characters who do not change throughout a narrative or play. See **dynamic characters.**

Stichic poems   See **stanza.**

Stock characters   Flat (simple) characters that are easily recognized conventions in dramas: the wily servant, the pretentious doctor, the gullible simpleton, the young lovers, the old cuckold.

Story   Everything that happens in a narrative and a play, arranged in chronological order. See **plot**, and **events**.

Stream of consciousness   The presentation of characters' preconscious or prespeech thoughts as an apparently incoherent "stream." See **reported thought, quoted monologue,** and **narrated monologue.**

Strophic poems   See **stanza.**

Structural divisions in plays   Units, such as acts and scenes, that are self-contained and that can be distinguished from other units in the play. See **formal structural divisions in plays** and **informal structural divisions in plays.**

Structuralism   A method of analyzing literature, arising from the linguistics of Ferdinand de Saussure, that focuses on similarities between the structure of language and the structure of literature.

Structure in works of literature   The way the parts of a work are organized into a coherent whole.

Style   The way writers and speakers use language.

Subgenres   Kinds of literature that have the typical features of a broad genre (like fiction, drama, and poetry) but that have further, more specific features. Detective fiction, for example, is a subgenre of fiction.

Subject   Something a work of literature seems to be about—genuine love, political integrity, financial corruption, bravery under fire, leadership. See **theme.**

Subordinate clause   Phrases within a sentence that do not stand alone as sentences, that are "dependent" on the independent clause of the sentence. See **simple sentence.**

Subtext in a play   The unspoken but discernable meanings of the written words, especially of the dialogue.

Summary narration   The narration of events and repeated actions that happen over time. Reading a summary narration takes much less time than for the events to occur: "For two years, Marcia attended concerts at Carnegie Hall, hoping against hope to see Raymond." See **scenic narration.**

Syllabic meter   See **meter.**

Syllogism   A unit of reasoning consisting of two claims that support a third claim. The two supporting claims are called *premises* and the third claim is called a *conclusion.*

Symbol An object, event, or character that signifies an abstract idea or ideas. The symbol's meaning is often interestingly vague, suggestive rather than precise. See **private symbols** and **public symbols.**

Symbolism The use of symbols in a work.

Syntax Sentence structure; the way words go together to make sentences. See **simple sentence** and **independent clause.**

Testimony Interpretive statements by literary critics that authors of research papers use to support their own lines of thought. See **research paper.**

Tetrameter A line of poetry consisting of four metrical feet. See **meter** and **foot.**

Theme An idea about the human condition that the audience extracts from works of literature. A theme is what the work seems to say about a subject. See **subject.**

Thesis of an essay The main claim of the essay, the one idea that unifies the essay.

Third person limited point of view In narrative fiction, the telling of a story by an apparently all-knowing ("omniscient") narrator who enters the mind of only one character. The narrator refers to all the characters in the third person, as "he" and "she."

Third person objective (dramatic) point of view In narrative fiction, the telling of a story by an apparently all-knowing ("omniscient") narrator who enters the mind of no characters. We learn about characters from the outside, just as we do when watching a play–thus the term "dramatic." The narrator refers to all the characters in the third person, as "he" and "she."

Third person omniscient point of view In narrative fiction, the telling of a story by an apparently all-knowing ("omniscient") narrator who enters the minds of more than one character and who refers to all the characters in the third person, as "he" and "she."

Tone A narrator's or writer's predominant attitude toward a subject. The subject can be a place, event, character, or idea.

Topoi Traditional patterns of thought, identified by Aristotle as *topoi,* "places" to discover meaning and to develop ideas. Topoi include definition, structure, process, cause and effect, and comparison.

Tragedy A subgenre of drama that, according to Aristotle, contains conventions such as a larger-than-life hero whose flaw brings about a precipitous fall and whose fate inspires pity and fear in the audience. See **comedy.**

Trimeter A line of poetry consisting of three metrical feet. See **meter** and **foot.**

Trochee A metrical foot consisting of an accented syllable followed by an unaccented syllable: lóvely. See **foot** and **meter.**

Trope Generally, the extension of the meanings of a word beyond its literal meaning. More specifically, a trope is an analogy such as metaphor and simile. See **figurative language, metaphor, simile,** and **analogy.**

Truth in literature The reflection in works of literature of aspects of the world outside the works.

Turn A point in a poem when the poet shifts from one meaning or mood to another. The turn in a Shakespearean sonnet typically occurs from the first twelve lines to the couplet. The turn in a Petrarchan sonnet takes place between the octave and sestet.

Typical characters Characters that typify real people.

Understatement A form of verbal irony that minimizes the nature of something while meaning the opposite. See **verbal irony.**

Unreliable narrators Narrators or "centers of consciousness" whose judgments and rendering of facts are untrustworthy.

Unstable situation The introduction of conflict at the beginning of a plot. See **Freytag pyramid.**

Usage The way English is used in mainstream publications, such as newspapers, magazines, books, advertisements, financial reports, business reports, and scholarly journals.

Verbal irony A statement of the opposite of what one means. See **irony.**

Villanelle A traditional form of poetry, originating in Italy and France, that has nineteen lines and six stanzas. Each stanza except the last has three lines; the last has four. The rhyme scheme is aba, aba, aba, aba, aba, abaa. The first and third lines of the poem are repeated throughout: the first line at the end of stanzas two and four, the third line at the end of stanzas three and five. At the end of the poem, these two lines form a couplet.

Visual poetry Poetry that must be seen as well as heard in order to be fully understood. Visual poetry is also called *pattern poetry.* Visual poetry has traditionally taken the appearance of recognizable objects like angels wings, love knots, hearts, crosses, animals, stars, and labyrinths.

Writing process The steps authors go through in order to write an essay: inventing, drafting, revising, and editing.

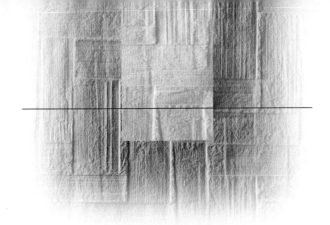

Credits

Chapter 3

Page 44 Source: Robison, Mary. "Yours." *An Amateur's Guide to the Night: Stories.* Boston: David R. Godine, 1989. © 1989 Mary Robison, reprinted with permission of Wylie Agency, Inc.

Chapter 5

Page 108 Source: Brontë, Emily Jane. "The Night is Darkening Round Me." *The Complete Poems of Emily Jane Brontë.* Ed. C.W. Hatfield. New York: Columbia University Press, 1941, p. 56.

Page 115 Source: Bogan, Louise. "Song for a Lyre." *The Sleeping Fury: Poems.* New York: Charles Scribners, 1937, p. 42.

Page 116 Source: Kenyon, Jane. "In the Nursing Home." *Otherwise: New and Selected Poems.* Saint Paul, MN: Graywolf Press, 1996. p. 13. © 1996 the estate of Jane Kenyon, reprinted with permission of Graywolf Press.

Page 132 Source: Brontë, Emily Jane. "The Night Is Darkening Round Me." *The Complete Poems of Emily Jane Brontë.* Ed. C.W. Hatfield. New York: Columbia University Press, 1941, p. 56.

Page 150 Source: *To Walk in Seasons: An Introduction to Haiku.* Ed. William Howard Cohen. Rutland, VT: Charles E. Tuttle Co., 1972. pp. 47, 56, 62. Reprinted with permission.

Page 154 Source: Hughes, Langston. "Vagabonds." *The Collected Poems of Langston Hughes.* © 1994 the estate of Langston Hughes, reprinted with permission of Alfred A. Knopf, a division of Random House, Inc.

Page 156 Source: Bishop, Elizabeth. "One Art." *The Complete Poems: 1927–1979.* © 1979, 1983 Alice Helen Methfessel. Reprinted with permission of Farrar, Straus, and Giroux, LLC.

Page 159 Source: cummings. e. e. *Complete Poems 1904–1962.* New York: Liveright Publishing, 1991. p. 673.

Page 159 Source: Brooks, Gwendolyn. "We Real Cool." *Selected Poems.* New York: Harper & Row. p. 73. © 1963 Harper & Row.

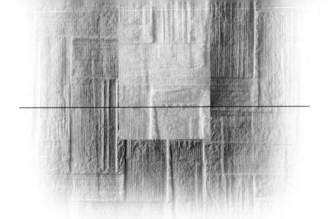

Index of Concepts and Terms

Index of Critics, Authors, and Works

Praise for *WAR DANCES:*

"Sherman Alexie is not a finicky writer. He is often messy and in-your-face in a way that can make you laugh (or shudder) when you least expect to. . . . *War Dances* is Alexie's fiercely freewheeling collection of stories and poems about the tragicomedies of ordinary lives."   —*O, the Oprah Magazine*

"Alexie has a wry, subversive sensibility. . . . The structure [in *War Dances*] is sophisticated yet playful, a subtle way to bring lightness to heavy topics such as senility, bigotry, cancer, and loneliness. . . . A mix tape of a book, with many voices, pieces of different length, shifting rhythms, an evolving story."

—Carolyn Kellogg, *Los Angeles Times*

"Smart modern stories interspersed with witty and deep-feeling verse."   —Alan Cheuse, *San Francisco Chronicle*

"Sherman Alexie mixes up comedy and tragedy, shoots it through with tenderness, then delivers with a provocateur's don't-give-a-damn flourish. He's unique, and his new book, *War Dances*, is another case in point."   —Mary Ann Gwinn, *Seattle Times*

"[With *War Dances*], Sherman Alexie enhances his stature as a multitalented writer and an astute observer of life among Native Americans in the Pacific Northwest. . . . [An] edgy and frequently surprising collection."   —Harvey Freedenberg, *Bookpage*

"Few other contemporary writers seem willing to deal with issues of race, class, and sexuality as explicitly as Alexie . . . ["War Dances" is] a virtuoso performance of wit and pathos, a cultural and familial critique and a son's quiet, worthless scream against the night as his father expires . . . [that] reminds me of the early twentieth-century master of the short form Akutagawa Riyunosuke. . . . Yet again Sherman Alexie has given us a hell of a ride."

—Anthony Swofford, Barnes & Noble Reviews

"Complex . . . Unpredictable . . . Thought-provoking."

—Michelle Peters, *Winnipeg Free Press*

"Alexie's works are piercing yet rueful. He writes odes to anguished pay-phone calls, to boys who would drive through blizzards to see a girl, to couples who need to sit together on airplane flights even though the computer thinks otherwise. . . . [A] marvelous collection."   —Connie Ogle, *The Miami Herald*

"Sherman Alexie is a rare creature in contemporary literature, a writer who can make you laugh as easily as he can make you cry. He's also frighteningly versatile, as a poet, screenwriter, short-story author, and novelist."   —Ben Fulton, *Salt Lake Tribune*

"*War Dances* is maybe the most personal book Alexie has ever published, and it's certainly one of his most readable. The closest thing to a historical precedent for this book is *Palm Sunday*, Kurt Vonnegut's wildly entertaining self-described 'autobiographical collage' of anecdotes, fiction, reminiscences, and other work. . . . Each piece firmly builds on some part of the other, like the songs on a good mix tape. . . . The asymmetrical collection on display in *War Dances* works as a supremely gratifying reading experience."
     —Paul Constant, *The Stranger*

"Alexie is a master storyteller whose prose is laced with metaphoric realities of life, mixed with triumph and tragedy. . . . *War Dances* is vintage Alexie . . . [and] should be savored. . . . Fans will not be disappointed."
     —Levi Rickert, *The Grand Rapids Press*

"Remarkable . . . Wonderful . . . [Alexie's] work reveals both the light and dark within Native American life. A paradox in his writing is that you can be in the middle of delighted laughter when he will hit you with a sentence so true to the core of a character's pain that you suck your breath or are startled to realize you are crying."
     —Gale Zoe Garnett, *The Globe and Mail*

"May be his best work yet . . . An odd grab bag of images, insights, and loose ends . . . yet each piece asks a similar set of questions: What's the point of all this? If there is a point, what's the point of that? And isn't life really goddamn funny? . . . A book about searching."   —Mike Dumke, *Chicago Reader*

"Hilarious. Tender. Brutal. These are the trademarks of one of America's most dazzling writers, Sherman Alexie. His latest book, *War Dances* . . . renders emotional landscapes—anger, joy, anxiety, grief, fear—with skill."
—Elizabeth DiNovella, *The Progressive* (Favorite Books of 2009)

"Beautiful . . . [Alexie] tells wryly amusing, bittersweet stories. . . . He makes you laugh, he makes you cry. Perfect reasons to read him." —Frank Zoretich, *Albuquerque Journal*

"Penetrating . . . Alexie unfurls highly expressive language . . . [in] this spiritedly provocative array of tragic comedies."
—*Publishers Weekly*

"Encounter [Alexie's work] once and you'll never forget it."
—*Library Journal*

"Alexie is at his best in this collection of hilarious and touching stories." —Geeta Sharma-Jensen, *Milwaukee Journal Sentinel*

"Funny, humane, sad, structurally interesting . . . Worth reading."
—Jacob Silverman, *Virginia Quarterly Review*

"If there is something that Sherman Alexie can't write, would you let me know? . . . [*War Dances*] will place him even further amongst the most compelling and talented American writers. . . . Fascinating . . . It's a pointed and provocative stance that makes his literature do what all good literature should do: transport us to another place that we would not necessarily go except in our darkest depths. . . . Alexie doesn't shy away from hard-nosed concern for his people and equal concern for the way in which others appropriate his people's horrors in order for them to show how far the white man has come—but it's never enough. And he never pretends that it's even close to being reconciled. So his work goes on, changing by the season, staying true to one thing: the honest depiction of the ability of human beings to deceive and, ultimately, redeem both themselves and the world that creates a context around their actions." —Jana Sicilian, Bookreporter.com

WAR DANCES

Also by Sherman Alexie

FICTION
The Absolutely True Diary of a Part-Time Indian

Flight

Ten Little Indians

The Toughest Indian in the World

The Lone Ranger and Tonto Fistfight in Heaven

Indian Killer

Reservation Blues

SCREENPLAYS
The Business of Fancy Dancing

Smoke Signals

POETRY
Face

Dangerous Astronomy

Il powwow della fine del mondo

One Stick Song

The Man Who Loves Salmon

The Summer of Black Widows

Water Flowing Home

Seven Mourning Songs for the Cedar Flute
I Have Yet to Learn to Play

First Indian on the Moon

Old Shirts & New Skins

I Would Steal Horses

The Business of Fancy Dancing

WAR DANCES

by

Sherman Alexie

Grove Press
New York

ISBN 978-0-8021-4489-8

Grove Press
an imprint of Grove/Atlantic, Inc.
154 West 14th Street
New York, NY 10011

Distributed by Publishers Group West
www.groveatlantic.com

15 16 17 18   6 5 4 3

For
Elisabeth, Morgan, Eric, and Deb

Contents

Contents

WAR DANCES

THE LIMITED

I saw a man swerve his car
And try to hit a stray dog,
But the quick mutt dodged
Between two parked cars

And made his escape.
God, I thought, did I just see
What I think I saw?
At the next red light,

I pulled up beside the man
And stared hard at him.
He knew that'd I seen
His murder attempt,

But he didn't care.
He smiled and yelled loud
Enough for me to hear him
Through our closed windows:

"Don't give me that face
Unless you're going to do
Something about it.
Come on, tough guy,

What are you going to do?"
I didn't do anything.
I turned right on the green.
He turned left against traffic.

I don't know what happened
To that man or the dog,
But I drove home
And wrote this poem.

Why do poets think
They can change the world?
The only life I can save
Is my own.

BREAKING AND ENTERING

Back in college, when I was first learning how to edit film—how to construct a scene—my professor, Mr. Baron, said to me, "You don't have to show people using a door to walk into a room. If people are already in the room, the audience will understand that they didn't crawl through a window or drop from the ceiling or just materialize. The audience understands that a door has been used—the eyes and mind will make the connection—so you can just skip the door."

Mr. Baron, a full-time visual aid, skipped as he said, "Skip the door." And I laughed, not knowing that I would always remember his bit of teaching, though of course, when I tell the story now, I turn my emotive professor into the scene-eating lead of a Broadway musical.

"Skip the door, young man!" Mr. Baron sings in my stories— my lies and exaggerations—skipping across the stage with a top hat in one hand and a cane in the other. "Skip the door, old friend! And you will be set free!"

"Skip the door" is a good piece of advice—a maxim, if you will—that I've applied to my entire editorial career, if not my entire life. To state it in less poetic terms, one would say, "An editor must omit all unnecessary information." So in telling you this story—with words, not film or video stock—in constructing its scenes, I will attempt to omit all unnecessary information. But oddly enough, in order to skip the door in telling this story, I am forced to begin with a door: the front door of my home on Twenty-seventh Avenue in the Central District neighborhood of Seattle, Washington.

One year ago, there was a knock on that door. I heard it, but I did not rise from my chair to answer. As a freelance editor, I work at home, and I had been struggling with a scene from a locally made film, an independent. Written, directed, and shot by amateurs, the footage was both incomplete and voluminous. Simply stated, there was far too much of nothing. Moreover, it was a love scene—a graphic sex scene, in fact—and the director and the producer had somehow convinced a naive and ambitious local actress to shoot the scene full frontal, graphically so. This was not supposed to be a pornographic movie; this was to be a tender coming-of-age work of art. But it wasn't artistic, or not the kind of art it pretended to be. This young woman had been exploited—with her permission, of course—but I was still going to do my best to protect her.

Don't get me wrong. I'm not a prude—I've edited and enjoyed sexual and violent films that were far more graphic—but I'd spotted honest transformative vulnerability in that young actress's performance. Though the director and the producer thought she'd just been acting—had created her fear and shame through technical skill—I knew better. And so, by editing out the more gratuitous nudity and focusing on faces and small pieces of dialogue—and by paying more attention to fingertips than to what those fingertips were touching—I was hoping to turn a sleazy gymnastic sex scene into an exchange that resembled how two people in new love might actually touch each other.

Was I being paternalistic, condescending, and hypocritical? Sure. After all, I was being paid to work with exploiters, so didn't that mean I was also being exploited as I helped exploit the woman? And what about the young man, the actor, in the scene? Was he dumb and vulnerable as well? Though he was allowed—was legally bound—to keep his penis hidden, wasn't he more exploited than exploiter? These things are hard to define. Still, even in the most compromised of situations, one must find a moral center.

But how could I find any center with that knocking on the door? It had become an evangelical pounding: *Bang, bang, bang, bang!* It had to be the four/four beat of a Jehovah's Witness or a Mormon. *Bang, cha, bang, cha!* It had to be the iambic pentameter of a Sierra Club shill or a magazine sales kid.

Trust me, nobody interesting or vital has ever knocked on a front door at three in the afternoon, so I ignored the knocking and kept at my good work. And, sure enough, my potential guest stopped the noise and went away. I could hear feet pounding down the stairs and there was only silence—or, rather, the relative silence of my urban neighborhood.

But then, a few moments later, I heard a window shatter in my basement. Is shatter too strong a verb? I heard my window break. But break seems too weak a verb. As I visualize the moment—as I edit in my mind—I add the sound track, or rather I completely silence the sound track. I cut the sounds of the city—the planes overhead, the cars on the streets, the boats on the lake, the televisions and the voices and the music and the wind through the trees—until one can hear only shards of glass dropping onto a hardwood floor.

And then one hears—feels—the epic thump of two feet landing on that same floor.

Somebody—the same person who had knocked on my front door to ascertain if anybody was home, had just broken and entered my life.

Now please forgive me if my tenses—my past, present, and future—blend, but one must understand that I happen to be one editor who is not afraid of jump cuts—of rapid flashbacks and flash-forwards. In order to be terrified, one must lose all sense of time and place. When I heard those feet hit the floor, I traveled back in time—I de-evolved, I suppose—and became a primitive version of myself. I had been a complex organism—but I'd turned into a two-hundred-and-two pound one-celled amoeba. And that amoeba knew only fear.

Looking back, I suppose I should have just run away. I could have run out the front door into the street, or the back door onto the patio, or the side door off the kitchen into the alley, or even through the door into the garage—where I could have dived through the dog door cut into the garage and made my caninelike escape.

But here's the salt of the thing: though I cannot be certain, I believe that I was making my way toward the front door—after all, the front door was the only place in my house where I could be positive that my intruder was *not* waiting. But in order to get from my office to the front door, I had to walk past the basement door. And as I walked past the basement door, I spotted the baseball bat.

It wasn't my baseball bat. Now, when one thinks of baseball bats, one conjures images of huge slabs of ash wielded by steroid-fueled freaks. But that particular bat belonged to my ten-year-old son. It was a Little League bat, so it was comically small. I could easily swing it with one hand and had, in fact, often swung it one-handed as I hit practice grounders to the little second baseman of my heart, my son, my Maximilian, my Max. Yes, I am a father. And a husband. That is information you need to know. My wife, Wendy, and my son were not in the house. To give me the space and time I needed to finish editing the film, my wife had taken our son to visit her mother and father in Chicago; they'd been gone for one week and would be gone for another. So, to be truthful, I was in no sense being forced to defend my family, and I'd never been the kind of man to defend his home, his property, his shit. In fact, I'd often laughed at the news footage of silly men armed with garden hoses as they tried to defend their homes from wildfires. I always figured those men would die, go to hell, and spend the rest of eternity having squirt-gun fights with demons.

So with all that information in mind, why did I grab my son's baseball bat and open the basement door? Why did I creep down the stairs? Trust me, I've spent many long nights awake, asking myself those questions. There are no easy answers. Of course, there are many men—and more than a few women—who believe I was fully within my rights to head down those stairs and confront my intruder. There are laws that define—that frankly encourage—the art of self-defense. But since I wasn't interested in defending my property, and since my family and I were not being directly threatened, what part of my self could I have possibly been defending?

In the end, I think I wasn't defending anything at all. I'm an editor—an artist—and I like to make connections; I am paid to make connections. And so I wonder. Did I walk down those stairs because I was curious? Because a question had been asked (Who owned the feet that landed on my basement floor?) and I, the editor, wanted to discover the answer?

So, yes, slowly I made my way down the stairs and through the dark hallway and turned the corner into our downstairs family room—the man cave, really, with the big television and the pool table—and saw a teenaged burglar. I stood still and silent. Standing with his back to me, obsessed with the task—the crime—at hand, he hadn't yet realized that I was in the room with him.

Let me get something straight. Up until that point I hadn't made any guesses as to the identity of my intruder. I mean, yes, I live in a black neighborhood—and I'm not black—and there had been news of a series of local burglaries perpetrated by black teenagers, but I swear none of that entered my mind. And when I saw him, the burglar, rifling through my DVD collection and shoving selected titles into his backpack—he was a felon with cinematic taste, I guess, and that was a strangely pleasing observation—I didn't think, There's a black teenager stealing from me. I only remembering being afraid and wanting to make my fear go away.

"Get the fuck out of here!" I screamed. "You fucking fucker!"

The black kid was so startled that he staggered into my television—cracking the screen—and nearly fell before he caught his balance and ran for the broken window. I could have—would have—let him make his escape, but he stopped and turned back toward me. Why did he do that? I don't know. He was young and scared and made an irrational decision. Or maybe it wasn't irrational at all. He'd slashed his right hand when he crawled through the broken window, so he must have decided the opening with its jagged glass edges was not a valid or safe exit—who'd ever think a broken window was a proper entry or exit—so he searched for a door. But the door was behind me. He paused, weighed his options, and sprinted toward me. He was going to bulldoze me. Once again, I could have made the decision to avoid conflict and step aside. But I didn't. As that kid ran toward me I swung the baseball bat with one hand.

I often wonder what would have happened if that bat had been made of wood. When Max and I had gone shopping for bats, I'd tried to convince him to let me buy him a wooden one, an old-fashioned slugger, the type I'd used when I was a Little Leaguer. I've always been a nostalgic guy. But my son recognized that a ten-dollar wooden bat purchased at Target was not a good investment.

"That wood one will break easy," Max had said. "I want the lum-a-lum one."

Of course, he'd meant to say *aluminum;* we'd both laughed at his mispronunciation. And I'd purchased the lum-a-lum bat.

So it was a metal bat that I swung one-handed at the black teenager's head. If it had been cheap and wooden, perhaps the bat would have snapped upon contact and dissipated the force. Perhaps. But this bat did not snap. It was strong and sure, so when it made full contact with the kid's temple, he dropped to the floor and did not move.

He was dead. I had killed him.

I fell to my knees next to the kid, dropped my head onto his chest, and wept.

I don't remember much else about the next few hours, but I called 911, opened the door for the police, and led them to the body. And I answered and asked questions.

"Did he have a gun or knife?"

"I don't know. No. Well, I didn't see one."

"He attacked you first?"

"He ran at me. He was going to run me over."

"And that's when you hit him with the bat?"

"Yes. It's my son's bat. It's so small. I can't believe it's strong enough to—is he really dead?"

"Yes."

"Who is he?"

"We don't know yet."

His name was Elder Briggs. Elder: such an unusual name for anybody, especially a sixteen-year-old kid. He was a junior at Garfield High School, a B student and backup point guard for the basketball team, an average kid. A good kid, by all accounts. He had no criminal record—had never committed even a minor infraction in school, at home, or in the community—so why had this good kid broken into my house? Why had he decided to steal from me? Why had he made all the bad decisions that had led to his death?

The investigation was quick but thorough, and I was not charged with any crime. It was self-defense. But then nothing is ever clear, is it? I was legally innocent, that much is true, but was I morally innocent? I wasn't sure, and neither were a significant percentage of my fellow citizens. Shortly after the police held the press conference that exonerated me, Elder's family— his mother, father, older brother, aunts, uncles, cousins, friends, and priest—organized a protest. It was small, only forty or fifty people, but how truly small can a protest feel when you are the subject—the object—of that protest?

I watched the live coverage of the event. My wife and son, after briefly returning from Chicago, had only spent a few days with me before they fled back to her parents. We wanted to protect our child from the media. An ironic wish, considering that the media were only interested in me because I'd killed somebody else's child.

"The police don't care about my son because he's black," Elder's mother, Althea, said to a dozen different microphones and as many cameras. "He's just another black boy killed by a white man. And none of these white men care."

As Althea continued to rant about my whiteness, some clever producer—and his editor—cut into footage of me, the white man who owned a baseball bat, walking out of the police station as a free man. It was a powerful piece of editing. It made me look pale and guilty. But all of them—Althea, the other protesters, the reporters, producers, and editors—were unaware of one crucial piece of information: I am not a white man.

I am an enrolled member of the Spokane Tribe of Indians. Oh, I don't look Indian, or at least not typically Indian. Some folks assume I'm a little bit Italian or Spanish or perhaps Middle Eastern. Most folks think I'm just another white guy who tans well. And since I'd just spent months in a dark editing room, I was at my palest. But I grew up on the Spokane Indian Reservation, the only son of a mother and father who were also Spokane Indians who grew up on our reservation. Yes, both of my grandfathers had been half-white, but they'd both died before I was born.

I'm not trying to be holy here. I wasn't a traditional Indian. I didn't dance or sing powwow or speak my language or spend my free time marching for Indian sovereignty. And I'd married a white woman. One could easily mock my lack of cultural connection, but one could not question my race. That's not true, of course. People, especially other Indians, always doubted my race. And I'd always tried to pretend it didn't matter—I was confident about my identity—but it did hurt my feelings. So when I heard Althea Riggs misidentify my race—and watched the media covertly use editing techniques to confirm her misdiagnosis—I picked up my cell phone and dialed the news station.

"Hello," I said to the receptionist. "This is George Wilson. I'm watching your coverage of the protests and I must issue a correction."

"Wait, what?" the receptionist asked. "Are you really George Wilson?"

"Yes, I am."

"Hold on," she said. "Let me put you straight through to the producer."

So the producer took the call and, after asking a few questions to further confirm my identity, he put me on live. So my voice played over images of Althea Riggs weeping and wailing, of her screaming at the sky, at God. How could I have allowed myself to be placed into such a compromising position? How could I have been such an idiot? How could I have been so goddamn callous and self-centered?

"Hello, Mr. Wilson," the evening news anchor said. "I understand you have something you'd like to say."

"Yes." My voice carried into tens of thousands of Seattle homes. "I am watching the coverage of the protest, and I insist on a correction. I am not a white man. I am an enrolled member of the Spokane Tribe of Indians."

Yes, that was my first official public statement about the death of Elder Briggs. It didn't take clever editing to make me look evil; I had accomplished this in one take, live and uncut.

I was suddenly the most hated man in Seattle. And the most beloved. My fellow liberals spoke of my lateral violence and the destructive influence of colonialism on the indigenous, while conservatives lauded my defensive stand and lonely struggle against urban crime. Local bloggers posted hijacked footage of the most graphically violent films I'd edited.

And finally, a local news program obtained rough footage of the film I'd been working on when Elder Briggs broke into my house. Though I had, through judicious editing, been trying to protect the young actress, a black actress, the news only played the uncut footage of the obviously frightened and confused woman. And when the reporters ambushed her—her name was Tracy—she, of course, could only respond that, yes, she felt as if she'd been violated. I didn't blame her for that; I agreed with her. But none of that mattered. I could in no way dispute the story—the cleverly edited series of short films—

that had been made about me. Yes, I was a victim, but I didn't for one second forget that Elder Briggs was dead. I was ashamed and vilified, but I was alive.

I spent most of that time alone in my basement, in the room where I had killed Elder Briggs. When one spends that much time alone, one ponders. And when one ponders, one creates theories—hypotheses, to explain the world. Oh, hell, forget rationalization; I was pissed, mostly at myself for failing to walk away from a dangerous situation. And I was certainly pissed at the local media, who had become as exploitative as any pornographic moviemaker. But I was also pissed at Althea and Elder Briggs.

Yes, the kid was a decent athlete; yes, the kid was a decent student; yes, the kid was a decent person. But he had broken into my house. He had smashed my window and was stealing my DVDs and, if I had not been home, would have stolen my computer and television and stereo and every other valuable thing in my house. And his mother, Althea, instead of explaining why her good and decent son had broken and entered a stranger's house, committing a felony, had instead decided to blame me and accuse me of being yet another white man who was always looking to maim another black kid—had already maimed generations of black kids—when in fact I was a reservation Indian who had been plenty fucked myself by generations of white men. So, Althea, do you want to get into a pain contest? Do you want to participate in the Genocidal Olympics? Whose tragic history has more breadth and depth and length?

Oh, Althea, why the hell was your son in my house? And oh, my God, it was a *Little League* baseball bat! It was only twenty inches long and weighed less than three pounds. I could have hit one hundred men in the head—maybe one thousand or one million—and not done anything more than given them a headache. But on that one day, on that one bitter afternoon, I took a swing—a stupid, one-handed, unlucky cut—and killed a kid, a son, a young man who was making a bad decision but who maybe had brains and heart and soul enough to stop making bad decisions.

Oh, Jesus, I murdered somebody's potential.

Oh, Mary, it was self-defense, but it was still murder. I confess: I am a killer.

How does one survive these revelations? One just lives. Or, rather, one just finally walks out of his basement and realizes that the story is over. It's old news. There are new villains and heroes, criminals and victims, to be defined and examined and tossed aside.

Elder Briggs and I were suddenly and equally unimportant.

My life became quiet again. I took a job teaching private-school white teenagers how to edit video. They used their newly developed skills to make documentaries about poor brown people in other countries. It's not oil that runs the world, it's shame. My Max was always going to love me, even when he began to understand my limitations, I didn't know what my wife thought of my weaknesses.

Weeks later, in bed, after lovemaking, she interrogated me.

"Honey," she said.

"Yes," I said.

"Can I ask you something?"

"Anything."

"With that kid, did you lose your temper?"

"What do you mean?" I asked.

"Well, you have lost your temper before."

"Just one time."

"Yes, but you broke your hand when you punched the wall."

"Do you think I lost my temper with Elder Briggs?" I asked.

My wife paused before answering, and in that pause I heard all her doubt and fear. So I got out of bed, dressed, and left the house. I decided to drive to see a hot new independent film—a gory war flick that pretended to be antiwar—but first stepped into a mini-mart to buy candy I could smuggle into the theater.

I was standing in the candy aisle, trying to decide between a PayDay and a Snickers, when a group of young black men walked into the store. They were drunk or high and they were cursing the world, but in a strangely friendly way. How is it that black men can make a word like *motherfucker* sound jovial?

There are people—white folks, mostly—who are extremely uncomfortable in the presence of black people. And I know plenty of Indians—my parents, for example—who are also uncomfortable around black folks. As for me? I suppose I'd always been the kind of nonblack person who celebrated himself for not being uncomfortable around blacks. But now, as I watched those black men jostle one another up and down the aisles, I was afraid—no, I was nervous. What if they recognized me? What if they were friends of Elder Briggs? What if they attacked me?

Nothing happened, of course. Nothing ever really happens, you know. Life is infinitesimal and incremental and inconsequential. Those young black men paid for their energy drinks and left the store. I paid for my candy bar, walked out to my car, and drove toward the movie theater.

One block later, I had to hit my brakes when those same black guys jaywalked across the street in front of me. All of them stared me down and walked as slowly as possible through the crosswalk. I'd lived in this neighborhood for years and I'd often had this same encounter with young black men. It was some remnant of the warrior culture, I suppose.

When it had happened before, I had always made it a point to smile goofily and wave to the black men who were challenging me. Since they thought I was a dorky white guy, I'd behave like one. I'd be what they wanted me to be.

But this time, when those black men walked in slow motion in front of me, I did not smile or laugh. I just stared back at them. I knew I could hit the gas and slam into them and hurt them, maybe even kill them. I knew I had that power. And I knew that I would not use that power. But what about these black guys? What power did they have? They could only make me wait at an intersection. And so I waited. I waited until they walked around the corner and out of my vision. I waited until another driver pulled up behind me and honked his horn. I was supposed to move, and so I went.

Go, Ghost, Go

At this university upon a hill,
    I meet a tenured professor
        Who's strangely thrilled
    To list all of the oppressors—
Past, present, and future—who have killed,
Are killing, and will kill the indigenous.
        O, he names the standard suspects—
            Rich, white, and unjust—
    And I, a red man, think he's correct,
But why does he have to be so humorless?

And how can he, a white man, fondly speak
    Of the Ghost Dance, the strange and cruel
        Ceremony
    That, if performed well, would have doomed
All white men to hell, destroyed their colonies,
And brought every dead Indian back to life?
    The professor says, "Brown people
        From all brown tribes
    Will burn skyscrapers and steeples.
They'll speak Spanish and carry guns and knives.

Sherman, can't you see that immigration
Is the new and improved Ghost Dance?"
All I can do is laugh and laugh
And say, "Damn, you've got some imagination.
You should write a screenplay about this shit—
About some fictional city,
Grown fat and pale and pretty,
That's destroyed by a Chicano apocalypse."
The professor doesn't speak. He shakes his head
And assaults me with his pity.
I wonder how he can believe
In a ceremony that requires his death.
I think that he thinks he's the new Jesus.
He's eager to get on that cross
And pay the ultimate cost
Because he's addicted to the indigenous.

Bird-watching at Night

What kind of bird is that?

An owl.

What kind of bird was that?

Another owl.

Oh, that one was too quick and small to be an owl. What was it?

A quick and small owl.

One night, when I was sixteen, I was driving with my girlfriend up on Little Falls Flat and this barn owl swooped down over the road, maybe fifty feet or so in front of us, and came flying straight toward our windshield. It was huge, pterodactyl-size, and my girlfriend screamed. And—well, I screamed, too, because that thing was heading straight for us, but you know what I did? I slammed on the gas and sped toward that owl. Do you know why I did that?

Because you wanted to play chicken with the owl?

Exactly.

So what happened?

When we were maybe a second from smashing into each other, that owl just flapped its wings, but barely. What's a better word than *flap*? What's a word that still means *flap*, but a smaller *flap*?

How about slant?

Oh, yes, that's pretty good. So, like I was saying, as that owl was just about to smash into our windshield, it slanted its wings, and slanted up into the dark. And it was so friggin' amazing, you know? I just slammed on the brakes and nearly slid into the ditch. And my girlfriend and I were sitting there in the dark with the engine *tick, tick, tick*ing like some kind of bomb, but an existential bomb, like it was just measuring out the endless nothingness of our lives because that owl had nearly touched us but was gone forever. And I said something like, "That was magnificent," and my girlfriend—you want to know what she said?

She said something like, "I'm breaking up with you."

Damn, that's exactly what she said. And I asked her, "Why are you breaking up with me?" And do you know what she said?

She said, "I'm breaking up with you because you are not an owl."

Yes, yes, yes, and you know what? I have never stopped thinking about her. It's been twenty-seven years, and I still miss her. Why is that?

Brother, you don't miss her. You miss the owl.

After Building the Lego *Star Wars* Ultimate Death Star

How many planets do you want to destroy?
Don't worry, Daddy, this is just a big toy,
And there is nothing more fun than making noise.

My sons, when I was a boy, I threw dirt clods
And snow grenades stuffed with hidden rocks, and fought
Enemies—other Indian boys—who thought,

Like me, that joyful war turned us into gods.

WAR DANCES

1. My Kafka Baggage

A few years ago, after I returned from a trip to Los Angeles, I unpacked my bag and found a dead cockroach, shrouded by a dirty sock, in a bottom corner. "Shit," I thought. "We're being invaded." And so I threw the unpacked clothes, books, shoes, and toiletries back into the suitcase, carried it out onto the driveway, and dumped the contents onto the pavement, ready to stomp on any other cockroach stowaways. But there was only the one cockroach, stiff and dead. As he lay on the pavement, I leaned closer to him. His legs were curled under his body. His head was tilted at a sad angle. Sad? Yes, sad. For who is lonelier than the cockroach without his tribe? I laughed at myself. I was feeling empathy for a dead cockroach. I wondered about its story. How had it got into my bag? And where? At the hotel in Los Angeles? In an airport baggage system? It didn't originate in our house. We've kept those tiny bastards away from our place for fifteen years. So what had happened to this little vermin? Did he smell something delicious in my bag—my musky deodorant or some crumb of chocolate Power Bar—and climb inside, only to be crushed by the shifts of fate and garment bags? As he died, did he feel fear? Isolation? Existential dread?

2. SYMPTOMS

Last summer, in reaction to various allergies I was suffering from, defensive mucous flooded my inner right ear and confused, frightened, untied, and unmoored me. Simply stated, I could not fucking hear a thing from that side, so I had to turn my head to understand what my two sons, ages eight and ten, were saying.

"We're hungry," they said. "We keep telling you."

They wanted to be fed. And I had not heard them.

"Mom would have fed us by now," they said.

Their mother had left for Italy with her mother two days ago. My sons and I were going to enjoy a boys' week, filled with unwashed socks, REI rock wall climbing, and ridiculous heaps of pasta.

"What are you going to cook?" my sons asked. "Why haven't you cooked yet?"

I'd been lying on the couch reading a book while they played and I had not realized that I'd gone partially deaf. So I, for just a moment, could only weakly blame the silence—no, the contradictory roar that only I could hear.

Then I recalled the man who went to the emergency room because he'd woken having lost most, if not all, of his hearing. The doctor peered into one ear, saw an obstruction, reached in with small tweezers, and pulled out a cockroach, then reached into the other ear, and extracted a much larger cockroach. Did you know that ear wax is a delicacy for roaches?

I cooked dinner for my sons—overfed them out of guilt—and cleaned the hell out of our home. Then I walked into the bathroom and stood close to my mirror. I turned my head and body at weird angles, and tried to see deeply into my congested ear. I sang hymns and prayed that I'd see a small angel trapped in the canal. I would free the poor thing, and she'd unfurl and pat dry her tiny wings, then fly to my lips and give me a sweet kiss for sheltering her metamorphosis.

3. THE SYMPTOMS WORSEN

When I woke at three a.m., completely unable to hear out of my clogged right ear, and positive that a damn swarm of locusts was wedged inside, I left a message for my doctor, and told him that I would be sitting outside his office when he reported to work.

This would be the first time I had been inside a health-care facility since my father's last surgery.

4. BLANKETS

After the surgeon cut off my father's right foot—no, half of my father's right foot—and three toes from the left, I sat with him in the recovery room. It was more like a recovery hallway. There was no privacy, not even a thin curtain. I guessed it made it easier for the nurses to monitor the postsurgical patients, but still, my father was exposed—his decades of poor health and worse decisions were illuminated—on white sheets in a white hallway under white lights.

"Are you okay?" I asked. It was a stupid question. Who could be okay after such a thing? Yesterday, my father had *walked* into the hospital. Okay, he'd shuffled while balanced on two canes, but that was still called walking. A few hours ago, my father still had both of his feet. Yes, his feet and toes had been black with rot and disease but they'd still been, technically speaking, feet and toes. And, most important, those feet and toes had belonged to my father. But now they were gone, sliced off. Where were they? What did they do with the right foot and the toes from the left foot? Did they throw them in the incinerator? Were their ashes floating over the city?

"Doctor, I'm cold," my father said.

"Dad, it's me," I said.

"I know who are you. You're my son." But considering the blankness in my father's eyes, I assumed he was just guessing at my identity.

"Dad, you're in the hospital. You just had surgery."

"I know where I am. I'm cold."

"Do you want another blanket?" Another stupid question. Of course, he wanted another blanket. He probably wanted me to build a fucking campfire or drag in one of those giant propane heaters that NFL football teams used on the sidelines.

I walked down the hallway—the recovery hallway—to the nurses' station. There were three women nurses, two white and one black. Being Native American-Spokane and Coeur d'Alene Indian, I hoped my darker pigment would give me an edge with the black nurse, so I addressed her directly.

"My father is cold," I said. "Can I get another blanket?"

The black nurse glanced up from her paperwork and regarded me. Her expression was neither compassionate nor callous.

"How can I help you, sir?" she asked.

"I'd like another blanket for my father. He's cold."

"I'll be with you in a moment, sir."

She looked back down at her paperwork. She made a few notes. Not knowing what else to do, I stood there and waited.

"Sir," the black nurse said. "I'll be with you in a moment."

She was irritated. I understood. After all, how many thousands of times had she been asked for an extra blanket? She was a nurse, an educated woman, not a damn housekeeper. And it was never really about an extra blanket, was it? No, when people asked for an extra blanket, they were asking for a time machine. And, yes, she knew she was a health care provider, and she knew she was supposed to be compassionate, but my father, an alcoholic, diabetic Indian with terminally damaged kidneys, had just endured an incredibly expensive surgery for what? So he could ride his motorized wheelchair to the bar and win bets by showing off his disfigured foot? I know she didn't want to be cruel, but she believed there was a point when doctors should stop rescuing people from their own self-destructive impulses. And I couldn't disagree with her but I could ask for the most basic of comforts, couldn't I?

"My father," I said. "An extra blanket, please."

"Fine," she said, then stood and walked back to a linen closet, grabbed a white blanket, and handed it to me. "If you need anything else—"

I didn't wait around for the end of her sentence. With the blanket in hand, I walked back to my father. It was a thin blanket, laundered and sterilized a hundred times. In fact, it was too thin. It wasn't really a blanket. It was more like a large beach towel. Hell, it wasn't even good enough for that. It was more like the world's largest coffee filter. Jesus, had health care finally come to this? Everybody was uninsured and unblanketed.

"Dad, I'm back."

He looked so small and pale lying in that hospital bed. How had that change happened? For the first sixty-seven years of his life, my father had been a large and dark man. And now, he was just another pale and sick drone in a hallway of pale and sick drones. A hive, I thought, this place looks like a beehive with colony collapse disorder.

"Dad, it's me."

"I'm cold."

"I have a blanket."

As I draped it over my father and tucked it around his body, I felt the first sting of grief. I'd read the hospital literature about this moment. There would come a time when roles would reverse and the adult child would become the caretaker of the ill parent. The circle of life. Such poetic bullshit.

"I can't get warm," my father said. "I'm freezing."

"I brought you a blanket, Dad, I put it on you."

"Get me another one. Please. I'm so cold. I need another blanket."

I knew that ten more of these cheap blankets wouldn't be enough. My father needed a real blanket, a good blanket.

I walked out of the recovery hallway and made my way through various doorways and other hallways, peering into the rooms, looking at the patients and their families, looking for a particular kind of patient and family.

I walked through the ER, cancer, heart and vascular, neuroscience, orthopedic, women's health, pediatrics, and surgical services. Nobody stopped me. My expression and posture were that of a man with a sick father and so I belonged.

And then I saw him, another Native man, leaning against a wall near the gift shop. Well, maybe he was Asian; lots of those in Seattle. He was a small man, pale brown, with muscular arms and a soft belly. Maybe he was Mexican, which is really a kind of Indian, too, but not the kind that I needed. It was hard to tell sometimes what people were. Even brown people guessed at the identity of other brown people.

"Hey," I said.

"Hey," the other man said.

"You Indian?" I asked.

"Yeah."

"What tribe?"

"Lummi."

"I'm Spokane."

"My first wife was Spokane. I hated her."

"My first wife was Lummi. She hated me."

We laughed at the new jokes that instantly sounded old.

"Why are you in here?" I asked.

"My sister is having a baby," he said. "But don't worry, it's not mine."

"Ayyyyyy," I said—another Indian idiom—and laughed.

"I don't even want to be here," the other Indian said. "But my dad started, like, this new Indian tradition. He says it's a thousand years old. But that's bullshit. He just made it up to impress himself. And the whole family just goes along, even when we know it's bullshit. He's in the delivery room waving eagle feathers around. Jesus."

"What's the tradition?"

"Oh, he does a naming ceremony right in the hospital. Like, it's supposed to protect the baby from all the technology and shit. Like hospitals are the big problem. You know how many babies died before we had good hospitals?"

"I don't know."

"Most of them. Well, shit, a lot of them, at least."

This guy was talking out of his ass. I liked him immediately.

"I mean," the guy said. "You should see my dad right now. He's pretending to go into this, like, fucking trance and is dancing around my sister's bed, and he says he's trying to, you know, see into her womb, to see who the baby is, to see its true nature, so he can give it a name—a protective name—before it's born."

The guy laughed and threw his head back and banged it on the wall.

"I mean, come on, I'm a loser," he said and rubbed his sore skull. "My whole family is filled with losers."

The Indian world is filled with charlatans, men and women who pretended—hell, who might have come to believe—that they were holy. Last year, I had gone to a lecture at the University of Washington. An elderly Indian woman, a Sioux writer and scholar and charlatan, had come to orate on Indian sovereignty and literature. She kept arguing for some kind of separate indigenous literary identity, which was ironic considering that she was speaking English to a room full of white professors. But I wasn't angry with the woman, or even bored. No, I felt sorry for her. I realized that she was dying of nostalgia. She had taken nostalgia as her false idol—her thin blanket—and it was murdering her.

"Nostalgia," I said to the other Indian man in the hospital.

"What?"

"Your dad, he sounds like he's got a bad case of nostalgia."

"Yeah, I hear you catch that from fucking old high school girlfriends," the man said. "What the hell you doing here anyway?"

"My dad just got his feet cut off," I said.

"Diabetes?"

"And vodka."

"Vodka straight up or with a nostalgia chaser?"

"Both."

"Natural causes for an Indian."

"Yep."

There wasn't much to say after that.

"Well, I better get back," the man said. "Otherwise, my dad might wave an eagle feather and change my name."

"Hey, wait," I said.

"Yeah?"

"Can I ask you a favor?"

"What?"

"My dad, he's in the recovery room," I said. "Well, it's more like a hallway, and he's freezing, and they've only got these shitty little blankets, and I came looking for Indians in the hospital because I figured—well, I guessed if I found any Indians, they might have some good blankets."

"So you want to borrow a blanket from us?" the man asked.

"Yeah."

"Because you thought some Indians would just happen to have some extra blankets lying around?"

"Yeah."

"That's fucking ridiculous."

"I know."

"And it's racist."

"I know."

"You're stereotyping your own damn people."

"I know."

"But damn if we don't have a room full of Pendleton blankets. New ones. Jesus, you'd think my sister was having, like, a dozen babies."

Five minutes later, carrying a Pendleton Star Blanket, the Indian man walked out of his sister's hospital room, accompanied by his father, who wore Levi's, a black T-shirt, and eagle feathers in his gray braids.

"We want to give your father this blanket," the old man said. "It was meant for my grandson, but I think it will be good for your father, too."

"Thank you."

"Let me bless it. I will sing a healing song for the blanket. And for your father."

I flinched. This guy wanted to sing a song? That was dangerous. This song could take two minutes or two hours. It was impossible to know. Hell, considering how desperate this old man was to be seen as holy, he might sing for a week. I couldn't let this guy begin his song without issuing a caveat.

"My dad," I said. "I really need to get back to him. He's really sick."

"Don't worry," the old man said and winked. "I'll sing one of my short ones."

Jesus, who'd ever heard of a self-aware fundamentalist? The son, perhaps not the unbeliever he'd pretended to be, sang backup as his father launched into his radio-friendly honor song, just three-and-a-half minutes, like the length of any Top 40 rock song of the last fifty years. But here's the funny thing: the old man couldn't sing very well. If you were going to have the balls to sing healing songs in hospital hallways, then you should logically have a great voice, right? But, no, this guy couldn't keep the tune. And his voice cracked and wavered. Does a holy song lose its power if its singer is untalented?

"That is your father's song," the old man said when he was finished. "I give it to him. I will never sing it again. It belongs to your father now."

Behind his back, the old man's son rolled his eyes and walked back into his sister's room.

"Okay, thank you," I said. I felt like an ass, accepting the blanket and the old man's good wishes, but silently mocking them at the same time. But maybe the old man did have some power, some real medicine, because he peeked into my brain.

"It doesn't matter if you believe in the healing song," the old man said. "It only matters that the blanket heard."

"Where have you been?" my father asked when I returned. "I'm cold."

"I know, I know," I said. "I found you a blanket. A good one. It will keep you warm."

I draped the Star Blanket over my father. He pulled the thick wool up to his chin. And then he began to sing. It was a healing song, not the same song that I had just heard, but a healing song nonetheless. My father could sing beautifully. I wondered if it was proper for a man to sing a healing song for himself. I wondered if my father needed help with the song. I hadn't sung for many years, not like that, but I joined him. I knew this song would not bring back my father's feet. This song would not repair my father's bladder, kidneys, lungs, and heart. This song would not prevent my father from drinking a bottle of vodka as soon as he could sit up in bed. This song would not defeat death. No, I thought, this song is temporary, but right now, temporary is good enough. And it was a good song. Our voices filled the recovery hallway. The sick and healthy stopped to listen. The nurses, even the remote black one, unconsciously took a few steps toward us. The black nurse sighed and smiled. I smiled back. I knew what she was thinking. Sometimes, even after all of these years, she could still be surprised by her work. She still marveled at the infinite and ridiculous faith of other people.

5. DOCTOR'S OFFICE

I took my kids with me to my doctor, a handsome man—a reservist—who'd served in both Iraq wars. I told him I could not hear. He said his nurse would likely have to clear wax and fluid, but when he scoped inside, he discovered nothing.

"Nope, it's all dry in there," he said.

He led my sons and me to the audiologist in the other half of the building. I was scared, but I wanted my children to remain calm, so I tried to stay measured. More than anything, I wanted my wife to materialize.

During the hearing test, I heard only 30 percent of the clicks, bells, and words—I apparently had nerve and bone conductive deafness. My inner ear thumped and thumped.

How many cockroaches were in my head?

My doctor said, "We need an MRI of your ear and brain, and maybe we'll find out what's going on."

Maybe? That word terrified me.

What the fuck was wrong with my fucking head? Had my hydrocephalus come back for blood? Had my levees burst? Was I going to flood?

6. HYDROCEPHALUS

Merriam-Webster's dictionary defines hydrocephalus as "an abnormal increase in the amount of cerebrospinal fluid within the cranial cavity that is accompanied by expansion of the cerebral ventricles, enlargement of the skull and especially the forehead, and atrophy of the brain." I define hydrocephalus as "the obese, imperialistic water demon that nearly killed me when I was six months old."

In order to save my life, and stop the water demon, I had brain surgery in 1967 when I was six months old. I was supposed to die. Obviously, I didn't. I was supposed to be severely mentally disabled. I have only minor to moderate brain damage. I was supposed to have epileptic seizures. Those I did have, until I was seven years old. I was on phenobarbital, a major league antiseizure medication, for six years.

Some of the side effects of phenobarbital—all of which I suffered to some degree or another as a child—include sleepwalking, agitation, confusion, depression, nightmares, hallucinations, insomnia, apnea, vomiting, constipation, dermatitis, fever, liver and bladder dysfunction, and psychiatric disturbance.

How do you like them cockroaches?

And now, as an adult, thirty-three years removed from phenobarbital, I still suffer—to one degree or another—from sleepwalking, agitation, confusion, depression, nightmares, hallucinations, insomnia, bladder dysfunction, apnea, and dermatitis.

Is there such a disease as post-phenobarbital traumatic stress syndrome?

Most hydrocephalics are shunted. A shunt is essentially brain plumbing that drains away excess cerebrospinal fluid. Those shunts often fuck up and stop working. I know hydrocephalics who've had a hundred or more shunt revisions and repairs. That's over a hundred brain surgeries. There are ten fingers on any surgeon's hand. There are two or three surgeons working on any particular brain. That means certain hydrocephalics have had their brains fondled by three thousand fingers.

I'm lucky. I was only temporarily shunted. And I hadn't suffered any hydrocephalic symptoms since I was seven years old.

And then, in July 2008, at the age of forty-one, I went deaf in my right ear.

7. CONVERSATION

Sitting in my car in the hospital parking garage, I called my brother-in-law, who was babysitting my sons.

"Hey, it's me. I just got done with the MRI on my head."

My brother-in-law said something unintelligible. I realized I was holding my cell to my bad ear. And switched it to the good ear.

"The MRI dude didn't look happy," I said.

"That's not good," my brother-in-law said.

"No, it's not. But he's just a tech guy, right? He's not an expert on brains or anything. He's just the photographer, really. And he doesn't know anything about ears or deafness or anything, I don't think. Ah, hell, I don't know what he knows. I just didn't like the look on his face when I was done."

"Maybe he just didn't like you."

"Well, I got worried when I told him I had hydrocephalus when I was a baby and he didn't seem to know what that was."

"Nobody knows what that is."

"That's the truth. Have you fed the boys dinner?"

"Yeah, but I was scrounging. There's not much here."

"I better go shopping."

"Are you sure? I can do it if you need me to. I can shop the shit out of Trader Joe's."

"No, it'll be good for me. I feel good. I fell asleep during the MRI. And I kept twitching. So we had to do it twice. Otherwise, I would've been done earlier."

"That's okay; I'm okay; the boys are okay"

"You know, before you go in that MRI tube, they ask you what kind of music you want to listen to—jazz, classical, rock, or country—and I remembered how my dad spent a lot of time in MRI tubes near the end of his life. So I was wondering what kind of music he always chose. I mean, he couldn't hear shit anyway by that time, but he still must have chosen something. And I wanted to choose the same thing he chose. So I picked country."

"Was it good country?"

"It was fucking Shania Twain and Faith Hill shit. I was hoping for George Jones or Loretta Lynn, or even some George Strait. Hell, I would've cried if they'd played Charley Pride or Freddy Fender."

"You wanted to hear the alcoholic Indian father jukebox."

"Hey, that's my line. You can't quote me to me."

"Why not? You're always quoting you to you."

"Kiss my ass. So, hey, I'm okay, I think. And I'm going to the store. But I think I already said that. Anyway, I'll see you in a bit. You want anything?"

"Ah, man, I love Trader Joe's. But you know what's bad about them? You fall in love with something they have—they stock it for a year—and then it just disappears. They had those wontons I loved and now they don't. I was willing to shop for you and the boys, but I don't want anything for me. I'm on a one-man hunger strike against them."

8. WORLD PHONE CONVERSATION, 3 A.M.

After I got home with yogurt and turkey dogs and Cinnamon Toast Crunch and my brother-in-law had left, I watched George Romero's *Diary of the Dead*, and laughed at myself for choosing a movie that featured dozens of zombies getting shot in the head.

When the movie was over, I called my wife, nine hours ahead in Italy.

"I should come home," she said.

"No, I'm okay," I said. "Come on, you're in Rome. What are you seeing today?"

"The Vatican."

"You can't leave now. You have to go and steal something. It will be revenge for every Indian. Or maybe you can plant an eagle feather and claim that you just discovered Catholicism."

"I'm worried."

"Yeah, Catholicism has always worried me."

"Stop being funny. I should see if I can get Mom and me on a flight tonight."

"No, no, listen, your mom is old. This might be her last adventure. It might be your last adventure with her. Stay there. Say Hi to the Pope for me. Tell him I like his shoes."

That night, my sons climbed into bed with me. We all slept curled around one another like sled dogs in a snowstorm. I woke, hour by hour, and touched my head and neck to check if they had changed shape—to feel if antennae were growing. Some insects "hear" with their antennae. Maybe that's what was happening to me.

9. VALEDICTION

My father, a part-time blue collar construction worker, died in March 2003, from full-time alcoholism. On his deathbed, he asked me to "Turn down that light, please."

"Which light?" I asked.

"The light on the ceiling."

"Dad, there's no light."

"It burns my skin, son. It's too bright. It hurts my eyes."

"Dad, I promise you there's no light."

"Don't lie to me, son, it's God passing judgment on Earth."

"Dad, you've been an atheist since '79. Come on, you're just remembering your birth. On your last day, you're going back to your first."

"No, son, it's God telling me I'm doomed. He's using the brightest lights in the universe to show me the way to my flame-filled tomb."

"No, Dad, those lights were in your delivery room."

"If that's true, son, then turn down my mother's womb."

We buried my father in the tiny Catholic cemetery on our reservation. Since I am named after him, I had to stare at a tombstone with my name on it.

10. BATTLE FATIGUE

Two months after my father's death, I began research on a book about our family's history with war. I had a cousin who had served as a cook in the first Iraq war in 1991; I had another cousin who served in the Vietnam War in 1964–65, also as a cook; and my father's father, Adolph, served in WWII and was killed in action on Okinawa Island, on April 5, 1946.

During my research, I interviewed thirteen men who'd served with my cousin in Vietnam but could find only one surviving man who'd served with my grandfather. This is a partial transcript of that taped interview, recorded with a microphone and an iPod on January 14, 2008:

Me: Ah, yes, hello, I'm here in Livonia, Michigan, to inter-view—well, perhaps you should introduce yourself, please?

Leonard Elmore: What?

Me: Um, oh, I'm sorry, I was asking if you could perhaps introduce yourself.

LE: You're going to have to speak up. I think my hearing aid is going low on power or something.

Me: That is a fancy thing in your ear.

LE: Yeah, let me mess with it a bit. I got a remote control for it. I can listen to the TV, the stereo, and the telephone with this thing. It's fancy. It's one of them blue tooth hearing aids. My grandson bought it for me. Wait, okay, there we go. I can hear now. So what were you asking?

Me: I was hoping you could introduce yourself into my re-corder here.

LE: Sure, my name is Leonard Elmore.

Me: How old are you?

LE: I'm eighty-five-and-a-half years old (laughter). My great-grandkids are always saying they're seven-and-a-half or nine-and-a-half or whatever. It just cracks me up to say the same thing at my age.

Me: So, that's funny, um, but I'm here to ask you some questions about my grandfather—

LE: Adolph. It's hard to forget a name like that. An Indian named Adolph and there was that Nazi bastard named Adolph. Your grandfather caught plenty of grief over that. But we mostly called him "Chief," did you know that?

Me: I could have guessed.

LE: Yeah, nowadays, I suppose it isn't a good thing to call an Indian "Chief," but back then, it was what we did. I served with a few Indians. They didn't segregate them Indians, you know, not like the black boys. I know you aren't supposed to call them boys anymore, but they were boys. All of us were boys, I guess. But the thing is, those Indian boys lived and slept and ate with us white boys. They were right there with us. But, anyway, we called all them Indians "Chief." I bet you've been called "Chief" a few times yourself.

Me: Just once.

LE: Were you all right with it?

Me: I threw a basketball in the guy's face.

LE: (laughter)

Me: We live in different times.

LE: Yes, we do. Yes, we do.

Me: So, perhaps you could, uh, tell me something about my grandfather.

LE: I can tell you how he died.

Me: Really?

LE: Yeah, it was on Okinawa, and we hit the beach, and, well, it's hard to talk about it—it was the worst thing—it was Hell—no, that's not even a good way to describe it. I'm not a writer like you—I'm not a poet—so I don't have the words—but just think of it this way—that beach, that island—was filled with sons and fathers—men who loved and were loved—American and Japanese and Okinawan—and all of us were dying—were being killed by other sons and fathers who also loved and were loved.

Me: That sounds like poetry—tragic poetry—to me.

LE: Well, anyway, it was like that. Fire everywhere. And two of our boys—Jonesy and O'Neal—went down—were wounded in the open on the sand. And your grandfather—who was just this little man—barely five feet tall and maybe one hundred and thirty pounds—he just ran out there and picked up those two guys—one on each shoulder—and carried them to cover. Hey, are you okay, son?

Me: Yes, I'm sorry. But, well, the thing is, I knew my grandfather was a war hero—he won twelve medals—but I could never find out what he did to win the medals.

LE: I didn't know about any medals. I just know what I saw. Your grandfather saved those two boys, but he got shot in the back doing it. And he laid there in the sand—I was lying right beside him—and he died.

Me: Did he say anything before he died?

LE: Hold on. I need to—

Me: Are you okay?

LE: It's just—I can't—

Me: I'm sorry. Is there something wrong?

LE: No, it's just—with your book and everything—I know you want something big here. I know you want something big from your grandfather. I knew you hoped he'd said something huge and poetic, like maybe something you could have written, and, honestly, I was thinking about lying to you. I was thinking about making up something as beautiful as I could. Something about love and forgiveness and courage and all that. But I couldn't think of anything good enough. And I didn't want to lie to you. So I have to be honest and say that your grandfather didn't say anything. He just died there in the sand. In silence.

11. ORPHANS

I was worried that I had a brain tumor. Or that my hydrocephalus had returned. I was scared that I was going to die and orphan my sons. But, no, their mother was coming home from Italy. No matter what happened to me, their mother would rescue them.

"I'll be home in sixteen hours," my wife said over the phone.

"I'll be here," I said. "I'm just waiting on news from my doctor."

12. COFFEE SHOP NEWS

While I waited, I asked my brother-in-law to watch the boys again because I didn't want to get bad news with them in the room.

Alone and haunted, I wandered the mall, tried on new clothes, and waited for my cell phone to ring.

Two hours later, I was uncomposed and wanted to murder everything, so I drove south to a coffee joint, a spotless place called Dirty Joe's.

Yes, I was silly enough to think that I'd be calmer with a caffeinated drink.

As I sat outside on a wooden chair and sipped my coffee, I cursed the vague, rumbling, ringing noise in my ear. And yet, when my cell phone rang, I held it to my deaf ear.

"Hello, hello," I said and wondered if it was a prank call, then remembered and switched the phone to my left ear.

"Hello," my doctor said. "Are you there?"

"Yes," I said. "So, what's going on?"

"There are irregularities in your head."

"My head's always been wrong,"

"It's good to have a sense of humor," my doctor said. "You have a small tumor that is called a meningioma. They grow in the meninges membranes that lie between your brain and your skull."

"Shit," I said. "I have cancer."

"Well," my doctor said. "These kinds of tumors are usually noncancerous. And they grow very slowly, so in six months or so, we'll do another MRI. Don't worry. You're going to be okay."

"What about my hearing?" I asked.

"We don't know what might be causing the hearing loss, but you should start a course of prednisone, the steroid, just to go with the odds. Your deafness might lessen if left alone, but we've had success with the steroids in bringing back hearing. There *are* side effects, like insomnia, weight gain, night sweats, and depression."

"Oh, boy," I said. "Those side effects might make up most of my personality already. Will the 'roids also make me quick to pass judgment? And I've always wished I had a dozen more skin tags and moles."

The doctor chuckled. "You're a funny man."

I wanted to throw my phone into a wall but I said good-bye instead and glared at the tumorless people and their pretty tumorless heads.

13. Meningioma

Mayoclinic.com defines "meningioma" as "a tumor that arises from the meninges—the membranes that surround your brain and spinal cord. The majority of meningioma cases are noncancerous (benign), though rarely a meningioma can be cancerous (malignant)."

Okay, that was a scary and yet strangely positive definition. No one ever wants to read the word "malignant" unless one is reading a Charles Dickens novel about an evil landlord, but "benign" and "majority" are two things that go great together.

From the University of Washington Medical School Web site I learned that meningioma tumors "are usually benign, slow growing and do not spread into normal brain tissue. Typically, a meningioma grows inward, causing pressure on the brain or spinal cord. It may grow outward toward the skull, causing it to thicken."

So, wait, what the fuck? A meningioma can cause pressure on the brain and spinal fluid? Oh, you mean, just like fucking hydrocephalus? Just like the water demon that once tried to crush my brain and kill me? Armed with this new information—with these new questions—I called my doctor.

"Hey, you're okay," he said. "We're going to closely monitor you. And your meningioma is very small."

"Okay, but I just read—"

"Did you go on the Internet?"

"Yes."

"Which sites?"

"Mayo Clinic and the University of Washington."

"Okay, so those are pretty good sites. Let me look at them." I listened to my doctor type.

"Okay, those are accurate," he said.

"What do you mean by accurate?" I asked. "I mean, the whole pressure on the brain thing, that sounds like hydrocephalus."

"Well, there were some irregularities in your MRI that were the burr holes from your surgery and there seems to be some scarring and perhaps you had an old concussion, but other than that, it all looks fine."

"But what about me going deaf? Can't these tumors make you lose hearing?"

"Yes, but only if they're located near an auditory nerve. And your tumor is not."

"Can this tumor cause pressure on my brain?"

"It could, but yours is too small for that."

"So, I'm supposed to trust you on the tumor thing when you can't figure out the hearing thing?"

"The MRI revealed the meningioma, but that's just an image. There is no physical correlation between your deafness and the tumor. Do the twenty-day treatment of Prednisone and the audiologist and I will examine your ear, and your hearing. Then, if there's no improvement, we'll figure out other ways of treating you."

"But you won't be treating the tumor?"

"Like I said, we'll scan you again in six to nine months—"

"You said six before."

"Okay, in six months we'll take another MRI, and if it has grown significantly—or has changed shape or location or anything dramatic—then we'll talk about treatment options. But if you look on the Internet, and I know you're going to spend a lot of time obsessing on this—as you should—I'll tell you what you'll find. About 5 percent of the population has these things and they live their whole lives with these undetected meningiomas. And they can become quite large—without any side effects—and are only found at autopsies conducted for other causes of death. And even when these kinds of tumors become invasive or dangerous they are still rarely fatal. And your tumor, even if it grows fairly quickly, will not likely become an issue for many years, decades. So that's what I can tell you right now. How are you feeling?"

"Freaked and fucked."

I wanted to feel reassured, but I had a brain tumor. How does one feel any optimism about being diagnosed with a brain tumor? Even if that brain tumor is neither cancerous nor interested in crushing one's brain?

14. Drugstore Indian

In Bartell's Drugs, I gave the pharmacist my prescription for Prednisone.

"Is this your first fill with us?" she asked.

"No," I said. "And it won't be the last."

I felt like an ass, but she looked bored.

"It'll take thirty minutes," she said, "more or less. We'll page you over the speakers."

I don't think I'd ever felt weaker, or more vulnerable, or more absurd. I was the weak antelope in the herd—yeah, the mangy fucker with the big limp and a sign that read, "Eat me! I'm a gimp!"

So, for thirty minutes, I walked through the store and found myself shoving more and more useful shit into my shopping basket, as if I were filling my casket with the things I'd need in the afterlife. I grabbed toothpaste, a Swiss Army knife, moisturizer, mouthwash, non-stick Band-Aids, antacid, protein bars, and extra razor blades. I grabbed pen and paper. And I also grabbed an ice scraper and sunscreen. Who can predict what weather awaits us in Heaven?

This random shopping made me feel better for a few minutes but then I stopped and walked to the toy aisle. My boys needed gifts: Lego cars or something, for a lift, a shot of capitalistic joy. But the selection of proper toys is art and science. I have been wrong as often as right and heard the sad song of a disappointed son.

Shit, if I died, I knew my sons would survive, even thrive, because of their graceful mother.

I thought of my father's life: he was just six when his father was killed in World War II. Then his mother, ill with tuberculosis, died a few months later. Six years old, my father was cratered. In most ways, he never stopped being six. There was no religion, no magic tricks, and no song or dance that helped my father.

Jesus, I needed a drink of water, so I found the fountain and drank and drank until the pharmacist called my name.

"Have you taken these before?" she asked.

"No," I said, "but they're going to kick my ass, aren't they?"

That made the pharmacist smile, so I felt sadly and briefly worthwhile. But another customer, some nosy hag, said, "You've got a lot of sleepless nights ahead of you."

I was shocked. I stammered, glared at her, and said, "Miss, how is this any of your business? Please, just fuck all the way off, okay?"

She had no idea what to say, so she just turned and walked away and I pulled out my credit card and paid far too much for my goddamn steroids, and forgot to bring the toys home to my boys.

15. Exit Interview for My Father

- True or False?: when a reservation-raised Native American dies of alcoholism it should be considered death by natural causes.

- Do you understand the term *wanderlust*, and if you do, can you please tell us, in twenty-five words or less, what place made you wanderlust the most?
- Did you, when drunk, ever get behind the tattered wheel of a '76 Ford three-speed van and somehow drive your family one thousand miles on an empty tank of gas?
- Is it true that the only literary term that has any real meaning in the Native American world is *road movie*?
- During the last road movie you saw, how many times did the characters ask, "Are we there yet?"
- How many times, during any of your road trips, did your children ask, "Are we there yet?"
- In twenty-five words or less, please define *there*.
- Sir, in your thirty-nine years as a parent, you broke your children's hearts, collectively and individually, 612 times and you did this without ever striking any human being in anger. Does this absence of physical violence make you a better man than you might otherwise have been?
- Without using the words *man* or *good*, can you please define what it means to be a good man?
- Do you think you will see angels before you die? Do you think angels will come to escort you to Heaven? As the angels are carrying you to Heaven, how many times will you ask, "Are we there yet?"
- Your son distinctly remembers stopping once or twice a month at that grocery store in Freeman, Washington, where you would buy him a red-white-and-blue rocket popsicle and purchase for yourself a pickled pig foot. Your son

distinctly remembers the feet still had their toenails and little tufts of pig fur. Could this be true? Did you actually eat such horrendous food?

- Your son has often made the joke that you were the only Indian of your generation who went to Catholic school on purpose. This is, of course, a tasteless joke that makes light of the forced incarceration and subsequent physical, spiritual, cultural, and sexual abuse of tens of thousands of Native American children in Catholic and Protestant boarding schools. In consideration of your son's questionable judgment in telling jokes, do you think there should be any moral limits placed on comedy?

- Your oldest son and your two daughters, all over thirty-six years of age, still live in your house. Do you think this is a lovely expression of tribal culture? Or is it a symptom of extreme familial codependence? Or is it both things at the same time?

- F. Scott Fitzgerald wrote that the sign of a superior mind "is the ability to hold two opposing ideas at the same time." Do you believe this is true? And is it also true that you once said, "The only time white people tell the truth is when they keep their mouths shut"?

- A poet once wrote, "Pain is never added to pain. It multiplies." Can you tell us, in twenty-five words or less, exactly how much we all hate mathematical blackmail?

- Your son, in defining you, wrote this poem to explain one of the most significant nights in his life:

MUTUALLY ASSURED DESTRUCTION

When I was nine, my father sliced his knee
With a chain saw. But he let himself bleed
And finished cutting down one more tree
Before his boss drove him to EMERGENCY.

Late that night, stoned on morphine and beer,
My father needed my help to steer
His pickup into the woods. "Watch for deer,"
My father said. "Those things just appear

Like magic." It was an Indian summer
And we drove through warm rain and thunder,
Until we found that chain saw, lying under
The fallen pine. Then I watched, with wonder,

As my father, shotgun-rich and impulse-poor,
Blasted that chain saw dead. "What was that for?"
I asked. "Son," my father said, "here's the score.
Once a thing tastes blood, it will come for more."

- Well, first of all, as you know, you did cut your knee with a chain saw, but in direct contradiction to your son's poem:

  A) You immediately went to the emergency room after injuring yourself.
  B) Your boss called your wife, who drove you to the emergency room.

C) You were given morphine but even you were not alcoholically stupid enough to drink alcohol while on serious narcotics.

D) You and your son did not get into the pickup that night.

E) And even if you had driven the pickup, you were not injured seriously enough to need your son's help with the pedals and/or steering wheel.

F) You never in your life used the word, *appear*, and certainly never used the phrase, *like magic*.

G) You also agree that Indian summer is a fairly questionable seasonal reference for an Indian poet to use.

H) What the fuck is "warm rain and thunder"? Well, everybody knows what warm rain is, but what the fuck is warm thunder?

I) You never went looking for that chain saw because it belonged to the Spokane tribe of Indians and what kind of freak would want to reclaim the chain saw that had just cut the shit out of his knee?

J) You also agree that the entire third stanza of this poem sounds like a Bruce Springsteen song and not necessarily one of the great ones.

K) And yet, "shotgun-rich and impulse-poor" is one of the greatest descriptions your son has ever written and probably redeems the entire poem.

L) You never owned a shotgun. You did own a few rifles during your lifetime, but did not own even so much as a pellet gun during the last thirty years of your life.

M) You never said, in any context, "Once a thing tastes your blood, it will come for more."

N) But you, as you read it, know that it is absolutely true and does indeed sound suspiciously like your entire life philosophy.

O) Other summations of your life philosophy include: "I'll be there before the next teardrop falls."

P) And: "If God really loved Indians, he would have made us white people."

Q) And: "Oscar Robertson should be the man on the NBA logo. They only put Jerry West on there because he's a white guy."

R) And: "A peanut butter sandwich with onions. Damn, that's the way to go."

S) And: "Why eat a pomegranate when you can eat a plain old apple. Or peach. Or orange. When it comes to fruit and vegetables, only eat the stuff you know how to grow."

T) And: "If you really want a woman to love you, then you have to dance. And if you don't want to dance, then you're going to have to work extrahard to make a woman love you forever, and you will always run the risk that she will leave you at any second for a man who knows how to tango."

U) And: "I really miss those cafeterias they use to have in Kmart. I don't know why they stopped having those. If there is a Heaven then I firmly believe it's a Kmart cafeteria."

V) And: "A father always knows what his sons are doing. For instance, boys, I knew you were sneaking that *Hustler* magazine out of my bedroom. You remember that one? Where actors who looked like Captain Kirk and

Lieutenant Uhura were screwing on the bridge of the *Enterprise*. Yeah, that one. I know you kept borrowing it. I let you borrow it. Remember this: men and pornography are like plants and sunshine. To me, porn is photosynthesis."

W) And: "Your mother is a better man than me. Mothers are almost always better men than men are."

16. REUNION

After she returned from Italy, my wife climbed into bed with me. I felt like I had not slept comfortably in years.

I said, "There was a rumor that I'd grown a tumor but I killed it with humor."

"How long have you been waiting to tell me that one?" she asked.

"Oh, probably since the first time some doctor put his fingers in my brain."

We made love. We fell asleep. But I, agitated by the steroids, woke at two, three, four, and five a.m. The bed was killing my back so I lay flat on the floor. I wasn't going to die anytime soon, at least not because of my little friend, Mr. Tumor, but that didn't make me feel any more comfortable or comforted. I felt distant from the world—from my wife and sons, from my mother and siblings—from all of my friends. I felt closer to those who've always had fingers in their brains.

And I didn't feel any closer to the world six months later when another MRI revealed that my meningioma had not grown in size or changed its shape.

"You're looking good," my doctor said. "How's your hearing?"

"I think I've got about 90 percent of it back."

"Well, then, the steroids worked. Good."

And I didn't feel any more intimate with God nine months later when one more MRI made my doctor hypothesize that my meningioma might only be more scar tissue from the hydrocephalus.

"Frankly," my doctor said. "Your brain is beautiful."

"Thank you," I said, though it was the oddest compliment I'd ever received.

I wanted to call up my father and tell him that a white man thought my brain was beautiful. But I couldn't tell him anything. He was dead. I told my wife and sons that I was okay. I told my mother and siblings. I told my friends. But none of them laughed as hard about my beautiful brain as I knew my father would have. I miss him, the drunk bastard. I would always feel closest to the man who had most disappointed me.

The Theology of Reptiles

We found a snake, dead in midmolt.
"It's almost like two snakes," I said.
My brother grabbed it by the head
And said, "It just needs lightning bolts."

Laughing, he jumped the creek and draped
The snake over an electric fence.
Was my brother being cruel? Yes,
But we were shocked when that damn snake

Spiraled off the wire and splayed,
Alive, on the grass, made a fist
Of itself, then, gorgeous and pissed,
Uncurled, stood on end, and swayed

For my brother, who, bemused and odd,
Had somehow become one snake's god.

Catechism

Why did your big brother, during one hot summer, sleep in the hall-way closet?

My mother, a Spokane Indian, kept bags of fabric scraps in that hallway closet. My brother arranged these scrap bags into shapes that approximated a mattress and pillows. My mother used these scraps to make quilts.

As an Indian, were you taught to worship the sun or the moon?

My mother was (and is) a Protestant of random varieties. My late father, a Coeur d'Alene, was a Catholic until the day that he decided to become an atheist. But it wasn't until twelve years after he decided to become an atheist that he made this information public.
MY MOTHER: "Why did you wait so long to tell us?"
MY FATHER: "I didn't want to make a quick decision."

Do you think that religious ceremony is an effective treatment for grief?

My mother once made a quilt from dozens of pairs of second- and third- and fourth-hand blue jeans that she bought at Goodwill, the Salvation Army, Value Village, and garage sales.

My late sister studied my mother's denim quilt and said, "That's a lot of pants. There's been a lot of ass in those pants. This is a blanket of asses."

If your reservation is surrounded on all sides by two rivers and a creek, doesn't that make it an island?

A Coeur d'Alene Indian holy man—on my father's side—received this vision: Three crows, luminescent and black, except for collars of white feathers, perched in a pine tree above my ancestor's camp and told him that three strangers would soon be arriving and their advice must be heeded or the Coeur d'Alene would vanish from the earth. The next day, the first Jesuits—three men in black robes with white collars—walked into a Coeur d'Alene Indian fishing camp.

Do you believe that God, in the form of his son, Jesus Christ, once walked the Earth?

Thus the Coeur d'Alene soon became, and remain, among the most Catholicized Indians in the country.

Has any member of the clergy ever given you a clear and concise explanation of this Holy Ghost business?

Therefore, nuns taught my father, as a child, to play classical piano.

Do you think that Beethoven was not actually deaf and was just having a laugh at his family's expense?

By the time I was born, my father had long since stopped playing piano.

ME: "Dad, what did the nuns teach you to play?"

HIM: "I don't want to talk about that shit."

After you catch a sliver from a wooden crucifix, how soon afterward will you gain superpowers?

When he was drunk, my father would sit at the kitchen table and hum an indecipherable tune while playing an imaginary keyboard.

Did your mother ever make a quilt that featured a real piano keyboard?

I have mounted my father's imaginary keyboard on my office wall.

ME: "And, here, on the wall, is my favorite work of art."

GUEST: "I don't see anything."

ME: "It's an installation piece created by my father."

GUEST: "I still can't see anything."

ME: "Exactly."

If you could only pick one word to describe your family, then what would that word be?

Honorificabilitudinitas.

Is that a real word?

Yes, Shakespeare used it. It means "The state of being able to achieve honors."

So you're stating your multisyllabic, overeducated, and pretentious belief that your family is and was in a state of being able to achieve honors?

Yep.

What kind of honors?

Whenever anybody in my family did something good, my mother would make an honor blanket. She used pieces of people's clothes and stitched in little photographs and images or important dates and names. Very ornate.

So if your mother were going to honor your family's religious history with an honor blanket, what shape would it take?

It wouldn't be an honor blanket. It would be a quilt of guilt.

Do you actually believe in God?

My mother kept scraps of God in our hallway closet. My big brother arranged these scraps of God into shapes that approximated a mattress and pillows, and slept in that closet. My mother once used these scraps of God to make an epic quilt. My late sister studied this quilt and said, "That's a lot of God. There's been a lot of God in this God. This is a blanket of God."

However, my late father, when drunk, would sit at the kitchen table and sing to an indecipherable God while playing an imaginary keyboard.

But what do you think about God?

I'm at my kitchen window, and I'm watching three crows perched on the telephone wire. I think they're talking trash about me.

ODE TO SMALL-TOWN SWEETHEARTS

O, when you are driving through a blizzard
    And your vision has been reduced—
        Has been scissored—
    Into two headlights and a noose,
How joyous to come upon the Wizard
Of Snowplows driving his glorious machine.
        Now you will survive if you ride
           In his slipstream.
        He pushes back the fear and ice.
This is not a time for prayer, so you scream

With joy (*Snowplow! Snowplow! Snowplow! Snowplow!*)
        As he leads you into the next
           Snowed-in town.
        You are not dead! You did not wreck!
And you know a family who live here—the Browns.
They run that little diner on Main Street.
        It must be shut at this dark hour—
           Quarter past three—
        But the son, Mark, plays power
Forward for the high school, the Wolverines—

And once broke your nose with a stray elbow
      While playing some tough-ass defense—
      And you know him and call him friend.
So you park your car and trudge through the snow—
Cursing and/or blessing this fierce winter—
      To find Mark and his dad awake
      And cooking chicken-fried steaks
For a dozen other survivors and sinners.
"Dang," Mark says. "Why are you out in this stuff?"
      "For a girl," you say. And Mark nods.
      Mortals have always fought the gods
And braved epic storms for love and/or lust.
So don't be afraid to speak honestly
      About how you obeyed beauty's call.
      And though your triumph was small,
You can still sing of your teenage odyssey.

THE SENATOR'S SON

I hadn't seen my best friend in sixteen years, half of our lives ago, so I didn't recognize him when I pulled him out of the car and hit him in the face. I'd taken a few self-defense classes, so I'd learned to strike with the heel of my open hand. It's too easy to break fingers if one slams a fist against the hard bones of the head. A good student, I also remembered to stand with my feet a shoulder's width apart, for maximum balance, and to twist my hips and shoulders back before I thrust forward, for maximum leverage and striking power. And so, maximally educated, I hit my best friend and snapped his nose.

It made an astonishing noise. I imagine it could have been heard a block away. And the blood! Oh, his red glow drenched my shirt. He screamed, slumped back against his car, and slid to the ground. After that, it would have been impossible to recognize him because his face was a bloody mask. Drunk and enraged, I tried to kick him and might have beaten him unconscious or worse, but Bernard, my old college friend and drinking buddy, wrapped me in a bear hug and dragged me away.

Meanwhile, on the other side of the car, a faggot was winning his fight with Spence and Eddie, my other friends. They'd picked the wrong guy to bash. He was a talented fighter and danced, ducked, and threw mean kicks and elbows that *snap-snap-snap*ped into my friends' faces. This guy had to be one of those ultimate fighters, a mixed-martial artist.

This was in Seattle, on a dark street on Capitol Hill, the Pacific Northwest center of all things shabby, leftist, and gay. What was I, a straight Republican boy, doing on Capitol Hill? Well, it's also the home of my favorite Thai joint. I love peanut sauce and Asian beer. So my friends and I had feasted in celebration of my new junior partnership in the law firm of Robber Baron, Tax Dodger & Guilt-ridden Pro Bono. I was cash-heavy, lived in a three-bedroom condo overlooking Elliott Bay, and drove a hybrid Lexus SUV.

My father was in his first term as U.S. senator from Washington State, and he was already being talked about as a candidate for U.S. president. "I'm something different," he said to me once. "This country wants Jimmy Stewart. And I am Jimmy Stewart."

It was true. My father was handsome without being beautiful, intelligent without being pretentious, and charming without being sexual. And he was a widower, a single father who'd raised an accomplished son. My mother had died of breast cancer when I was six years old, and my father, too much in love with her memory, had never remarried. He was now as devoted and loyal to curing breast cancer as he had been to my mother.

A University of Washington Law graduate, he had begun life as the only son of a wheat farmer and his schoolteacher wife. Eagle Scout, captain of the basketball team, and homecoming king, my father was the perfect candidate. He was a city commissioner, then a state representative, and then he ran for the U.S. Senate. After decades of voting for the sons and grandsons of privilege, the state's conservatives were excited, even proud, to vote for a public school veteran, a blue-collar prince, a farmer's son, a boy with dirt in his shoes.

His best moment during his senatorial campaign was during the final debate with his Democratic rival. "My opponent keeps talking about how hard he's worked for his country, for our state. And I'm sure he has. But my grandfather and my father taught me how to be a farmer. They taught me how to plant the seed and grow the wheat that feeds our country. I worked so hard that my hands bled; look, you can still see my scars. And I promise you, my fellow Washingtonians, that I will work hard for you. And I will work hard *with* you."

My father lost liberal King County by a surprisingly close margin but kicked ass in the rest of the state and was declared senator at 9:35 P.M. on the night of the election.

Yes, my father had become Jefferson Smith and had marched into the other Washington as the first real populist in decades.

I'm not ashamed to admit that I cried a little on the night my father was elected. You've seen the photograph. It was on the cover of the *Seattle Times* and was reprinted all over the country. Everybody assumed that I was happy for my father. Overjoyed, in fact. But I was also slapped hard by grief. I desperately missed my mother, but I desperately missed my father as well. You see, he was now a U.S. senator with presidential ambitions, and that meant he belonged to everybody. I knew I'd forever lost a huge part of his energy and time and, yes, his love; I'd have to share my father with the world. I also knew I'd lost my chance to ever be anything other than an all-star politician's son.

But who wants to hear the sob story of a senator's son? The real question is this: Why the hell would I risk my reputation and future and my father's political career—the entire meaning of his life—for a street fight—for a gay bashing? I don't know, but it was high comedy.

So I laughed while that tough faggot beat Spence and Eddie into the pavement. And I laughed as Bernard dragged me toward his car, shoved me into the backseat, and slammed the door shut. Then he popped open his trunk, grabbed his tire iron, and ran back toward the fight.

I powered down the window and watched Bernard race up to that black-belt fag and threaten him with the tire iron.

"Stop this shit," Bernard yelled. "Or I'll club you."

"Why the hell are you waving that thing at me?" he screamed back. "You started it."

It was true, playground true. Spence, Eddie, Bernie, and I had started it. We'd been drunkenly ambling down the street, cussing and singing, when Spence spotted the amorous boys in their car.

"Lookit," he said. "I hate them fucking fags."

That's all it took. With banshee war cries, Spence and Eddie flung open the driver's door and dragged out the tough guy. I dragged my best friend (whom I didn't recognize) from the passenger seat and broke his nose.

And now, I was drunk in Bernard's car and he was waving a tire iron at the guy we'd assaulted.

"Come on, Spence, Eddie," Bernard said.

Bloodied and embarrassed by their beating, Spence and Eddie staggered to their feet and made their way to the car. Still waving that tire iron, Bernard also came back to me. I laughed as Spence and Eddie slid into the backseat beside me. I laughed when Bernard climbed into the driver's seat and sped us away. And I was still laughing when I looked out the rear window and saw the tough guy tending to his broken and bloody lover boy. But even as I laughed, I knew that I had committed an awful and premeditated crime: I had threatened my father's career.

Sixteen years before I dragged him out of his car and punched him in the face, my best friend Jeremy and I were smart, handsome, and ambitious young Republicans at Madison Park School in Seattle. Private and wealthy, Madison Park was filled with leftist children, parents, and faculty. Jeremy and I were the founders and leaders of the Madison Park Carnivores, a conservative club whose mission was to challenge and ridicule all things leftist. Our self-published newspaper was called *Tooth & Claw*, borrowed from the poem by Alfred Tennyson, of course, and we filled its pages with lame satire, poorly drawn cartoons, impulsive editorials, and gushing profiles of local conservative heroes, including my father, a Republican city commissioner in a Democratic city.

Looking back, I suppose I became a Republican simply because my father was a Republican. It had never occurred to me to be something different. I loved and respected my father and wanted to be exactly like him. If he'd been a plumber or a housepainter, I suppose I would have followed him into those careers. But my father's politics and vocation were only the outward manifestations of his greatness. He was my hero because of his strict moral sense. Simply put, my father kept his promises.

Jeremy, a scholarship kid and the only child of a construction worker and a housewife, was far more right wing than I was. He worried that my father, who'd enjoyed bipartisan support as city commissioner, was a leftist in conservative disguise.

"He's going to Souter us," Jeremy said. "Just you watch, he's going to Souter us in the ass."

Jeremy and I always made fun of each other's fathers. Since black kids told momma jokes, we figured we should do the opposite.

"I bet your daddy sucks David Souter's dick," Jeremy said.

Jeremy hated Supreme Court Justice David Souter, who'd been named to the court by the first President Bush. Thought to be a typical constitutional conservative, Souter had turned into a moderate maverick, a supporter of abortion rights and opponent of sodomy laws, and was widely seen by the right as a political traitor. Jeremy thought Souter should be executed for treason. Was it hyperbole? Sure, but I think he almost meant it. He was a romantic when it came to political assassination.

"When I close one eye, you look just like Lee Harvey," I said.

"I'm not Oswald," he said. "Oswald was a communist. I'm more like John Wilkes Booth."

"Come on, man, read your history. Booth killed Lincoln over slavery."

"It wasn't about slavery. It was about states' rights."

Jeremy had always enjoyed a major-league hard-on for states' rights. If it had been up to him, the United States would be fifty separate countries with fifty separate interpretations of the Constitution.

Yes, compared to Jeremy, I was more Mao than Goldwater.

It was in January of our sophomore year at Madison Park that Jeremy stole me out of class and drove me to the McDonald's in North Bend, high up in the Cascade Mountains, more than thirty miles away from our hometown of Seattle.

"What are we doing way up here?" I asked.

"Getting lunch," he said.

So we ordered hamburgers and fries from the drive-thru and ate in the car.

"I love McDonald's fries," he said.

"Yeah, they're great," I said. "But you know the best thing about them?"

"What?"

"I love that McDonald's fries are exactly the same everywhere you go. The McDonald's fries in Washington, DC, are exactly like the fries in Seattle. Heck, the McDonald's fries in Paris, France, are exactly like the fries in Seattle."

"Yeah, so what's your point?" Jeremy asked.

"Well, I think the McDonald's fries in North Bend are also exactly like the fries in Washington, DC, Paris, and Seattle. Do you agree?"

"Yeah, that seems reasonable."

"Okay, then," I said. "If all the McDonald's fries in the world are the same, why did you drive me all the way up into the mountains to buy fries we could have gotten anywhere else in the world and, most especially, in Seattle?"

"To celebrate capitalism?"

"That's funny, but it's not true," I said. "What's really going on?"

"I have something I need to tell you," Jeremy said.

"And you couldn't have told me in Seattle?"

"I didn't want anybody to hear," he said.

"Oh, nobody is going to hear anything up here," I said.

Jeremy stared out the window at Mount Si, a four-thousand-foot-tall rock left behind by one glacier or another. I usually don't pay attention to such things, but I did that day. Along with my best friend, I stared at the mountain and wondered how old it was. That's the thing: the world is old. Ancient. And humans are so temporary. But who wants to think about such things? Who wants to feel small?

"I'm getting bored," I said.

"It's beautiful up here," he said. "So green and golden."

"Yeah, whatever, Robert Frost. Now tell me why we're here."

He looked me in the eye. Stared at me for a long time. *Regarded* me.

"What?" I said, and laughed, uncomfortable as hell.

"I'm a fag," he said.

"What?" I said, and laughed.

"I'm a fag," he repeated.

"That's not funny," I said, and laughed again.

"It's kind of funny."

"Okay, yeah, it's a little funny, but it's not true."

"Yes, it is. I am a fag."

I looked into his eyes. I stared at him for a long time. I *regarded* him.

"You're telling the truth," I said.

"Yeah."

"You're a fag."

"Yeah."

"Wow."

"That's all you have to say?"

"What else am I supposed to say?" I asked.

"I was hoping you would say more than 'Wow.'"

"Well, 'Wow' is all I got."

"Damn," he said. "And I had this all planned out."

He'd been thinking about coming out to me, his unveiling, for months. At first, he'd thought about telling me while we were engaged in some overtly masculine activity, like shouting out "I'm gay!" while we were butchering a hog. Or whispering, "I'm a really good shot—for a homosexual," while we were duck hunting. Or saying, "After I'm done with Sally's vagina, it's penis and scrotum from now on," as we were screwing twin sisters in their living room.

"I'm not gay," I said.

"I know."

"I'm just saying it, so it's out there, I'm not gay. Not at all."

"Jeez, come on, I'm not interested in you like that," he said. "I'm gay, but I'm not blind."

"That's funny," I said, but I didn't laugh. I was pissed. I felt betrayed. I'd been his best friend since we were five years old, and he'd never told me how he felt. He'd never told me who he was. He'd lied to me all those years. It made me wonder what else he had lied about. After all, don't liars tell lies about everything? And sure, maybe he'd lied to protect himself from hatred and judgment. And, yes, maybe he lied because he was scared of my reaction. But a lie is a lie, right? And lying is contagious.

"You're a liar," I said.

"I know," he said, and cried.

"Ah, man," I said, "don't cry."

And then I realized how many times I'd said that to girls, to *naked* girls. I mean, don't get me wrong. I'd seen him cry before—we'd wept together at baseball games and funerals—but not in that particular context.

"I'm getting sick to my stomach," I said, which made him cry all that much harder. It felt like I was breaking up with him or something.

Maybe I wasn't being fair. But all you ever hear about are gay people's feelings. What about the feelings of the gay people's friends and family? Nobody talks about our rights. Maybe people are born gay, okay? I can deal with that, but maybe some people, like me, are born afraid of gay people. Maybe that fear is encoded in my DNA.

"I'm not gay," I said.

"Stop saying that," he said.

But I couldn't help it. I had to keep saying it. I was scared. I wondered if I was gay and didn't know it. After all, I was best friends with a fag, and he'd seen me naked. I'd seen him naked so often I could have described him to a police sketch artist. It was crazy.

"I can't take this," I said, and got out of the car. I walked over to a picnic bench and sat.

Jeremy stayed in the car and stared through the windshield at me. He wanted my love, my sweet, predictable, platonic love, the same love I'd given to him for so many years. He'd chosen me as his confessor. I was supposed to be sacred for him. But I felt like God had put a shotgun against my head and pulled the trigger. I was suddenly Hamlet, and all the uses of the world were weary, stale, flat, and unprofitable.

Jeremy stared at me. He waited for me to take action. And yes, you can condemn me for my inaction and fear. But I was only sixteen years old. Nobody had taught me how to react in such a situation. I was young and terrified and I could not move. Jeremy waited for several long minutes. I sat still, so he gave me the finger and shouted, "Fuck off!" I gave him the finger and shouted, "Fuck off!" And then Jeremy drove away.

I sat there for a few hours, bewildered. Yes, I was bewildered. When was the last time a white American male was truly bewildered or would admit to such a thing? We had taken the world from covered wagons to space shuttles in seventy-five years. After such accomplishment, how could we ever get lost in the wilderness again? How could we not invent a device to guide our souls through the darkness?

I prayed to Our Father and I called my father. And one father remained silent and the other quickly came to get me.

In that North Bend parking lot, in his staid sedan, my father trembled with anger. "What the hell are you doing up here?" he asked. He'd left a meeting with the lame-duck mayor to rescue me.

"Jeremy drove me up."

"And where is Jeremy?"

"We got in a fight. He left."

"You got into a fight?" my father asked. "What are you, a couple of girls?"

"Jeremy is a fag," I said.

"What?"

"Jeremy told me he's a fag."

"Are you homosexual?" my father asked.

I laughed.

"This is not funny," he said.

"No, it's just that word, *homosexual;* it's a goofy word."

"You haven't answered the question."

"What question?"

"Are you homosexual?"

I knew that my father still loved me, that he was still my defender. But I wondered how strong he would defend me if I were indeed gay.

"Dad, I'm not a fag. I promise."

"Okay."

"Okay."

We sat there in silence. A masculine silence. Thick and strong. Oh, I'm full of shit. We were terrified and clueless.

"Okay, Dad, what happens next?"

"I was hoping to tell you this at a better time, but I'm going to run for the State House."

"Oh, wow," I said. "Congratulations."

"I'm happy you're happy. I hated to make the decision without your input, but it had to be that way."

"I understand."

"Yes, I knew you would. And I hope you understand a few other things."

And so my father, who'd never been comfortable with my private school privilege, transferred me from Madison Park to Garfield High, a racially mixed public school in a racially mixed neighborhood.

Let my father tell you why: "The Republican Party has, for decades, silently ignored the pernicious effects of racial segregation, while simultaneously resisting any public or private efforts at integration. That time has come to an end. I am a Republican, and I love my fellow Americans, regardless of race, color, or creed. But, of course, you've heard that before. Many Republicans have issued that same kind of lofty statement while living lives entirely separate from people of other races, other classes, and other religions. Many Republicans have lied to you. And many Democrats have told you those same lies. But I will not lie, in word or deed. I have just purchased a house in the historically black Central District neighborhood of Seattle, and my son will attend Garfield High School. I am moving because I believe in action. And I am issuing a challenge to my fellow Republicans and to all Democrats, as well: Put your money, and your house, where your mouth is."

And so my father, who won the state seat with 62 percent of the vote, moved me away from Jeremy, who also left Madison Park and was homeschooled by his mother. Over the next year or so, I must have called his house twenty times. But I always hung up when he or his parents answered. And he called my private line more than twenty times, but would stay on the line and silently wait for me to speak. And then it stopped. We became rumors to each other.

Five hours after I punched Jeremy in the face, I sat alone in the living room of my childhood home in Seattle. Bernard, Spence, and Eddie were gone. I felt terrible. I prayed that I would be forgiven. No, I didn't deserve forgiveness. I prayed that I would be fairly judged. So I called the fairest man I know—my father—and told him what I had done.

The sun was rising when my father strode alone into the room and slapped me: once, twice, three times.

"Shit," he said, and stepped away.

I wiped the blood from my mouth.

"Shit," my father said once more, stepped up close to me, and slapped me again.

I was five inches taller, thirty years younger, and forty pounds heavier than my father and could have easily stopped him from hitting me. I could have hurt him. But I knew that I deserved his anger. A good son, I might have let him kill me. And, of course, I know that you doubt me. But I believe in justice. And I was a criminal who deserved punishment.

"What did you do?" my father asked.

"I don't know," I said. "I was drunk and stupid and—I don't know what happened."

"This is going to ruin everything. You've ruined me with this, this *thing*, do you understand that?"

"No, it's okay. I'll confess to it. It's all my fault. Nobody will blame you."

"Of course they'll blame me. And they *should* blame me. I'm your father."

"You're a great father."

"No, I'm not. I can't be. What kind of father could raise a son who is capable of such a thing?"

I wanted to rise up and tell my father the truth, that his son was a bloody, bawdy villain. A remorseless, treacherous, lecherous, kindless villain. But such sad and selfish talk is reserved for one's own ears. So I insulted myself with a silence that insulted my father as well.

"Don't just sit there," he said. "You can't just sit there. You have to account for yourself."

My father had always believed in truth, and in the real and vast differences between good and evil. But he'd also taught me, as he had learned, that each man is as fragile and finite as any other.

On the morning of September 11, 2001, my father prayed aloud for the victims. All day, the media worried that the body count might reach twenty or thirty thousand, so my father's prayers were the most desperate of his life. But, surprisingly, my father also prayed for the nineteen men who'd attacked us. He didn't pray for their forgiveness or redemption. No, he believed they were going to burn in a real hell. After all, what's the point of a metaphorical hell? But my father was compassionate and Christian enough to know that those nineteen men, no matter how evil their actions and corrupt their souls, could have been saved.

This is what my father taught me on that terrible day: "We are tested, all of us. We are constantly and consistently given the choice. Good or evil. Light or darkness. Love or hate. Some of those decisions are huge and tragic. Think of those nineteen men and you must curse them. But you must also curse their mothers and fathers. Curse their brothers and sisters. Curse their teachers and priests. Curse everybody who failed them. I pray for those nineteen men because I believe that some part of them, the original sliver of God that still resided in them, was calling out for guidance, for goodness and beauty. I pray for them because they chose evil and thus became evil, and I pray for them because nobody taught them how to choose goodness and become good."

Of course, my father, being a politician, could never have uttered those words in public. His supporters would not have understood the difference between empathy for a lost soul and sympathy with a terrorist's politics. Make no mistake: My father was no moral relativist. He wanted each criminal to be judged by his crimes, not by his motivations or biography.

My father refused to believe that all cultures were equal. He believed that representative democracy was a God-given gift to humans.

"I think that our perfect God will protect us in a perfect afterlife," he was fond of saying in public. "But in this highly imperfect world, we highly imperfect humans need to be protected from one another, and only a progressive republican government can guarantee any sort of protection."

In private, my father said this: "Fuck the fucking leftists and their fucking love of secularism and communism. Those bastards haven't yet figured out that the secular Hitler and the communist Stalin slaughtered millions and millions of people."

Don't get me wrong. My father knew that the world was complicated and unpredictable—and that only God knew the ultimate truth—but he also knew that each citizen of that world was ultimately responsible for his actions. My father staked his political career, his entire life, on one basic principle: An unpredictable world demands a predictable moral code.

"Son," my father said to me many a time in the years after September 11, "a thief should be judged by the theft. A rapist should be judged by the rape. A murderer should be judged by the murder. A terrorist should be judged by the terror."

And so I sat, a man capable of inexplicable violence against an innocent, eager to be judged by my God and by my father. I wanted to account and be held accountable.

"I'm sorry," I said. "I shouldn't have attacked those men. I shouldn't have walked away from the scene. At least, I should have gone back to the scene. I should go back now and turn myself in to the police."

"But you're not telling me why you did it," my father said. "Can you tell me that? Why did you do it?"

I searched my soul for an answer and could not find one. I could not make sense of it. But if I'd known that it was Jeremy I'd assaulted, I could have spoken about Cain and Abel and let my father determine the moral of the story.

"Spence and Eddie—"

"No," my father interrupted. "This is not about them. This is about you."

"Okay," I said. "I'm really confused here, Dad. I'm trying to do the right thing. And I need you to help me. Tell me what the right thing is. Tell me what I'm supposed to do."

And so my father told me what he had learned from confidential sources. The gay men had reported the assault but, obviously shocked and confused, had provided conflicting descriptions of Spence, Eddie, and Bernard and no description of me other than "white male, twenties to thirties, five-eight to six feet, one-eighty to two hundred pounds." In other words, I could have been almost any Caucasian guy in Seattle. The victims didn't catch the license plate of the suspects' car and could only describe it as a "dark four-door." There were no other witnesses to the assault as of yet. Most curious, the victims disagreed on whether or not the perpetrators brandished guns.

"What do the police think?" I asked.

"They think the victims are hiding something," my father said.

"They're just scared and freaked out."

"No. I agree with the police. I think they're hiding something."

"No, they're not hiding anything, Dad. They're just confused. I'd be confused if somebody attacked me like that."

"No, they're hiding the fact that they started the fight and they don't want the police to know it."

I was shocked. Was this really my father or his lying twin? Was I talking to my father or his murderous brother?

"Listen," he said. "I don't think the police really have anything to go on. And I don't think they're going to pursue this much further. But we're going to monitor the investigation very closely. And we're going to be preemptive if we sense any real danger."

"What are you talking about? Are you going to hurt them?"

More enraged than ever before, my father grabbed me by the shirt. "Don't you say such things. Don't you dare! This is the United States of America, not some third world shit heap! I am not in the business of intimidation or violence. I am not in the business of murder."

It was true. My father believed in life, the sacred spark of humans, more strongly than any other man I'd ever known. As a Republican, he was predictably antiabortion, but he was also against capital punishment. His famous speech: "It is the business of man to judge and punish on this mortal Earth; but it is the business of God to give and take away life. I believe that abortion is a great evil, but it is just as evil to abandon any child to the vagaries of economics. I believe it is evil to murder another human being, but it is just as evil for a government to kill its citizens based on the vagaries of justice."

Yes, this was the man I had accused of conspiracy. I had insulted my father. I'd questioned his honor. I'd deemed him capable of murder. He was right to shake me.

"I'm sorry," I said. "I'm sorry. I'm just confused. Help me. Please, Daddy, help me. I love you. Please, please help me."

And so he held me while I wept.

"I love you, son," he said. "But you have to listen to me. You have to understand. I know that you were wrong to do what you did. It was a mortal sin. You sinned against God, against those men, and against me. And you should pay for those sins."

My good father wanted me to be a good man.

"But it's not that easy," my father said. "If you turn yourself in to the police, I will also pay for your sins. And I know I should pay for your sins because I am your father, and I have obviously failed to raise you well. But I will also pay for your sins as a U.S. senator, so our state and country will also pay for them. A scandal like this will ruin my career. It will ruin our party. And it will ruin our country. And though I know I will be judged harshly by God, I can't let you tell the truth."

My father wanted me to lie. No, he was forcing me to lie.

"William, Willy," he said. "If we begin to suspect that you might be implicated in this, we're going to go on the offensive. We're going to kill their reputations."

If it is true that children pay for the sins of their fathers, is it also true that fathers pay for the sins of their children?

Three days later, I returned to my condominium in downtown Seattle and found a message waiting on my voice mail.

"Hey, William, it's—um, me, Jeremy. You really need to call me."

And so I called Jeremy and agreed to meet him at his house in Magnolia, an upper-class neighborhood of Seattle. It was a small but lovely house, painted blue and chocolate.

I rang the doorbell. Jeremy answered. His face and nose were swollen purple, yellow, and black; his eyes were blood-shot and tear-filled.

"It was you," I said, suddenly caught in an inferno of shame.

"Of course it was me. Get your ass in here."

Inside, we sat in his study, a modernist room decorated with beautiful and useless furniture. What good is a filing cabinet that can only hold an inch of paperwork?

"I'm so sorry, Jeremy," I said. "I didn't know it was you."

"Oh, so I'm supposed to be happy about that? Things would be okay if you'd beaten the shit out of a fag you didn't know?"

"That's not what I meant."

"Okay, then, what did you mean?"

"I was wrong to do what I did. Completely wrong."

"Yes, you were," he said.

He was smiling. I recognized that smile. Jeremy was giving me shit. Was he going to torture me before he killed me?

"Why didn't you tell the police it was me?" I asked.

"Because the police don't give a shit about fags."

"But we assaulted you. We could have killed you."

"Doubtful. James had already kicked the crap out of your friends. And he would have kicked the crap out of you and the guy with the tire iron. Let's just call it a split decision."

"You didn't tell James it was me, did you?"

"No, of course not. I told the police a completely different story than James did. And I was the one with the broken face, so they believed me."

"But what about James? What's he going to do?"

"Oh, who cares? I barely knew him."

"But it was a hate crime."

"Aren't all crimes, by definition, hate crimes? I mean, people don't rob banks because they love tellers."

"I don't understand you. Why haven't you gone public with this? You could destroy my father. And me."

Jeremy sighed.

"Oh, William," he said. "You're still such an adolescent. And so romantic. I haven't turned you in because I'm a Republican, a good one, and I think your father is the finest senator we've ever had. I used to think he was a closet Democrat. But he's become something special. This kind of shit would completely fuck his chance at the presidency."

Jesus, was this guy more a son to my father than I was?

"And, okay, maybe I'm a romantic, too," Jeremy said. "I didn't turn you in because we were best friends and because I still consider you my best friend."

"But my father hates gay people."

"It's more complicated than that."

And so Jeremy explained to me that his sexual preference had nothing to do with his political beliefs.

"Hey," he said. "I don't expect to be judged negatively for my fuck buddies. But I don't want to be judged positively, either. It's just sex. It's not like it's some specialized skill or something. Hell, right now, in this house, one hundred thousand bugs are fucking away. In this city, millions of bugs are fucking at this very moment. And, hey, probably ten thousand humans—and registered voters—are fucking somewhere in this city. Four or five of them might even be married."

"So what's your point?"

"Anybody who thinks that sex somehow relates to the national debt or terrorism or poverty or crime or moral values or any kind of politics is just an idiot."

"Damn, Jeremy, you've gotten hard."

"That's what all the boys say."

"And what does James say? What if he goes to the press? What if he sees my face in the newspapers or on TV and recognizes me?"

"James is a little fag coffee barista from Bumfuck, Idaho. Nobody cares what he has to say. Little James could deliver a Martian directly to the White House and people would think it was a green poodle with funny ears."

I wondered if I'd completely scrambled Jeremy's brains when I punched him in the head.

"Will you listen to me?" I said. "My father will destroy your life if he feels threatened."

"Did you know your father called my father that day up in North Bend?" Jeremy asked.

"What day?" I asked. But I knew.

"Don't be obtuse. After I told you I was gay, you told your father, and your father told my father. And my father beat the shit out of me."

"You're lying," I said. But I knew he wasn't.

"You think my face looks bad now? Oh, man, my dad broke my cheekbone. Broke my arm. Broke my leg. A hairline fracture of the skull. A severe concussion. I saw double for two months."

"How come you didn't go to the police?"

"Oh, my dad took me to the police. Said a gang of kids did it to me. Hoodlums, he called them."

"How come you didn't tell the police the truth?"

"Because my dad said he'd kill my mom if I told the truth."

"I don't think I believe any of this."

"You can believe what you want. I know what happened. My father beat the shit out of me because he was ashamed of me. And I let him because I was ashamed of me. And because I loved my mom."

I stared at him. Could he possibly be telling the truth? Are there truths as horrible as this one? In abandoning him when he was sixteen, did I doom him to a life with a violent father and a beaten mother?

"But you know the best thing about all of this?" he asked.

I couldn't believe there'd be any good in this story.

"When my father was lying in his hospital bed, he asked for me," Jeremy said. "Think about it. My father was dying of cancer. And he called for me. He needed me to forgive him. And you know what?"

"What?" I asked, though I didn't want to know.

"I went into his room, hugged him and told him I forgave him and I loved him, and we cried and then he died."

"I can't believe any of this."

"It's all true."

"You forgave your father?" I asked.

"Yeah," Jeremy said. "It really made me wish I was Roman or Greek, you know? A classical Greek god would have killed his lying, cheating father and *then* given him forgiveness. And a classical Greek god would have better abs, too. That's what Greek gods are all about, you know? Patricide and low body fat."

How could anybody be capable of that much forgiveness? I was reminded of the black man, the convicted rapist, who'd quietly proclaimed his innocence all during his thirty years in prison. After he was exonerated by DNA evidence and finally freed, that black man completely forgave the white woman who'd identified him as her rapist. He said he forgave her because it would do him no good to carry that much anger in his heart. I often wonder if that man was Jesus come back.

"The thing is, Willy," Jeremy said, "you've always been such a moral guy. Six years old, and you made sure that everybody got equal time on the swings, on the teeter-totter, on the baseball field. Even the losers. And you learned that from your father."

"My father is a great man," I said, but I wasn't sure I believed it. I had to believe it, though, or my foundations would collapse.

"No," Jeremy said. "Your father has great ideas, but he's an ordinary man, just like all of us. No, your father is more of an asshole than usual. He likes to hit people."

"He's only hit me a couple of times."

"That you can remember."

"What does that mean?"

"We wouldn't practice denial if it didn't work."

"Fuck you," I said.

"Oh, you're scary. What are you going to do, punch me in the face?"

We laughed.

"It comes down to this," Jeremy said. "You can't be a great father and a great politician at the same time. Impossible. Can't be a great father and a great writer, either. Just ask Hemingway's kids."

"I prefer Faulkner."

"Yeah, there's another candidate for Father of the Year."

"Okay, okay, writers are bad dads. What's your point?"

"Your father is great because of his ideas. And those great ideas will make him a great president."

"Why do you believe in him so much?"

"It's about sacrifice. Listen, I am a wealthy American male. I can't campaign for something as silly and fractured as gay marriage when there are millions of Muslim women who can't even show their ankles. Your daddy knows that. Everybody knows it."

"I don't know anything."

"I hate to sound like a campaign worker or something, but listen to me. I believe in him so much that I'll pay ten bucks for a gallon of gas. I believe in him so much that I'm going to let you go free."

I wondered if Jeremy had been beaten so often that it had destroyed his spirit. Had he lost the ability to defend himself? How many times could he forgive the men who had bloodied and broken him? Is there a finite amount of forgiveness in the world? Was there a point after which forgiveness, even the most divinely inspired, is simply the act of a coward? Or has forgiveness always been used as political capital?

"Jeremy," I asked, "what am I supposed to do with all this information?"

"That's up to you, sweetheart."

Oh, there are more things in heaven and earth than can be explained by *Meet the Press*.

Jeremy and I haven't talked since that day. We agreed that our friendship was best left abandoned in the past. My crime against him was also left in the past. As expected, the police did not pursue the case, and it was soon filed away. There was never any need to invent a story.

I cannot tell you what happened to James, or to Eddie and Spence, or to Bernard. We who shared the most important moment of our lives no longer have any part in the lives of the others. It happens that way. I imagine that someday one of them might try to tell the whole story. And I imagine nobody would believe them. Who would believe any of them? Or me? Has a liar ever told the truth?

As for my father, he lost his reelection bid and retired to the relatively sad life of an ex-senator. He plays golf three times a week. State leaders beg for his advice.

My father and I have never again discussed that horrible night. We have no need or right to judge each other for sins that might have already doomed us to a fiery afterlife. Instead, we both silently forgave each other, and separately and loudly pray to God for his forgiveness. I'll let you know how that works out.

ANOTHER PROCLAMATION

When
Lincoln
Delivered
The
Emancipation
Proclamation,
Who
Knew

that, one year earlier, in 1862, he'd signed and approved the
order for the largest public execution in United States history?
Who did they execute? "Mulatto, mixed-bloods, and Indians."
Why did they execute them? "For uprisings against the State
and her citizens." Where did they execute them? Mankato,
Minnesota. How did they execute them? Well, Abraham Lincoln thought it was good

And
Just
To
Hang
Thirty-eight
Sioux

simultaneously. Yes, in front of a large and cheering crowd, thirty-eight Indians dropped to their deaths. Yes, thirty-eight necks snapped. But before they died, thirty-eight Indians sang their death songs. Can you imagine the cacophony of thirty-eight different death songs? But wait, one Indian was pardoned at the last minute, so only thirty-seven Indians had to sing their death songs. But, O, O, O, O, can you imagine the cacophony of that one survivor's mourning song? If he taught you the words, do you think you would sing along?

Invisible Dog on a Leash

1.

In 1973, my father and I saw *Enter the Dragon*, the greatest martial arts movie of all time. I loved Bruce Lee. I wanted to be Bruce Lee. Afterward, as we walked to our car, I threw punches and kicks at the air.

"Hey, Dad," I asked, "is Bruce Lee the toughest guy in the world?"

My father said, "No way. There are five guys in Spokane who could probably kick Bruce Lee's ass."

"Really? You mean in a fair fistfight and everything?"

"Who said anything about fair? And who'd want to throw punches with Bruce Lee? I'm not talking about fists. I'm saying there are at least five guys in Spokane who, if they even saw Bruce Lee, they'd walk up to him and just sucker punch him with a baseball bat or a two-by-four or something."

"That's not right."

"You didn't ask me about right. You asked me about tough."

"Are you tougher than Bruce Lee?"

"Well, I'm tough in some ways, I guess. But I'm not the kind of guy who will knock somebody in the head with a baseball bat. I'm not going to do that to Bruce Lee. But let me tell you, there are more than five guys in Spokane who would do that. As I'm thinking more and more about it, I'm thinking there are probably fifty crazy guys who'd sneak up behind Bruce Lee at a restaurant and just knock him out with a big frying pan or something."

"Okay, Dad, that's enough."

"And I haven't even talked about prison dudes. Shoot, every other guy in prison would be happy to sucker punch Bruce Lee. They'd wait in a dark corner for a week, just waiting to ambush Bruce Lee with a chain saw or something. Man, those prison guys aren't going to mess around with a Jeet Kune Do guy like Bruce Lee. No way. Those prison dudes would build a catapult and fling giant boulders at Bruce Lee."

"Okay, Dad, I believe you. I've heard enough. Stop it, Dad, stop it!"

"Okay, Okay, I'm sorry. I'm just telling you the truth."

2.

On TV, Uri Geller was bending spoons
With just his mind. "Wow," I said. "That's so cool."

Then, three days later, as I browsed through Rick's
Pawn Shop, I picked up a book of magic tricks

And learned how to bend spoons almost as well.
I called my act URI GELLER IS GOING TO HELL.

3.

At Expo '74, in Spokane, I saw my first invisible dog on a leash. A hilarious and agile Chinese man was selling them.

"My dog is fast," he said. And his little pet, in its leash and harness, dragged him across the grass. I thought it was real magic. I didn't know it was just an illusion. I didn't know that thick and flexible wires had been threaded through the leash and harness and then shaped to look like a dog—an invisible dog. In fact, I didn't discover the truth until two years later at our tribe's powwow, when a felonious-looking white man tried to sell me an invisible dog with a broken leash. Without a taut leash, that invisible dog didn't move or dance in its harness. The magic was gone. I was an emotional kid, so I started to cry, and the felonious dude said, "Shit, kid, take it, I found it in the garbage anyway."

4.

In '76, I also saw the remake of *King Kong*. It was terrible. Even my father, who loved the worst drive-in exploitation crap, said, "It's Kong, man. What went so wrong?" But that does remind me of a drive-in flick whose name I can't recall. It's about a herd of Sasquatch who sneak into a biker gang's house and kidnap all of the biker women. Later, the biker gang puts spiked wheels on their rods, roars into the woods, somehow finds the Sasquatch, and battles for the women. As the Sasquatch fight and fall and pretend to die, two or three of them lose their costume heads. Their furry masks just go sailing but the actors playing Sasquatch, and the other actors, and the director, and the writer, and the producers, and God just keep on going as if it didn't matter. And I suppose, for the sake of budget, it *didn't* matter, but I stood on the top of our van and shouted, "It's not real. It's not real. It's not real. It's not real!" And some politically aware but unseen dude shouted from out of the dark, "Okay, Little Crazy Horse, we know it's not real, so get your ass back in your van."

5.

Speaking of Sasquatch, I met the love of my life in 1979, in Redding, California, the heart of Bigfoot Country. Okay, she wasn't the love of my life, she just happened to be the first world-class beauty I'd ever seen. Honestly. She could have been on the cover of *Glamour* magazine. But she was just a teenage girl from Redding, California, which, like I said, was the heart of Bigfoot Country. And I was obsessed with Bigfoot, with the real Sasquatch, not the fake biker-gang-fighting and biker-chick-kidnapping type. So, as this gorgeous girl asked me what I wanted (my family had stopped to eat at some fast-food joint on our way to Disneyland), I said, "Isn't it cool to live in Bigfoot Country? In the heart of Bigfoot Country. In the heart of the heart of Bigfoot Country."

"Oh," she said. "That stuff ain't real. It's my two uncles— Little Jim and Big Jim—who make all those footprints with these big wooden feet they carved out and tie up on their boots."

"What?"

"Yeah. If you've ever seen that movie *Planet of the Apes*, you've seen my uncles, because they played gorillas."

"Are you kidding?"

"No, my uncles used to work at the San Francisco Zoo when they were in college. They helped feed the gorillas and monkeys and chimps and stuff. So they really learned how to walk around like apes. But those Hollywood people didn't appreciate them, you know? Didn't pay them hardly anything for being in that first *Planet* movie. So my uncles didn't work on any of the sequels."

"I can't believe what I'm hearing."

"Well, it's all true. You can even go visit my uncles if you want. They've got a bunch of those fake Bigfoot feet you can buy. And if you tell them I sent you over, they'll even show you their Bigfoot costumes."

"They have costumes?"

"Yeah, and you will not believe how much those costumes look like a real Bigfoot. It was Big Jim who was playing Bigfoot in that famous movie. You've seen that one, right? The one where Bigfoot is walking across the riverbed? Yeah, whenever I see that video on TV, I scream, "Hey, Uncle Big Jim!" Anyway, I have to remember my job. What do you want to eat, little man?"

"A corn dog, I guess."

6.

O, the '70s broke my heart. No,
The '70s broke my heart's ass.

Home of the Braves

When my female friends are left
By horrid spouses and lovers,
I commiserate. I send gifts—
Powwow songs and poems—and wonder

Why my gorgeous friends cannot find
Someone who knows them as I do.
Is the whole world deaf and blind?
I tell my friends, "I'd marry you

Tomorrow." I think I'm engaged
To thirty-six women, my harem:
Platonic, bookish, and enraged.
I love them! But it would scare them—

No, of course, they already know
That I can be just one more boy,
A toy warrior who explodes
Into silence and warpaths with joy.

THE BALLAD OF
PAUL NONETHELESS

In Chicago's O'Hare Airport, walking east on a moving sidewalk, Paul saw a beautiful woman walking west. She'd pulled her hair back into a messy ponytail, and her blue jeans were dark-rinsed boot-cut, and her white T-shirt was a size too small, and her pale arms were muscular. And—ah, she wore a pair of glorious red shoes. Pumas. Paul knew those shoes. He'd seen them in an ad in a fashion magazine, or maybe on an Internet site, and fallen in love with them. Allegedly an athletic shoe, the red Pumas were really a thing of beauty. On any woman, they'd be lovely; on this woman, they were glorious. Who knew that Paul would someday see those shoes on a woman's feet and feel compelled to pursue her?

Paul wanted to shout out, *I love your Pumas!* He wanted to orate it with all the profundity and passion of a Shakespearean couplet, but that seemed too eccentric and desperate and—well, literate. He wanted the woman to know he was instantly but ordinarily attracted to her, so he smiled and waved instead. But bored with her beauty, or more likely bored with the men who noticed her beauty, she ignored Paul and rolled her baggage on toward the taxi or parking shuttle or town car.

"'She's gone, she's gone.'" Paul sang the chorus of that Hall & Oates song. He sang without irony, for he was a twenty-first-century American who'd been taught to mourn his small and large losses by singing Top 40 hits.

There was a rule book: When a man is rebuffed by a beautiful stranger he must sing blue-eyed soul; when a man is drunk with the loneliness of being a frequent flyer he must sing Mississippi Delta blues; when a man wants revenge he must whistle the sound track of *The Good, the Bad, and the Ugly*. When a man's father and mother die within three months of each other, he must sing Rodgers and Hammerstein: "Oklahoma! Oklahoma Okay!"

Despite all the talk of diversity and division—of red and blue states, of black and white and brown people, of rich and poor, gay and straight—Paul believed that Americans were shockingly similar. How can we be so different, thought Paul, if we all know the lyrics to the same one thousand songs? Paul knew the same lyrics as any random guy from Mobile, Alabama, or woman from Orono, Maine. Hell, Paul had memorized, without effort or ever purchasing or downloading one of their CDs—or even one of their songs—the complete works of Garth Brooks, Neil Diamond, and AC/DC. And if words and music can wind their way into and around our DNA strands—and Paul believed they could—wouldn't American pop music be passed from generation to generation as easily as blue eyes or baldness? Hadn't pop music created a new and invisible organ, a pituitary gland of the soul, in the American body? Or were these lies and exaggerations? Could one honestly say that Elvis is a more important figure in American history than Einstein? Could one posit that Aretha Franklin's version of "Respect" was more kinetic and relevant to American life than Dwight D. Eisenhower's 1961 speech that warned us about the dangers of a military-industrial complex? Could a reasonable person think that Madonna's "Like a Prayer" was as integral and universal to everyday life as the fork or wheel? Paul believed all these heresies about pop music but would never say them aloud for fear of being viewed as a less-than-serious person.

Or wait, maybe Paul wasn't a serious person. Maybe he was an utterly contemporary and callow human being. Maybe he was an American ironic. Maybe he was obsessed with pop music because it so perfectly reflected his current desires. And yet, Paul sold secondhand clothes for a living. He owned five vintage clothing stores in the Pacific Northwest and was currently wearing a gray tweed three-piece suit once owned by Gene Kelly. So Paul was certainly not addicted to the present day. On the contrary, Paul believed that the present, past, and future were all happening simultaneously, and that any era's pop culture was *his* pop culture. And sure, pop culture could be crass and manipulative, and sometimes evil, but it could also be magical and redemptive.

Take Irving Berlin, for example. He was born Israel Baline in Russia in 1888, emigrated with his family in 1893 to the United States, and would eventually write dozens, if not hundreds, of classic tunes, including, most famously, "Alexander's Ragtime Band." Yes, it was a Russian Jew who wrote the American love song that suggested we better hurry and meander at the same time. Can a person simultaneously hurry and meander? Yes, in the United States a romantic is, by definition, a person filled with those contradictions. And, the romantic American is in love with his contradictions. And the most romantic Americans (see Walt Whitman) want to have contradictory sex. Walt Whitman would have wanted to have sex with Irving Berlin. Paul loved Irving Berlin and Walt Whitman. He loved the thought of their sexual union. And most of all, Paul loved the fact that Irving Berlin had lived a long and glorious life and died in 1989, only sixteen years earlier.

Yes, Irving Berlin was still alive in 1989. It's quite possible that Irving Berlin voted for Michael Dukakis for United States president. How can you not love a country and a culture where that kind of beautiful insanity can flourish? But wait— did any of this really matter anyway? Was it just the musical trivia of a trivial man in a trivial country? And beyond all that, why was Paul compelled to defend his obsessions? Why was he forced to define and self-define? After all, one doesn't choose his culture nearly as much as one trips and falls into it.

Splat! Paul was a forty-year-old man from Seattle, Washington, who lived only ten minutes from the house where Kurt Cobain shotgunned himself, and only fifteen minutes from the stretch of Jackson Street where Ray Charles and Quincy Jones began their careers in bygone jazz clubs. *Splat!* Paul's office, and the headquarters of his small used-clothes empire, was down the street from a life-size statue of Jimi Hendrix ripping an all-weather solo. *Splat!* Paul bought his morning coffee at the same independent joint where a dozen of Courtney Love's bounced checks decorated the walls.

Paul believed American greatness and the ghosts of that greatness surrounded him. But who could publicly express such a belief and not be ridiculed as a patriotic fool? Paul believed in his fellow Americans, in their extraordinary decency, in their awesome ability to transcend religion, race, and class, but what leftist could state such things and ever hope to get laid by any other lefty? And yet Paul was the perfect example of American possibility: He made a great living (nearly $325,000 the previous tax year) by selling secondhand clothes.

For God's sake, Paul was flying to Durham, North Carolina, for a denim auction. A Baptist minister had found one hundred pairs of vintage Levi's (including one pair dating back to the nineteenth century that was likely to fetch $25,000 or more!) in his father's attic, and was selling them to help raise money for the construction of a new church. Blue jeans for God! Blue jeans for Jesus! Blue Jeans for the Holy Ghost!

Used clothes for sale! Used clothes for sale! That was Paul's capitalistic war cry. That was his mating song.

Thus unhinged and aroused, Paul turned around and ran against the moving sidewalk. He chased after the beautiful woman—in her gorgeous red Pumas—who had rebuffed him. He wanted to tell her everything that he believed about his country. No, he just wanted to tell her that music—pop music— was the most important thing in the world. He would show her the top twenty-five songs played on his iPod, and she'd have sex with him in the taxi or parking shuttle or town car.

And there she was, on the escalator above him, with her perfect jeans and powerful yoga thighs. Paul could hear her denim singing friction ballads across her skin. Paul couldn't remember the last time he'd had sex with a woman who wore red shoes. Paul dreamed of taking them off and taking a deep whiff. Ha! He'd instantly developed a foot fetish. He wanted to smell this woman's feet. Yes, that was the crazy desire in his brain and his crotch when he ran off the escalator and caught the woman outside of the security exit.

"Excuse me, I'm sorry, hello," Paul said.

She stared at him. She studied his face, wondering if she knew him, or if he was a gypsy cab driver, or if he was a creep.

"I saw you back there on the moving sidewalk," Paul said.

Wow, that was a stupid thing to say. That meant nothing. No, that meant Paul had noticed the lovely shapes of her green eyes, breasts, and ass—their mystical geometry—and that made him as ordinary, if slightly more mathematical, as any other man in the airport. He needed to say something extraordinary, something poetic, in order to make her see that he was capable of creating, well, extraordinary poetry. Could he talk about her shoes? Was that a convincing way to begin this relationship? Or maybe he could tell her that Irving Berlin's real name was Israel.

"I mean," Paul said, "well, I wanted to—well, the thing is, I saw you—no, I mean—well, I did see you, but it wasn't sight that made me chase after you, you know? I mean—it wasn't really any of my five senses that did it. It was something beyond that. You exist beyond the senses; I just know that without really knowing it, you know?"

She smiled. The teeth were a little crowded. The lines around her eyes were new. She was short, a little over five feet tall, and, ah, she wore those spectacular red shoes. If this didn't work out, Paul was going to run home and buy the DVD version of that movie about the ballerina's red dance slippers. Or was he thinking of the movie about the kid who lost his red balloon? Somewhere there must be a movie about a ballerina who ties her dance shoes to a balloon and watches them float away. *Jesus*, Paul said to himself. *Focus, focus.*

"You have a beautiful smile," Paul said to the stranger. "And if your name is Sara, I'm going to lose my mind."

"My name isn't Sara," she said. "Why would you think my name is Sara?"

"You know, great smile, name is Sara. 'Sara Smile'? The song by Hall and Oates."

"Oh, yeah, that's a good one."

"You've made me think of two Hall and Oates songs in, like, five minutes. I think that's a sign. Of what, I don't know, but a sign nonetheless."

"I think that's the first time I've ever heard a man say *nonetheless* in normal conversation."

Was she mocking him? Yes, she was. Was that a positive step in their relationship? Did it imply a certain familiarity or the desire for a certain familiarity? And, by the way, when exactly had he become the kind of man who uses *nonetheless* in everyday conversation?

"Listen," Paul said to the beautiful stranger. "I don't know you. And you don't know me. But I want to talk to you—and listen to you; that's even more important—I want to talk and listen to you for a few hours. I want to share stories. That's it. That's it exactly. I think you have important stories to tell. Stories I need to hear."

She laughed and shook her head. Did he amuse her? Or bemuse her? There was an important difference: Women sometimes slept with bemusing men, but they usually *married* amusing men.

"So, listen," Paul said. "I am perfectly willing to miss my flight and have coffee with you right here in the airport—and if that makes you feel vulnerable, just remember there are dozens of heavily armed security guards all around us—so, please, if you're inclined to spend some time with a complete but devastatingly handsome stranger, I would love your company."

"Well," she said. "You *are* cute. And I like your suit."

"It used to belong to Gene Kelly. He wore it in one of his movies."

"*Singin' in the Rain?*"

"No, one of the bad ones. When people talk about the golden age of Hollywood musicals, they don't realize that almost all of them were bad."

"Are you a musician?"

"Uh, no, I sell used clothes. Vintage clothes. But only the beautiful stuff, you know?"

"Like your suit."

"Yes, like my suit."

"Sounds like a cool job."

"It *is* a cool job. I have, like, one of the coolest lives ever. You should know that."

"I'm sure you are a very cool individual. But I'm married, and my husband is waiting for me at baggage claim."

"I don't want this to be a comment on the institution of marriage itself, which I believe in, but I want you to know that your marriage, while great for your husband and you, is an absolute tragedy for me. I'm talking Greek tragedy. I'm talking mothers-killing-their-children level of tragedy. If you listened to my heart, you'd hear that it just keeps beating *Medea, Medea, Medea*. And yes, I know the rhythm is off on that. Makes me sound like I have a heart murmur."

She laughed. He'd made her laugh three or four times since they'd met. He'd turned the avenging and murderous Medea into a sexy punch line. How many men could do that?

"Hey," she said. "Thank you for the—uh—attention. You've made my day. Really. But I must go. I'll see you in the next life."

She turned to leave, but then she paused—*O, che sarà!*— leaned in close to Paul, and gave him a soft kiss on the cheek. Then she laughed again and walked away. No, it wasn't just a walk. It was a magical act of transportation. Delirious, Paul watched her leave. He marveled at the gifts of strangers, at the way in which a five-minute relationship can be as gratifying and complete (and sexless!) as a thirteen-year marriage. Then he made his way back through security and to his gate, caught his flight to North Carolina, and bought a pair of 1962 Levi's for $1,250.

Of course, Paul was a liar, a cheater, and a thief. He'd pursued the beautiful airport stranger without giving much thought to his own marriage. And sure, he was separated, and his wife and three teenage daughters were living in the family home while Paul lived in a one-bedroom on Capitol Hill, but he was still married and wanted to remain married. He loved his wife, didn't he? Well, of course he did. She was lovely (was more than that, really) and smart and funny and all those things an attractive human being is supposed to be, and she in turn thought Paul was a lovely, smart, funny, and attractive human being. They had built a marriage based on their shared love of sixties soul music on vinyl—and vintage clothes, of course. Or perhaps

Paul had built this life and his wife had followed along. In any case, they were happy, extraordinarily happy, right? Jesus, it was easy to stay happy in a first-world democracy. What kind of madman would stay that long in an unhappy marriage, especially in an age when people divorced so easily? Yes, Paul loved his wife; he was in love with her. He was sure he could pass a lie-detector test on that one. And he loved his three daughters. He was more sure about that.

But if he was so happy, if he was so in love with his wife and daughters, why was he separated from them? Sadly, it was all about sex—or, rather, the lack of sex. Simply and crudely stated, Paul had lost the desire to fuck his wife. How had that happened? Paul didn't know, exactly. And he couldn't talk to anybody about it. How could he tell his friends, his circle of men, that he had no interest in sleeping with the sexiest woman any of them had ever met? She was so beautiful that she intimidated many of his friends. His best friend, Jacob, had once drunkenly confessed that he still couldn't look her directly in the eyes.

"I've known her, what, almost twenty years?" Jacob had said. "And I still have to look at her out of the corner of my eye. I'm the godfather to your daughters, and I have to talk to their mother with my sideways vision. You remember the time we all got drunk and naked in my hot tub? She was so amazing, so perfect, that I had to run around the corner and throw up. Your wife was so beautiful she made me sick. I hope you know how lucky you are, you lucky bastard."

Yes, Paul knew he was lucky: He had a great job, great daughters, and a great wife that he didn't want to fuck. And so he, the lucky bastard, had sex with every other possible partner. During his marriage, Paul had had sex with eight other women: two employees, three ex-girlfriends, two of his friends' wives, and a woman with one of the largest used-clothing stores on eBay.

After that last affair, a clumsy and incomplete coupling in a San Francisco apartment crowded with vintage sundresses and UPS boxes, Paul had confessed to his wife. Oh, no, he didn't confess to all his infidelities. That would have been too much. It would have been cruel. Instead, he only admitted to the one but carefully inserted details of the other seven, so that his confession would be at least fractionally honest. His wife had listened silently, packed him a bag, and kicked him out of the house. What was the last thing she'd said? "I can't believe you fucked somebody from eBay."

And so, for a year now, Paul had lived apart from his family. And had been working hard to win back their love. He'd been chaste while recourting his wife. But he was quite sure that she doubted his newly found fidelity—he traveled too damn much ever to be thought of as a good candidate for stability—and he'd heard from his daughters that a couple of men, handsome strangers, had come calling on his wife. He couldn't sleep some nights when he thought about other men's hands and cocks and mouths touching his wife. How strange, Paul thought, to be jealous of other men's lust for the woman who had only wanted, and had lost, her husband's lust. And stranger and more contradictory, Paul vanquished his jealousy by furiously masturbating while fantasizing about his dream wife fucking dream men. Feeling like a fool, but hard anyway, Paul stroked as other

men—nightmares—pushed into his wife. And when those vision men came hard, Paul also came hard. Everybody was
arched and twisted. And oh, Paul was afraid—terrified—of
how good it felt. What oath, what marital vow, did he break
by imagining his wife's infidelity? None, he supposed, but he
felt primitive, like the first ape that fell from the high trees and,
upon landing, decided to live upright, use tools, and evolve.
Dear wife, Paul wanted to say, *I'm quite sure that you will despise
me for these thoughts, and I respect your need to keep our lives private,
to relock the doors of our home, but I, primal and vain, still need to boast
about my fears and sins. Inside my cave, I build fires to scare away the
ghosts and keep the local predators at bay, or perhaps I build fires to
attract hungry carnivores. Could I be that dumb? Dear wife, watch
me celebrate what I lack. I am as opposable as my thumbs.* Ah, Paul
thought, who cares about the color of a man's skin when his true
identity is much deeper—subterranean—and far more diverse
and disturbing than the ethnicity of his mother and father? And
yet, nobody had ever argued for the civil rights of contradictory masturbators. "Chances are," Paul often sang to himself
while thinking of his marriage. "Chances are." And he was
singing that song in a Los Angeles International Airport
bookstore—on his way home from the largest flea market in
Southern California—when he saw the beautiful stranger who
had rebuffed him three months earlier at O'Hare.

"Hey," he said. "It's Sara Smile."

She looked up from the book she was skimming—some
best-selling and clever book about the one hundred greatest
movies ever made—and stared at Paul. She was puzzled at first,
but then she remembered him.

"Hey," she said. "It's Nonetheless."

Paul was quite sure this was the first time in the history of English that the word *nonetheless* had caused a massive erection. He fought mightily against the desire to kiss the stranger hard on the mouth.

"Wow," she said. "This is surprising, huh?"

"I can't believe you remember me," Paul said.

"I can't believe it either," she said. Then she quickly set down the book she'd been browsing. "These airport books, you know? They're entertaining crap."

Her embarrassment was lovely.

"I don't underestimate the power of popular entertainment," Paul said.

"Oh, okay, I guess," she said. "Wait, no. Let me amend that. I actually have no idea what you're talking about."

"I guess I don't either," Paul said. "I was trying to impress you with some faux philosophy."

She smiled. Paul wanted to lick her teeth. Once again, she was wearing blue jeans and a white T-shirt. Why is it that some women can turn that simple outfit into royal garb? God, he wanted her. *Want, want, want.* Can you buy and sell *want* on eBay?

"Are you still married?" he asked.

She laughed.

"Damn," she said. "You're as obvious as a thirteen-year-old. When are you going to start pawing at my breasts?"

"It's okay that you're married," he said. "I'm married, too."

"Oh, well, now, you didn't mention that the last time we met."

She was teasing him again. Mocking. Insulting. But she was not walking away. She had remembered him, had remembered a brief encounter from months earlier, and she was interested in him, in his possibilities. Wasn't she?

"No, I didn't mention my marriage," he said. "But I didn't mention it because I'm not sure how to define it. Technically speaking, I'm separated."

"Are you separated because you like to hit on strangers in airports?" she asked.

Wow. How exactly was he supposed to respond to that? He supposed his answer was going to forever change his life. Or at least decide if this woman was going to have sex with him. But he was not afraid of rejection, so why not tell the truth?

"Strictly speaking," he said, "I am not separated because I hit on strangers in airports. In fact, I can't recall another time when I hit on anybody in an airport. I am separated because I cheated on my wife."

Paul couldn't read her expression. Was she impressed or disgusted by his honesty?

"Do you have kids?" she asked.

"Three daughters. Eighteen, sixteen, and fifteen. I am surrounded by women."

"So you cheated on your daughters, not just your wife?"

Yes, it was true. Paul hated to think of it that way. But he knew his betrayal of his wife was, in some primal way, the lesser crime. What kind of message was he sending to the world when he betrayed the young women—his offspring—who would carry his name—his DNA—into the future?

"Yes," Paul said. "I cheated on my daughters. And that's pathetic. It's like I've put a letter in a bottle, and I've dropped it in the ocean, and it will someday wash up onshore, and somebody will find it, open it, and read it, and it will say, *Hello, People of the Future, my name is Paul Nonetheless, and I was a small and lonely man.*"

"You have a wife and three daughters and you still feel lonely?"

"Yes," he said. "It's true. Sad and true."

"Do you think you're as lonely, let's say, as a Russian orphan sleeping with thirty other orphans in a communal crib in the basement of a hospital in Tragikistan or somewhere?"

"No," Paul said. "I am not that lonely."

"Last week, outside of Spokane, a man and his kids got into a car wreck. He was critically injured, paralyzed from the neck down, and all five of his kids were killed. They were driving to pick up the mother at the train station. So tell me, do you think you are as lonely as that woman is right now?"

Wow, this woman had a gift for shaming!

"No," Paul said. "I am not that lonely. Not even close."

"Okay, good. You do realize that, grading on a curve, your loneliness is completely average."

"Yes, I realize that. Compared to all the lonely in the world, mine is pretty boring."

"Good," she said. "You might be an adulterous bastard, but at least you're a self-aware adulterous bastard."

She waited for his response, but he had nothing to say. He couldn't dispute the accuracy of her judgment of his questionable morals, nor could he offer her compelling evidence of his goodness. He was as she thought he was.

"My father cheated on us, too," she said. "We all knew it. My mother knew it. But he never admitted to it. He kept cheating and my mother kept ignoring it. They were married for fifty-two years and he cheated during all of them. Had to go on the damn Viagra so he could cheat well into his golden years. I think Viagra was invented so that extramarital assholes could have extra years to be assholes.

"But you know the worst thing?" she asked. "At the end, my father got cancer and he was dying and you'd think that would be the time to confess all, to get right with God, you know? But nope, on his deathbed, my father pledged his eternal and undying love to my mother. And you know what?"

"What?"

"She believed him."

Paul wanted to ask her why she doubted her father's love. Well, of course, Paul knew why she doubted it, but why couldn't her father have been telling the truth? Despite all the adultery and lies, all the shame and anger, perhaps her father had deeply and honestly loved her mother. If his last act on earth was a declaration of love, didn't that make him a loving man? Could an adulterous man also be a good man? But Paul couldn't say any of this, couldn't ask these questions. He knew it would only sound like the moral relativism of a liar, a cheater, and a thief.

"Listen to me," she said. "I can't believe I'm saying this stuff to you. I don't say this stuff to anybody, and here I am, talking to you like we're friends."

Paul figured silence was the best possible response to her candor.

"Okay, then," she said, "I guess that's it. I don't want to miss my flight. It was really nice to see you again. I'm not sure why. But it was." .

She walked away. He watched her. He knew he should let her go. What attraction could he have for her now? He was the cheating husband of a cheated wife and the lying father of deceived daughters. But he couldn't let her go. Not yet. So he chased after her again.

"Hey," he said, and touched her shoulder.

"Just let me go," she said. A flash of anger. Her first flash of anger at him.

"Listen," he said. "I was going to let you go. But I couldn't. I mean, don't you think it's amazing that we've run into each other twice in two different airports?"

"It's just a coincidence."

"It's more than that. You know it's more than that. We've got some connection. I can feel it. And I think you can feel it, too."

"I have a nice ass. And a great smile. And you have pretty eyes and good hair. And you wear movie stars' clothes. That's why we noticed each other. But I have news for us, buddy, there's about two hundred women in this airport who are better-looking than me, and about two hundred and one men who are better-looking than you."

"But we've seen each other twice. And you remembered me."

"We saw each other twice because we are traveling salespeople in a capitalistic country. If we paid attention, I bet you we would notice the same twelve people over and over again."

Okay, so she was belittling him and their magical connection. And insulting his beloved country, too. But she was still talking to him. She'd tried to walk away, but he'd caught her, and she was engaged in a somewhat real conversation with him. He suddenly realized that he knew nothing of substance about this woman. He only knew her opinions of his character.

"Okay," he said. "We're making progress. I sell clothes. But you already knew that. What do you sell?"

"You don't want to know," she said.

"Yes, I do."

"No, you don't."

"Tell me."

"It will kill your dreams," she said.

That hyperbole made Paul laugh.

"Come on, it can't be that bad."

"I work for a bank," she said.

"So, wow, you're a banker," Paul said, and tried to hide his disappointment. She could have said that she did live-animal testing—smeared mascara directly into the eyes of chimpanzees—and Paul would have felt better about her career choice.

"But I'm not the kind of banker you're thinking about," she said.

"What kind of banker are you?" Paul asked, and studied her casual, if stylish, clothing. What kind of banker wore blue jeans? Perhaps a trustworthy banker? Perhaps the morality of any banker was inversely proportional to the quality of his or her clothing?

"Have you ever heard of microlending?" she asked.

"Yeah, that's where you get regular people to loan money to poor people in other countries. To start small businesses and stuff, right?"

"Basically, yes, but my company focuses on microlending to unique entrepreneurs in the United States."

"Ah, so what's your bank called?"

"We're in the start-up phase, so I don't want to get into that quite yet."

He was a little insulted, but then he realized that he was a stranger, after all, so her secrecy was understandable.

"You're just starting out then?" Paul asked. "That's why you're traveling so much?"

"Yes. We have initial funding from one source," she said, "and I'm meeting with other potential funders around the country."

"Sounds exciting," Paul said. He lied. Paul didn't trust the concept of using money to make more money. He believed it was all imaginary. He preferred his job—the selling of tangible goods. Paul trusted his merchandise. He knew a pair of blue jeans would never betray him.

"It's good work, but it's not exciting," she said. "Fund-raising is fucking humiliating. You know what I really do? You know what I'm good at? I'm good at making millionaires cry. And crying millionaires are generous with their money."

"I'm a millionaire," Paul said, "and you haven't made me cry yet."

"I haven't tried to," she said. She patted Paul on the cheek—let the hounds of condescension loose!—and walked out of the bookstore.

After she left, Paul bought the book she'd been browsing—the list of the greatest movies of all time—and read it on the flight back to Seattle. It was a book composed entirely of information taken from other sources. But Paul set it on his nightstand, then set his alarm clock on the book, and thought about the beautiful microbanker whenever he glanced at the time.

On a Tuesday, a year and a half into their separation, while sitting in their marriage counselor's office, Paul turned to his wife and tried to tell the truth.

"I love you," he said. "You're my best friend. I can't imagine a life without you as my wife. But, the thing is, I've lost my desire—my sexual desire—for you."

Could there be a more painful thing to say to her? To say to anyone? *You are not desirable.* That was a treasonous, even murderous, statement inside of a marriage. What kind of person could say that to his wife? To the person who'd most often allowed herself to be naked and vulnerable in front of him? Paul supposed he was being honest, but fuck honesty completely, fuck honesty all the way to the spine, and fuck the honest man who tells the truth on his way out the door.

"How can you say this shit to me?" she asked. "We've been separated for almost two years. You keep telling me you don't want a divorce. You keep begging me for another chance. For months, you have begged me. So here we are, Paul, this is your chance. And all you can say is that you don't desire me? What are you talking about?"

"I remember when we used to have sex all day and night," he said. "I remember we used to count your orgasms."

It was true. On a cool Saturday in early April, in the first year of their marriage, Paul had orgasmed six times while his wife had come eleven times. What had happened to those Olympian days?

"Is that the only way you can think about a marriage?" she asked. "Jesus, Paul, we were young. Our marriage was young. Everything is easier when you're young."

Paul didn't think that was true. His life had steadily improved over the years and, even in the middle of a marital blowup, Paul was still pleased with his progress and place in the world.

"I don't know why I feel the way I do," Paul said. "I just feel that way. I feel like we have gone cold to each other."

"I haven't gone cold," she said. "I'm burning, okay? You know how long it's been since I've had sex? It's been almost four years. Four years! And you know what? I'm ashamed to say that aloud. Listen to me. I'm ashamed that I'm still married to the man who has not fucked me in four years."

Paul looked to the marriage counselor for help. He felt lost in the ocean of his wife's rage and needed a friggin' lifeguard. But the counselor sat in silence. In *learned* silence, the bastard.

"Don't you have anything to say?" she asked Paul. "I'm your wife. I'm the mother of your children. I deserve some respect. No, I demand it. I demand your respect."

He wanted to tell her the truth. He wanted to tell himself the truth, really. But was he capable of such a thing? Could he tell her what he suspected? Could he share his theory about the loss of desire? If he sang to her, would that make it easier? Is honesty easier in four/four time?

"Are you just going to sit there?" she asked. "Is this what it comes down to, you sitting there?"

My love, he wanted to say to her, I began to lose my desire for you during the birth of our first child, and it was gone by the birth of our third. Something happened to me in those delivery rooms. I saw too much. I saw your body do things— I saw it change—and I have not been able to look at you, to see you naked, without remembering all the blood and pain and fear. *All the changes.* I was terrified. I thought you were dying. I felt like I was in the triage room of a wartime hospital, and there was nothing I could do. I felt so powerless. I felt like I was failing you. I know it's irrational. Jesus, I know it's immature and ignorant and completely irrational. *I know it's wrong.* I should have told you that I didn't want to be in the delivery room for the first birth. And I should have never been in the delivery room during the second and third. Maybe my desire would have survived, would have recovered, if I had not seen the second and third births. Maybe I wouldn't feel like such a failure. But how was I supposed to admit to these things? In the twenty-first-century United States, what kind of father and husband chooses not to be in the delivery room?

My love, Paul wanted to say, I am a small and lonely man made smaller and lonelier by my unspoken fears.

"Paul!" his wife screamed. "Talk to me!"

"I don't know," Paul said. "I don't know why I feel this way. I just do."

"Paul." The counselor finally spoke, finally had an opinion. "Have you considered that your lack of desire might be a physical issue? Have you consulted a doctor about this? There are—"

"He has no problem fucking other women," she said. "He's fucked plenty of other women. He just has a problem fucking me."

She was right. Even now, as they fought to save their marriage, Paul was thinking of the woman in the airport. He was thinking about all other women and not the woman in his life.

That night, on eBay, Paul bid on a suit once worn by Sean Connery during the publicity tour for *Thunderball*. It would be too big for Paul; Connery is a big man. But Paul still wanted it. Maybe he'd frame it and put it on the wall of his apartment. Maybe he'd drink martinis and stare at it. Maybe he'd imagine that a crisp white pocket square made all the difference in the world. But he lost track of the auction and lost the suit to somebody whose screen name was Shaken, Not Stirred.

Jesus, Paul thought, I'm wasting my life.

After the divorce, Paul's daughters spent every other weekend with him. It was not enough time. It would never be enough. And he rarely saw them during his weekends anyway because they were teenagers. Everywhere he looked, he saw happy men—good and present fathers—and he was not one of them. A wealthy man, an educated man, a privileged man, he had failed his family—his children—as easily and brutally as the poorest, most illiterate, and helpless man in the country. And didn't that prove the greatness of the United States? All of us wealthy and imperial Americans are the children of bad fathers! Ha! thought Paul. Each of us—rich and poor, gay and straight, black and white—we are fragile and finite. We all go through this glorious life without guarantees, without promise of rescue or redemption. We have freedom of speech and religion, and the absolute freedom to leave behind our loved ones, to force them to unhappily pursue us. How can I possibly protect my daughters from their nightmares, from their waking fears, Paul thought, if I am not sleeping in the room next door? Oh, God, he missed them! Pure and simple, he ached. But who has sympathy for the failed father? Who sings honor songs for the monster?

And what could he do for his daughters? He could outfit them in gorgeous vintage clothing. So he gave them dresses and shoes and pants that were worn by Doris Day, Marilyn Monroe, and Audrey Hepburn.

"Who is Audrey Hepburn?" his youngest daughter had asked.

"She was perfect," Paul said.

"But who is she?"

"An actress. A movie star."

"What movies has she been in?"

"I don't think you've seen any of them."

"If I don't know who she is, why did you buy me her dress?"

It was a good question. Paul didn't have an answer. He just looked at this young woman in front of him—his daughter—and felt powerless.

"I thought maybe if you wore different clothes at school," Paul said, "maybe you could start a trend. You'd be original."

"Oh, my God," she said. "It's high school, Dad. People get beat up for being original."

Jesus, Paul had thought he was giving her social capital. He thought he could be a microlender of art—the art of the pop song. So he gave music to his daughters. Yes, he'd once romanced their mother with mix tapes, dozens of mix tapes, so he'd romance his daughters—in an entirely different way—with iPods. So Paul bought three iPods and loaded them with a thousand songs each. Three iPods, three thousand songs. Instead of just a few songs on a CD or a cassette tape, Paul had made epic mixes. Paul had given each daughter a third of his musical history. And, oh, they were delighted—were ecstatic—when they opened their gifts and saw new iPods, but, oh, how disappointed—how disgusted—they were when they discovered that their new iPods were already filled with songs, songs chosen by their father. By their sad and desperate father.

"Daddy," his eldest daughter said. "Why did you put all *your* music on here?"

"I chose all those songs for you," he said. "They're specifically for you."

"But all these songs are *your* songs," she said. "They're not mine."

"But if you listen to them," he said, "if you learn them, then maybe they can become *our* songs."

"We don't have to love the same things," she said.

"But I want you to love what I love."

Did I say that? Paul asked himself. Did I just sound that love starved and socially inept? Am I intimidated by my own daughter? In place of romantic love for my wife, am I trying to feel romantic love for my daughters? No, no, no, no, Paul thought. But he wasn't sure. How could he be sure? He was surrounded by women he did not understand.

"It's okay, Daddy," she said. "I can just load my music over your music. Thank you for the iPod."

She shook her head—a dismissive gesture she'd learned from her mother—kissed her incompetent father on the cheek, and left the room.

Three years after his divorce had finalized, after two of his daughters had gone off to college, one to Brown and the other to Oberlin, and his third daughter had disowned him, Paul saw Sara Smile again in the Detroit Airport. They saw each other at the same time, both walking toward a coffee kiosk.

"Sara Smile," he said.

"Excuse me?" the woman said.

"It's me," he said. "Paul Nonetheless."

"I'm sorry," she said. "Do I know you?"

He realized this woman only looked like his Sara Smile. It would have been too much to ask for a third chance meeting. If he'd run into Sara Smile again, they would have had to make their way over to the airport hotel—the Hyatt or Hilton or whatever it was—and get a room. He could imagine them barely making it inside the door before their hands were down each other's pants. God, he'd drop to his knees, unbutton her pants, pull them down to her ankles, and kiss her thighs. He'd pull aside her panties and push his mouth against her crotch and she'd want it for a few moments—she'd moan her approvals—and then she'd remember her husband and her life—substantial—and she'd push Paul away. She'd pull up her pants and apologize and rush out of the room. And Paul would be there, alone again, on his knees again, in a room where thousands of people had slept, eaten, fucked, and made lonely phone calls home. And who would Paul call? Who was waiting for his voice on the line? But wait, none of this had happened. It wasn't real. Paul was still standing in the Detroit Airport next to a woman—a stranger—who only strongly resembled Sara Smile.

"Are you going to call this coincidental now?" he asked this stranger.

"You have me confused with somebody else," she said. She was smiling. She was enjoying this odd and humorous interaction with the eccentric man in his old-fashioned suit.

"Can I buy you a coffee?" he asked. He knew she was the wrong woman. But he wasn't going to let that become an impediment.

"Sir," she said. "I'm not who you think I am."

She wasn't smiling now. She realized that something was wrong with this man. Yes, she was in an airport, surrounded by people—by security—but she was still a little afraid.

"How's your marriage?" he asked.

"Sir, please," she said. "Stop bothering me."

She walked away, but Paul followed her. He couldn't stop himself. He needed her. He walked a few feet behind her.

"Me asking about your marriage is just a way of talking about my marriage," he said. "But you knew that, right? Anyway, I'm divorced now."

"Sir, if you don't leave me alone, I am going to find a cop."

She stopped and put her hands up as if to ward off a punch.

"My wife left me," Paul said. "Or I left her. We left each other. It's hard to say who left first."

Paul shrugged his shoulders. And then he sang the first few bars of "She's Gone." But he couldn't quite hit Daryl Hall's falsetto notes.

"I can't hit those high notes," Paul said. "But it's not about the notes, is it? It's about the heat behind the notes."

"What's wrong with you?" the woman asked.

Two hours later, Paul sat in a simple room at a simple table while two men in suits leaned against the far wall and studied him.

"I'm not a terrorist," Paul said. "If that's what you're thinking."

The men didn't speak. Maybe they couldn't speak. Maybe there were rules against speaking. Maybe this was some advanced interrogation technique. Maybe they were silent because they knew Paul would want to fill the room with his voice.

"Come on, guys," he said. "I got a little carried away. I knew it wasn't her. I knew it wasn't Sara. I just needed to pretend for a while. Just a few moments. If she'd let me buy her some coffee or something. If she'd talked to me, everything would have been okay."

The men whispered to each other.

Paul decided it might be best if he stopped talking, if he stopped trying to explain himself.

Instead he would sing. Yes, he would find the perfect song for this situation and he would sing it. And these men—police officers, federal agents, mysterious suits—would recognize the song. They certainly wouldn't (or couldn't) sing along, but they'd smile and nod their heads in recognition. They'd share a moment with Paul. They'd have a common history, maybe even a common destiny. Rock music had that kind of power. But what song? What song would do?

And Paul knew—understood with a bracing clarity—that he must sing Marvin Gaye's "What's Going On." And so he began to hum at first, finding the tune, before he sang the first few lyrics—mumbled them, really, because he couldn't quite remember them—but when he came to the chorus, Paul belted it out. He sang loudly, and his imperfect, ragged vocals echoed in that small and simple room.

What's going on?
What's going on?
What's going on?

And, yes, Paul recognized that his singing—his spontaneous talent show—could easily be seen as troublesome. It could even be seen as crazy. Paul knew he wasn't crazy. He was just sad, very sad. And he was trying to sing his way out of the sadness.

What's going on?
What's going on?
What's going on?

The men kept staring at Paul. They wouldn't smile. They wouldn't even acknowledge the song. Why not? But then Paul remembered what had happened to Marvin Gaye. Broken, depressed, alcoholic, drug-addicted, Marvin had ended up living back home with his parents. Even as his last hit, "Sexual Healing," was selling millions of copies, Marvin was sleeping in his parents' house.

And, oh, how Marvin fought with his father. Day after day, Marvin Gaye Sr. and Marvin Gaye Jr. *screamed* at each other.

"What happened to you?"

"It's all your fault."

"You had it all and you lost it."

"You're wasting your life."

"Where's my money?"

"You have stolen from me."

"You owe me."

"I don't owe you shit."

Had any father and son ever disappointed each other so completely? But Paul couldn't stop singing. Even as he remembered that Marvin Gaye Sr. had shot and killed his son—killed his song.

What's going on?

What's going on?

What's going on?

And then it was over. Paul stopped singing. This was the wrong song. Yes, it was the worst possible song to be singing at this moment. There had to be a better one, but Paul couldn't think of it, couldn't even think of another inappropriate song. *What's wrong with me? Why can't I remember?* Paul laughed at himself as he sat in the airport interrogation room. How had he come to this? Wasn't Paul a great man who lived in a great country? Hadn't he succeeded? Jesus, he was good at everything he had ever attempted. Well, he had failed at marriage, but couldn't he be good at grief? Couldn't he be an all-star griever? Couldn't he, through his own fierce tears, tell his captors that he wasn't going to die? Couldn't he survive? Couldn't he pause now and rest his voice—rest his soul—and then start singing again when he felt strong enough? Could he do that? Was he ever going to be that strong?

"Officers," Paul said, "I'm very tired. Can I please have some time? The thing is, I'm sorry for everything. And I know this is no excuse, but I think—I realize now that I want to remember everything—every song, every article of clothing—because I'm afraid they will be forgotten."

One of the men shook his head; the other turned his back and spoke into a cell phone.

Paul bowed his head with shame.

And then he spoke so softly that he wasn't sure the men heard him. Paul thought of his wife and his daughters, of Sara Smile, and he said, "I don't want to be forgotten. I don't want to be forgotten. Don't forget me. Don't forget me. Don't forget me. Don't forget me."

ON AIRPLANES

I am always amused
By those couples—

Lovers and spouses—
Who perform and ask

Others to perform
Musical chairs

Whenever they, by
Random seat selection,

Are separated
From each other.

"Can you switch
Seats with me?"

A woman asked me.
"So I can sit

With my husband?"
She wanted me,

A big man, who
Always books early,

And will gratefully
Pay extra for the exit row,

To trade my aisle seat
For her middle seat.

By asking me to change
My location for hers,

The woman is actually
Saying to me:

"Dear stranger, dear
Sir, my comfort is

More important than yours.
Dear solitary traveler,

My love and fear—
As contained

Within my marriage—
Are larger than yours."

O, the insult!
O, the condescension!

And this is not
An isolated incident.

I've been asked
To trade seats

Twenty or thirty times
Over the years.

How dare you!
How dare you

Ask me to change
My life for you!

How imperial!
How colonial!

But, ah, here is
The strange truth:

Whenever I'm asked
To trade seats

For somebody else's love,
I do, I always do.

Big Bang Theory

After our earliest ancestors crawled out of the oceans, how soon did they feel the desire to crawl back in?

At age nine, I stepped into the pool at the YWCA. I didn't know how to swim, but the other Indian boys had grown salmon and eagle wings and could fly in water and sky.

Wouldn't the crow, that ubiquitous trickster, make a more compelling and accurate national symbol for the United States than the bald eagle?

Okay, that Indian-boy salmon-and-eagle-wings transformation thing is bullshit, but I'm trying to tell a creation story here, and by definition all creation stories are bullshit. Scientifically speaking, we all descend from one man and woman who lived in what we now call Africa—yes, we are all African at our cores—but why should we all live with the same metaphorical creation story? The Kiowa think they were created when lightning struck the mud inside a log. I think the Hopis are crash-landed aliens who are still waiting for a rescue mission. Christians think God built everything in a week—well, in six days—and then rested. Yeah, like God created the universe in anticipation of the Sunday funny pages.

Q: In the singles bar, over nonalcoholic beer, what did the Palestinian say to the Israeli?
A: "Your holy war or mine?"

But wait, before I get too critical or metaphysical, let me return to that YWCA on Maple Street in Spokane, Washington. I stood alone in the shallow end while my big brother, cousins, best friend, and little warrior enemies swam in the deep end. I was so ashamed, but then our female swim instructors shouted my name and challenged me to dive off the five-foot board. Fuck that! I jumped out of the pool and ran into the locker room.

There is a myth that drowning is a peaceful death. I've heard people say, "I would just open my mouth and breathe death in." In truth, drowning is torture. The fear of drowning is used as torture.

At the YWCA, I quickly dressed and waited for the other Indian boys, who mocked me for my aquatic cowardice and locked me in a towel bin. But I escaped and made it onto the bus that took us to the Fox Theater for a matinee showing of *Jaws,* the blockbuster that changed the way our country looks at sharks and at films.

Did you know that when a shark stops swimming, it dies?

As we walked past the endless line of movie lovers, the other boys kept pitching me crap, but then our female swim instructors, one Japanese and one Korean, shouted my name again and insisted that I join them in the line. "But what about us?" my brother asked. "You go to the deep end," the Japanese girl said.

A wise man once said that revenge is not more important than love or compassion. Until it is.

I was nine. The Asian girls were sixteen. I sat between them and they each held one of my hands as we watched a great white shark devour people. At one point, when a little boy was in danger, I hid my face in the Korean girl's chest. Oh, it was the first time I had ever been that close to a woman's breast.

Do you think the universe is expanding or contracting?

I wish I knew what happened to those Asian girls. Are they still living in Spokane? Do you realize how much they mean to me? Did they love me? Or was I just a sad-ass kid who needed their help? If I could talk to them, I would tell them this creation story: "A bonnethead shark in Omaha, Nebraska, conceived and gave birth to a baby that soon died. But this mother shark had never shared water with a male. Scientists were puzzled. So they performed a DNA test and discovered the dead baby only had its mother's DNA. Yes, that bonnethead shark had given virgin birth. Do you think this is amazing? Well, it's not. Dozens of species of insects give virgin birth. Crayfish give virgin birth. Some honeybees give virgin birth. And Komodo dragons—yeah, those big lizards give virgin birth, too. Jeez, one human gives virgin birth and that jump-starts one of the world's great religions. But when a Komodo dragon gives virgin birth, do you know what it's thinking? It's thinking, *This is Tuesday, right? I think this is Tuesday. What am I going to do on Wednesday?*

ODE FOR PAY PHONES

All

That

Autumn,

I walked from

The apartment (shared

With my sisters) to that pay phone

On Third Avenue, next to a sleazy gas station

And down the block from the International House of Pan-
cakes. I was working the night

Shift at a pizza joint and you were away at college. You dated a
series of inconsequential boys. Well, each boy meant little on his

Own, but their cumulative effect devastated my brain and
balls. I wanted you to stop kissing relative strangers, so I called
you at midnight as often as I could afford. If I talked to you
that late, I knew

(Or hoped) you couldn't rush into anybody's bed. But, O, I still recall the misery of hearing the *ring, ring, ring, ring*

Of your unanswered phone. These days, I'd text you to find you, but where's the delicious pain

In that? God, I miss standing in the mosquito dark

At this or that pay phone. I wish

That I could find one

And call back

All that

I

Loved.

FEARFUL SYMMETRY

When he was eighteen and a senior in high school, Sherwin Polatkin and a group of his schoolmates jumped into two cars and drove into Spokane to see *The Breakfast Club*. Sherwin sat next to Karen, a smart and confident sophomore—a farm-town white girl with the sun-bleached hair and tanned skin of a harvest truck driver. She'd never been of romantic interest, so Sherwin slouched in his seat and munched on popcorn. It was just the random draw of a dozen friends choosing seats.

But near the end of the movie, as Molly Ringwald and Judd Nelson were making out in a supply closet, Sherwin was surprised to discover that Karen was holding his hand and even more surprised when she started playing with his fingers. Their friends had no idea this was happening. Karen lightly ran her fingertips along Sherwin's palm, the backs of his fingers, and his wrist. It was simple—and nearly innocent—but it still felt like sex.

Sherwin was not a virgin—he'd had sex with three girls—but this was the first time a girl had been so indirect with her desires. He'd touched naked women, but this hand-holding—this skin against skin—seemed far more intimate. He loved it. He was a Spokane Indian, the lead singer for his drum group, and had a sudden urge to sing an honor song for Karen—for her tenderness. He was nervous they'd be discovered. He knew their friends would be both titillated and slightly offended by this contact. It seemed like a betrayal of what was otherwise a platonic gathering. But Sherwin could not stop it. And Karen certainly didn't want to stop it. He would never touch her again, and they would never speak of the moment and would not see each other again after high school, but Sherwin always considered it one of the best moments of his life.

So, years later, when he became a professional writer, Sherwin would tell curious journalists that he loved movies and his favorite movie of all time was *The Breakfast Club*, but he would never tell them why. He knew that the best defense against fame was keeping certain secrets. He hoped that Karen, wherever she was, would someday read an interview with him and smile when she read about his cinematic preference.

On August 11, 1948, sixteen smoke jumpers, led by a taciturn man named Wayne Ford, parachuted into Sirois Canyon, a remote area near Wenatchee, Washington, to fight a small wildfire. However, the fire, unpredictable as such fires can be, exploded into a fifty-foot-tall wall of flame, jumped the canyon, and chased the smoke jumpers up a steep and grassy hillside. Fifteen smoke jumpers tried to outrun the fire, an impossible race to win, but Wayne Ford didn't run. Instead, he did something that was new and crazy: He built the first U.S. Forest Service escape fire.

Did you know that you can escape a fire by setting another fire at your feet? You might seem to be building a funeral pyre, but you're creating a circle of safety. In order to save your endangered ass, all you have to do is burn down the grass surrounding you, lie facedown in the ash, and pray that the bigger fire will pass over you like a flock of blind and burning angels.

I know you're thinking, *You're crazy. There's no way I'm going to set a fire when another fire is already chasing me.* And that's exactly what Wayne Ford's men thought. They had never seen any firefighter set one fire to escape another. It was unprecedented— for white folks. Indians had set many such escape fires before white men had arrived in the Americas, but Wayne Ford and his men had no way of knowing this.

Wise Wayne Ford—who before the fire had the same color and sinewy bite as one hundred and fifty pounds of deer jerky— could never fully explain why he set his escape fire. All he ever said is that it just made sense. Ford's men tried to outrun the murderous flames, but one by one they all succumbed to the fire and smoke. Ford calmly lay down in the ash, in his circle of safety, and lived.

Thirty years after the Sirois Canyon fire, Harris Tolkin, a former smoke jumper, began to write a nonfiction chronicle of the tragedy, *Fearful Symmetry: The True Story of the Sirois Canyon Fire*. Tolkin borrowed the title of his book from the first and last stanzas of William Blake's most famous poem:

> Tyger! Tyger! burning bright
> In the forests of the night,
> What immortal hand or eye
> Could frame thy fearful symmetry?

In exploring the meanings of the Sirois Canyon fire and its aftermath, Tolkin relied heavily on William Blake's notions of *innocence* and *experience* and on the dichotomies of joy and sorrow, childhood and adulthood, religious faith and doubt, and good and evil. Tolkin died before completing the book, but it was edited by his daughter, Diane Tolkin, and was posthumously published in 2002 and was a surprise *New York Times* best seller for twenty-six weeks. In 2003, Tesla Studios, fresh off a Best Picture Oscar for their Civil War epic, *Leaves of Grass*, approached a hot young short-story writer, poet and first-time screenwriter, Sherwin Polatkin, to adapt *Fearful Symmetry* for the big screen.

Sitting in the Tesla offices, Sherwin stared through a glass desk at the bare feet of the executive producer, a short thin man who was otherwise completely dressed in a gorgeous bespoke suit.

"So, Sherwin," the producer said, "why are you here?"

That was a strange question, considering that Sherwin had been invited. He decided that it must be an existential query. Or no, maybe it was just the first question of a job interview. This was Hollywood, yes, but Sherwin was really just a typist—a *creative* typist—trying to get a job.

"Well, number one," Sherwin said, "I know fire like no other screenwriter in this town. I was a hotshot, a forest firefighter, for ten summers. It's how I paid for college."

That was a lie. Sherwin had only fought one fire in his life—a burning hay bale—and he'd only had to pour ten buckets of water on it. But this executive had no way of knowing Sherwin was a liar. Wasn't everybody in Hollywood a liar? Maybe Sherwin could only distinguish himself by the quality of his lies and not their quantity.

"And number two, I'm a Native American," Sherwin said. "I'm indigenous to the West, to the idea of the West, and you're not going to find that sort of experience in film school."

That couldn't be true. Wasn't Hollywood filled with small-town folks from the West—hell, from everywhere? Wasn't Hollywood filled with nomads? Yes, Jewish folks, those original nomads, created the movie business, and it had not really changed in all the decades since, had it? Wasn't Sherwin really just one more nomad in a business filled with nomads? How could he really distinguish himself?

"Listen," Sherwin said to the executive, "I'm nervous and I'm exaggerating, and I'm sounding like an arrogant bastard, so let's just start over. Is that okay? Can we call *cut* and start this scene over? Can we do a reshoot?"

The executive smiled and tugged at his toes. Yes, they were well-manicured toes, but it was still disconcerting, in the context of a business meeting, to see something—ten things—so naked and—well, toelike.

"We've had about a dozen screenwriters work on this project," the executive said. "And had three different directors attached. And none of them could crack this thing. So tell me, how are you going to crack it?"

Sherwin didn't quite understand the terminology. He assumed it had something to do with secret codes and languages. So he went with that.

"Well, the book itself is a tragedy." Sherwin said.

"Tragedies are fucked at the box office," the executive said.

Sherwin didn't know if that was true. It didn't feel true. Or maybe it was truer than Sherwin wanted to believe. Weren't

Americans afraid of tragedy? As a Native American, Sherwin was, by definition, trapped in a difficult but lustful marriage with tragedy. But that cultural fact wouldn't get him this job.

"I think there's redemption in this story," Sherwin said. "I know I can find the redemption."

"Redemption," the executive said. "Yes, that's exactly what we need."

Thus hired on the basis of one word—one universal concept—Sherwin tried to transform a tragedy into a redemptive action-adventure movie. How did he go about his task? First he pulled the story out of the past and reset it in the present. Why? Because the studio thought the audience wouldn't watch another period piece, and because the director—an old studio pro who was rumored to have had sex with at least three of the actresses who'd starred in *Dallas*, the TV series—wanted his Chinese girlfriend to play the female lead. Ah, the things one does for diversity!

But in changing the time frame of the Sirois Canyon fire at the behest of the capitalistic studio and the love-struck director, Polatkin was confronted with a logical problem. If the fictional Wayne Ford were to set an escape fire in 2003 and still be ignored by his crew members for such a crazy idea, Polatkin would have to pretend that forest-fire fighters still didn't know about escape fires. This, of course, was a nasty insult to the intelligence of firefighters. So Polatkin only had one option. He had to change the narrative and eliminate Wayne Ford's escape fire—or, rather, the concept of a man setting the first escape fire in U.S. Forest Service history. But Harris Tolkin's book revolves around the revolutionary nature of this escape fire. Thus, by eliminating the escape fire and its aftermath, Polatkin created a screenplay that had little connection to the narrative and moral concerns of the sourcebook.

Such are the dangers of creating art based on other art. Such are the dangers of Hollywood, where it is contractually understood that screenwriters will write first drafts with verve, and then, with each revision, lose more nerve and individuality. It's fucked, but Polatkin got paid five hundred thousand bucks to write a first draft where the killing fire burned as brightly as William Blake's tygers. In fact, Wayne Ford, younger and renamed for the film, saw tygers inside the flames as they chased his team up the steep slope. The others lost all innocence and hope and died before they reached the summit. But Ford reached the top and made the mad plummet down the back slope with the fire tygers in pursuit. He didn't build an escape fire—no time for that old tactic—he just ran, and he survived because he was so damn fast.

There is real inspiration for this fictional flight from fiery death. On July 3, 1999, near Boulder, Colorado, another relatively small wildfire exploded into a conflagration and chased sixteen firefighters up a steep slope and killed fifteen of them. Only Richard McPhee, an experienced smoke jumper out of Bonners Ferry, Idaho, was able to outrun the flames. Later, when researchers did the math, they estimated that McPhee ran the equivalent of a hundred-yard dash in nine seconds. That would be a world-record speed on a *flat* surface, but McPhee ran it while carrying a forty-pound backpack up a heavily forested sixty-degree slope. The man *wanted* to live. It gives one pleasure to take the measure of a man's fight to survive. Ask yourself: Could I have run that fast and won the right to live? This might be glib, but certain men are born to be stars—to be at their best when faced with death. Richard McPhee only believes he was lucky.

"Yeah, I've got speed," he said. "But hell, what if I had fallen or tripped or just hit some bad luck? What if I had started in back and had to run past everyone? I lived because nobody was running slowly in front of me."

Richard McPhee refuses to be called a hero, which makes him the perfect real-life model for a cinematic star. So, in writing his first-draft screenplay, Polatkin blended aspects of Wayne Ford and Richard McPhee's heroism and created an entirely fictional smoke jumper, now named Joseph Adams, who survived a murderous inferno but was emotionally and spiritually crippled by survivor's guilt. Angry and drinking alcoholically, Joseph Adams falls apart in the first act, staggers his way through the second act, and finds redemption in the third act when he again faces a monster fire but sacrifices his own life to save his entire team, including the love of his life, a Vietnamese-American smoke jumper named Grace. Yes, Sherwin decided that the director's Chinese girlfriend would cross over racial borders and play a Vietnamese-American woman, a first-generation immigrant, who had fled the Vietnam War and was adopted and raised by a white American family. And yes, Polatkin, the possessor of a reservation-inspired messiah complex ("I am the smartest Indian in the universe and I will save all you other Indians!"), decided that the hero, Joseph Adams, should die so that others might live.

Okay, Polatkin wasn't writing Shakespeare, but he did write an interesting screenplay, maybe even a good one. But as he'd feared, the studio had notes. They wanted to change a few things so Polatkin flew to Hollywood, met his town-car driver, and was driven to a meeting room in L.A. Sherwin kept thinking of Survivor's eighties hit, "Eye of the Tiger," as twenty studio executives shuttled into the room. The director, angry because his other project had been scuttled, rolled in late, stuffed his face with a muffin, and said, while spewing food, "This screenplay is seriously flawed, but it's nothing we can't fix."

The director was wearing cargo shorts. Sherwin was convinced that nobody over the age of thirty-three should ever wear cargo shorts.

For the rest of the day, the director and the executives made suggestions and demands: "The hero can't die. Get rid of the William Blake shit. And you need more action, more fistfights and fucking. Maybe you could write a scene where the hero fucks his girl in the ash after a fire. The hero could leave ashy handprints on his girl's back—on her whole body. That would be primal and hot. Jesus, it would be poetry."

Polatkin fought for his screenplay's survival, but it was a pathetic and lonely battle. He was a writer-for-hire and was contractually bound to follow studio orders or he would be fired and replaced. So, feeling hollow and violated, he took careful notes as a roomful of businessmen wrested art into commodity. He thought of how much he had always loved movies and how, for most his life, he'd had no idea how they were made. He thought of the boy he had been, sitting in that dark theater with Karen, the girl from high school, and how innocent it was.

Not perfect, not at all, but better—cleaner—than this meeting. How had the boy who loved movies become so different from this man who wrote them?

And then Sherwin saw the latest issue of *The New Yorker,* crisp and unread, on the table. He had just published his first short story in the magazine. It's every fiction writer's wish to be published in the same magazine that has published Cheever, Munro, Yates, and ten thousand other greats and near-greats and goods.

"Hey," Sherwin said. "I've got a short story in that *New Yorker.*"

The director flipped through the magazine, coughed and sighed, and said, "You should let me be your editor because you would win the fucking Pulitzer if I were in charge of your career."

The room went cold and silent. The professionally cold studio executives couldn't believe that any human being, even a film director, had said something so deluded and imperial.

Polatkin was baffled. No, it was worse than that. At that moment, something broke inside him. He didn't know it at the time, but he'd fractured some part of his soul. He only realized the extent of his spiritual injuries a few months later. While writing nine drafts of the screenplay, Sherwin—who had already taken out the concept of the first escape fire set in U.S. Forest Service history—discovered that he could not take the William Blake out of a book whose title and themes were based on Blake's poetry.

"I can't do it," he said to the director. "The book is about Blake. How can you take Blake out if the book is about Blake?"

"Fuck Blake," the director said. "And fuck this book. Do you think this book is the fucking Bible? Do you think it's sacred? Jesus, we're making a movie, and that's more fucking important than this book. I'm going to make a movie that's ten times—a hundred times—greater than this fucking book. So are you going to take out the fucking Blake or what?"

"I can't do it," Sherwin said.

"Then fuck you. You're fired."

It was easy to fire screenwriters. But Sherwin was not just a screenwriter. He was also the author of a book of short stories and two volumes of poetry, and he still wanted to explore the notion of heroic self-sacrifice, so he decided to write a series of sonnets dedicated to smoke jumpers. At his home in San Francisco, he sat at his computer and stared at the blank screen. He sat, silent and unworking, for hours, for weeks, for months. Every time he tried to write a word, a metaphor, a line of poetry, he could only hear the critical voices of the studio executives and the director: *The hero can't die. Get rid of the William Blake shit.* Sherwin had fallen victim to his own imagination. He couldn't create anything on the page, but he was fully capable of creating fictional and aural ghosts who prevented him from writing.

Desperate, he decided the computer's advanced technology was creating the impediment. He decided to go back to the beginning—to the Adam and Eve of writing—the pen and paper. Yes, he tried to write by hand. He reasoned that if Herman Melville could write *Moby-fucking-Dick* with an inky feather, he could write one measly goddamn sonnet with a felt tip pen and graph paper. But he could still hear the executives and director talking. *The hero can't die. Get rid of the William Blake shit.* He was suffering from Hollywood-induced schizophrenia and couldn't produce a word. Polatkin had always mocked those folks who'd claimed to suffer from writer's block. But now, he was a writer . . .

Who could not produce one goddamn word.
The poems had migrated like goddamn birds.
And no matter what you may have heard,
Writer's block causes physical hurt.
The fool couldn't wear a goddamn shirt
Because the cotton scratched, bruised, and burned
His skin. His stomach ached; his vision blurred.
What happens to a soul that's shaken *and* stirred?

What happens to a writer who can't write?
Who flees his office and drives through the night,
In search of some solace, some goddamn streetlight
That will illuminate and give back his life,
His odes and lyrics? The desperate fool tried
Every workshop trick. The agnostic fool cried
To God for relief. God, can a man die
Of writer's block? Well, the fool did survive

. . . the early and most painful stages of his creative disease. Sherwin grew numb. He became strangely complacent with the idea that he would never write again. Oh, Sherwin still loved words, but he found other ways to play with them. He discovered the magic and terror of crossword puzzles. He read dictionaries and encyclopedias that promised to help him solve the most difficult ones. He soon became good at crossword puzzles. By testing himself using the same crosswords the best puzzlers solved in competition, Sherwin learned that he was probably one of the best five hundred crossword puzzle solvers in the English-speaking world.

He'd become that good after only six months of part-time work. How good could he become if he dedicated himself fully to the task? He figured that by living even more frugally than he had for the last decade, he had enough cash to survive for one more decade. So he decided to become, for lack of a better term, a crossword monk. But instead of praying, instead of keeping a diary, instead of transcribing by hand every page of some holy book, Sherwin made lists of words, the most common crossword-puzzle answers:

AREA	OLE
ERA	IRE
ERE	ESE
ELI	ENE
ALE	ARE
ALOE	ATE
EDEN	NEE
ALI	ALA
ETA	AGE
ESS	IRA
ERIE	ACE
ANTE	ELSE
ARIA	ODE

ERR	EVE
ADO	ETNA
IDEA	ASEA
EEL	ASH
END	ANTI
ANT	EAR
APE	ARI
ACRE	ETAL
EST	

That was just the short list. There were a thousand or more common answers. They were the building blocks of crossword puzzles. But the quality—the comedy and tragedy—of a puzzle often had less to do with the answers than with the clues. A great solver understood the poetry of the clues. The most difficult puzzles used puns, misdirection, verb-noun elision, and camouflage in their clueing.

Sherwin believed himself to be a great solver, so he traveled to the American Crossword Puzzle Championship in Stamford, Connecticut.

When he stepped into the conference room, crowded with solvers who all seemed to know one another, Sherwin was nervous and vaguely ashamed of himself. Was this what his life had come to? He'd been flying first class to Hollywood, and now he was paying too much for a king bed nonsmoking in a Hilton in Connecticut? Yes, it was a wealthy, lovely, and privileged part of the state, but it still felt like a descent.

But wait, Sherwin thought, stop judging people. These solvers were a group of people who had to be clever. These people were thinkers. Yes, there had to be plenty of eccentrics—compulsive hand-washers, functioning autistics, encyclopedia readers, and compulsive cat collectors—but didn't that actually make them a highly attractive group of people? When had Sherwin been anything other than a weird fucker? Didn't he get paid to be a weird fucker?

"Hello," he said to the woman at the registration desk. She wore a name tag with her name, *Sue*, spelled out on a crossword grid.

"Hello," Sue said. "Welcome to the tournament. Are you a contestant or a journalist?"

"A contestant."

"So this must be your first time here?" she asked.

"How do you know that?"

"Oh, this is a family, really, a highly dysfunctional family." She laughed. "I know everybody. But I don't know you. So that makes you new."

"You've got me."

"Okay, I'll sign you up for the C Group."

"C? What's that?"

"It's for new solvers."

"I'm new," Sherwin said, "but I'm good."

"Oh, first-timers are always C Group. If you do well enough on the first few puzzles, they'll consider moving you up right away, but that rarely happens."

"Why not?"

"Because the puzzles are always more difficult than you'd expect. And because the pressure—well, first-timers have no idea how much pressure there is. And—well, they tend to choke a bit."

Sue laughed again.

"Are you laughing at me?" Sherwin asked.

"Oh, no," she said. "I'm sorry. I'm laughing at myself. I've been coming to this tournament for seventeen years and I'm still a C Group. I keep choking year after year."

"I'm used to pressure."

"Oh, I'm not judging you. It's all supposed to be fun. It *is* fun. Just sign up with the C Group and have fun. This is your first time. You have years of fun ahead of you."

Years of fun? When had anybody ever said such a thing and meant it? Sue meant it. Sherwin shrugged and signed up for C Group.

Later that afternoon, he sat at a long table in a room filled with long tables. He had four pencils and a good eraser. He sat beside an elderly Korean woman who looked as if she'd been born in her sweater.

"Hello," she said. "You must be new?"

She had a slight accent, so she was probably a first-generation immigrant. She'd probably been in the United States for twenty-five years. She'd been here long enough to become a crossword solver. Sherwin realized that he had no idea if crossword puzzles were written in other languages. Were other languages flexible enough?

"Are you new?" the Korean woman asked again. She was missing a lower front tooth. This made her look somehow younger, even impish. Don't be condescending, Sherwin chastised himself.

"Yes, I'm new," he said. "C Group."

"Welcome, welcome," she said. "We're like a family here."

"So I've heard."

"Yes, just like a family. Like my family. My big sister is a legendary bitch. Just like that bitch over there."

She pointed a pencil at another elderly woman, a white woman wearing thick glasses. Didn't she know that one could purchase plastic lenses these days?

"Why is she a bitch?" Sherwin asked.

"Because she always beats me. And because she always apologizes for beating me. Young man, you must never apologize for being good. It makes the rest of us feel worse about ourselves."

"Okay, good advice," Sherwin said. "So I guess I should tell you that I really don't belong in Group C. I'm better than that."

"So you think you can beat me?"

"I've timed myself with puzzles. I'm fast."

"I'm sure you are."

A volunteer set the first puzzle—freshly printed on fine cotton paper—facedown on the table in front of Sherwin.

"So what happens now?" Sherwin asked.

"When they say *go*, you turn over the paper and do your puzzle. When you're finished, raise your hand, and somebody will mark your time, and then they'll collect your puzzle and check it for accuracy. And they'll measure your score against all the other C Group puzzlers."

"The woman said they'd move me up to B if I did well enough."

"Why don't you just do the first puzzle and see what happens? What's your name anyway?"

"Sherwin."

"I'm Mai. What do you do when you aren't solving puzzles?"

"I'm a writer."

"Oh. Have you written anything I might have heard of?"

"Doubtful. I wrote poems and short stories. I never sold much. And never won any awards. I wrote a couple of movies, too. But they never got made."

"What are you working on now?"

"Oh, I don't write anymore."

"Why not?"

"My talent dried up and blew away in the wind," Sherwin said. "I am the Dust Bowl."

"I'm sorry to hear that."

"I'm sorry to say it."

Sherwin had never before confessed aloud his fears that his talent was gone forever. And now that he had, he realized that he would never write again. Not like he had. Was that so bad? He'd written two decent books and two bad ones. How many people in the world had written and published anything? Because he'd stopped writing, Sherwin had been thinking of himself as a failure. But perhaps that wasn't it. Perhaps he had only been destined to be a writer for that brief period of time. After all, there must be at least one person in the world who had loved his books—who still loved his work—so perhaps that made it all worthwhile. Wasn't everything temporary anyway?

"Okay, wait, Sherwin, enough of the biography," the Korean woman said. "Here we go."

"Puzzlers," the emcee said, "start your puzzles."

Sherwin and the Korean woman, and a few hundred other puzzlers, flipped over their papers and started working. Sherwin quickly filled three Across answers and one Down, but then stalled. He read through the clues and found that he didn't know any of them offhand. He was stuck already. Thirty seconds into his first puzzle and he was frozen. Words were failing him. Again and again, they failed him. He stared blankly at his mostly empty grid for one minute and three seconds and was shocked when the Korean woman raised her hand.

"You're done?" he asked.

"You're not supposed to talk," she said.

"But you're really done that fast?"

"Yes, but that bitch up there beat me again."

Sherwin checked out of the hotel, caught a taxi to the airport, and the flight to Chicago that would connect him to the flight back home to San Francisco.

On the second leg, somewhere over Wyoming, Sherwin pulled out the *New York Times* and found the crossword. It was Saturday, so this puzzle would probably be difficult to solve. Sherwin vowed to solve it, quickly and accurately. He wanted redemption. Here, in the airplane, he was able to fill in a few boxes, but not many. The puzzle remained mostly unsolved.

He was ready to crumple the paper into a ball and stuff it into the seat pocket in front of him when he became aware that he was being watched. One row behind him, to the left and across the aisle, a man was simultaneously working the airline magazine crossword puzzle and watching Sherwin work his *New York Times* puzzle. The airline magazine puzzles were embarrassingly easy. But the man was obviously struggling and was embarrassed by his struggles.

"I'll figure this out," he said to Sherwin, "but you, man, you're working the *Times* puzzle. You must be a genius."

"Maybe," Sherwin said.

Wanting to confirm the man's opinion, Sherwin again studied the puzzle. He tentatively filled in one answer. It was wrong, surely it was wrong; ALPINE could not be the right answer. It made no sense. But it fit the squares. It put ink on the page. Sherwin felt good about that, so he filled in another answer with the wrong word. And then he filled in another. In a minute, he finished the puzzle. He'd filled nearly all the boxes with incorrect and random words like *music* and *screenwriter* and *fear* but the man behind him could not tell that Sherwin was faking it. He could only see Sherwin finishing the difficult puzzle in record time. Wow, the man thought, he's barely even reading the clues. He's a crossword machine. He's a crossword cyborg. He's a crossword killer. He's a crossword Terminator.

When Sherwin filled in the last blank, he sighed with satisfaction, folded the paper in half, and slid it into the seat pocket in front of him. Then he looked back at the man behind him and smiled. The man gave him a thumbs-up. It was such an eager and innocent gesture that Sherwin felt guilty for his deception. But then he laughed at himself, at his gift for lying.

I am a lying genius, Sherwin thought. And what is lying but a form of storytelling? Sherwin realized that he'd told a story, the first story he'd told in public for any kind of audience since he left Hollywood. But wait, did this really count as story-telling? Well, he'd entertained one man, right? And then Sherwin realized what he'd truly just done. And he roared with laughter and startled a few of his fellow passengers with the volume of his joy.

Sherwin realized that, for years, he'd been running away from a wildfire, an all-consuming inferno that had turned his words into cinder and ash, but he'd just now set an escape fire; he'd told a lie, a story, that convinced him he might be capable of putting a story on the page. Or was this all delusion? Sherwin knew there was a pen in his left inside coat pocket. He could feel it there. And there was paper everywhere on this airplane. He had ink; he could get paper. Oh, he wondered, oh, do I have the strength to begin again? Do I have the courage to step into a dark theater, hold hands with a beautiful woman, and fall back in love with my innocence?

ODE TO MIX TAPES

These days, it's too easy to make mix tapes.
CD burners, iPods, and iTunes
Have taken the place
Of vinyl and cassette. And, soon
Enough, clever introverts will create
Quicker point-and-click ways to declare
One's love, lust, friendship, and favor.
But I miss the labor
Of making old-school mix tapes—the midair

Acrobatics of recording one song
At a time. It sometimes took days
To play, choose, pause,
Ponder, record, replay, erase,
And replace. But there was no magic wand.
It was blue-collar work. A great mix tape
Was sculpture designed to seduce
And let the hounds loose.
A great mix tape was a three-chord parade

Led by the first song, something bold and brave,
　　　A heat-seeker like Prince with "Cream,"
　　　Or "Let's Get It On," by Marvin Gaye.
The next song was always Patsy Cline's "Sweet Dreams,"
or something by Hank. But O, the last track
　　　Was the vessel that contained
　　　The most devotion and pain
And made promises that you couldn't take back.

Roman Catholic Haiku

Humans

In 1985, while attending Gonzaga University—a Jesuit institution—students shared the dining hall with fifty or sixty nuns who lived in a dormitory-turned-convent. We students didn't think positively or negatively about this situation. We barely had any interaction with the holy women, though a few of us took to shouting, "Get thee to a nunnery!" at one another— but never at the nuns—after we took a Shakespeare class. I'm sure the nuns must have heard us shouting Hamlet's curse at one another, but being a rather scholarly bunch, they were probably more amused than insulted.

Nature

The brown recluse spider is not an aggressive spider and attacks only when hurt or threatened. Its bite, however, contains a very aggressive poison that can form a necrotizing ulcer that destroys soft tissue and sometimes bone. So this six-eyed spider is passive and dangerous. And it's strangely beautiful. It often has markings on its stomach and back that resemble violins. Yes, this spider could be thought of as a tattooed musician.

COLLISION

While waiting in the lunch line behind a nun, I noticed a brown recluse spider perched on her shoulder. I reflexively slapped the arachnid to the floor. The nun must have thought I'd slapped her in jest or cruelty because she turned and glared at me. But then I pointed at the brown recluse spider scuttling across the floor away from us. At first, the nun stepped back, but then she took two huge steps forward and crushed the spider underfoot. The nun gasped; I gasped. Mortified, she looked at me and said, "I'm sorry." And then she looked down at the mutilated spider and said, "You, too."

Looking Glass

On October 5, 1877, in Montana's Bear Paw Mountains, the starved and exhausted Nez Perce ended their two-thousand-mile flight and surrendered to General Oliver Howard and his Ninth Cavalry. When the legendary Nez Perce leader, Chief Joseph, stood and said, "My heart is sick

And
Sad.
From
Where
The
Sun
Now
Stands,

I
Will
Fight
No
More
Forever"

he thought they were his final words. He had no idea that he would live for another twenty-seven years. First, he watched

hundreds of his people die of exile in Oklahoma. Then Joseph
and his fellow survivors were allowed to move back to the
Pacific Northwest but were forced to live on the Colville Indian Reservation, hundreds of miles away from their tribe's
ancestral home in Oregon's Wallowa Valley. Exiled twice,
Joseph still led his tribe into the twentieth century, though he
eventually died of depression. But my grandmother, who was
born on the Colville Indian Reservation, always said she remembered Joseph as a kind and peaceful man. She always said
that Chief Joseph was her favorite babysitter.

Yes,
He
Would
Sit
In
His
Rocking
Chair

And
Braid
My
Grandmother's
Epic
Hair.

SALT

I wrote the obituary for the obituaries editor. Her name was Lois Andrews. Breast cancer. She was only forty-five. One in eight women get breast cancer, an epidemic. Lois's parents had died years earlier. Dad's cigarettes kept their promises. Mom's Parkinson's shook her into the ground. Lois had no siblings and had never been married. No kids. No significant other at present. No significant others in recent memory. Nobody remembered meeting one of her others. Some wondered if there had been any others. Perhaps Lois had been that rarest of holy people, the secular and chaste nun. So, yes, her sexuality was a mystery often discussed but never solved. She had many friends. All of them worked at the paper.

I wasn't her friend, not really. I was only eighteen, a summer intern at the newspaper, moving from department to department as need and boredom required, and had only spent a few days working with Lois. But she'd left a note, a handwritten will and testament, with the editor in chief, and she'd named me as the person she wanted to write her obituary.

"Why me?" I asked the chief. He was a bucket of pizza and beer tied to a broomstick.

"I don't know," he said. "It's what she wanted."

"I didn't even know her."

"She was a strange duck," he said.

I wanted to ask him how to tell the difference between strange and typical ducks. But he was a humorless white man with power, and I was a reservation Indian boy intern. I was to be admired for my ethnic tenacity but barely tolerated because of my callow youth.

"I've never written an obituary by myself," I said. During my hours at her desk, Lois had carefully supervised my work.

"It may seem bureaucratic and formal," she'd said. "But we have to be perfect. This is a sacred thing. We have to do this perfectly."

"Come on," the chief said. "What did you do when you were working with her? She taught you how to write one, didn't she?"

"Well, yeah, but—"

"Just do your best," he said and handed me her note. It was short, rather brutal, and witty. She didn't want any ceremony. She didn't want a moment of silence. Or a moment of indistinct noise, either. And she didn't want anybody to gather at a local bar and tell drunken stories about her because those stories would inevitably be romantic and false. And she'd rather be forgotten than inaccurately remembered. And she wanted me to write the obituary.

It was an honor, I guess. It would have been difficult, maybe impossible, to write a good obituary about a woman I didn't know. But she made it easy. She insisted in her letter that I use the standard fill-in-the-blanks form.

"If it was good enough for others," she'd written, "it is good enough for me."

A pragmatic and lonely woman, sure. And serious about her work. But, trust me, she was able to tell jokes without insulting the dead. At least, not directly.

That June, a few days before she went on the medical leave that she'd never return from, Lois had typed *surveyed* instead of *survived* in the obituary for a locally famous banker. That error made it past the copy editors and was printed: *Mr. X is surveyed by his family and friends.*

Mr. X's widow called Lois to ask about the odd word choice.

"I'm sorry," Lois said. She was mortified. It was the only serious typo of her career. "It was my error. It's entirely my fault. I apologize. I will correct it for tomorrow's issue."

"Oh, no, please don't," the widow said. "My husband would have loved it. He was a poet. Never published or anything like that. But he loved poems. And that word, *survey*—well, it might be accidental, but it's poetry, I think. I mean, my husband would have been delighted to know that his family and friends were surveying him at the funeral."

And so a surprised and delighted Lois spent the rest of the day thinking of verbs that more accurately reflected our interactions with the dead.

Mr. X is assailed by his family and friends.
Mr. X is superseded by his family and friends.
Mr. X is superimposed by his family and friends.
Mr. X is sensationalized by his family and friends.
Mr. X is shadowboxed by his family and friends.

Lois laughed as she composed her imaginary obituaries. I'd never seen her laugh that much, and I suspected that very few people had seen her react that strongly to anything. She wasn't remote or strained, she was just private. And so her laughter—her public joy—was frankly erotic. Though I'd always thought of her as a sexy librarian—with her wire-rimmed glasses and curly brown hair and serious panty hose and suits—I'd never really thought of going to bed with her. Not to any serious degree. I was eighteen, so I fantasized about having sex with nearly every woman I saw, but I hadn't obsessed about Lois. Not really. I'd certainly noticed that her calves were a miracle of muscle—her best feature—but I'd only occasionally thought of kissing my way up and down her legs. But at that moment, as she laughed about death, I had to shift my legs to hide my erection.

"Hey, kid," she said, "when you die, how do you want your friends and family to remember you?"

"Jeez," I said. "I don't want to think about that stuff. I'm eighteen."

"Oh, so young," she said. "So young and handsome. You're going to be very popular with the college girls."

I almost whimpered. But I froze, knowing that the slightest movement, the softest brush of my pants against my skin, would cause me to orgasm.

Forgive me, I was only a kid.

"Ah, look at you," Lois said. "You're blushing."

And so I grabbed a random file off her desk and ran. I made my escape. But, oh, I was in love with the obituaries editor. And she—well, she taught me how to write an obituary.

And so this is how I wrote hers:

Lois Andrews, age 45, of Spokane, died Friday, August 24, 1985, at Sacred Heart Hospital.

There will be no funeral service. She donated her body to Washington State University. An only child, Lois Anne Andrews was born January 16, 1940, at Sacred Heart Hospital, to Martin and Betsy (Harrison) Andrews. She never married. She was the obituaries editor at the *Spokesman-Review* for twenty-two years. She is survived by her friends and colleagues at the newspaper.

Yes, that was the story of her death. It was not enough. I felt morally compelled to write a few more sentences, as if those extra words would somehow compensate for what had been a brief and solitary life.

I was also bothered that Lois had donated her body to science. Of course, her skin and organs would become training tools for doctors and scientists, and that was absolutely vital, but the whole process still felt disrespectful to me. I thought of her, dead and naked, lying on a gurney while dozens of students stuck their hands inside of her. It seemed—well, pornographic. But I also knew that my distaste was cultural.

Indians respect dead bodies even more than the live ones.

Of course, I never said anything. I was young and frightened and craved respect and its ugly cousin, approval, so I did as I was told. And that's why, five days after Lois's death and a few minutes after the editor in chief had told me I would be writing the obituaries until they found "somebody official," I found myself sitting at her desk.

"What am I supposed to do first?" I asked the chief.

"Well, she must have unfiled files and unwritten obits and unmailed letters."

"Okay, but where?"

"I don't know. It was *her* desk."

This was in the paper days, and Lois kept five tall filing cabinets stuffed with her job.

"I don't know what to do," I said, panicked.

"Jesus, boy," the editor in chief said. "If you want to be a journalist, you'll have to work under pressure. Jesus. And this is hardly any pressure at all. All these people are dead. The dead will not pressure you."

I stared at him. I couldn't believe what he was saying. He seemed so cruel. He was a cruel duck, that's what he was.

"Jesus," he said yet again, and grabbed a folder off the top of the pile. "Start with this one."

He handed me the file and walked away. I wanted to shout at him that he'd said Jesus three times in less than fifteen seconds. I wasn't a Christian and didn't know much about the definition of blasphemy, but it seemed like he'd committed some kind of sin.

But I kept my peace, opened the file, and read the handwritten letter inside. A woman had lost her husband. Heart attack. And she wanted to write the obituary and run his picture. She included her phone number. I figured it was okay to call her. So I did.

"Hello?" she said. Her name was Mona.

"Oh, hi," I said. "I'm calling from the *Spokesman-Review*. About your—uh, late husband?"

"Oh. Oh, did you get my letter? I'm so happy you called. I wasn't sure if anybody down there would pay attention to me."

"This is sacred," I said, remembering Lois's lessons. "We take this very seriously."

"Oh, well, that's good—that's great—and, well, do you think it will be okay for me to write the obituary? I'm a good writer. And I'd love to run my husband's photo—his name was Dean— I'd love to run his photo with the—with his—with my remembrance of him."

I had no idea if it was okay for her to write the obituary. And I believed that the newspaper generally ran only the photographs of famous dead people. But then I looked at the desktop and noticed Lois's neatly written notes trapped beneath the glass. I gave praise for her organizational skills.

"Okay, okay," I said, scanning the notes. "Yes. Yes, it's okay if you want to write the obituary yourself."

I paused and then read aloud the official response to such a request.

"Because we understand, in your time of grieving, that you want your loved one to be honored with the perfect words—"

"Oh, that's lovely."

"—but, and we're truly sorry about this, it will cost you extra," I said.

"Oh," she said. "Oh, I didn't know that. How much extra?"

"Fifty dollars."

"Wow, that's a lot of money."

"Yes," I said. It was one-fifth of my monthly rent.

"And how about running the photograph?" Mona asked. "How much extra does that cost?"

"It depends on the size of the photo."

"How much is the smallest size?"

"Fifty dollars, as well."

"So it will be one hundred dollars to do this for my husband?"

"Yes."

"I don't know if I can afford it. I'm a retired schoolteacher on a fixed income."

"What did you teach?" I asked.

"I taught elementary school—mostly second grade—at Meadow Hills for forty-five years. I taught three generations." She was proud, even boastful. "I'll have you know that I taught the grandchildren of three of my original students."

"Well, listen," I said, making an immediate and inappropriate decision to fuck the duck in chief. "We have a special rate for—uh, retired public employees. So the rate for your own obituary and your husband's photograph is—uh, let's say twenty dollars. Does that sound okay?"

"Twenty dollars? Twenty dollars? I can do twenty dollars. Yes, that's lovely. Oh, thank you, thank you."

"You're welcome, ma'am. So—uh, tell me, when do you want this to run?"

"Well, I told my daughters and sons that it would run tomorrow."

"Tomorrow?"

"Yes, the funeral is tomorrow. I really want this to run on the same day. Is that okay? Will that be possible?"

I had no idea if it was possible. "Let me talk to the boys down in the print room," I said, as if I knew them. "And I'll call you back in a few minutes, okay?"

"Oh, yes, yes, I'll be waiting by the phone."

We said our good-byes and I slumped in my chair. In Lois's chair. What had I done? I'd made a promise I could not keep. I counted to one hundred, trying to find a cool center, and walked over to the chief's office.

"What do you want?" he asked.

"I think I screwed up."

"Well, isn't that a surprise," he said. I wanted to punch the sarcasm out of his throat.

"This woman—her husband died," I said. "And she wanted to write the obituary and run his photo—"

"That costs extra."

"I know. I read that on Lois's desk. But I read incorrectly, I think."

"How incorrectly?"

"Well, I think it's supposed to cost, like, one hundred dollars to run the obit and the size photo she wants—"

"How much did you tell her it would cost?"

"Twenty."

"So you gave her an eighty-percent discount?"

"I guess."

He stared at me. Judged me. He'd once been a Pulitzer finalist for a story about a rural drug syndicate.

"And there's more," I said.

"Yes?" His anger was shrinking his vocabulary.

"I told her we'd run it tomorrow."

"Jesus," he said. "Damn it, kid."

I think he wanted to fire me, to throw me out of his office, out of his building, out of his city and country. I suddenly realized that he was grieving for Lois, that he was angry about her death. Of course he was. They had worked together for two decades. They were friends. So I tried to forgive him for his short temper. And I did forgive him, a little.

"I'm sorry," I said.

"Well, shit on a rooster," he said, and leaned back in his chair. "Listen. I know this is a tough gig here. This is not your job. I know that. But this is a newspaper and we measure the world by column inches, okay? We have to make tough decisions about what can fit and what cannot fit. And by telling this woman—this poor woman—that she could have this space tomorrow, you have fucked with the shape of my world, okay?"

"Yes, sir," I said.

He ran his fingers through his hair (my father did the same thing when he was pissed), made a quick decision, picked up his phone, and made the call.

"Hey, Charlie, it's me," he said. "Do we have any room for another obituary? With a photo?"

I could hear the man screaming on the other end.

"I know, I know," the chief said. "But this is an important one. It's a family thing."

The chief listened to more screaming, then hung up on the other guy.

"All right," he said. "The woman gets one column inch for the obit."

"That's not much," I said.

"She's going to have to write a haiku, isn't she?"

I wanted to tell him that haikus were not supposed to be elegies, but then I realized that I wasn't too sure about that literary hypothesis.

"What do I do now?" I asked.

"We need the obit and the photo by three o'clock."

It was almost one.

"How do I get them?" I asked.

"Well, you could do something crazy like get in a car, drive to this woman's house, pick up the obit and the photo, and bring them back here."

"I don't have a car," I said.

"Do you have a driver's license?"

"Yes."

"Well, then, why don't you go sign a vehicle out of the car pool and do your fucking job?"

I fled. Obtained the car. And while cursing Lois and her early death, and then apologizing to Lois for cursing her, I drove up Maple to the widow's small house on Francis. A green house with a white fence that was maybe one foot tall. A useless fence. It couldn't keep out anything.

I rang the doorbell and waited a long time for the woman—Mona, her name was Mona—to answer. She was scrawny, thin-haired, dark for a white woman. At least eighty years old. Maybe ninety. Maybe older than that. I did the math. Geronimo was still alive when this woman was born. An old raven, I thought. No, too small to be a raven. She was a starling.

"Hello," she said.

"Hi, Mona," I said. "I'm from the *Spokesman;* we talked on the phone."

"Oh, yes, oh, yes, please come in."

I followed her inside into the living room. She slowly, painfully, sat on a wooden chair. She was too weak and frail to lower herself into a soft chair, I guess. I sat on her couch. I looked around the room and realized that every piece of furniture, every painting, every knickknack and candlestick, was older than me. Most of the stuff was probably older than my parents. I saw photographs of Mona, a man I assumed was her husband, and five or six children, and a few dozen grandchildren. Her children and grandchildren, I guess. Damn, her children were older than my parents. Her grandchildren were older than me.

"You have a nice house," I said.

"My husband and I lived here for sixty years. We raised five children here."

"Where are your children now?"

"Oh, they live all over the country. But they're all flying in tonight and tomorrow for the funeral. They loved their father. Do you love your father?"

My father was a drunken liar.

"Yes," I said. "I love him very much."

"That's good, you're a good son. A very good son."

She smiled at me. I realized she'd forgotten why I was there.

"Ma'am, about the obituary and the photograph?"

"Yes?" she said, still confused.

"We need them, the obituary you wrote for your husband, and his photograph?"

And then she remembered.

"Oh, yes, oh, yes, I have them right here in my pocket."

She handed me the photograph and the obit. And yes, it was clumsily written and mercifully short. The man in the photograph was quite handsome. A soldier in uniform. Black hair, blue eyes. I wondered if his portrait had been taken before or after he'd killed somebody.

"My husband was a looker, wasn't he?" she asked.

"Yes, very much so."

"I couldn't decide which photograph to give you. I mean, I thought I might give you a more recent one. To show you what he looks like now. He's still very handsome. But then I thought, No, let's find the most beautiful picture of them all. Let the world see my husband at his best. Don't you think that's romantic?"

"Yes, you must have loved him very much," I said.

"Oh, yes, he was ninety percent perfect. Nobody's all perfect, of course. But he was close, he was very close."

Her sentiment was brutal.

"Listen, ma'am," I said. "I'm sorry, but I have to get these photographs back to the newspaper if they're going to run on time."

"Oh, don't worry, young man, there's no rush."

Now I was confused. "But I thought the funeral was tomorrow?" I asked.

"Oh, no, silly, I buried my husband six months ago. In Veterans' Cemetery. He was at D-Day."

"And your children?"

"Oh, they were here for the funeral, but they went away."

But she looked around the room as if she could still see her kids. Or maybe she was remembering them as they had been, the children who'd indiscriminately filled the house and then, just as indiscriminately, had moved away and into their own houses. Or maybe everything was ghosts, ghosts, ghosts. She scared me. Maybe this house was lousy with ghosts. I was afraid that Lois's ghost was going to touch me on the shoulder and gently correct my errors.

"Mona, are you alone here?" I asked. I didn't want to know the answer.

"No, no—well, yes, I suppose. But my Henry, he's buried in the backyard."

"Henry?"

"My cat. Oh, my beloved cat."

And then she told me about Henry and his death. The poor cat, just as widowed as Mona, had fallen into a depression after her husband's death. Cat and wife mourned together.

"You know," she said. "I read once that grief can cause cancer. I think it's true. At least, it's true for cats. Because that's what my Henry had, cancer of the blood. Cats get it all the time. They see a lot of death, they do."

And so she, dependent on the veterinarian's kindness and charity, had arranged for her Henry to be put down.

"What's that big word for killing cats?" she asked me.

"Euthanasia," I said.

"Yes, that's it. That's the word. It's kind of a pretty word, isn't it? It sounds pretty, don't you think?"

"Yes."

"Such a pretty word for such a sad and lonely thing," she said.

"Yes, it is," I said.

"You can name your daughter Euthanasia and nobody would even notice if they didn't know what the word meant."

"I suppose," I said.

"My cat was too sick to live," Mona said.

And then she told me how she'd held Henry as the vet injected him with the death shot. And, oh, how she cried when Henry's heart and breath slowed and stopped. He was gone, gone, gone. And so she brought him home, carried him into the backyard, and laid him beside the hole she'd paid a neighbor boy to dig. That neighbor boy was probably fifty years old.

"I prayed for a long time," she said. "I wanted God to know that my cat deserved to be in Heaven. And I didn't want Henry to be in cat heaven. Not at all. I wanted Henry to go find my husband. I want them both to be waiting for me."

And so she prayed for hours. Who can tell the exact time at such moments? And then she kneeled beside her cat. And that was painful because her knees were so old, so used—like the ancient sedan in the garage—and she pushed her Henry into the grave and poured salt over him.

"I read once," she said, "that the Egyptians used to cover dead bodies with salt. It helps people get to Heaven quicker. That's what I read."

When she poured the salt on her cat, a few grains dropped and burned in his eyes.

"And let me tell you," she said. "I almost fell in that grave when my Henry meowed. Just a little one. I barely heard it. But it was there. I put my hand on his chest and his little heart was beating. Just barely. But it was beating. I couldn't believe it. The salt brought him back to life."

Shit, I thought, the damn vet hadn't injected enough death juice into the cat. Shit, shit, shit.

"Oh, that's awful," I said.

"No, I was happy. My cat was alive. Because of the salt. So I called my doctor—"

"You mean you called the vet?"

"No, I called my doctor, Ed Marashi, and I told him that it was a miracle, that the salt brought Henry back to life."

I wanted to scream at her senile hope. I wanted to run to Lois's grave and cover her with salt so she'd rise, replace me, and be forced to hear this story. This was her job; this was her responsibility.

"And let me tell you," the old woman said. "My doctor was amazed, too, so he said he'd call the vet and they'd both be over, and it wasn't too long before they were both in my home. Imagine! Two doctors on a house call. That doesn't happen anymore, does it?"

It happens when two graceful men want to help a fragile and finite woman.

And so she told me that the doctors went to work on the cat. And, oh, how they tried to bring him back all the way, but there just wasn't enough salt in the world to make it happen. So the doctors helped her sing and pray and bury her Henry. And, oh, yes—Dr. Marashi had sworn to her that he'd tried to help her husband with salt.

"Dr. Marashi said he poured salt on my husband," she said. "But it didn't work. There are some people too sick to be salted."

She looked around the room as if she expected her husband and cat to materialize. How well can you mourn if you continually forget that the dead are dead?

I needed to escape.

"I'm really sorry, ma'am," I said. "I really am. But I have to get back to the newspaper with these."

"Is that my husband's photograph?" she asked.

"Yes."

"And is that his obituary?"

"Yes," I said. "It's the one you wrote."

"I remember, I remember."

She studied the artifacts in my hands.

"Can I have them back?" she asked.

"Excuse me?"

"The photo, and my letter, that's all I have to remember my husband. He died, you know?"

"Yes, I know," I said.

"He was at D-Day."

"If I give you these back," I said. "I won't be able to run them in the newspaper."

"Oh, I don't want them in the newspaper," she said. "My husband was a very private man."

Ah, Lois, I thought, you never told me about this kind of death.

"I have to go now," I said. I wanted to crash through the door and run away from this house fire.

"Okay, okay. Thank you for visiting," she said. "Will you come back? I love visitors."

"Yes," I said. I lied. I knew I should call somebody about her dementia. She surely couldn't take care of herself anymore. I knew I should call the police or her doctor or find her children and tell them. I knew I had responsibilities to her—to this grieving and confused stranger—but I was young and terrified.

So I left her on her porch. She was still waving when I turned the corner. Ah, Lois, I thought, are you with me, are you with me? I drove the newspaper's car out of the city and onto the freeway. I drove for three hours to the shore of Soap Lake, an inland sea heavy with iron, calcium, and salt. For thousands of years, my indigenous ancestors had traveled here to be healed. They're all gone now, dead by disease and self-destruction. Why had they believed so strongly in this magic water when it never protected them for long? When it might not have protected them at all? But you, Lois, you were never afraid of death, were you? You laughed and played. And you honored the dead with your brief and serious prayers.

Standing on the shore, I prayed for my dead. I praised them. I stupidly hoped the lake would heal my small wounds. Then I stripped off my clothes and waded naked into the water.

Jesus, I don't want to die today or tomorrow, but I don't want to live forever.

FOOD CHAIN

This is my will:

Bury me
In an anthill.

After one week
Of this feast,

Set the ants on fire.
Make me a funeral pyre.

Let my smoke rise
Into the eyes

Of those crows
On the telephone wire.

Startle those birds
Into flight

With my last words:
I loved my life.